# Introducti

**ALSO AVAILABLE IN THE BANKING CERTIFICATE SERIES**

PRELIMINARY SECTION

**Banking: The Business**
Geoffrey Lipscombe
ISBN 0 273 03192 9

**Business Calculations for Bankers***
Helen Coult
ISBN 0 273 02884 7

**Business Communication for Bankers**
Gill Kelly
ISBN 0 273 03325 5

FINAL SECTION

**Banking Operations – UK Lending and International Business (2nd Edition)***
Audrey Davies and Martin Kearns
ISBN 0 273 03846 X

**Customer Services – Marketing and the Competitive Environment***
Carol Mayall and Sally Palmer
ISBN 0 273 03994 6

**Economics and the Banks' Role in the Economy (2nd Edition)***
Geoffrey Lipscombe
ISBN 0 273 03250 X

**Banking: the Legal Environment** (2nd Edition)*
David Palfreman
ISBN 0 273 03701 3

**Supervisory Skills (2nd Edition)***
Brian Stone
ISBN 0 273 03501 0

**PITMAN BOOKS FOR THE BANKING DIPLOMA (SERIES EDITOR: B J BEECHAM)**

**Management in Banking**
Helen Coult
ISBN 0 273 03218 6

**Accountancy**
Peter MacNamara
ISBN 0 273 03216 X

**The Monetary and Financial System**
B J Beecham
ISBN 0 273 03245 3

**Law Relating to Banking Services**
Paul Raby
ISBN 0 273 03217 8

** Published in association with the Chartered Institute of Bankers*

# INTRODUCTION TO ACCOUNTING

SECOND EDITION

**Karl Harper BA(Hons), ACIB, MCIM, Cert Ed**

Series Editor: David Palfreman BA, FCIB

To Joshua, my second edition

PITMAN PUBLISHING
128 Long Acre, London WC2E 9AN
A Division of Longman Group UK Limited



First published in Great Britain 1991
Second edition 1994

**British Library Cataloguing in Publication Data**
A catalogue record for this book is available from the British Library

ISBN 0 273 60202 0



Printed and bound in Great Britain by Clays Ltd, St Ives plc

The publisher's policy is to use **paper manufactured from sustainable forests**

# Contents

*Preface* ix

*Acknowledgements* ix

**1 An introduction to accounting** **1**

Objectives – Introduction – What is accountancy? – What financial information do we need to record? – Why do we need to record financial information? – How do businesses record their financial information? – Summary – Self-assessment questions

**2 The balance sheet** **6**

Objectives – Introduction – The balance sheet format – Buying and selling on credit – Drawings – Summary – Self-assessment questions

**3 Double entry bookkeeping** **16**

Objectives – Introduction – How does a company maintain records? – Double entry bookkeeping – Expenses – Carriage In and Carriage Out – Stock – Day books or journals – Returns In and Returns Out – Discounts – Balancing off the ledgers – Trial balance – Summary – Self-assessment questions

**4 Errors and control accounts** **31**

Objectives – Introduction – Errors which affect the trial balance – Control accounts – Sales ledger control account – Purchase ledger control account – Conclusion – Summary – Self-assessment questions

**5 Trading profit and loss account** **38**

Objectives – Introduction – Producing a Trading Profit and Loss Account – Returns In and Returns Out – Carriage In and Carriage Out – Discount allowed and discount received – Producing a Trading Profit and Loss Account and Balance Sheet – Errors and the reported profit figure – Summary – Self-assessment questions

**6 Trading profit and loss account and balance sheet - extra matters** **51**

Objectives – Introduction – Vertical format – Accounting concepts and conventions – Dealing with prepayments and accruals – Prudence – Provision for bad and doubtful debts – Summary – Self-assessment questions

**7 Depreciation** **72**

Objectives – Introduction – What is depreciation? – Causes of depreciation – Methods of calculating depreciation – The effects of depreciation on the Trading Profit and Loss Account and Balance Sheet – Procedure for dealing with depreciation – The disposal or scrapping of a fixed asset – Dealing with disposals in the trial balance – Summary – Self-assessment questions

**8 Sole trader revision** **90**

Objectives – Dealing with adjustments – Specimen layout of a Trading Profit and Loss Account and Balance Sheet of a sole trader

**9 Partnership accounts** **98**

Objectives – Introduction – Definition – Producing the final accounts of a partnership – Specimen layout of partnership accounts – Partnership agreements – Summary – Self-assessment questions

**10 The admission or retirement of a partner** **108**

Objectives – Introduction – Goodwill – The admission of a new partner – Goodwill as an intangible asset – Retirement or death of a partner – Revaluation of assets – Summary – Self-assessment questions

**11 Limited company accounts** **121**

Objectives – Introduction – Accounts – Principles of a Balance Sheet – Conclusion – Summary – Self-assessment questions

**12 Manufacturing accounts** **138**

Objectives – Introduction – Calculating the cost of manufacture – Producing a Trading Profit and Loss Account for manufacturing businesses – Producing a Balance Sheet for manufacturing businesses – Summary – Self-assessment questions

**13 Statements of Standard Accounting Practice (SSAPs) and Financial Reporting Standards (FRSs)** **149**

Objectives – Introduction - syllabus and examination requirements – What are Statements of Standard Accounting Practice (SSAPs) and Financial Reporting Standards (FRSs)? – Why do we need SSAPs and FRSs? – How do SSAPs and FRSs solve the problem? – What authority do SSAPs and FRSs have? – Taxation – Inflation – Summary – Self-assessment questions

**14 Cash flow forecasts** **169**

Objectives – Introduction - What is a cash flow forecast? – What is the purpose of producing such forecasts? – How are they constructed? – Producing a forecast Trading Profit and Loss Account and Balance Sheet from a cash flow forecast – Summary – Self-assessment questions

**15 Cash and working capital** **181**

Objectives – Introduction - what is working capital? – Assessing a company's working capital position – Cash cycle/flow of funds – The cost of maintaining working capital – How do you keep working capital to a minimum? – Conclusion - the importance of working capital – Summary – Self-assessment questions

**16 Cash flow statements** **190**

Objectives – Introduction – Cash flows: in and out – Example presentation – Preparing a cash flow statement – The purchase and sale of fixed assets during the year – Analysis of the Cash Flow Statement – Summary – Self-assessment questions

**17 Reconciliation statements** **204**

Objectives – Introduction - what are reconciliation statements? – Bank reconciliation statements – Updating the cash book – Different opening balances – Reconciling the opening and closing bank/cash balance – Summary – Self-assessment questions

**18 Ratio analysis** **217**

Objectives – Introduction – what is ratio analysis? – Calculating accounting ratios – Interpretation of account ratios – Limitation of ratio analysis – Conclusion – Summary – Self-assessment questions

**19 Break even analysis** **227**

Objectives – Introduction - what is break even analysis? – Fixed and variable costs – Calculating the break even point – Contribution/sales ratio – Break even charts – Margin of safety – The effect of changes in sales volume and costs – The use of break even analysis as a decision making tool and planning aid – Assumptions/limitations – Summary – Self-assessment questions

**20 Examination preparation/revision** **244**

Objectives – Introduction - examination format – Examination tips – From Trial Balance to Final Accounts – Cash Flow Statements: make sure you are ready – Mock examination

*Appendix A: Answers to progress tests* 264

*Appendix B: Answers to self-assessment questions* 292

*Index* 323

# 1 An introduction to accounting

**OBJECTIVES**

**After studying this chapter you should be able to:**

**1 Understand the nature and purpose of accounting;**
**2 List the financial information recorded by businesses;**
**3 Explain the importance of recording financial information;**
**4 Appreciate that while trading profitability is important, so too is a company's cashflow position.**

## ■ INTRODUCTION

You are now about to start the final section of the Banking Certificate and possibly wondering why you need to study accountancy; after all you are bankers not accountants.

The aim of this course, however, is not to turn you into accountants – preparing accounts for customers and helping them with their tax problems – but to help you to become better bankers, more capable of understanding a customer's financial position through an examination of their *accounts* (i.e. their financial information).

As banks have a variety of customers, we will examine the accounts of individuals trading as shopkeepers, taxi-drivers etc, and also of partnerships and limited companies first, through the recording of their financial information, and then through the interpretation and use of this information in order to make decisions, assess loan applications and assist your customers.

## ■ WHAT IS ACCOUNTANCY?

As you may well be aware accountancy is concerned with *the recording of financial information*, but what financial information do we need to record and why?

## ■ WHAT FINANCIAL INFORMATION DO WE NEED TO RECORD?

Imagine that you have started your own business, let us say a clothes shop; what financial information would you record? Before reading any further, see if you can make a list of the information you would record.

Now let us see how our lists compare.

1 Details of any *items you purchased* in order to commence business such as:

- premises;
- fixtures and fittings (carpets, etc);

- equipment (cashtill);
- van (to collect your stock);
- stock of clothes.

2 *Your source of finance* (where you obtained the money to purchase such items). Most new businesses need to borrow money either to start their operation or to see them through the first year until the company is generating sufficient cash of its own. A loan may therefore be one of the company's sources of finance. Before agreeing to provide such finance the manager of your bank would wish to see that the owners of the company have also invested some of their own money in the business, i.e. capital. Your sources of finance may therefore be a combination of your own money, capital and loans.
3 *Cash received* in respect of sales.
4 *Cash paid out* in respect of further purchases of stock and overheads such as gas, electricity and wages.
5 As a banker I am sure you will realise that not everybody pays for goods in cash, and you will therefore need to record details of *all cheque and credit card transactions* which you both receive and pay.
6 Hopefully, after a period of trading you will be able to purchase your stock on credit, and therefore *purchases made on credit* are another item that needs to be recorded.
7 After a while you may decide to allow your regular customers to buy on credit and only a fool would fail to record details of *sales made on credit.*

## ■ WHY DO WE NEED TO RECORD FINANCIAL INFORMATION?

Now that we have outlined the financial information we need to record, see if you can make a list of the reasons for recording such information. Look back at the list of information in order to assist you, then compare your list with mine. While some of the points are obvious, others are more obscure, so don't worry if you don't manage to get all the points.

1 *To determine whether your clothes shop has achieved a profit or suffered a loss.* More sophisticated bookkeeping could be used to indicate the strong and weak areas of your business, e.g. to determine whether the ladies' section of your shop is profitable.
2 *To determine whether or not the business will be able to meet its financial commitments as they fall due,* through an examination of the company's *cashflow position* (i.e. the flow of cash in and out of the business).
3 *To determine the financial strength and health of the business.*
4 *Credit given to customers* must be recorded to ensure payment is received on the due date, and *credit received* must be recorded to ensure we have the necessary funds available when payment is required.
5 In order to *assess your past performance.*
6 To enable you to *exercise control over your future progress.*
7 *To assist your decision-making.* While you may feel that the ladies' section of your shop is running at a loss, the financial information will provide the answer and

therefore assist, or even make, your decision to discontinue this side of your business.

8 *In order to comply with the law.* As you will later discover, limited companies are required by law to publish an audited set of accounts.

9 The financial information *provides a valuable source of information* and is of interest to a number of people:

(a) shareholders; or

(b) partners – as the owners or joint owners, they are entitled to a share of the profits;

(c) potential creditors; purchases and shareholders;

(d) existing creditors;

(e) banks;

(f) financial institutions – all of whom wish to see whether or not the company is financially healthy before they either invest in the company or provide credit or finance;

(g) Inland Revenue – who are keen to see that the company meets its full tax liability at the appropriate date;

(h) auditors – who are responsible for checking the accounts of the company;

(i) managers within the company – who will be keen to monitor the profitability of their section.

## ■ HOW DO BUSINESSES RECORD THEIR FINANCIAL INFORMATION?

As you have discovered, a considerable amount of information needs to be recorded. It is the accountant's task to collate all the information and to present it in a meaningful manner so that one can determine the profit or loss, whether or not the business will be able to meet its financial commitments, the financial strength and health of the business and so on.

Just how this is done is the subject of this book. The initial chapters are primarily concerned with the recording of financial information for various businesses – sole traders (i.e. someone who is the sole owner of a business, say a shopkeeper), partnerships and limited companies, in order to establish the profit or loss and demonstrate the financial position of the business through the Balance Sheet, which is the subject of Chapter 2.

## ■ SUMMARY

1 Accountancy is concerned with the recording, collating and presenting of financial information in a meaningful manner.

2 The following financial information needs to be recorded:

(a) items purchased to commence business, such as premises, equipment, stock, etc;

(b) your sources of finance (where you obtained the money to purchase such items);

(c) the amount of capital (money contributed by the owners of the business);
(d) cash received;
(e) cash paid out;
(f) cheques and credit card transactions;
(g) purchases on credit;
(h) sales on credit.

3 You need to record financial information in order to:

(a) determine your profit or loss;
(b) assess whether or not the business will be able to meet its financial commitments as they fall due through an examination of the company's cashflow position;
(c) determine the financial strength and health of the business;
(d) ensure payment is received from customers buying on credit on the due date;
(e) ensure you have adequate funds available to meet demands from suppliers who have allowed you to buy on credit;
(f) assess past performance;
(g) exercise control over future progress;
(h) assist management in decision-making;
(i) comply with the law;
(j) provide information to interested parties.

4 Cashflow refers to the flow of cash in and out of the business.

5 The financial position of a company is of interest to the following people:

(a) shareholders;
(b) partners;
(c) potential creditors, purchasers and shareholders;
(d) creditors;
(e) banks;
(f) financial institutions;
(g) Inland Revenue;
(h) auditors;
(i) managers.

6 A sole trader is someone who is the sole owner of a business.

## ■ SELF-ASSESSMENT QUESTIONS

1 Make a list of financial information a businessman would need to record.

2 What is meant by a company's source of finance?

3 What is capital?

4 To which types of customer are businesses likely to offer credit facilities?

5 Make a list of the reasons for recording financial information.

6 What is meant by a company's cashflow position?

7 Why is it important for companies to monitor their cashflow position?

8 Who is interested in a company's financial position?

9 Bert is the owner of a small hotel. Describe three pieces of financial information which you think he should have so that he can exercise control over his business. Explain why these would be important to him in his day-to-day work.

10 'In very few businesses could one obtain an accurate view of the profit or loss for a period by the simple study of cash receipts and payments for that accounting period.' Comment on this statement.

True need what is still saleable, outstanding, produced orders.

11 List six separate reasons why businesses maintain financial records, and explain for each one why such records are needed.

1) Income Expenditure, Stock, sales, Capital, withdrawals, debts, Creditors, Cash, fixtures fittings.

2) Starting Capital 3) Money injected into business by owner/partners to start bus

4) Good long lasting, well established

5) Give info to you, bank, accountant, tax office, creditors,

6) Cashflow. Liquid position

7) Make sure what is in and out agrees,

8) Owners

9)

# 2 The balance sheet

**OBJECTIVES**

**After studying this chapter you should be able to:**

**1 Explain in simple terms the nature and purpose of a Balance Sheet;**
**2 Define various accounting terms such as assets, liabilities, capital, etc;**
**3 Distinguish between fixed and current assets, current and long-term liabilities;**
**4 Understand what happens when a business buys or sells goods on credit;**
**5 Produce a Balance Sheet in a horizontal format.**

## ■ INTRODUCTION

You will recall from Chapter 1 that two important pieces of information recorded by businesses are:

1 details of *items purchased* in order to commence or continue in business, such as premises, equipment and stock, i.e. items the business *owns*; and
2 *the source of finance* (where they obtained the money to purchase such items). So far we have considered two sources:

(a) *capital* (money contributed by the owners) and
(b) *loans* (possibly from a bank), i.e. items the business owes.

You may be wondering why capital is considered to be money owed by the business; after all, it represents money contributed by the owners.

The reason for this is because we make a distinction between the owners and the business, treating each one separately.

*Capital is therefore money owed by the business to the owners of the business.*

## ■ THE BALANCE SHEET FORMAT

So we have two pieces of information:

1 Items the business *owns*, which are known as *assets*.
2 Items the business *owes*, which may take the form of:

(a) *capital* (owed to the owners);
(b) *liabilities* (owed to outside providers of finance).

The Balance Sheet is a record of these details with *assets* on one side and the *capital* and *liabilities* on the other. It therefore reflects the company's financial position at a particular date.

*Balance Sheet of example as at 1.9.X0*

| Items the business owns | Source of finance/money owed |
|---|---|
| *Assets* | *Capital (owners)* |
| | *Liabilities (outside providers)* |

Let us look at an example.

Mr Davenport has just won £50 000 on the football pools and wishes to use the money to start his own business, designing and constructing conservatories (i.e. the £50 000 is a *source of finance*, and as it is contributed by himself it is known as *capital*).

Having done some research he realises that he needs a further £10 000 and therefore approaches the bank for a loan. As his plans for the business appear sound and in view of his creditworthiness the bank agrees to the loan but asks for a mortgage on his house as security (i.e. if Mr Davenport fails to repay the loan, the bank will be able to look towards the sale of the house for repayment). The loan is therefore another *source of finance*, but as it is contributed by someone other than the owners it is known as a *liability*. With the money Mr Davenport purchases the following *assets*:

| | |
|---|---|
| Premises | £30 000 |
| Fixtures | £5 000 |
| Equipment | £2 000 |
| Stock of material | £2 000 |

The Balance Sheet being a record of these details would appear as follows:

*Balance Sheet of Davenport Conservatories (a) as at 31.9.X9 (b)*

| | £ | £ | | £ |
|---|---|---|---|---|
| (c) *Fixed assets* | | | Capital | 50 000 |
| Premises | 30 000 | | | |
| Fixtures | 5 000 | | | |
| Equipment | 2 000 | 37 000 | | |
| | | | *Liabilities* | |
| (c) *Current assets* | | | Loan | 10 000 |
| Stock | 3 000 | | | |
| Cash | 20 000 | 23 000 | | |
| | | 60 000 | (d) | (d) 60 000 |

The important points to note are:

(a) *Title*

*The title should always indicate whose balance sheet it is*, in our case Davenport Conservatories, which is not the same as Mr Davenport. As a result Mr Davenport's house, an asset owned by him does not appear on the Balance Sheet, despite its importance to the bank. The only items in the Balance Sheet of a business are those owned or owed by the business. This is known as the *Business Entity Concept*.

(b) *Date*

*The Balance Sheet is like a photograph of the business's financial position* **as at** *a particular date only.*

(c) *There are two types of asset*

(i) *Fixed Assets*

Items of a permanent or semi-permanent nature, necessary for carrying out the business activities and therefore not normally changed in day-to-day trading. These are listed above Current Assets in order of permanence.

(ii) *Current Assets*

Items acquired or produced for resale and conversion into cash – the least liquid being listed first.

(d) *A balance sheet must always balance*

This is because one side represents the source of finance and the other what you have done with that money *plus*, in our case, the remaining cash of £20 000. After all, the remaining is something owned by the business and therefore an asset.

We can therefore say that:

ASSET = CAPITAL + LIABILITIES
(items owned) = (source of finance)

(e) *Layout*

This balance sheet is in a horizontal format, but as you will see later there are other ways of presenting the information.

The important thing is to be neat.

*(i)* underline titles such as 'fixed assets' etc;
*(ii)* do not simply list fixed and current assets in one column, use two, so the reader can see the sub-total for fixed and current assets at a glance;
*(iii)* list the items in their correct order;
*(iv)* put the total on the same line;
*(v)* do not forget the heading.

Accountancy is concerned with conveying information and as a result marks are often to be gained in the examination by paying attention to these points. They take little understanding, so do not lose these marks.

## PROGRESS TEST 1

Now try the following exercises. The answers are given in Appendix A, so check that you are correct before continuing.

(a) Complete the table

| | Assets | Capital | Liabilities |
|---|---|---|---|
| | £ | £ | £ |
| (i) | 7 500 | 5 000 | |
| (ii) | | 26 500 | 11 000 |
| (iii) | 15 000 | | 2 500 |
| (iv) | 25 000 | 15 750 | |

(b) Rearrange the following items to produce the balance sheet of Costa's Bakery as at 30.9.Y0. Unfortunately, Costa forgot to advise you of the amount of capital, but remember, a balance sheet always balances.

| | £ |
|---|---|
| Fixtures and fittings | 7 000 |
| Cash | 2 000 |
| Loan | 12 000 |
| Premises | 56 500 |
| Equipment | 5 000 |
| Stock | 2 000 |

## ■ BUYING AND SELLING ON CREDIT

### Buying on credit

Let us assume that Mr Davenport now decides to purchase another £2 000 of material (stock). On this occasion, however, he manages to secure credit terms of two months. How will this affect his balance sheet, shown on page 7?

Well, the first thing, which I am sure you have realised, is that stock will increase from £3 000 to £5 000 and with it the total of the assets.

*Balance Sheet of Davenport Conservatories as at 31.10.X9*

| | £ | £ | | £ |
|---|---|---|---|---|
| *Fixed assets* | | | Capital | 50 000 |
| Premises | 30 000 | | | |
| Fixtures | 5 000 | | | |
| Equipment | 2 000 | 37 000 | *Liabilities* | |
| | | | Loan | 10 000 |
| *Current assets* | | | | |
| **Stock** | **5 000** | | | |
| Cash | 20 000 | 25 000 | | |
| | | 62 000 | | 60 000 |

The problem now is that the assets equal £62 000 and the capital plus liabilities equal £60 000, i.e. the Balance Sheet does *not* balance, and as you know *a balance sheet must always balance.*

The reason for this is that, while we have recorded the increase in stock, we have not recorded the fact that Mr Davenport owes £2 000 to his supplier (i.e. we have another *liability*).

In this case the liability is known as a *creditor* (someone to whom we owe money following the purchase of goods) and as the debt is repayable within one year the liability is a *current liability.*

Debts repayable after more than one year are known as *deferred or long-term liabilities.*

So if we record our creditor of £2 000 and the increase in stock of £2 000, the balance sheet will appear as follows:

*Balance Sheet of Davenport Conservatories as at 31.1.X9*

| | £ | £ | | £ |
|---|---|---|---|---|
| *Fixed assets* | | | Capital | 50 000 |
| Premises | 30 000 | | | |
| Fixtures | 5 000 | | *Deferred liabilities* | |
| Equipment | 2 000 | 37 000 | Loan | 10 000 |
| *Current assets* | | | *Current liabilities* | |
| **Stock** | **5 000** | | **Creditors** | **2 000** |
| Cash | 20 000 | 25 000 | | |
| | | 62 000 | | 62 000 |

***Current and deferred liabilities***

In the Balance Sheet above I have assumed that the loan is over a period of more than twelve months and is therefore a deferred or long-term liability.

What is the position, however, with an *overdraft*? Obviously, it is a liability (money owed by the business), but is it current or deferred? After all, many businesses have overdrafts outstanding for many years. As you will discover from your studies of *Banking, the Legal Environment* (David Palfreman, Pitman Publishing, 1991), an overdraft is normally repayable on demand and is therefore considered a *current liability*.

**Selling on credit**

Suppose Mr Davenport now designs and erects a conservatory for a customer at a price of £5 000, but with payment being at one month's credit, as the sale is to a friend. The materials and stock originally cost £2 000 and Mr Davenport will therefore earn a profit of £3 000 from this job.

Let us look at how this will affect the Balance Sheet. First of all, stock will obviously reduce by £2 000, as stock is recorded in the Balance Sheet at the cost price. But what else are we going to do to make the Balance Sheet balance?

Well, we need to record the profit of £3 000, earned by the business. As this belongs to the owners of the business, the amount is added to the capital, making the Balance Sheet appear as follows:

*Balance Sheet of Davenport Conservatories as at 31.11.X9*

| | £ | £ | | £ |
|---|---|---|---|---|
| *Fixed assets* | | | Capital | 50 000 |
| Premises | 30 000 | | **Profits** | **3 000** |
| Fixtures | 5 000 | | | |
| Equipment | 2 000 | 37 000 | *Deferred liabilities* | |
| | | | Loan | 10 000 |
| *Current assets* | | | *Current liabilities* | |
| **Stock** | **3 000** | | Creditors | 2 000 |
| Cash | 20 000 | 23 000 | | |
| | | 60 000 | | 65 000 |

Once again the Balance Sheet does not balance because we have failed to record something. We have failed to record the fact that £5 000 is owed to the business, i.e. there is a *debtor* of £5 000 (someone who owes the business money).

As *debtors* are, hopefully, converted into cash in the near future they are a *current asset.*

The completed Balance Sheet appears as follows:

*Balance Sheet of Davenport Conservatories as at 31.12.X9*

| | £ | £ | | £ |
|---|---|---|---|---|
| *Fixed assets* | | | Capital | 50 000 |
| Premises | 30 000 | | **Profits** | **3 000** |
| Fixtures | 5 000 | | | 53 000 |
| Equipment | 2 000 | 37 000 | *Deferred liabilities* | |
| | | | Loan | 10 000 |
| *Current assets* | | | *Current liabilities* | |
| **Stock** | **3 000** | | Creditors | 2 000 |
| **Debtors** | **5 000** | | | |
| Cash | 20 000 | 28 000 | | |
| | | 65 000 | | 65 000 |

**PROGRESS TEST 2**

Now complete the following table before checking your answer (in Appendix A).

| | Effect upon: Assets | Capital | Liabilities |
|---|---|---|---|
| e.g. | | | |
| (a) Purchased stock for £3 000 cash | Stock + £3 000<br>Cash – £3 000 | | |
| (b) Paid a creditor by cheque £4 000 | | | |
| (c) Obtained a loan for £1 000 | | | |
| (d) The owner injected a further £5 000 into the business | | | |

## ■ DRAWINGS

When we calculated Mr Davenport's profit of £3 000 we simply stated that material (stock) originally cost £2000 and could be sold as a conservatory for £5 000. We have therefore ignored at this stage any money spent by Mr Davenport on overheads such as gas, electricity and wages paid to employees. Such expenses do not directly appear in the Balance Sheet but the Trading Profit and Loss Account, which we shall examine in Chapter 4.

Suppose, however, Mr Davenport wanted to withdraw £2 000 for his own living expenses. How would we deal with this item? It would be easy to think that it is dealt with in the same way as wages paid to employees in the Trading Profit and Loss Account but this is *not* the case.

Money withdrawn by the owners of a business, for their own personal use is known as *drawings* and is reflected in the Balance Sheet as a deduction from the money owed to them, i.e. from capital and profits.

A withdrawal, or *drawings* of £2000 would therefore be represented by the Balance Sheet as follows:

*Balance Sheet of Davenport Conservatories as at 31.1.Y0*

| | £ | £ | | £ |
|---|---|---|---|---|
| *Fixed assets* | | | Capital | 50 000 |
| Premises | 30 000 | | + Profits | 3 000 |
| Fixtures | 5 000 | | | 53 000 |
| Equipment | 2 000 | 37 000 | **– Drawings** | **2 000** |
| | | | | 51 000 |
| *Current assets* | | | *Deferred liabilities* | |
| Stock | 3 000 | | Loan | 10 000 |
| Debtors | 5 000 | | *Current liabilities* | |
| **Cash** | **18 000** | 26 000 | Creditor | 2 000 |
| | | 63 000 | | 63 000 |

Note how cash has reduced by £2000 as a result of the drawing. A *double effect*, you might say, causing us to make a *double entry*.

In the next chapter we shall examine the double effect of transactions when we look at *Double Entry Bookkeeping*, a subject with which some of you may be familiar from your studies of *Business Calculations* (Helen V Coult, Pitman Publishing, 1990) (Preliminary Certificate).

## ■ SUMMARY

1 A Balance Sheet reflects the financial position of a business at a particular date only.

2 The title to the Balance Sheet should indicate whose accounts it represents.

3 The only items to appear in the balance sheet of a company are the items owned or owed by the business *not* the personal assets of the owners. This is the *Business Entity Concept*.

4 A Balance Sheet in the horizontal format shows assets on one side and capital plus liabilities (source of finance) on the other.

5 Assets = Capital + Liabilities.

6 A Balance Sheet must always balance.

7 Assets are items *owned* by the business, e.g. premises.

8 Fixed assets are of a permanent or semi-permanent nature, necessary for the continuation of the business and therefore not normally changed in the day-to-day trading.

9 Current assets are items acquired or produced for resale and conversion into cash.

10 Capital is the amount contributed by the owners of the business.

11 Profits are owed by the business to the owners and are therefore added to capital.

12 Drawings represent the money withdrawn by the owners and are deducted from capital plus profits.

13 Liabilities are amounts owed by the business.

14 Long-term liabilities are debts that are repayable after more than one year.

15 Current liabilities are debts that are repayable within one year.

16 Overdrafts are normally repayable on demand and are therefore considered to be a *current liability.*

17 Creditors are people to whom the business owes money and are hence a liability, and if repayable within one year a current liability.

18 Debtors are people who owe the business money and are hence a *current asset.*

## ■ SELF-ASSESSMENT QUESTIONS

1 Define the following terms:

- Drawings
- Deferred liability
- Current assets
- Debtors
- Creditors

2 Complete the table:

| | Assets | Capital | Liabilities |
|---|---|---|---|
| | £ | £ | £ |
| (a) | 50 000 | | 10 000 |
| (b) | 62 000 | 40 000 | |
| (c) | | 20 000 | 30 000 |
| (d) | 17 500 | | 2 000 |
| (e) | | 25 000 | 10 000 |
| (f) | 15 000 | 10 000 | |

3 What is meant when a Balance Sheet is described as a photograph of a company?

4 What do you understand by the term 'Business Entity Concept'?

**5** Complete the table:

| | Effect upon: Assets | Capital | Liabilities |
|---|---|---|---|
| e.g. (a) Purchased stock on credit £2 000 | Stock + £2 000 | | Creditors + £2 000 |
| (b) Purchased a van for £5 000 in cash | | | |
| (c) The owner puts a further £2 500 cash into the business | | | |
| (d) Sold goods originally costing £1 000 for £3 000, on credit terms | | | |
| (e) Obtained a bank loan for £7 000 | | | |
| (f) Debtors of £1 000 pay their debts by cheque | | | |

**6** Indicate whether the following items are fixed assets; current assets; current liabilities, etc.

- Creditors
- Debtors
- Drawings
- Bank loan
- Bank overdraft
- Cash
- Stock
- Profits

**7** Rearrange these items in their correct order:

| *Current assets* | £ |
|---|---|
| Bank | 1 000 |
| Stock | 2 000 |
| Cash | 500 |
| Debtors | 5 000 |

8 Produce a Balance Sheet for Mr J Cartwright's greengrocery business, 'The Spud Shop' as at 30.9.Y0. Unfortunately, Mr Cartwright has mixed his personal and business information.

| | | £ |
|---|---|---|
| Capital | | 31 000 |
| Amounts due from suppliers | | 2 000 |
| Amounts due from customers | | 5 000 |
| Bank: | Current account J Cartwright | 2 000 |
| | Loan account J Cartwright | 1 000 |
| | Loan account Spud Shop | 10 000 |
| Shop premises | | 30 000 |
| Drawings | | 1 000 |
| Stock of goods | | 5 000 |
| Private house | | 68 000 |
| Equipment | | 2 000 |

ACCOUNTS OF THE SPUD SHOP AS AT. 30.9.Y0.

| | | | | | |
|---|---|---|---|---|---|
| FIXED ASSETS. | | | CAPITAL | 31000 | |
| PREMISES. | 30 000 | | + PROFIT | 2000 | |
| EQUIPMENT | 2 000 | 32000 | – DRAWINGS. | 1000 | 32000 |
| CURRENT ASSETS | | | LONG TERM LIABILITIES. | | |
| STOCK OF GOODS | 5000 | | LOAN | 10 000 | |
| DEBTORS | 7000 | | LOAN | 1 000 | 11 000 |
| BANK/CASH | 0000 | 12000. | SHORT TERM LIAB. | | |
| | | | CREDITORS | | |
| | | | OVERDRAFT | 1000 | 1000 |
| | | 44000 | | | 44 000 |

# 3 Double entry bookkeeping

**OBJECTIVES**

**After studying this chapter you should be able to:**

**1 Understand the nature of double entry bookkeeping;**

**2 Produce a trial balance from a number of bookkeeping entries;**

**3 Outline the purpose of a trial balance.**

## ■ INTRODUCTION

In the last chapter we followed the activities of Mr Davenport and witnessed his Balance Sheet change with every business transaction.

Imagine the situation if Mr Davenport and other businesses such as Marks & Spencer drew up a new Balance Sheet after every transaction, 'Sir we've just sold another Chicken Kiev, I mean another two, sorry three...'. Obviously it would be impossible to do so.

Fortunately, it is also unnecessary as companies only need to draw up a Balance Sheet once a year at the end of their accounting period.

While they only need to produce a Balance Sheet once a year they will still need to record certain accounting information on a regular basis in order to keep control over their business.

For example, you would not simply wait until the balance-sheet date to calculate your debtors, you need to see how much is owed and by whom on any one day.

## ■ HOW DOES A COMPANY MAINTAIN RECORDS?

The recording of such information will differ from company to company. A newsagent may simply have a book with each customer's name on a separate page listing the amounts owed. Other companies may have their debtors listed on computer, with each debtor having a separate file or page.

Then at the end of the accounting period, when the company wishes to produce its Balance Sheet, it can either manually total up the amounts owed from each debtor or ask the computer to produce a figure which could be transferred to the Balance Sheet.

As you can imagine, in practice it is a lot more difficult than I have outlined. When the accounts of a company such as Marks & Spencer are published, they may well be a few months old.

## ■ DOUBLE ENTRY BOOKKEEPING

So far I have only mentioned the need to monitor debtors on a day-to-day basis, but the same could be said for creditors, cash and many other items.

You will therefore need a separate record or ledger for each item so the up-to-date position of each can be seen at any time.

These ledgers are often known as 'T' accounts and may be drawn as follows:

| *Debit* | | | *Cash* | *Credit* | |
|---|---|---|---|---|---|
| Date | Transaction | Amount | Date | Transaction | Amount |

The terms *debit* and *credit* simply mean left and right and should *not* be confused with their meaning in banking.

*Debit side records:* Money / goods **in**
and / or Items you own (as in the Balance Sheet)

*Credit side records:* Money / goods **out**
and / or Money owed (as in the Balance Sheet)

| *Debit* | *Credit* |
|---|---|
| Money/Goods **in**<br>Items owned<br>(as per Balance Sheet) | Money/Goods **out**<br>Money owed<br>(as per Balance Sheet) |

**Example**

Let us follow the transactions of Mr O'Neil of Wonder Records.

*Oct 1 Commenced business with £30 000 in the bank.*

Mr O'Neil will need to record the amount of capital he has contributed and is therefore *owed* by the business *and* the cash the business has received.
He will therefore need two separate records:

*Bank*

| | | | |
|---|---|---|---|
| Oct 1 Capital | £30 000 | | |

*Capital*

| | | | |
|---|---|---|---|
| | | Oct 1 Bank | £1 000 |

*Bank* is recorded on the left-hand side (Debit) as it is money going *into* the business.
*Capital* is recorded on the right-hand side (Credit) as it is money *owed* by the business.
The narrative is simply a cross-reference to the other book, describing the transaction.

*Oct 1 Transferred £1000 from the bank to the petty cash.*

*Bank*

| | | | |
|---|---|---|---|
| Oct 1 Capital | £30 000 | Oct 1 Cash | £1 000 |

*Cash*

| | | | |
|---|---|---|---|
| Oct 1 Bank | £1 000 | | |

*Bank* is a credit entry as it is money going *out*.
*Cash* is a debit entry as it is money going *in*.

*This is not a misprint*. Remember, in accounts debit and credit simply mean left and right, a point which often confuses bankers.

*Oct 2 Purchased equipment for £5000 by cheque.*

*Bank*

| | | | |
|---|---|---|---|
| Oct 1 Capital | £30 000 | Oct 1 Cash | £1 000 |
| | | Oct 2 Equipment | £5 000 |

*Equipment*

| | | | |
|---|---|---|---|
| Oct 2 Cash | £5 000 | | |

*Bank* is a credit entry it is money going *out*.
*Equipment* is a debit entry as it is something you *own*.

As you will discover, each transaction has a *double effect*, with one entry being made on the debit side (left-hand side) of one ledger and another entry being made on the credit side (right-hand side) of another ledger. For every debit there is a credit. Hence the name *double entry bookkeeping*. Remember money coming in or items purchased are on the debit side, while money going out and money owed are on the credit side.

**PROGRESS TEST 1**

Enter the following transactions in their various ledgers.

Oct 1 Started business with £20 000 cash
Oct 2 Purchased: Van £10 000
Equipment £2 000
Fittings £2 000
Oct 3 Obtained a bank loan of £10 000, and opened up a bank account for the business.
Oct 4 Transferred £3 000 cash into the banks.

## ■ EXPENSES

So far we have ignored expenses such as gas, electricity etc, let us examine how we would deal with these in the case of Mr O'Neil.

*Oct 3 Paid rent of £150 by cheque.*
*Oct 4 Paid wages £200 by cheque.*

*Bank*

| | | | | | |
|---|---|---|---|---|---|
| | | | | | £ |
| Oct 1 | Capital | £30 000 | Oct 1 | Cash | 1 000 |
| | | | 2 | Equipment | 5 000 |
| | | | 3 | Rent | 150 |
| | | | 4 | Wages | 200 |

*Rent*

| | | | |
|---|---|---|---|
| Oct 3 | Cash | £150 | |

*Wages*

| | | | |
|---|---|---|---|
| Oct 4 | Cash | £200 | |

*Bank* the amounts are recorded on the right-hand side as cash going out.
*Expenses paid* are recorded on the left-hand side *the opposite side to cash going out.*

Remember entries are always on one side of one ledger and the other side of another in order to make both sides balance.

## ■ CARRIAGE IN AND CARRIAGE OUT

These terms simply refer to transport costs relating to the transport of goods in or out, they are therefore dealt with like any other expenses when entering details in the ledgers.

However, as you shall see later, *Carriage In*, being an expense incurred as a direct result of purchasing, is dealt with differently from other expenses when it comes to the Trading Profit and Loss Account.

## ■ STOCK

*Oct 5 Purchased a stock of 5000 records for £5 000 (i.e. £1 each) on two months' credit from A Black*

*Purchases*

| | | | |
|---|---|---|---|
| Oct 5 | A Black | £5 000 | |

*A Black (Creditor)*

| | | | |
|---|---|---|---|
| | Oct 5 | Purchases | £5 000 |

As you can see we do not have a ledger for stock, instead we have:

(i) a purchases ledger
(ii) a sales ledger.

This is because goods are purchased at cost price while sold at a profit.

*Oct 6 Sold 2 500 records for £5 000 (i.e. £2 each) payment by cheque.*

*Sales*

| | | | |
|---|---|---|---|
| | | Oct 6 Bank | £5 000 |

*Bank*

| | £ | | £ |
|---|---|---|---|
| Oct 1 Capital | 30 000 | Oct 1 Cash | 1 000 |
| 6 Sales | 5 000 | 2 Equipment | 5 000 |
| | | 3 Rent | 150 |
| | | 4 Wages | 200 |

If we did not have separate ledgers for purchases and sales, the stock ledger would appear as though we had no stock left, which is not the case.

*Stock*

| | | | |
|---|---|---|---|
| Oct 5 A Black (i.e. 5 000 records @ £1 each) | £5 000 | Oct 6 Bank (i.e. 2 500 records @ £2 each) | £5 000 |

## ■ DAY BOOKS OR JOURNALS

Where companies buy and sell a large number of items on credit the purchases and sales ledger may well become cluttered. To avoid this such companies may use Day Books or Journals to record all credit transactions.

### Sales day book

Credit sales are entered in the Day Book at the point of sale. Then at the end of the accounting period the Day Book is totalled up and the balance transferred to the Sales Ledger.

*Forrester Ltd Sales Day Book*

| *Date* | | *Debtor* | *Invoice No* | £ |
|---|---|---|---|---|
| Jan | 1 | Mather | 1810 | 1 000 |
| | 5 | Jennings | 1911 | 5 100 |
| | 8 | Knowles | 1812 | 2 610 |
| | 11 | Peters | 1813 | 4 200 |
| | 15 | Gilzean | 1814 | 650 |
| | 26 | Hunt | 1815 | 810 |
| | 31 | Rogers | 1816 | 2 000 |
| | 31 | Transfer to Sales Ledger | | 16 370 |

*Sales*

| | | | |
|---|---|---|---|
| | | Jan 31 Credit sales for the month | £16 370 |

NB: The double entries will therefore be:

(a) Enter the sale in the Sales Day Book.
(b) Debit each individual debtors' ledger at the time of sale.

For example:

*Mather (Debtor)*

| | | |
|---|---|---|
| Jan 1 Sales | £1 000 | |

*Jennings (Debtor)*

| | | |
|---|---|---|
| Jan 5 Sales | £5 100 | |

**Other day books**

Day books are also kept for:

(a) Purchase Day Book – credit purchases are listed in the Purchases Day Book and at the end of the accounting period the balance is transferred to the Purchase Ledger;
(b) Returns Inwards Day Book;
(c) Returns Outwards Day Book.

As the questions and examples which follow do not involve many transactions you will not be required to enter items in the day books.

Let us now return to Mr O'Neil and Wonder Records.

## ■ RETURNS IN AND RETURNS OUT

(a) *Returns In* refers to goods which have been returned to us possibly because they are faulty.
(b) *Returns Out* refers to goods we have returned to our suppliers.

Let us see how we would deal with these.

*Oct 7 Returned goods of £1000 to A Black, which were faulty.*

*Returns out*

| | | | |
|---|---|---|---|
| | | Oct 7 A Black | £1 000 |

*A Black (Creditor)*

| | | | |
|---|---|---|---|
| Oct 7 Ret Out | £1 000 | Oct 5 Purchases | £4 000 |

(a) Open a new ledger for Returns Out (remember every item has its own ledger).
(b) Credit the Returns Out ledger – goods going *out*.
(c) Debit A Black – his ledger will therefore show that we originally owed him £5 000 but have since returned goods of £1 000, indicating that we now owe him only £4 000.

*Oct 8 Customer returns faulty goods to us of £100 in return for a cash refund.*

*Cash*

| | | | |
|---|---|---|---|
| Oct 1 Bank | £1 000 | Oct 5 Returns In | £100 |

*Returns in*

| | | | |
|---|---|---|---|
| Oct 8 Cash | £100 | | |

## ■ DISCOUNTS

In business there are two types of discount:

(a) *Trade discount* – given to customers who buy in bulk.

e.g. *Oct 10 Sales of goods £500 to V Ahmed on credit terms of 1 month, with a trade discount of 5%.*

| | £ |
|---|---|
| Sales of goods | 500 |
| Less discount 5% | 25 |
| Net amount due | 475 |

*V Ahmed*

| | | | |
|---|---|---|---|
| Oct 10 Sales | £475 | | |

*Sales*

| | | | |
|---|---|---|---|
| | | Oct 10 V Ahmed | £475 |

In this case the discount is deducted at the time of sale and therefore only the net amount appears in the ledger.

(b) *Cash discount* – given to customers for prompt payment. Here the customer will have originally been invoiced for the total amount.

e.g. *Oct 11 Sale of goods £100 to S Broady on credit terms of 3 months, with a 5% cash discount for prompt payment.*

Original entries:

*S Broady*

| | | | |
|---|---|---|---|
| Oct 11 Sales | £100 | | |

*Sales*

| | | | |
|---|---|---|---|
| | | Oct 11 S Broady | £100 |

*Oct 20 S Broady has unexpectedly received some money and calls to pay his bill early by cheque.*

This will qualify him for the 5% cash discount, i.e. 5% of £100 = £5. He therefore needs to pay only £95 (£100 – 5).

*S Broady*

| | | | | | |
|---|---|---|---|---|---|
| Oct 11 | Sales | £100 | Oct 20 | Cash | £95 |

*Cash*

| | | | | | |
|---|---|---|---|---|---|
| Oct 20 | Broady | £95 | | | |

As you can see, S Broady's ledger still indicates that he owes £5. We therefore need to record details of the discount we have *allowed* him.

The transaction is therefore completed in the following manner:

*Discounts allowed*

| | | | | | |
|---|---|---|---|---|---|
| Oct 20 | S Broady | £5 | | | |

*S Broady*

| | | | | | |
|---|---|---|---|---|---|
| Oct 11 | Sales | £100 | Oct 20 | Cash | £95 |
| | | | 20 | Dis. All. | £5 |

Mr O'Neil may also *receive discounts*, i.e. from suppliers, either for bulk orders (trade discount) or for prompt payment (cash discount).

e.g. *Oct 30 Paid A Black in full by cheque after deducting £100 for prompt payment.*

*A Black (Creditor)*

| | | | | | |
|---|---|---|---|---|---|
| Oct 7 | Ret. Out | £1 000 | Oct 5 | Purchases | £5 000 |
| 9 | Dis. Revd. | £100 | | | |

*Discount received*

| | | | | | |
|---|---|---|---|---|---|
| | | | Oct 9 | A Black | £100 |

The balance to pay is £3 900 (£5 000 – (1 000 + 100) and the transaction is therefore completed as follows:

*A Black (Creditor)*

| | | | | | |
|---|---|---|---|---|---|
| | | £ | | | |
| Oct 7 | Returns Out | 1 000 | Oct 5 | Purchases | 5 000 |
| 9 | Discount received | 100 | | | |
| 30 | Bank | 3 900 | | | |

*Bank*

| | | | | | |
|---|---|---|---|---|---|
| | | £ | | | £ |
| Oct 1 | Capital | 30 000 | Oct 1 | Cash | 1 000 |
| 6 | Sales | 5 000 | 2 | Equipment | 5 000 |
| 20 | S Broady | 95 | 3 | Rent | 150 |
| | | | 4 | Wages | 200 |
| | | | 30 | A Black | 3 900 |

So:

*Discounts allowed* – represents cash discounts we have allowed our customers.
*Discounts received* – represents cash discounts we have received from our customers.

**PROGRESS TEST 2**

Complete the following table.

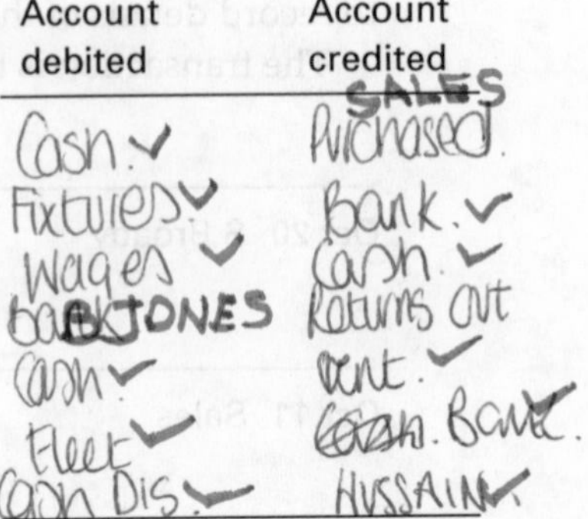

| | Account debited | Account credited |
|---|---|---|
| (a) Sold goods for £1 000 cash | | |
| (b) Bought fixtures by cheque for £3 000 | | |
| (c) Paid wages of £200 cash | | |
| (d) Returned goods to B Jones for £150 | | |
| (e) Received rent of £100 in cash in respect of premises sub-let | | |
| (f) Paid electricity £200 by cheque | | |
| (g) Allowed Mr Hussain £50 *cash* discount | | |

## ■ BALANCING OFF THE LEDGERS

Earlier in the chapter I mentioned that companies need to produce a Balance Sheet only at the end of their accounting period and that in the meantime they will record details of their transactions in ledgers.

Suppose Mr O'Neil has now come to the end of his accounting period and wishes to produce his final accounts.

First of all he must balance off the ledgers by adding up the greater side, which then forms the total of the ledger, i.e. £35 095.

*Bank*

| | | £ | | | £ |
|---|---|---|---|---|---|
| Oct | 1 Capital | 30 000 | Oct | 1 Cash | 1 000 |
| | 6 Sales | 5 000 | | 2 Equipment | 5 000 |
| | 20 S Broady | 95 | | 3 Rent | 150 |
| | | | | 4 Wages | 200 |
| | | | | 30 A Black | 3 900 |
| | | | | 30 Balance | 24 945 |
| | | 35 095 | | | 35 095 |
| Nov | 1 Balance c/o | £24 700 | | | |

He must then make the other side equal £35 095 by inserting a balancing figure of £24 945 which represents the money left in the bank account.

The balance is then carried over as the starting balance of the next accounting period and is the amount entered in the trial balance.

## ■ TRIAL BALANCE

The trial balance is a summary of the balances remaining in the various ledgers, with debits on one side and credits on the other. You may not be surprised to notice that the trial balance balances. This, you will recall is because an entry has been made on one side of one ledger and the other side of another, i.e. for every debit there is a credit.

Obviously, if it does not balance, then we have made a mistake, and the trial balance therefore provides a check on the accuracy of the accounts. Unfortunately, that does not necessarily mean that our accounts are accurate if the trial balance does balance. We may have:

1 omitted to enter details of a transaction on either side;
2 entered details twice;
3 entered the wrong amount in both ledgers;
4 entered the correct amount but in the wrong ledgers.

These types of error will be considered in the next chapter, but for now let us concentrate on entering details in the ledgers and constructing a trial balance.

A full recap of Mr O'Neil's transaction, together with a record of his ledgers are given below, illustrating:

(a) the recording of entries;
(b) the balancing of ledger;
(c) the construction of a trial balance.

*Mr O'Neil of Wonder Records*

Oct 1 Commenced business with £30 in the bank.
1 Transferred £1 000 from the bank to the petty cash.
2 Purchased equipment for £5 000 by cheque.
3 Paid rent of £150 by cheque.
4 Paid gas £50 and wages £200 by cheque.
5 Purchased a stock of 5 000 records for £5 000 on two months' credit from A Black.
6 Sold 2 500 records for £5 000, payment by cheque.
7 Returned goods of £1 000 to A Black which were faulty.
8 Customers returned faulty goods to us of £100 in exchange for cash refund.
10 Sale of goods £500 to V Ahmed on credit terms of 1 month with a trade discount of 5%.
11 Sale of goods £100 to S Broady on credit terms of 3 months, with a 5% cash discount for prompt payment.
20 S Broady unexpectedly received some money and calls to pay his bill early by cheque.
30 Paid A Black in full by cheque, after deducting £100 for prompt payment.

### Bank

| | | £ | | | £ |
|---|---|---|---|---|---|
| Oct 1 | Cash | 30 000 | Oct 1 | Cash | 1 000 |
| 6 | Sales | 5 000 | 2 | Equipment | 5 000 |
| 20 | S Broady | 95 | 3 | Rent | 150 |
| | | | | Wages | 200 |
| | | | 30 | Bank | 3 900 |
| | | | 31 | Balance | 24 845 |
| | | 35 095 | | | 35 095 |
| Nov 1 | Balance c/o | 24 845 | | | |

### Capital

| | | £ | | | £ |
|---|---|---|---|---|---|
| Oct 31 | Balance c/o | 30 000 | Nov 1 | Bank | 30 000 |
| | | | 1 | Balance c/o | 30 000 |

### Cash

| | | £ | | | £ |
|---|---|---|---|---|---|
| Oct 1 | | 1 000 | Oct 8 | Return In | 100 |
| | | | 31 | Balance | 900 |
| | | 1 000 | | | 1 000 |
| Nov 1 | Balance c/o | 900 | | | |

### Equipment

| | | £ | | | £ |
|---|---|---|---|---|---|
| Oct 2 | Bank | 5 000 | Oct 31 | Balance | 5 000 |
| Nov 1 | Balance c/o | 5 000 | | | |

### Rent

| | | £ | | | £ |
|---|---|---|---|---|---|
| Oct 31 | Bank | 150 | Oct 31 | Balance | 150 |
| Nov 1 | Balance c/o | 150 | | | |

### Wages

| | | £ | | | £ |
|---|---|---|---|---|---|
| Oct 3 | Bank | 200 | Oct 31 | Balance | 200 |
| Nov 1 | Balance c/o | 200 | | | |

### Purchases

| | | £ | | | £ |
|---|---|---|---|---|---|
| Oct 5 | A Black | 5 000 | Oct 31 | Balance | 5 000 |
| Nov 1 | Balance c/o | 5 000 | | | |

*A Black*

| | | £ | | | £ |
|---|---|---|---|---|---|
| Oct 7 | Returns Out | 1 000 | Oct 5 | Purchases | 5 000 |
| 30 | A Black | 100 | | | |
| 30 | Bank | 3 900 | | | |
| | | 5 000 | | | 5 000 |

*Sales*

| | | £ | | | £ |
|---|---|---|---|---|---|
| | | | Oct 6 | Bank | 5 000 |
| | | | 10 | Ahmed | 475 |
| Oct 31 | Balance | 5 575 | 11 | S Broady | 100 |
| | | 5 575 | | | 5 575 |
| | | | Nov 1 | Balance c/o | 5 575 |

*Returns out*

| | | £ | | | £ |
|---|---|---|---|---|---|
| Oct 31 | Balance | 1 000 | Oct 7 | A Black | 1 000 |
| | | | Nov 1 | Balance c/o | 1 000 |

*Returns in*

| | | £ | | | £ |
|---|---|---|---|---|---|
| Oct 8 | Cash | 100 | Oct 31 | Balance | 100 |
| Nov 1 | Balance c/o | 100 | | | |

*V Ahmed*

| | | £ | | | £ |
|---|---|---|---|---|---|
| Oct 10 | Sales | 475 | Oct 31 | Balance | 475 |
| Nov 1 | Balance c/o | 475 | | | |

*S Broady*

| | | £ | | | £ |
|---|---|---|---|---|---|
| Oct 11 | Sales | 100 | Oct 20 | Discount allowed | 5 |
| | | | 20 | Bank | 95 |
| | | 100 | | | 100 |

*Discount allowed*

| | | £ | | | £ |
|---|---|---|---|---|---|
| Oct 20 | S Broady | 5 | Oct 31 | Balance | 5 |
| Nov 1 | Balance c/o | 5 | | | |

*Discount received*

| | £ | | £ |
|---|---|---|---|
| Oct 31 Balance | 100 | Oct 30 A Black | 100 |
| | | Nov 1 Balance c/o | 100 |

*Trial Balance of Wonder Records as at 31.10.Y0*

| | £ | £ |
|---|---|---|
| Bank | 24 845 | |
| Capital | | 30 000 |
| Cash | 900 | |
| Equipment | 5 000 | |
| Rent | 150 | |
| Wages | 200 | |
| Purchases | 5 000 | |
| A Black | | |
| Sales | | 5 575 |
| Returns out | | 1 000 |
| Returns in | 100 | |
| V Ahmed (Debtor) | 475 | |
| S Broady | | |
| Discounts allowed | 5 | |
| Discounts received | | 100 |
| | 36 675 | 36 675 |

**PROGRESS TEST 3**

Enter the following transactions in the appropriate ledgers and draw up the trial balance of Nigel Cripps.

Nov 1 Started business with £2 000 in the bank.
2 Purchased goods for £175 on credit from M Lowe.
3 Bought a second-hand van for £1 000 by cheque.
4 Sold goods for cash £1 000.
5 Returned faulty goods to M Lowe for £50.
8 Sold goods on credit to P Daubney £500.
10 Nigel withdrew £500 cash to buy a new car phone for his BMW.
12 Paid electricity bill of £36 in cash.
16 Paid rent of £50 by cheque.
19 Purchased goods of £1 000 on credit from N Rose.
20 Paid M Lowe by cheque after deducting £20 for a cash discount.
26 Sold goods for £300 cash.
29 P Daubney returned £100 of goods to use.
30 Obtained a bank loan of £5 000 placing the money in the bank account.

## ■ SUMMARY

1 A company will only draw up its balance sheet at the end of its accounting period, usually once a year.

2 Double entry bookkeeping is a system of record keeping which enables a business to record its daily transactions.

3 A separate record or *ledger* is kept for each item.

4 The left-hand side of the ledger is known as the debit side.

5 The right-hand side of the ledger is known as the credit side.

6 Debit and credit simply mean left and right and should not be confused with their meaning in banking.

7 Generally, money/goods coming into the business are recorded on the debit side.

8 Generally, money/goods going out of the business and money owed are recorded on the credit side.

9 For each transaction there are two entries – one on the credit side of one ledger and one on the debit side of another, i.e. for every debit there is a credit.

10 Expenses paid, such as gas, wages etc are recorded on the debit side, as the double entry to cash/cheques paid out which is recorded on the credit side.

11 Carriage In refers to the cost of transporting goods into the business and is considered to be an expense incurred as a result of purchasing.

12 Carriage Out refers to the cost of transporting goods from the business.

13 The purchase of stock is recorded in a purchases ledger at the cost price and not a stock ledger.

14 The sale of stock is recorded in a sales ledger at the sale price.

15 Returns In refers to goods which have been returned to us possibly because they are faulty.

16 Returns Out refers to goods we have returned to our suppliers.

17 Where companies buy and sell a large number of items on credit they may enter details of purchases and sales in a purchases day book and sales day book.

18 The balance in the day books is then transferred to the purchases and sales ledger at the end of the accounting period.

19 Companies may also have day books for Returns Inwards and Return Outwards.

20 Trade discounts are often given to customers who buy in bulk. Such a discount will be deducted at the time of sale and will therefore not appear in the ledger.

21 Cash discounts may be given for prompt payment and will be recorded in the ledger of the company as either a discount allowed or a discount received.

22 Discount Allowed is the discount we allow to customers.

23 Discount Received is the discount we receive from our creditors.

24 At the end of the accounting period the ledgers are balanced off and the balance transferred to a trial balance.

25 The trial balance is a summary of the balances of the ledgers.

26 A trial balance always balances.

27 If the trial balance does not balance it indicates that an error has been made in the bookkeeping.

28 Even if the trial balance does balance, mistakes may have been made (see Chapter 4).

## SELF-ASSESSMENT QUESTIONS

1 Complete the table.

| | Account debited | Account credited |
|---|---|---|
| (a) Purchased stock for £5 000 cash | PURCHASES | CASH. |
| (b) Returned goods to A Barlow for £100 | A.BARLOW. | RETURNS OUT. |
| (c) Paid wages £500 cash | WAGES. | CASH. |
| (d) The owner puts an extra £10 000 cash into the business | BANK | CAPITAL. |
| (e) Repaid £5 000 of a loan by cheque | LOAN. | BANK. |

2 Record the following transactions in the appropriate ledgers and draw up the trial balance of 'Dave's Pantry' a local shopkeeper.

Sept 1 Started the business with £40 000 cash.
2 Transferred £29 000 into a bank account.
3 Obtained a bank loan of £10 000 which was paid into the bank account.
4 Purchased a van for £8 000; equipment for £3 000 and fixtures and fittings for £3 000 paying by cheque.
5 Bought stock of goods for £2 000 by cheque.
9 Sold goods for £200 cash.
10 Purchased more equipment for £500 on credit terms of one month from Delta Equipment Co.
11 Sold goods of £100 on credit to A Iqbal.
12 Mr Pantry withdrew £2 000 cash to buy clothes for his wife.
15 Purchased goods for £1 000 on credit from C Wainwright.
16 Paid rent £50, gas £30 and wages of £400 in cash.
20 Mr Pantry withdrew another £2 000 cash to buy clothes for his wife.
22 Sold goods for £500 cash.
23 Sold goods for £300 on credit to B White.
26 Paid Delta Equipment in full, by cheque after deducting £20 cash discount.
28 Paid wages of £300 cash.

3 Define the following:

(a) Returns In
(b) Discount Allowed
(c) Carriage In
(d) Returns Out
(e) Discounts Received
(f) Carriage Out

# 4 Errors and control accounts

**OBJECTIVES**

**After studying this chapter you should be able to:**

**1 Distinguish between errors which affect the trial balance and those which do not;**

**2 Explain what action you would take upon discovering a difference in the trial balance;**

**3 Describe the purpose of control accounts;**

**4 Prepare control accounts in order to rectify errors.**

## ■ INTRODUCTION

From our look at double entry bookkeeping you may well have discovered how easy it is to make a mistake. It is even possible to get the trial balance to balance despite having made mistakes! For example:

(a) *Error of omission*: completely forgetting to enter a transaction in either ledger.
(b) *Error of commission*: where an entry is made in the wrong person's ledger, e.g. Sale to G Smith entered in E Smith's account.
(c) *Error of principle*: where an entry is made in the wrong class of account, e.g. purchase of a van is entered in the purchases ledger.
(d) *Reversal of entries*: you debit the entry you should have credited and vice versa.
(e) *Error of original entry*: where the incorrect amount is entered in both ledgers.
(f) *Compensating errors*: two separate errors which cancel each other out.

Should you discover such an error you will, obviously, need to pass correcting entries which will depend upon the nature of the error. With an error of omission this will mean entering the transaction, whereas for other errors you will just need to cancel the incorrect entry and pass correcting entries. For example:

Jan 1 Purchased a van for £5 000 by cheque.
Feb 1 Discovered that the purchase had been entered in the purchases ledger in error.

*Purchases*

| | | | | | |
|---|---|---|---|---|---|
| Jan 1 | Bank | £5 000 | Feb 1 | Purchase of van entered in error | £5 000 |

*Bank*

| | | | | | |
|---|---|---|---|---|---|
| | | | Jan 1 | Van | £5 000 |

*Van*

| | | |
|---|---|---|
| Feb 1 Bank (1 Jan) | £5 000 | |

An entry should also be made in what is called *The Journal*, to explain the error.

*The Journal*

| | Dr £ | Cr £ |
|---|---|---|
| Van | 5 000 | |
| Purchases | | 5 000 |
| Correction of error: purchase of van entered in the purchase ledger. | | |

## ■ ERRORS WHICH AFFECT THE TRIAL BALANCE

I would imagine that, like me, you discovered these for yourself when faced with double entry questions, e.g.

- entering an item in only one ledger;
- entering different amounts in each ledger.

When this happens in practice a Suspense Account/Ledger must be opened to account for the difference, for example:

*Trial balance of Miss Take as at 31.12.X0*

| | Dr £ | Cr £ |
|---|---|---|
| Totals | 19 950 | 20 000 |
| Suspense account | 50 | |
| | 20 000 | 20 000 |

*Suspense account*

| | | |
|---|---|---|
| 31.12.X0 Difference as per trial balance | £50 | |

Every effort must then be made to find the error. Should the error not be found before the final accounts are drawn up, then the suspense account balance will appear as a current asset if it is a debit balance, and a current liability if it is a credit balance. When the error is found correcting entries must be passed with an entry explaining the error made in the Journal.

e.g. Purchases undercast by £50

*Suspense*

| | | | |
|---|---|---|---|
| 31.12.X0 Difference as per trial balance | £50 | Purchases | £50 |

*Purchase*

| | | |
|---|---|---|
| Suspense | £50 | |

*The Journal*

| | Dr | Cr |
|---|---|---|
| | £ | £ |
| Purchases | 50 | |
| Suspense | | 50 |
| Purchases undercast by £50 | | |

**PROGRESS TEST 1**

Upon balancing the trial balance you found the total to be:

| | Dr | Cr |
|---|---|---|
| Totals | 100 000 | 95 000 |

Investigations revealed the following errors and you are asked to pass correcting entries:

(a) Purchases overcast £1 000.
(b) Creditors undercast by £300.
(c) £1 400 received from a debtor entered only in the cash book and not in B Brown's ledger.
(d) Purchase of a van £3 000 by cheque entered only in the van ledger.
(e) Goods returned for £700 by A Arkwright entered only in Arkwright's ledger.

## ■ CONTROL ACCOUNTS

When the trial balance does not balance the company may need to check a large number of entries in many ledgers before the mistake is found.

Control accounts are set up to check the accuracy of certain ledgers and thereby avoid the unnecessary checking of other ledgers in a similar way to the following problem.

***Problem***

You have nine snooker balls, one of which weighs more than the others. You also have a set of scales which you can use only twice.

How do you find the heaviest ball?

***Answer***

Put three balls on one side of the scales and three on the other side. If one side weighs more, the heavy ball is in that set and we can forget the other balls. Then put one of the three from the heavier set on one side of the scales and another of the three on the other side. If this does not reveal the heavy ball then it is the ball not used.

So, if the trial balance revealed an error of £50 and a control account set up to check the accuracy of certain ledgers revealed a similar error, we would know that the error was in this area and therefore avoid unnecessarily checking all the many other ledgers.

## ■ SALES LEDGER CONTROL ACCOUNT

This is the control account set up to check the accuracy of the sales ledger, and hence the debtors, by listing the total of all amounts owed by debtors on one side and the total of all amounts received by debtors or which would reduce the amount outstanding on the other. For example:

*Sales ledger control account*

| | | £ | | £ | |
|---|---|---|---|---|---|
| | Opening bal. | 10 000 | Cash received | 17 000 | *Amounts received or* |
| *Amounts owing* | Sales | 100 000 | Cheques received | 80 000 | *reducing the debt* |
| | Interest | 5 000 | | | |
| | Unpaid cheques | 1 000 | Returns in | 2 000 | |
| | | | Bad debts written off | 1 000 | |
| | | | Balance c/f | 16 000 | |
| | | 116 000 | | 116 000 | |

The total of the debtor ledgers should, therefore, come to £16 000, i.e. the amount still outstanding. If it does not, we must start to check the individual debtor ledgers, but if it does, the error probably lies elsewhere and we can then go on to produce a Purchase Ledger Control Account to check the accuracy of the purchase ledgers.

## ■ PURCHASE LEDGER CONTROL ACCOUNT

This works in the same manner as the Sales Ledger Control Account but checks the accuracy of the purchases ledger.

It might appear as follows:

*Purchase ledger control account*

| | | £ | | £ | |
|---|---|---|---|---|---|
| *Amounts repaid or reducing the debt* | Cash paid | 5 000 | Opening bal. | 5 000 | *Amounts owing* |
| | Cheques paid | 5 000 | Purchases | 10 000 | |
| | Discount received | 1 000 | Interest | 2 000 | |
| | Returns out | 1 000 | | | |
| | Balance c/f | 5 000 | | | |
| | | 17 000 | | 17 000 | |

Where a company has a large sales or purchase ledger the control account could be sub-divided according to the debtor's or creditor's surname, e.g. A-D; E-G, etc.

**PROGRESS TEST 2**

According to its records, Wilshaws Ltd has a total debtor's balance of £21 706 and a total creditor's balance of £31 059. Produce a Sales and Purchase Ledger Control Account from the following information to check the accuracy of these figures.

| | £ |
|---|---|
| Opening debtors | 3 705 |
| Opening creditors | 21 000 |
| Purchases | 200 000 |
| Sales | 150 000 |
| Cheques received | 120 000 |
| Cheques paid | 190 000 |
| Cash received | 7 468 |
| Cash paid | 3 441 |
| Returns in | 5 000 |
| Returns out | 500 |
| Discounts allowed | 2 000 |
| Discount received | 1 000 |
| Bad debts written off | 3 107 |
| Unpaid cheques | 576 |
| Interest charged by Wilshaws | 5 000 |
| Interest charged by supplier | 4 000 |

## ■ CONCLUSION

Control accounts also provide a means of guarding against fraud as different people are responsible for the original entry and the preparation of the control account.

## ■ SUMMARY

1 There are certain errors which, though present, will not affect the balancing of the trial balance, such as:

- error of omission;
- error of commission
- error of principle;
- reversal of entries;
- error of original entry;
- compensating errors.

2 Other errors will affect the trial balance, such as:

- entering an item in only one ledger;
- entering different amounts in each ledger.

3 When the trial balance does not balance, a Suspense Account Ledger should be opened to account for the difference.

4 Once errors are discovered, correcting entries should be passed and a note explaining the error made in the Journal.

5 Control accounts are set up to check the accuracy of certain ledgers and thereby avoid the unnecessary checking of other ledgers.

6 Control accounts also provide a means for guarding against fraud.

## ■ SELF-ASSESSMENT QUESTIONS

1 What do you understand by:

(a) error of principle;
(b) compensating error;
(c) error of commission;
(d) error of original entry.

2 Upon balancing the trial balance you found the totals to be:

| | Dr | Cr |
|---|---|---|
| | £ | £ |
| Totals | 15 000 | 14 000 |

(a) Outline what will happen if the error cannot be found.
(b) Investigations revealed the following errors:

(i) Sales undercast £5 000.
(ii) £16 000 paid not entered in the ledger of D Black, but entered in the bank ledger.
(iii) Purchase of a machine for £14 000 by cheque entered only in the machine ledger.
(iv) Cash, £2 000, received from a creditor not entered in the cash book but entered in the creditor's ledger.

3 (a) Define the terms 'day book', 'ledger' and 'trial balance' in the context of the double entry system of book-keeping.
(b) Explain *two* ways in which the trial balance is used.
(c) State and describe *four* ways in which a trial balance may show equal totals for debits and credits and yet still contain errors.

4 Rocker Ltd keeps control accounts for its sales and purchases ledgers which it balances at the end of each month. The balances on these accounts at 31 March 1990 were:

| | Debit | Credit |
|---|---|---|
| | £ | £ |
| Purchases ledger | 782 | 78 298 |
| Sales ledger | 95 617 | 613 |

The following transactions and adjustments took place during April 1990:

| | £ |
|---|---|
| Sales on credit | 759 348 |
| Purchases on credit | 621 591 |
| Cash sales | 202 651 |
| Returns from credit customers | 3 549 |
| Returns to credit suppliers | 4 581 |
| Cash received from credit customers | 703 195 |
| Cash paid to credit suppliers | 612 116 |
| Discounts received | 8 570 |
| Discounts allowed | 23 355 |
| Bad debts written off | 5 123 |
| Provision for doubtful debts increased by | 458 |

At 30 April 1990, there were credit balances on the sales ledger totalling £161 and debit balances on the purchases ledger totalling £329.

*Required*
Prepare the sales ledger control account and purchases ledger control account of Rocker Ltd for April 1990, carrying down the balances as at 30 April 1990.

# 5 Trading profit and loss account

**OBJECTIVES**

**After studying this chapter you should be able to:**

1. **Distinguish between items appearing in a Trading Profit and Loss Account and items appearing in a Balance Sheet;**
2. **Define capital and revenue expenditure;**
3. **Explain what is meant by gross and net profit;**
4. **Calculate gross and net profit;**
5. **Produce both a Trading Profit and Loss Account and a Balance Sheet from a Trial Balance.**

## ■ INTRODUCTION

In Chapter 3 we recorded details of transactions in ledgers before producing a Trial Balance. The Trial Balance is then used as the starting point in the construction of the final accounts.

If you look back at the Trial Balance you produced in answer to Progress test 3, I am sure you will recognise many of the items as those appearing in a Balance Sheet.

But what about *income* received in the form of sales or discounts received and *expenses* such as rent and electricity. Where do those appear?

The answer is the *Trading Profit and Loss Account* which is drawn up to determine the profit or loss of a company by deducting a company's expenses from their income. So from a Trial Balance we now have two statements to produce:

(a) *Trading Profit and Loss Account* – to determine the profit or loss of the business.
(b) *Balance Sheet* – which reflects the assets and liabilities of the business.

Assuming the company uses Day Books, the account procedure from invoice to Balance Sheet may take the pattern as illustrated in Fig. 1.

## ■ PRODUCING A TRADING PROFIT AND LOSS ACCOUNT

One of the problems in producing a Trading Profit and Loss Account is separating those items which appear in the Trading Profit and Loss Account from those which appear in the Balance Sheet.

As I have stated, the Trading Profit and Loss Account is concerned with a company's *income* and *expenses*, but let us look closer at these two items.

(a) *Income* – as we are trying to establish whether our business is profitable we are concerned with income generated from business, i.e. sales and not with money received in the form of loans or capital. You will no doubt recall that loans and

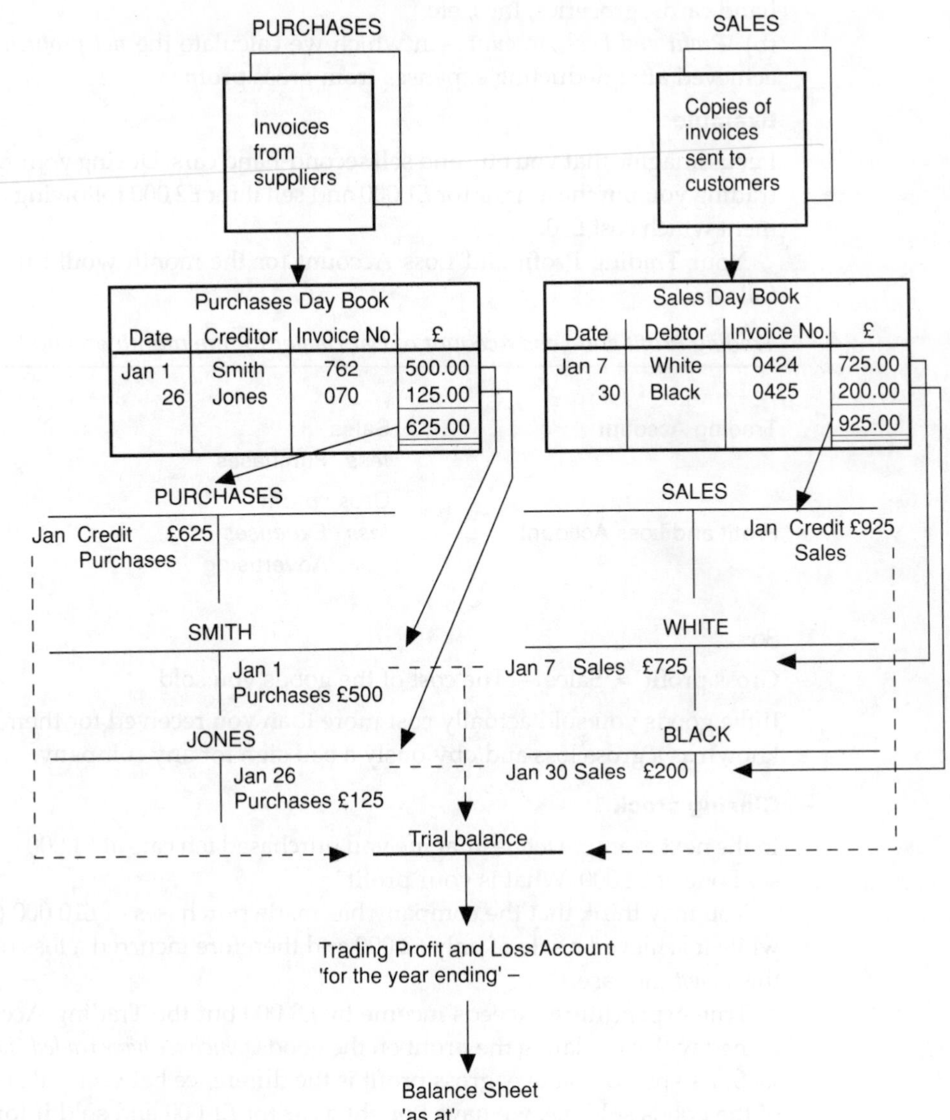


**Figure 1 The accounting procedure – invoice to balance sheet**

capital represent a company's source of finance which enables it to commence or continue in business and hence appear in the Balance Sheet.

(b) *Expenses* – while both the purchase of machinery and the payment of rent can be considered as expenditure, the Trading Profit and Loss Account is concerned only with expenditure incurred in the day-to-day running of the company, e.g. rent, rates, gas, etc., i.e. *revenue expenditure.*

The purchase of machinery or equipment etc. represent the purchase of *assets* which will be reflected in the Balance Sheet, i.e. *capital expenditure.*

The Trading Profit and Loss Account can be broken up into two parts:

(a) *Trading Account* – in which we calculate the *Gross profit*, i.e. the profit achieved on *trading* (buying and selling the goods of your business which could be second-hand cards, groceries, toys, etc.)

(b) *Profit and Loss Account* – in which we calculate the *net profit*, i.e. the profit achieved after deducting expenses from gross profit.

**Example**

Let us imagine that you buy and sell second-hand cars. During your first month of trading you purchase a car for £1 000 and sell it for £2 000 following an advertisement which cost £50.

Your Trading Profit and Loss Account for the month would therefore be as follows:

*Trading Profit and Loss Account of Car Dealer for the month ending 31.10.X8*

| | | £ |
|---|---|---|
| Trading Account | Sales | 2 000 |
| | *less* Purchases | 1 000 |
| | Gross profit | 1 000 |
| Profit and Loss Account | *less Expenses* | |
| | Advertising | 50 |
| | | 950 |

So:

Gross profit = Sales – The cost of the goods you sold

If the goods you sold actually cost more than you received for them, then this is known as a gross loss and obviously a bad sign for any company.

**Closing stock**

In the next example let us imagine you purchased ten cars at £1 000 each and then sold one at £2 000. What is your profit?

You may think that the company has made purchases of £10 000 (10 × £1 000) while it achieved a sale of only £2 000 and therefore incurred a loss of £8 000. But this is *not* the case.

True expenditure exceeds income by £8 000 but the Trading Account is concerned with calculating the profit on the goods *which we have traded (i.e. bought and sold)*. As spelt out above, gross profit is the difference between sales and the cost of the goods sold, i.e. we have bought a car for £1 000 and sold it for £2 000 and therefore achieved a gross profit of £1 000 on *that* car. We are then left with nine cars in stock which cost a total of £9 000 and represent an *asset* owned by the company.

This is shown in the Trading Account as follows:

| | £ | £ |
|---|---|---|
| Sales | | 2 000 |
| *less Cost of goods sold* | | |
| Purchases | 10 000 | |
| *less* Closing stock | 9 000 | 1 000 |
| Gross profit | | 1 000 |

and reveals the complete story to the reader.

Yes, more money has been spent on the purchase of goods than actually received from sales.

But, we have a closing stock of £9 000 worth of goods which can, hopefully, be sold in the future.

The cost of the goods we sold was £1 000 (£10 000 – £9 000).

The company is able to trade profitably, having sold goods for £2 000 which cost them only £1 000.

Before we go on to look at opening stock, can you think where else the closing stock might be reflected? Remember the stock left at the end of the accounting period is something of value, owned by the business.

Well, the answer I am looking for is the *Balance Sheet* as a *current asset*. As we do not have a ledger for stock, the value of the closing stock is found by counting and checking the number of items in stock, i.e. stocktaking, in itself a useful role to ensure no stock is going missing.

**Opening stock**

The closing stock of a company's first year in business will of course be its opening stock of year two.

Suppose a company starts its second year with a stock of goods which cost £5 000, and over the year purchased a further £20 000 worth of goods, and received £40 000 from sales. What is the company's gross profit if they have a closing stock of £10 000?

Let us recap for a moment.

| Gross profit = Sales – The cost of the goods you sold |
|---|

We must first find the total cost of *all* our purchases,

i.e. Opening stock + Purchases

and from this deduct the value of goods we have left. In this way we will find the *cost of the goods sold.*

The formula is therefore:

| | £ |
|---|---|
| Opening stock | 5 000 |
| + Purchases | 20 000 |
| | 25 000 |
| – Closing stock | 10 000 |
| | 15 000 |

and the Trading Account therefore appears as follows:

*Trading Account of AB Co. for the year ending 31.12.X8 (a)*

| | £ | £ |
|---|---|---|
| Sales | | 40 000 |
| *less Cost of goods sold* | | |
| Opening stock | 5 000 | |
| + Purchases | 20 000 | |
| | 25 000 | |
| – Closing stock | 10 000 | 15 000 |
| Gross profit | (b) | 25 000 |

*Note:*

(a) As we are calculating the profit achieved over a certain period, the title should always reflect this.

(b) Use two columns to improve the presentation.

**PROGRESS TEST 1**

1 Produce a Trading Account in each of the following cases.

| | *Closing stock* | *Opening stock* | *Sales* | *Purchases* |
|---|---|---|---|---|
| | £ | £ | £ | £ |
| (a) | 40 000 | 30 000 | 100 000 | 5 000 |
| (b) | 10 000 | 25 000 | 50 000 | 10 000 |
| (c) | 47 950 | 52 105 | 135 950 | 87 769 |
| (d) | 10 000 | 40 000 | 80 000 | 60 000 |

2 Produce a Trading Profit and Loss Account for the year ended 31.10.X9 from the following information supplied by M Reid.

| | £ |
|---|---|
| Purchases | 12 107 |
| Opening stock | 7 815 |
| Rent | 105 |
| Electricity | 205 |
| Sales | 20 959 |
| Insurance | 75 |
| Closing stock | 4 810 |

## ■ RETURNS IN AND RETURNS OUT

Can you remember what we mean by Returns In and Returns Out?

Just in case you cannot, let us recap and consider how they are dealt with in the Trading Profit and Loss Account.

*Returns In* are goods you have previously sold but which have since been returned to you, possibly because they are faulty. They are therefore shown *as a deduction from sales.*

*Returns Out* are goods you previously purchased but which you have since returned to your supplier and are shown *as a deduction from purchases.*

| | £ | £ | £ |
|---|---|---|---|
| Sales | | | 50 000 |
| **Less Returns In** | | | 2 000 |
| | | | 48 000 |
| *Less cost of goods sold* | | | |
| Opening stock | | 10 000 | |
| + Purchases | 35 000 | | |
| **Less Returns Out** | 1 000 | 34 000 | |
| | | 44 000 | |
| – Closing stock | | 20 000 | 24 000 |
| Gross profit | | | 24 000 |

*Note*

The third column is used to calculate the net figure for purchases which is then carried over and added to opening stock. *Do not* add opening stock to purchases and then deduct returns out. Returns out are deducted from purchases to find the next purchase figure.

## ■ CARRIAGE IN AND CARRIAGE OUT

These are another two items introduced previously, can you remember what they are and what is particular about Carriage In.

*Carriage Out* is the cost of transporting goods out and is treated as any other expense such as rent, rates etc. and is therefore *listed as an expense* deducted from gross profit to determine the net profit.

*Carriage In* is the cost of transporting goods in and, as it is incurred as a direct result of purchasing and not selling, it is dealt with differently than other expenses and is therefore one to watch out for. As an expense incurred as a result of purchase *it is added to purchases.*

| | £ | £ | £ |
|---|---|---|---|
| Sales | | | 50 000 |
| *less* Returns In | | | 2 000 |
| | | | 48 000 |
| *less Cost of goods sold* | | | |
| Opening stock | | 10 000 | |
| + Purchases | 35 000 | | |
| *less* Returns Out | 1 000 | | |
| | 34 000 | | |
| **Plus Carriage In** | 500 | 34 500 | |
| | | 44 500 | |
| – Closing stock | | 20 000 | 24 500 |
| Gross profit | | | 23 500 |
| *less Expenses* | | | |
| Rent | | 1 000 | |
| **Carriage Out** | | 250 | |
| Wages | | 5 000 | 6 250 |
| Net profit | | | 17 250 |

**PROGRESS TEST 2**

1 Produce a Trading Profit and Loss Account for the year ended 31.10.X8 from the following information supplied by B West.

| | £ |
|---|---|
| Purchases | 27 108 |
| Sales | 73 955 |
| Rent | 200 |
| Rates | 800 |
| Returns In | 515 |
| Carriage In | 70 |
| Opening stock | 11 518 |
| Returns Out | 205 |
| Wages | 5 801 |
| Closing stock | 5 809 |
| Carriage Out | 175 |

## ■ DISCOUNT ALLOWED AND DISCOUNT RECEIVED

*Discount allowed:* is an expense incurred by a company, being the amount of discount they allow their customers. *They are therefore listed with all other expenses.*

*Discount received* is a form of income received and is therefore *added to gross profit* before deducting the expenses.

*Trading Profit and Loss Account for Example Company for the year ending 31.10.X8*

| | £ | £ | £ |
|---|---|---|---|
| Sales | | | 50 000 |
| *less* Returns In | | | 2 000 |
| | | | 48 000 |
| *less Cost of goods sold* | | | |
| Opening stock | | 10 000 | |
| + Purchases | 35 000 | | |
| – Returns Out | 1 000 | | |
| | 34 000 | | |
| + Carriage In | 500 | 34 500 | |
| | | 44 500 | |
| – Closing stock | | 20 000 | 24 500 |
| Gross profit | | | 23 500 |
| *add Income* | | | |
| **Discount received** | | 1 000 | |
| Rents received | | 500 | |
| Interest received | | 250 | 1 750 |
| | | | 25 250 |
| *less Expenses* | | | |
| Rent | | 1 000 | |
| Carriage Out | | 250 | |
| Wages | | 5 000 | |
| **Discount allowed** | | 300 | 6 550 |
| Net profit | | | 18 700 |

Other examples of this form of income are rents received or interest received making the completed trading profit and loss format for Example Company as shown above.

## ■ PRODUCING A TRADING PROFIT AND LOSS ACCOUNT AND BALANCE SHEET

So, as you can see, there are a number of items which appear in a Trading Profit and Loss Account. The real problem comes when you are asked to produce both a Trading Profit and Loss Account and a Balance Sheet from a trial balance similar to that below:

*Trial Balance of E Loughlan as at 31.10.X8*

| Code | | Dr | Cr |
|---|---|---|---|
| CAP | Capital | | 60 000 |
| ✓TRADE | Sales | | 55 950 |
| ✓TRADE | Stock at 1.1.89 | 17 105 | |
| CAP | Drawings | 5 000 | |
| /FA | Premises | 50 000 | |
| ✓TRADE | Returns In | 210 | |
| /CA | Debtors | 3 105 | |
| /CL | Creditors | | 8 410 |
| TRADE | Carriage In | 309 | |
| /DL | Loan | | 20 000 |
| ✓TRADE | Returns Out | | 108 |
| ✓TRADE | Purchases | 41 807 | |
| /EXP | Rates | 1 000 | |
| /EXP | Discounts allowed | 410 | |
| /EXP | Electricity | 300 | |
| /INC | Interest received | | 250 |
| /FA | Fixtures and fittings | 15 000 | |
| /FA | Van | 5 000 | |
| /CL | Bank | | 2 923 |
| /EXP | Wages | 6 000 | |
| /EXP | Insurance | 500 | |
| /CA | Cash | 1 895 | |
| | | 147 641 | 147 641 |

Closing stock: £15 000

*Note*

If 'Bank' is a credit balance it is a bank overdraft and therefore a current liability.

It would be very easy to forget to use one of the items or remember that you should have added Carriage In to Purchases when you come to list the expenses. I would therefore suggest the following procedure:

1 Code each item in the trial balance (*as shown above*), e.g.

INC (Income)
EXP (Expenses)
CAP (Relating to Capital in the Balance Sheet)
LTL (Long-term liabilities)
CL (Current liabilities)
FA (Fixed assets)
CA (Current assets)

This is most important. If you can get this right, drawing up the Trading Profit and Loss Account and Balance Sheet is simply like doing a jigsaw. Place the pieces in the right place and it will balance. It is therefore also important to learn the layout.

2 Rearrange the items to produce:
(a) *Trading Profit and Loss Account*
then
(b) *Balance Sheet* – do not forget that the net profit you have calculated in the Trading Profit and Loss Account is added to Capital.

3 Place a tick against each item as you use it. Then if you forget to use an item, it will clearly stand out.

4 If you do not balance, find the difference and check whether there is an item for this amount which you have forgotten.

**PROGRESS TEST 3**

Produce a Trading Profit and Loss Account for the year ending 31.10.X8 and Balance Sheet as at 31.10.X8 from the Trial Balance of E Loughlan, shown above.

## ■ ERRORS AND THE REPORTED PROFIT FIGURE

In the last chapter we examined the situation where the trial balance did not balance, e.g.

*Trial Balance of Miss Take as at 31.12.X0*

| | Dr | Cr |
|---|---|---|
| | £ | £ |
| Totals | 19 950 | 20 000 |
| Suspense accounts | 50 | |
| | 20 000 | 20 000 |

You will remember that we therefore opened a Suspense Account and took steps to find the error possibly using Sales and Purchase Ledger Control Accounts.

*Suspense account*

| | |
|---|---|
| 3.12.X0 Difference as per trial balance £50 | |

In our example the error was found to be an undercasting of the purchases figure by £50, and correcting entries were therefore passed.

If the final accounts had been produced before this error was detected, then the company would have needed to produce a Statement of Corrected Net Profit, e.g.

| | £ |
|---|---|
| Reported net profit | 2 000 |
| *less* Purchases undercast | 50 |
| Corrected net profit | 1 950 |

## ■ SUMMARY

1 The Trading Profit and Loss Account is drawn up to determine the profit or loss of a company for a particular period.

2 Revenue Expenditure is the expenditure incurred in the day-to-day running of the company, e.g. rent, electricity.

3 Capital Expenditure relates to the purchase or improvement of a company's assets and is reflected in the Balance Sheet.

4 Trading Account shows the calculation of gross profit.

5 Gross Profit is the profit achieved on trading (i.e. on buying and selling the goods of your business).

6 Sales – Cost of goods sold = Gross profit.

7 Profit and Loss Account shows the calculation of net profit.

8 Net Profit is the profit achieved after deducting expenses from gross profit plus any other revenue received, such as discounts received.

9 Returns In, being goods previously sold but since returned, are shown as a deduction from sales.

10 Returns Out, being goods previously purchased but since returned to suppliers, are shown as a deduction from purchases.

11 Carriage In is the cost of transporting goods in and, as an expense incurred as a direct result of purchasing, it is added to purchases and not listed with other expenses.

12 Carriage Out is treated in the same way as other expenses and deducted from gross profit.

13 Discount Allowed is the amount of discount allowed to customers and treated in the same way as other expenses.

14 Discount Received, like rent received and interest received, is a form of income which is added to gross profit before deducting expenses.

15 A Trading Profit and Loss Account is 'for the year ending ...' or 'for the month ending ...' etc., as it reflects the profit or loss for that period.

16 A Balance Sheet, being like a photograph of a company's assets and liabilities, is always, 'as at' a particular date.

17 Questions will normally reveal the way the final accounts are to be headed

up by asking for a Trading Profit and Loss Account for the year ending ... and a Balance Sheet as at a particular date, but try to remember this, it is important and often worth a mark in the examination.

18 Where errors are not detected until after the profit figure is published, a Statement of Corrected Profit must be produced.

*NB.* An example layout of a Trading Profit and Loss Account is given on page 44.

## ■ SELF-ASSESSMENT QUESTIONS

1 Define the following:
   (a) Capital expenditure;
   (b) Revenue expenditure;
   (c) Gross profit;
   (d) Net profit.

2 When preparing a Trading Profit and Loss Account how would you deal with the following?
   (a) Returns In;
   (b) Discount Allowed;
   (c) Carriage Out;
   (d) Returns Out;
   (e) Carriage In;
   (f) Discount Received;
   (g) Money spent on fixtures and fittings.

3 Produce a Trading Profit and Loss Account for R Ford for the year ending 31.10.X9 and a Balance Sheet as at 31.10.X9 from the following trial balance.

*Trial Balance as at 31.10.X9*

| | Dr | Cr |
|---|---|---|
| Sales | | 279 105 |
| Purchases | 104 829 | |
| Premises | 100 000 | |
| Fittings | 24 000 | |
| Van | 26 000 | |
| Stock at 1.11.X8 | 57 955 | |
| Wages | 31 106 | |
| Electricity | 991 | |
| Rent | 1 000 | |
| Rates | 1 500 | |
| Gas | 350 | |
| Insurance | 200 | |
| Carriage Out | 107 | |
| Discount Allowed | 500 | |
| Debtors | 5 105 | |
| Creditors | | 8 138 |
| Loan | | 30 000 |
| Drawings | 60 000 | |
| Bank | 3 500 | |
| Cash | 100 | |
| Capital | | 100 000 |
| | 417 243 | 417 243 |
| Closing stock (found from stocktaking) | 41 295 | |

4 From the following Trial Balance produce a Trading Profit and Loss Account for the year ending 31.11.X9 and a Balance Sheet as at 31.11.X9 for Mr D Eyles.

*Trial Balance as at 31.11.X9*

| | Dr | Cr |
|---|---|---|
| | £ | £ |
| Capital | | 500 000 |
| Drawings | 200 676 | |
| Carriage in | 616 | |
| Discounts | 750 | 215 |
| Returns | 814 | 519 |
| Rates | 5 100 | |
| Wages | 25 900 | |
| Electricity | 3 908 | |
| Interest received | | 100 |
| Rent received | | 1 898 |
| Purchases and sales | 72 108 | 510 927 |
| Motor expenses | 1 287 | |
| Stock at 1.12.X8 | 39 509 | |
| Debtors and creditors | 51 000 | 56 100 |
| Bank overdraft | | 10 000 |
| Loan | | 30 000 |
| Land and buildings | 450 000 | |
| Machinery | 200 000 | |
| Fixtures | 39 871 | |
| Van | 10 129 | |
| Cash | 7 591 | |
| Carriage out | 500 | |
| | 1 109 759 | 1 109 759 |
| Stock at 31.11.X9 | £21 509 | |

5 From the following Trial Balance produce a Trading Profit and Loss Account for the year ending 31.12.X9 and a Balance Sheet as at 31.12.X9 for A Jackson.

*Trial Balance as at 31.12.X9*

| | Dr | Cr |
|---|---|---|
| | £ | £ |
| Sales | | 101 995 |
| Purchases | 52 379 | |
| Stock at 1.1.X8 | 36 109 | |
| Premises | 50 000 | |
| Debtors and creditors | 15 000 | 26 105 |
| Bank | | 10 616 |
| Motor expenses | 2 005 | |
| Fixtures | 6 698 | |
| Insurance | 1 000 | |
| Rent | 5 105 | |
| Equipment | 8 213 | |
| Rates | 2 000 | |
| Wages | 17 000 | |
| Carriage In | 300 | |
| Electricity | 1 510 | |
| Discount Allowed | 3 000 | |
| Carriage Out | 397 | |
| Returns In | 3 000 | |
| Loan | | 15 000 |
| Capital | | 50 000 |
| | 203 716 | 203 716 |
| Stock at 31.12.X9 | £11 810 | |

# 6 Trading profit and loss account and balance sheet – extra matters

**OBJECTIVES**

**After studying this chapter you should be able to:**

1. **Produce a Trading Profit and Loss Account and a Balance Sheet in vertical format;**
2. **Understand why this is the preferred form of presentation;**
3. **Appreciate that the construction of accounts is governed not only by tradition or fashion, but also by rules known as Statements of Standard Accounting Practice (SSAPs);**
4. **Explain the importance of matching revenue and related expenditure;**
5. **Appreciate the time at which revenue is recognised;**
6. **Recognise and explain the need for prudence;**
7. **Produce Trading Profit and Loss Accounts and Balance Sheets dealing with the above principles.**

## ■ INTRODUCTION

In the last chapter we constructed a Trading Profit and Loss Account and Balance Sheet from a trial balance.

If you look back at your answer to Progress test 3, you will see that the Trading Profit and Loss Account is written in a *vertical* format with the details running down the page.

Sales
*less Cost of goods sold*
**Gross profit**
*less Expenses*
**Net profit**

while the balance sheet is written in a *horizontal* format with assets on one side and capital and liabilities on the other:

*Balance Sheet of E Laughlan as at 31.10.X8*

| | £ | £ | | £ | £ |
|---|---|---|---|---|---|
| *Fixed assets* | | | Capital | | 60 000 |
| Premises | 50 000 | | + Net profit | | 3 667 |
| Fixtures | 15 000 | | | | 63 667 |
| Van | 5 000 | 70 000 | – Drawings | | 5 000 |
| *Current assets* | | | | | |
| Stock | 15 000 | | *Deferred liabilities* | | |
| Debtors | 3 105 | | Loan | | 20 000 |
| Cash | 1 895 | 20 000 | *Current liabilities* | | |
| | | | Creditors | 8 410 | |
| | | | Bank overdraft | 2 923 | 11 333 |
| | | 90 000 | | | 90 000 |

## ■ VERTICAL FORMAT

It is now more common to present both the Trading Profit and Loss Account and Balance Sheet in a *vertical* format. We therefore need to change the presentation of the balance sheet.

This can be done quite simply as follows, by moving the assets above the capital and liabilities.

*Balance Sheet of E Laughlan as at 31.10.X8*

| | £ | £ |
|---|---|---|
| *Fixed assets* | | |
| Premises | 50 000 | |
| Fixtures | 15 000 | |
| Van | 5 000 | 70 000 |
| *Current assets* | | |
| Stock | 15 000 | |
| Debtors | 3 105 | |
| Cash | 1 895 | 20 000 |
| | | 90 000 |
| Capital | | 60 000 |
| + Net Profit | | 3 667 |
| | | 63 667 |
| – Drawings | | 5 000 |
| | | 58 667 |
| *Long-term liabilities* | | |
| Loan | | 20 000 |
| *Current liabilities* | | |
| Creditors | 8 410 | |
| Bank overdraft | 2 923 | 11 333 |
| | | 90 000 |

But if we rearrange the order of the components, we are able to gain a better picture of the company's position.

Rather than present the Balance Sheet as shown above we should therefore present the information in the format shown below:

*Balance Sheet of E Laughlan as at 31.10.X8*

| | | £ | £ | |
|---|---|---|---|---|
| *Fixed assets* | | | | |
| Premises | | 50 000 | | |
| Fixtures | | 15 000 | | |
| Van | | 5 000 | 70 000 | Fixed assets |
| *Current assets* | | | | |
| Stock | | 15 000 | | |
| Debtors | | 3 105 | | |
| Cash | | 1 895 | | |
| | | 20 000 | | + |
| less | | | | |
| *Current liabilities* | | | | |
| Creditors | 8 410 | | | |
| Bank overdraft | 2 923 | 11 333 | 8 667 | Working Capital |
| | | | 78 667 | * |
| Financed by: | | | | |
| Capital | | | 60 000 | Financed by |
| + Net profit | | | 3 667 | |
| | | | 63 667 | |
| – Drawings | | | 5 000 | |
| | | | 58 667 | Capital |
| *Long-term liabilities* | | | | + |
| Loan | | | 20 000 | Long-term liabilities |
| | | | 78 667 | * |

While the Balance Sheet now balances to a different figure – this does not matter.

This form of presentation is preferred as it indicates the company's *working capital* (i.e. the difference between current assets and current liabilities).

| Working Capital = Current Assets – Current Liabilities |
|---|

Working capital examines the company's liquidity and trading position by deducting current liabilities (money the company owe and must repay within twelve months) from current assets (cash, or items the company can convert into cash in the near future).

We shall examine the importance on working capital later (Chapter 15), but for now let's just concentrate on using the new form of presentation which reveals the working capital.

**PROGRESS TEST 1**

Produce a Trading Profit and Loss Account for the year ending 31.11.X9 and a Balance Sheet as at 31.11.X9 in *vertical format* for N Cunningham from the following Trial Balance:

*Trial Balance as at 31.11.X9*

| | Dr<br>£ | Cr<br>£ |
|---|---|---|
| Purchases and sales | 9 959 | 31 705 |
| Stock as at 1.12.X8 | 13 201 | |
| Wages | 5 000 | |
| Carriage out | 317 | |
| Carriage in | 200 | |
| Discounts allowed | 250 | |
| Electricity | 700 | |
| Returns out | | 100 |
| Rates | 500 | |
| Insurance | 1 049 | |
| Premises | 30 000 | |
| Motor vehicles | 10 000 | |
| Debtors and creditors | 12 109 | 6 755 |
| Machinery | 5 000 | |
| Fixtures and fittings | 7 000 | |
| Bank | 754 | |
| Cash | 121 | |
| Capital | | 50 000 |
| Drawings | 11 400 | |
| Loan | | 19 000 |
| | 107 560 | 107 560 |

*Note*:
Closing stock £7 500

When we examine the published accounts of Public Limited Companies (Chapter 11) we shall see that they present their Balance Sheets in yet another manner. This should not worry you; with practice you will be able to use any format.

## ■ ACCOUNTING CONCEPTS AND CONVENTIONS

The way in which accounts are drawn are not only governed by tradition or fashion but also by Accounting Concepts and Conventions, as well as Statements of Standard Accounting Practice (SSAPs) and Financial Reporting Standards (FRSs) which are considered in Chapter 13.

The concepts and conventions upon which accounts are based are:

1 *Business entity*
The accounts show the activities of the *business* not the owner. The organisation should be seen as a separate business entity.
2 *Historical cost*
The accepted basis for recording goods or services acquired by the business is to record

them at historical cost – cost price. This is the most objective method of valuation, but has led to problems in terms of high rates of inflation. (*See* Chapter 13.)

3 *Materiality*

When deciding on how to treat an item of expenditure we will consider the material needs of the organisation. For example, the purchase of a stapling machine (even though it may last for several years) will be written off profits in the period in which it was purchased.

4 *Money measurement*

All items must be expressed in terms of money values. Accounting reports deal only with aspects of business which can be reduced to monetary terms. For example, one cannot record the values that a business may place on its workforce, even though this may affect the results of the business.

5 *Realisation*

Revenue is recognised when the goods or services concerned have been transferred to the customer, and an equivalent asset has been received already, or the right to receive it has been established. (*See* Prudence concept.)

The fundamental accounting concepts which should be considered at greater length are:

6 *Going concern;*
7 *Consistency;*
8 *Matching concept;*
9 *Accruals concept;*
10 *Prudence.*

**Going concern**

This means that the accounts are drawn up on the basis that the business is a going concern and will continue to trade for the foreseeable future.

The accountant preparing the accounts will, of course, need to satisfy himself that this is the case.

If the business was not a going concern the Balance Sheet would alter significantly, e.g.

- *Assets* may lie idle and therefore lose their value; stock may have to be sold at reduced prices.
- *Liabilities* may increase, such as penalty payments under contracts.

**Consistency**

Companies are expected to adopt the same accounting treatment of items each year. As we shall discover later, a change in the way we treat certain items can have a dramatic effect on the profit figure – and it would be unfair to increase profits by simply changing the way in which we draw up the accounts. That does not mean that changes are not allowed, but that any changes must be clearly stated. The effect on the year's results should also be identified and the previous year's figure restated to provide a comparison. (*See* SSAP 6 Chapter 13.)

**Matching concept**

A Trading Profit and Loss Account reflects a company's performance for a particular account period, e.g. for the year ending 31.12.90.

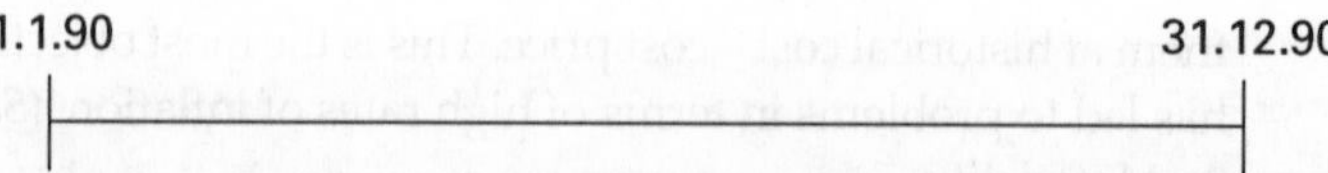


We therefore need to *match* the revenue earned during this period with the expenditure incurred during this period.

**Accruals concept**

The Accruals concept is closely linked to the matching concept. Let us consider the position of Mario's Restaurant for a moment. Mario needs to calculate his net profit for the year ending 31.12.X8.

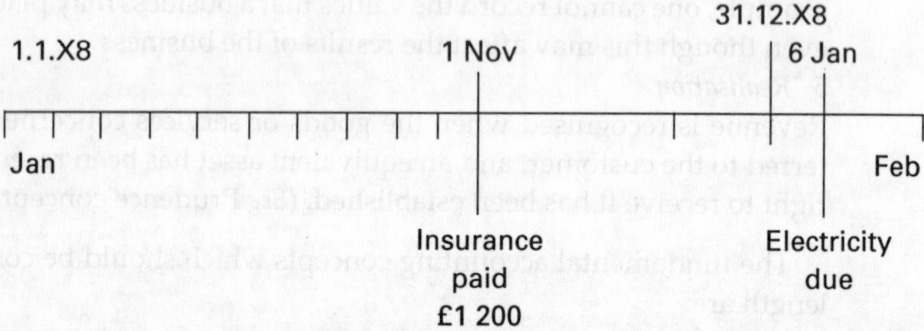


(a) His annual insurance premium is due for payment on 1 November but this relates to November and December of this accounting year and ten months of the next, i.e. at the end of the accounting year Mario will have paid his insurance bill in advance – *prepayment.*

(b) Mario pays for his electricity quarterly and expects to receive a bill at the beginning of January in respect of October, November and December, i.e. at the end of the accounting year Mario will still owe money for this bill – *accrual.*

The question is, do we simply include the full amount paid for insurance and forget the electricity bill as it is not payable until next year?

You may feel this would be fair as the next year's accounts would suffer in the same way and therefore even things up. Unfortunately, however, we are not allowed to simply ignore such matters, otherwise we would over- or under-estimate the profit figure for the year.

*SSAP 2 requires us to match all income relating to a particular period with the expenditure incurred which relates to that period and not the cash receipts and payments.*

We therefore need to *include* a charge for the electricity used during October, November and December, while reducing the insurance cost so that it only represents the cost of this accounting period.

## ■ DEALING WITH PREPAYMENTS AND ACCRUALS

Let us once again consider Mario's position:

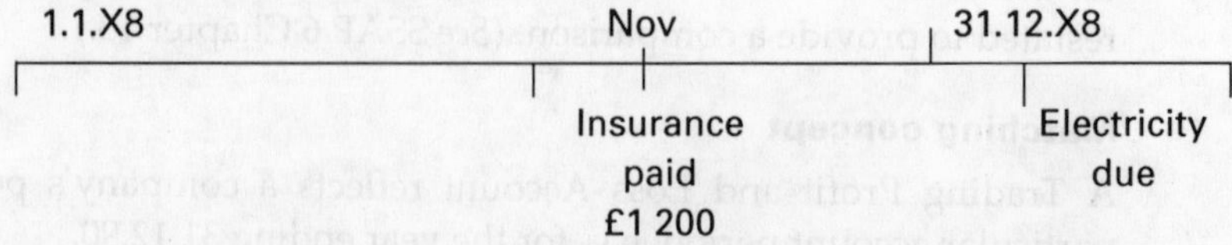

(a) *Prepayments, e.g. insurance*
(i) On 1 November Mario paid £1 200 to his insurance company by cheque.

*Bank*

| | | | | |
|---|---|---|---|---|
| Bal c/d | £6 000 | 1.11.X8 | Insurance | £1 200 |

*Insurance*

| | | | |
|---|---|---|---|
| 1.11.X8 | Bank | £1 200 | |

(ii) On 31.12.X8 Mario's accountant sets about preparing the Trading Profit and Loss Account for the year, i.e. for the year ending 31.12.X8.

*Remember* he only needs to include *the expenditure incurred which relates to that period* and not the full cash payment of £1 200, e.g. £200 (2/12 of £1 200).

(iii) He therefore enters £200 in the insurance ledger as the amount being transferred to the Trading Profit and Loss Account as an expense, and balances the account by including the prepayment of £1 000.

*Insurance*

| | | £ | | | £ |
|---|---|---|---|---|---|
| 1.11.X8 | Bank | 1 200 | 31.12.X8 | Profit and loss | 200 |
| | | | 31.12.X8 | Prepayment | 1 000 |
| | | 1 200 | | | 1 200 |
| 1.1.X9 | Prepayment | 1 000 | | | |

(iv) *Final accounts*
*(a)* £200 appears as an expense in the Trading Profit and Loss Account. In effect we have *deducted the amount of prepayment* from the amount paid.
*(b)* £1 000, the balance of the ledger, appears as a *current asset* labelled *prepayment*. If you think about it, as at 31.12.X8, the insurance company owe Mario £1 000 and are therefore similar to debtor.

(b) *Accruals, e.g. electricity*
(i) On 31.12.X8 Mario's electricity ledger appears as follows:

*Electricity*

| | | £ | |
|---|---|---|---|
| 31.3.X8 | Bank | 300 | |
| 4.7.X8 | Bank | 200 | |
| 6.10.X8 | Bank | 200 | |

(ii) The next electricity bill is not payable until January 19X9. While payable in the next accounting period, it *relates to expenditure incurred during October, November and December of this accounting period* and therefore an estimate of the *amount owing (accrual)* must be entered in the accounts, e.g. £400.

*Electricity*

| | | £ | | £ |
|---|---|---|---|---|
| 31.3.X8 | Bank | 300 | Profit and Loss Account | 1 100 |
| 4.7.X8 | Bank | 200 | | |
| 6.10.X8 | Bank | 200 | | |
| 31.12.X8 | Owing | 400 | | |
| | | 1 100 | | 1 100 |
| | | | 1.1.X9 Owing | 400 |

(iii) *Final accounts*

*(a)* £1 100 appears as an expense in the Trading Profit and Loss Account. In effect *we add the accrual* to the amount paid.

*(b)* £400, the balance of the ledger, appears as a *current liability* labelled *accrual* as it represents money owed by the company as at the 31.12.X8.

Let us now look at how prepayments and accruals may appear in a question which asks you to produce a Trading Profit and Loss Account and Balance Sheet.

*Trial balance as at 31.12.X9*

| | Dr £ | Cr £ |
|---|---|---|
| Capital | | 50 000 |
| Sales | | 150 000 |
| Purchases | 95 000 | |
| Rent | 1 100 | |
| Rates | 3 000 | |
| Electricity | 200 | |
| Gas | 100 | |
| Telephone | 50 | |
| Debtors | 12 170 | |
| Creditors | | 10 980 |
| Premises | 60 000 | |
| Fixtures | 20 000 | |
| Vehicles | 19 360 | |
| | 210 980 | 210 980 |

*Notes*:

| | |
|---|---|
| 1 Closing stock | £20 000 |
| 2 Rate prepaid | £100 |
| 3 Telephone owing | £20 |

Remember:

(a) *The trial balance* indicates the amounts actually paid.

(b) *The notes* will inform you of the prepaid and amount owing.

Therefore:

1 *Rates prepaid*

(i) Reduce rates by £100 (the amount prepaid).

(ii) Create a prepayment of £100 which will be shown as a current asset in the Balance Sheet.

2 *Telephone owing*

(i) Add the amount owing, £20, to the amount paid.

(ii) Create an accrual of £20 which will be shown as a current liability.

I would suggest you make a note of this action on the Trial Balance, as follows:

*Trial balance as at 31.12.X9*

| | DR | CR |
|---|---|---|
| | £ | £ |
| Capital | | 50 000 |
| Sales | | 150 000 |
| Purchases | 95 000 | |
| Rent | 1 100 | |
| Rates (–100) | 3 000 | |
| Electricity | 200 | |
| Gas | 100 | |
| Telephone (+20) | 50 | |
| Debtors | 12 170 | |
| Creditors | | 10 980 |
| Premises | 60 000 | |
| Fixtures | 20 000 | |
| Vehicles | 19 360 | |
| | 210 980 | 210 980 |
| Prepaid: Rates | 100 | |
| Accruals: Telephones | | 20 |

In this way you will not forget to adjust the expenses so they reflect the expenditure incurred, or to include prepayments and accruals in the Balance Sheet.

*NB.* When dealing with any notes like this, and there are more to come, you must ensure that the Trial Balance still balances after your adjustments. If it does not, then your Balance Sheet will not balance.

**PROGRESS TEST 2**

(a) Complete the Trading Profit and Loss Account for the year ending 31.12.X9 and a Balance Sheet as at 31.12.X9 for A Johnson, in *vertical format,* from the Trial Balance above.

(b) Produce a Trading Profit and Loss Account for the year ending 31.12.X9 and a Balance Sheet as at 31.12.X9 for S Smith, in *vertical format,* from the Trial Balance below.

*Trial Balance as at 31.12.X9*

| | Dr £ | Cr £ |
|---|---|---|
| Purchases and sales | 81 400 | 150 295 |
| Capital | | 50 000 |
| Drawings | 8 410 | |
| Loan | | 5 000 |
| Carriage inwards | 298 | |
| Motor van | 5 298 | |
| Office equipment | 21 095 | |
| Land and buildings | 84 889 | |
| Rent | 215 | |
| Rates | 1 009 | |
| Motor expenses | 109 | |
| Returns | 210 | 518 |
| Insurance | 75 | |
| Office expenses | 510 | |
| Carriage out | 109 | |
| Wages and salaries | 3 176 | |
| Creditors | | 3 095 |
| Debtors | 2 105 | |
| | 208 908 | 208 908 |

*Notes:*

1 Closing stock £21 598
2 Expenses owing:
   Rent £410
   Office expenses £218
3 Expenses prepaid:
   Insurance £109
   Wages £300

**Prepayments and accruals at the beginning and end of the accounting period**

This is possibly the most complicated situation you will be asked to deal with concerning prepayments and accruals.

***Example***

John has come to the end of his accounting period and therefore wishes to produce his Trading Profit and Loss Account and Balance Sheet.

During the year ending 31.12.X9 he has paid £10 000 in respect of office expenses.

At 31.12.X8 certain office expenses had been prepaid amounting to £500, while others amounting to £200 were outstanding.

At 31.12.X9 the prepaid office expenses are £100 with £150 still outstanding for other office expenses.

How much does John include as office expenses in his Trading Profit and Loss Account?

Hopefully, by now you are aware that we are concerned not simply with the amount of cash payment of £10 000. The figure to be included in the Trading Profit and Loss Account should *reflect the expenditure incurred which relates to the accounting period concerned* and *not* the cash payment, unless they are the same.

The ledger will therefore appear as follows, showing that the actual expenditure incurred was £10 350.

*Office expenses*

| | £ | | £ |
|---|---|---|---|
| Opening Balance prepaid | 500 | Opening Balance owing | 200 |
| Amount paid | 10 000 | Expenditure incurred | 10 350 |
| Closing Balance owing | 150 | Closing Balance prepaid | 100 |
| | 10 650 | | 10 650 |

***Procedure***

1 Personally I find it easier to look at the situation as follows:

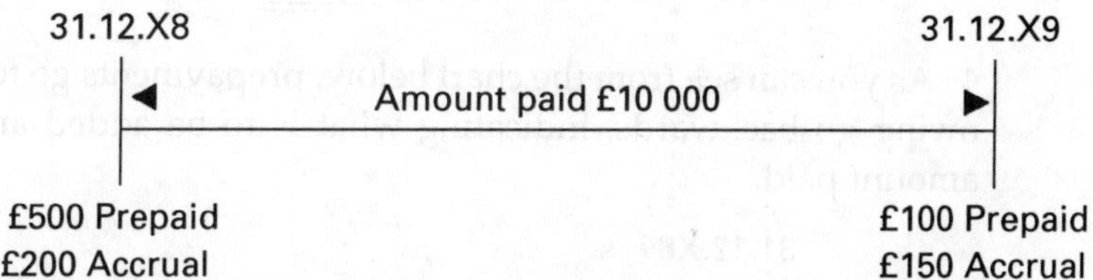


2 Let us first of all deal with the items at *31.12.X9*

(a) *£100 Prepaid.* This is in respect of next year's office expenses.

While it has been paid this year and is therefore part of the £10 000, it is *not* part of the expenditure incurred in this accounting period which is what we are trying to determine.

We must therefore deduct the £100 prepayment from the amount paid.

(b) *£150 Accrued.* This is the amount still outstanding which John should have paid for expenditure incurred.

We must therefore add £150 to the amount paid.

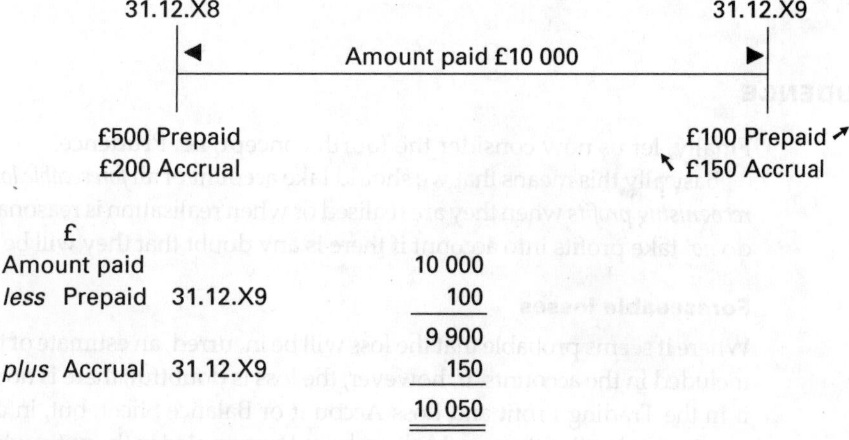


| | | £ |
|---|---|---|
| Amount paid | | 10 000 |
| *less* Prepaid | 31.12.X9 | 100 |
| | | 9 900 |
| *plus* Accrual | 31.12.X9 | 150 |
| | | 10 050 |

3 *Items as at 31.12.X8*

(a) *£500 Prepaid* – was paid last year but in respect of this accounting period and must therefore be added to the amount paid.

(b) *£200 Accrued* – was paid last year but in respect of this accounting period, and must therefore be deducted from the amount paid.

*Expenditure incurred*

| | £ |
|---|---|
| Amount Paid | 10 000 |
| less pre-paid 31.12.X9 | 100 |
| | 9 900 |
| plus accrual 31.12.X9 | 150 |
| | 10 050 |
| plus pre-paid 31.12.X8 | 500 |
| | 10 500 |
| less accrual 31.12.X8 | 200 |
| | 10 350 |

4 As you can see from the chart below, prepayments go forward while amounts owing go backwards, indicating what is to be added and deducted from the amount paid.

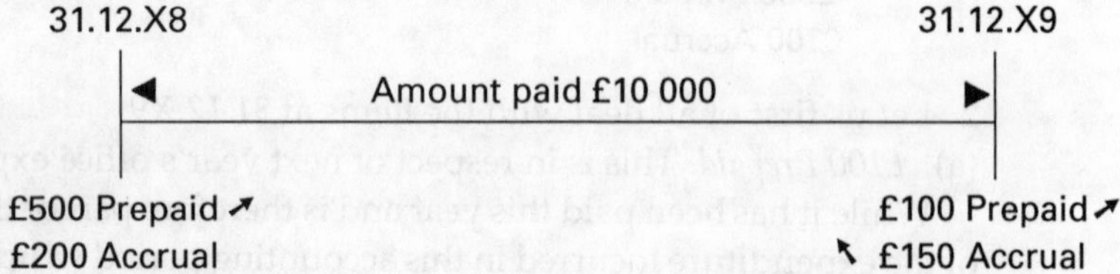


5 *Remember*
(a) the Closing Prepaid element (£100) appears as a current asset in the Balance Sheet, as it represents money owed *to* John;
(b) the Closing Accrual element (£150) appears as a current liability in the Balance Sheet, as it represents money owed *by* John.

## ■ PRUDENCE

Finally, let us now consider the fourth concept, i.e. Prudence.

Basically this means that we should take account of all *foreseeable losses*, while only *recognising profits* when they are realised or when realisation is reasonably certain. We do *not* take profits into account if there is any doubt that they will be realised.

### Foreseeable losses

Where it seems probable that the loss will be incurred, an estimate of the loss must be included in the accounts. If, however, the loss is doubtful, there is no need to include it in the Trading Profit and Loss Account or Balance Sheet, but, in order to remain prudent, a detail of the possible loss should be revealed in the notes which accompany the final accounts, e.g. guarantees given for loans granted to third parties.

As there is a possibility of the company being called upon to pay under their guarantee, then details of such must be revealed.

### Recognition of profits

Profits can be recognised when they are realised *or* when realisation is reasonably certain. It is therefore possible for businesses to recognise profits:

(a) when customers place an order,
(b) when the order is accepted,
(c) when goods are received by the customer,

*provided*, in all cases, the business is reasonably certain of receiving payment. Alternatively, businesses may recognise profits:

(d) when they actually receive the cash.

Where they trade on credit terms of many months, this may seem too prudent and therefore they may recognise profits:

(e) when the goods are sold, irrespective of when payment is received.

If we go back to double entry bookkeeping for a moment, you will recall that a sale on credit is entered in the ledgers as follows:

For example, Dec 1: Sale of £5 000 to A White on credit of 3 months.

*A White*

| | | |
|---|---|---|
| Dec 1 Sales | £5 000 | |

*Sales*

| | | |
|---|---|---|
| | Dec 1 A White | £5 000 |

At the end of the accounting period the ledgers are balanced off and the balances transferred to the trial balance. The sale of £5 000 to A White will form part of the total sales figure in the Trading Profit and Loss Account, and as a result contribute towards the profit calculation, despite the fact that A White's account is still outstanding. The balance of A White's account will form part of the Debtors figure appearing in the Balance Sheet.

We have therefore recognised the profit before it has been realised on the basis that realisation (payment) is reasonably certain.

Most businesses who trade on credit terms will, however, suffer from bad debts, i.e. some of their *debtors* will fail to pay. As a result the business should make a provision for some of their debtors failing to pay in order to account for all foreseeable losses, i.e. they should create a *provision for bad and doubtful debts.*

Consequently the normal time for recognising profits is *when the goods are sold with a provision being made for bad and doubtful debts and future interest payments.*

By making such a provision we are also attempting to match the bad debts which result from the sales of the same period (i.e. Matching Concept).

## ■ PROVISION FOR BAD AND DOUBTFUL DEBTS

The problem with creating a provision for bad and doubtful debts is that while we realise some debts will go bad we don't know which debts, and therefore how much will go bad.

An estimate must therefore be made, based on past experience. But an estimate of what? Well, an estimate of the people who owe the business money, i.e. of the debtors.

The estimate may well take into consideration how long the debts have been outstanding, as shown below:

| *Length outstanding* | *Amount* | *Estimate of bad and doubtful debts* | |
|---|---|---|---|
| | | | *Amount* |
| | £ | % | £ |
| 0–3 months | 15 000 | 1 | 1 500 |
| 3–6 months | 10 000 | 5 | 500 |
| 6–9 months | 7 000 | 10 | 700 |
| 9–12 months | 1 000 | 15 | 150 |
| Over 12 months | 500 | 20 | 100 |
| | 33 500 | | 2 950 |

Let us now look at a company who simply make a provision based on the outstanding debtors. From past experience they have found that 5 per cent of their debts turn bad and at the end of the year their debtors equal £40 000.

i.e. Debtors £40 000

Provision for bad and doubtful debts = 5% = £2 000

*Provision for bad and doubtful debts*

| | | | |
|---|---|---|---|
| | 31.12.X8 | Profit and Loss | £2 000 |

The £2 000 is then included:

(a) as an expense for the year in the Trading Profit and Loss Account,
(b) as a deduction from Debtors in the Balance Sheet.

*Example of Balance Sheet Extract*

| *Current assets* | £ | £ |
|---|---|---|
| Stock | | 20 000 |
| Debtors | 40 000 | |
| *less* Provision for bad and doubtful debts | 2 000 | 38 000 |
| Bank | | 1 000 |
| Cash | | 500 |
| | | 59 500 |

At the end of the following year the trial balance may appear as follows, with, you will note, the inclusion of the Provision for Bad and Doubtful Debts balance of £2 000.

*Trial Balance as at end of Year 2*

| | £ | £ |
|---|---|---|
| Purchases and sales | 100 000 | 200 000 |
| Stock at 1.1.X9 | 20 000 | |
| Rent | 3 000 | |
| Rates | 1 000 | |
| **Provision for bad and doubtful debts** | | 2 000 |
| Other expenses | 20 000 | |
| Premises | 80 000 | |
| Van | 15 000 | |
| Debtors | 42 000 | |
| Creditors | | 4 000 |
| Capital | | 75 000 |
| | 281 000 | 281 000 |

*Notes:*

1 Closing Stock at 31.12.X9 £15 000

2 Create a provision for bad and doubtful debts of 5 per cent of Debtors i.e. 5% of £42 000 = £2 100

We are once again asked to create a provision for bad and doubtful debts of 5 per cent, i.e. of £2 100.

As the balance of the provision ledger is already £2 000, we simply need to increase the provision this year by £100, making it the required £2 100.

*Provision for bad and doubtful debts*

| | | | | | |
|---|---|---|---|---|---|
| | | | 31.12.X8 | Profit and loss | £2 000 |
| | | | 31.12.X9 | Profit and loss | £100 |

We therefore need to adjust the Trial Balance as follows:

(i) increase the provision by £100,

(ii) include this year's provision of £100 at the foot of the Trial Balance, to be picked up as an expense.

*Trial Balance as at end of Year 2*

| | £ | £ |
|---|---|---|
| Purchases and sales | 100 000 | 200 000 |
| Stock at 1.1.X9 | 20 000 | |
| Rent | 3 000 | |
| Rates | 1 000 | |
| **Provision for bad and doubtful debts** | (+100) | 2 000 |
| Other expenses | 20 000 | |
| Premises | 80 000 | |
| Van | 15 000 | |
| Debtors | 42 000 | |
| Creditors | | 4 000 |
| Capital | | 75 000 |
| | 281 000 | 281 000 |
| Provision for bad debt (Year 2) | 100 | |

When drawing up the final accounts we therefore:

(i) deduct £2 100 from Debtors in the Balance Sheet (i.e. balance of the provision account);

(ii) include £100 as an expense in the Trading Profit and Loss Account.

Let us suppose the Debtors at the end of Year 3 are only £10 000 and we are asked once again to make a provision for bad and doubtful debts of 5 per cent, i.e. £500.

The balance of the provision for bad and doubtful debts appearing in the Trial Balance will be £2 100. We therefore need *to reduce* the provision by £1 600, leaving £500 in the account which will then be deducted from debtors of £10 000 in the Balance Sheet.

*Provision for bad and doubtful debts*

| | | £ | | | £ |
|---|---|---|---|---|---|
| 31.12.Y0 | Profit and loss | 1 600 | 31.12.X8 | Profit and loss | 2 000 |
| | | | 31.12.X9 | Profit and loss | 100 |
| 31.12.X9 | Balance | 500 | | | |
| | | 2 100 | | | 2 100 |
| | | | 1.1.Y1 | Balance c/o | 500 |

What, however, do we do with the reduction in provision of £1 600?

As we have reduced the provision rather than increased it, the £1 600 is added back to gross profit rather than deducted from it.

| | £ |
|---|---|
| Gross profit | 25 000 |
| *add provision for bad and doubtful debts* | 1 600 |
| | 26 600 |
| *less expenses* | |

So, the rule is:

(a) the amount of the provision made for the year is entered in the Trading Profit and Loss Account as an expense, and
(b) the balance of the account appears in the Balance Sheet as a deduction from Debtors, and
(c) if there is a reduction in the provision, the reduction is added to gross profit.

**Bad debts**

Where a sale actually goes bad, we can simply write this off immediately and no provision needs to be made.

e.g. Jan 1 Sale of goods to V Iqbal £2 000

*V Iqbal*

| | | | | | |
|---|---|---|---|---|---|
| Jan 1 | Sales | £2 000 | | | |

*Sales*

| | | | | | |
|---|---|---|---|---|---|
| | | | Jan 1 | V Iqbal | £2 000 |

March 1 We are advised that V Iqbal has been declared bankrupt and that unsecured creditors will not receive a dividend.

Therefore, we write off the debt of £2 000 in V Iqbal's ledger and create a bad debt which is included as an expense in the Trading Profit and Loss Account.

*V Iqbal*

| | | | | | |
|---|---|---|---|---|---|
| Jan 1 | Sales | £2 000 | Mar 1 | Bad Debts | £2 000 |

*Bad debts*

| | | | | | |
|---|---|---|---|---|---|
| Mar 1 | V Iqbal | £2 000 | | | |

As a result you may therefore see both Bad Debts and Provision for Bad and Doubtful Debts in a trial balance – treat each one separately.

**PROGRESS TEST 3**

Produce a Trading Profit and Loss Account for the year ending 31.3.X9 and a Balance Sheet as at 31.3.X9, in vertical format, for Mrs A Bowden.

*Trial Balance at 31.3.X9*

| | Dr £ | Cr £ |
|---|---|---|
| Purchases and sales | 60 297 | 100 000 |
| Stock at 31.3.X9 | 40 109 | |
| Premises | 70 000 | |
| Equipment | 21 000 | |
| Debtors and creditors | 20 109 | 17 109 |
| Bank | | 2 700 |
| Provision for bad and doubtful debts | | 1 500 |
| Cash | 170 | |
| Wages | 20 105 | |
| Rent and rates | 4 000 | |
| Insurance | 1 500 | |
| Electricity | 715 | |
| Office expenses | 951 | |
| Bad debts | 700 | |
| Capital | | 140 115 |
| Drawings | 21 768 | |
| | 261 424 | 261 424 |

*Notes*:

1 Stock at 31.3.X9 £61 206
2 Rent and rates prepaid £700
3 Insurance owing £500
4 Increase provision for bad debts to £2 000

## ■ SUMMARY

1 Working Capital = Current Assets – Current Liabilities.

2 Working Capital examines the company's liquidity and trading position by deducting current liabilities (money the company owe and must repay within twelve months) from current assets (cash, or items which the company can convert into cash in the near future).

3 Accounts are based on accounting concepts and conventions, e.g.

- Business entity,
- Historic cost,
- Materiality,
- Money measurement,
- Realisation.

4 The fundamental accounting concepts are:

(a) going concern;
(b) consistency;
(c) accruals (matching concept);
(d) prudence.

5 The Matching Concept is concerned with matching all income relating to a particular period with the expenditure incurred which relates to that period, not the cash receipts and payments.

6 Prepayments are money paid in advance, which appear as a *current asset* in the Balance Sheet.

7 Accruals are money owed which appear as a *current liability* in the Balance Sheet.

8 In dealing with prepayments:

(a) reduce the item concerned,
(b) create a prepayment as part of current assets.

9 In dealing with accruals:

(a) increase the item concerned,
(b) create an accrual as part of current liabilities.

10 Prudence means that we should take account of all *foreseeable losses* while only *recognising profits* when they are realised or realisation is reasonably certain.

11 Foreseeable Losses are included in the final accounts if their payment is probable or simply as a note to the accounts if their payment is doubtful.

12 Recognition of Profits is normally made when the goods are sold with a provision being made for bad and doubtful debts and future interest payments.

13 Provision for Bad and Doubtful Debts is an estimate of the amount of debts (debtors) which will turn bad, based on past experience and the length of time debts have been outstanding.

14 In dealing with provision for bad and doubtful debts:

(a) include the amount of the provision as an expense in the Trading Profit and Loss Account,
(b) the balance of the provision account appears in the Balance Sheet as a deduction from Debtors;
(c) any reduction in the provision is added to gross profit.

15 Bad debts may also appear as an expense and relate to debts which have actually turned bad.

16 Where there are prepayments and accruals at the beginning and end of the account period, we can determine the expenditure incurred in the following manner:

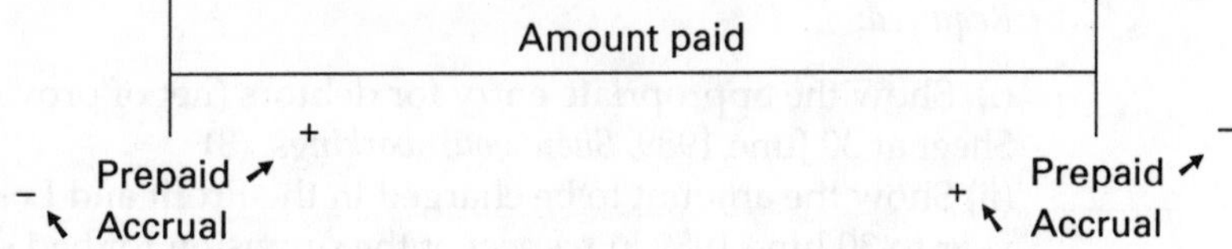


*Remember*:
The closing prepayment is a current asset.
The closing accrual is a current liability.

## ■ SELF-ASSESSMENT QUESTIONS

1 What do you understand by the term 'Working Capital'?

2 Statement of Standard Accounting Practice No. 2 (Disclosure of Accounting Policies) identifies the following four fundamental accounting concepts:

- going concern;
- accruals;
- consistency;
- prudence.

Explain what you understand by *each* of these concepts and give an example of the application of *each one* to the preparation of the annual accounts of a limited company. (20)
(CIB May 1990)

3 In a business which is buying and selling goods – where sales are made for cash, on credit terms and on hire-purchase terms – it would be possible to recognise profit or revenue at various times.

*Required*:
Identify *three* different times at which profit or revenue might be recognised. State, with reasons, which *one* of these three you would use. (20)
(CIB May 1989)

4 Balance Sheets are usually prepared on a 'going concern' basis. What does this statement mean? What effect does this basis have on the inclusion or exclusion of particular items, and on the valuation of certain assets? (10)
(CIB May 1988)

5 (a) A trader has total debtors of £35 208 at his Balance Sheet date of 30 June 1989. An analysis of the debtors at 30 June 1989 shows the following:

| | |
|---|---|
| Invoiced within the last month | £24 906 |
| Invoiced 1–2 months ago | £8 476 |
| Invoiced over 2 months ago | £1 826 |

The company accountant knows from past experience that 5 per cent of debts over two months old, 3 per cent of debts between one and two months old, and 1 per cent of debts less than one month old turn out to be bad. The balance on the Provision for Bad Debts Account at 30 June 1988 was £450 (credit).

*Required*:

(i) Show the appropriate entry for debtors (net of provisions) in the Balance Sheet at 30 June 1989. *Show your workings*. (3)
(ii) Show the amount to be charged in the Profit and Loss Account for the year to 30 June 1989 in respect of the provision for bad debts. (3)

(b) On 1 April 1989 Charles borrowed £5 000 for his business from a finance company. The terms of the loan were that he would make monthly capital repayments of £200 plus interest at the rate of 1.5 per cent per month on the outstanding capital balance starting on 1 May 1989.

*Required*:

What charge for loan interest in connection with this transaction would you expect to find in his Profit and Loss Account for the year ended 31 July 1989, and what entry would you expect to find in his Balance Sheet at 31 July 1989 in respect of the amount still outstanding?
*Show your workings* (9)

(c) A grocer's telephone bill has been fairly consistent in recent years. It rises during summer months as he has to make more calls to hotels and holiday camps to take orders.

He always receives his quarterly accounts in the first week of January, April, July and October and pays them two weeks after receipt. Recent bills have been as follows:

| | |
|---|---|
| April 1988 | £ 87 |
| July 1988 | £124 |
| October 1988 | £138 |
| January 1989 | £ 94 |
| April 1989 | £93 |
| July 1989 | £144 |
| October 1989 | £168 |

The accrued charge for telephones in his Balance Sheet dated 31 August 1988 was £92.

*Required*:

If you were preparing the grocer's annual accounts for the twelve months ended 31 August 1989, state the amounts you would show for telephone charges in:

(i) the Profit and Loss Account;
(ii) the Balance Sheet at 31 August 1989.

*Show your workings*. (5)
(Total marks for question – 20)
(CIB May 1989)

6 Prepare a Trading Profit and Loss Account for the year ending 31.12.89 and a Balance Sheet as at 31.12.89 in *vertical format*, for F Norman.

*Trial Balance of F Norman as at 31.12.89*

| | £ | £ |
|---|---|---|
| Purchases and sales | 79 210 | 169 421 |
| Stock as at 1.1.89 | 36 108 | |
| Discount received | | 1 100 |
| Rent | 269 | |
| Rates | 1 500 | |
| Office expenses | 269 | |
| Insurance | 670 | |
| Returns out | | 410 |
| Wages | 7 500 | |
| Premises | 70 000 | |
| Machinery | 40 000 | |
| Fixtures and fittings | 20 686 | |
| Debtors and creditors | 12 000 | 20 000 |
| Bank | 7 510 | |
| Cash | 100 | |
| Capital | | 100 000 |
| Drawings | 36 109 | |
| Loan | | 20 000 |
| Provision for bad debts | | 1 000 |
| | 311 931 | 311 931 |

*Notes*:

1 Stock as at 31.12.89 £20 000
2 Increase provision for bad debts by £1 000
3 Insurance prepaid £100
4 Office expenses owing £80.

# 7 Depreciation

**OBJECTIVES**

**After studying this chapter you should be able to:**

**1 Outline the nature and purpose of depreciation;**

**2 Calculate rates of depreciation using the following methods;**
 **(a) straight line,**
 **(b) reducing balance;**

**3 Explain the nature of the various methods of calculating depreciation;**

**4 Construct Trading Profit and Loss Accounts and Balance Sheets which require the provision for depreciation;**

**5 Take the appropriate action required on the disposal or scrapping of fixed assets;**

**6 Identify the profit or loss arising upon the disposal of scrapping of fixed assets.**

## ■ INTRODUCTION

In the last chapter we made adjustments for prepayments and accruals as well as providing for the possibility of bad and doubtful debt in order to match all the income relating to a particular period with the expenditure incurred which relates to that period and not simply the cash receipts and payments. In other words we adopted the matching concept in order to calculate the true profit figure for the accounting period.

Depreciation is yet another item we must consider if we are to calculate the true profit figure.

## ■ WHAT IS DEPRECIATION?

The easiest way to think of depreciation is to think of a car. How often do you hear people talk about how much the value of their car has depreciated?

So depreciation is concerned with the reduction in value of an asset, or to put it into accounting terms, it is:

'The measure of wearing out, consumption, other reduction in useful economic life of a fixed asset, whether through use, effluxion of time or obsolescence through technological change.'

*SSAP 12 'Accounting for Depreciation'*

which, put more simply, means:

depreciation is the amount by which an asset has reduced during the period of use by the firm.

For example:

| | |
|---|---|
| Motor van Cost 19X1 | £5 000 |
| Motor van sold 19X5 | £1 000 |
| *Depreciation* | £4 000 |

## ■ CAUSES OF DEPRECIATION

1 *Wear and tear* – signifies loss of value arising from use.
2 *Obsolescence* – machinery made obsolete by later inventions and better models, e.g. computers, robots in the car industry.
3 *Inadequacy* – when the asset becomes useless because the firm has grown or changed its requirements.
4 *Depletion* – if an asset is of a wasting nature.
5 *Time factor* – when assets depreciate through passage of time or if the asset is for a fixed period of time, e.g. a lease on premises.

The amount of depreciation can obviously be determined when we sell a fixed asset, but we cannot simply wait until the date of sale to account for depreciation; otherwise we would not be obeying the matching concept, and as a result we would be overstating the profit achieved over the life of the asset. The year in which the sale takes place would also bear the full reduction in value.

The matching concept requires the depreciation cost to be charged to the accounting periods which benefit from the use of the asset, i.e. if the motor van is expected to last for three years then the depreciation should be spread over the three years, as each year will benefit from its use and should therefore share in the cost and not just Year 3 when the van is scrapped or sold.

## ■ METHODS OF CALCULATING DEPRECIATION

The basis of calculation is arbitrary, i.e. there are a number of methods which are acceptable to SSAP 12, which outlines recommendations for *'Accounting for Depreciation'*.

While SSAP 12 leaves the choice of method to the company's discretion, it does indicate the types of asset which should be depreciated and the information to be disclosed, i.e. the method of depreciation, the amounts, the assets depreciated and their gross value.

The most common methods are:

(a) straight line;
(b) reducing balance;
(c) sum of years.

Each method is based on the historical cost of the asset and requires an estimate of the expected life and the residual value of the asset.

*Estimated Residual Value* is the estimated value at the end of the van's expected life with the owner, i.e. what the owner feels he will be able to sell the van for, if it lasts three years, as expected.

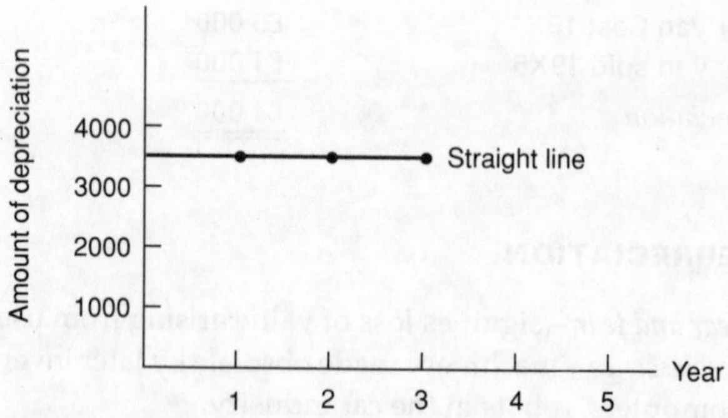


**Figure 2 The straight line method**

The residual value and expected life may differ considerably in reality.

### (a) Straight line method

The straight line method charges an equal amount of depreciation in each year of the asset's life. For example:

Van cost £12 000
Expected life 3 years
Estimated residual value £1 500

*Calculation*

Total depreciation = £12 000 − £1 500 = £10 500

∴ Annual depreciation = $\frac{£10\,500}{3}$ = £3 500

or expressed as a formula:

$$\frac{\text{Cost} - \text{Estimated value}}{\text{Number of years of expected life}} = \text{Annual depreciation}$$

This is known as the straight line method, as the depreciation charge, when plotted graphically, forms a straight line (*see* Fig. 2).

***Advantages of straight line method***

1 Easy to operate.
2 Ideal for an asset with a definite life and whose value is *nil* at the end of that life, i.e. a lease on premises.

***Disadvantages***

1 Not liked by the Inland Revenue.
2 A separate calculation is required for each asset.

### (b) Reducing balance method

This method applies a fixed percentage each year.

***Example***

Rather than depreciate £3 500 each year, as in the straight line method, the company may choose to depreciate by 50 per cent each year on the balance remaining.

| | £ |
|---|---|
| Cost | 12 000 |
| End Year 1 Depreciation 50% | 6 000 |
| Net book value Year 1 | 6 000 |
| End Year 2 Depreciation 50% | 3 000 |
| Net book value Year 2 | 3 000 |
| End Year 3 Depreciation 50% | 1 500 |
| Net book value Year 3 | 1 500 |

i.e. we are *reducing the balance* by 50 per cent each year.

While both methods show the same estimated residual value of £1 500 at the end of three years, a comparison of the two methods reveals that different amounts of depreciation are charged each year.

| *Straight line* | Cost | *Reducing balance* |
|---|---|---|
| £ | | £ |
| 12 000 | Cost | 12 000 |
| 3 500 | End year 1 | 6 000 |
| 8 500 | | 6 000 |
| 3 500 | End Year 2 | 3 000 |
| 5 000 | | 3 000 |
| 3 500 | End Year 3 | 1 500 |
| 1 500 | | 1 500 |

The reducing balance method charges more depreciation in the earlier years which, for certain assets such as motor vans, may be considered more realistic.

The choice of method will, of course, affect the amount of depreciation charged to each year's accounts, and as a result the profit calculation for the year, as well as the reported value of the fixed asset in the Balance Sheet, as we shall see later.

The rate used in the reducing balance method is found by the following complicated formula.

$r = 1 - \sqrt[n]{s/c}$

where r = rate of depreciation to be used
n = number of years (estimated life)
s = net residual value
c = cost of asset

***Example***

$r = 1 - \sqrt[3]{\frac{1\,500}{12\,000}}$

$= 1 - \sqrt[3]{0.125}$

$= 1 - 0.5$

$= 0.5$ or 50%

If you are ever asked to determine a percentage rate for the reducing balance method in the examination, you may as well adopt a trial and error approach, using just one rate, then another until you find a rate close enough.

**PROGRESS TEST 1**

1 (a) What do you understand by the term 'depreciation'?

(b) Outline the causes of depreciation.

(c) A motor car which cost £10 000 is estimated to have a useful economic life of five years, by which time it will have an estimated value of £3 000.

Using two different methods of depreciation calculate the depreciation charge for each of the five years. Work to the nearest £, and don't worry if your answers do not arrive at a scrap value of exactly £500.

(2) (a) Define and distinguish between the terms 'fixed assets' and 'current assets', and explain why this distinction is important when preparing final accounts.

(b) In relation to fixed assets, define the term 'annual depreciation charge'.

(c) Describe and compare the impact on annual profit measurement of:

(i) the straight line method of calculating depreciation;

(ii) the reducing balance method of calculating depreciation. Your answer should be illustrated with the example of an asset which cost £10 000, has a life of five years and a residual value of £1 681; the reducing balance rate is 30%. (CIB May 1991)

## ■ THE EFFECTS OF DEPRECIATION ON THE TRADING PROFIT AND LOSS ACCOUNT AND BALANCE SHEET

As we have seen, depreciation is charged to the accounting periods which benefit from the use of the asset.

If a motor van is expected to last for three years, then the depreciation is spread over the three years, as each year benefits from use of the asset and should therefore share in its reduction in value, which is usually calculated using one of the following methods:

(a) straight line;
(b) reducing balance;

The depreciation charge for the year is then included as an expense in the Trading Profit and Loss Account for that year, and is deducted from the cost of the asset in the Balance Sheet.

Let us now consider our example of the van which initially cost £12 000, and assume the owners used the straight line method for calculating depreciation. This method gave an annual depreciation charge of £3 500.

The accounts would therefore appear as follows:

*Trading Profit and Loss Extract end of Year 1*

| | £ | £ |
|---|---|---|
| Gross profit | | 20 000 |
| *less Expenses* | | |
| Rent | 5 000 | |
| Rates | 2 000 | |
| **Provision for depreciation** | 3 500 | |

*Balance Sheet Extract as at end of Year 1*

| | £ | £ |
|---|---|---|
| *Fixed assets* | | |
| Land and buildings | | 120 000 |
| Motor van (at cost) | 12 000 | |
| – **Provision for depreciation** | **3 500** | 8 500 |
| | | 128 500 |

The following year the accounts would appear as:

*Trading Profit and Loss Extract end of Year 2*

| | £ | £ |
|---|---|---|
| Gross profit | | 30 000 |
| *less Expenses* | | |
| Rent | 6 000 | |
| Electricity | 3 000 | |
| **Provision for depreciation** | **3 500** | |

*Balance Sheet Extract as at end Year 2*

| | £ | £ |
|---|---|---|
| Fixed assets | | |
| Land and buildings | | 120 000 |
| Motor van (at cost) | 12 000 | |
| – **Provision for depreciation** | **7 000** | 5 000 |
| | | 125 000 |

The important points to note are:

(a) the trading profit and loss account *includes only the charge for the year* (i.e. £3 500 each year),
(b) the balance sheet shows:
(i) the asset at *cost*
less (ii) *the total amount of depreciation which has been charged against the assets over its life,* i.e. *the net book value.*

At the end of Year 3, the Trading Profit and Loss Account will once again show an expense of £3 500 for depreciation, while the Balance Sheet will show:

*Balance Sheet Extract as at Year 3*

| | £ | £ |
|---|---|---|
| Fixed assets | | |
| Land and buildings | | 120 000 |
| Motor van (at cost) | 12 000 | |
| – **Provision for depreciation** | **10 500** | 1 500 |
| | | 121 500 |

**Examination questions**

The need to provide for depreciation is often part of a question asking you to produce a Trading Profit and Loss Account and Balance Sheet from a trial balance, with the instruction given by way of a note.

***Example***

*Trial Balance of L Peat as at 31.12.X9*

| | Dr | Cr |
|---|---|---|
| | £ | £ |
| Purchases and sales | 179 841 | 200 000 |
| Stock as at 1.1.X9 | 21 679 | |
| Capital | | 75 000 |
| Creditors | | 36 000 |
| Machinery | 30 000 | |
| Premises | 60 000 | |
| Debtors | 20 000 | |
| Carriage inwards | 510 | |
| Telephone | 216 | |
| Loan | | 2 328 |
| Electricity | 313 | |
| Rates | 1 000 | |
| Rent | 518 | |
| Office expenses | 821 | |
| Discount | 1 000 | 2 500 |
| Returns | 105 | 175 |
| | 316 003 | 316 003 |

*Notes:*

1 Stock as at 31.12.X9 £29 887.
2 Electricity accrued £105.
3 Office expenses prepaid £300.
4 Create a provision for bad debts of 5 per cent of debtors.
5 **Depreciation of machinery is 10 per cent on cost.**

## ■ PROCEDURE FOR DEALING WITH DEPRECIATION

1 *Calculate the amount of depreciation for the year*, i.e. 10% of 30 000 = £3 000

The £3 000 is then entered in the Provision for Depreciation Ledger and *not* the Machinery Ledger which remains at cost price.

*Provision for depreciation: machinery*

| | | | | | |
|---|---|---|---|---|---|
| | | | 31.12.X9 | Profit and loss | £3 000 |

*Machinery*

| | | | | | |
|---|---|---|---|---|---|
| 1.12.X9 | Bank | £30 000 | | | |

2 The double entry to the entry in the Provision for Depreciation Ledger is to include the amount as an expense in the Trading Profit and Loss Account.

I have therefore included the provision, as a new expense, at the foot of the trial balance below so that I don't forget to include it when drawing up the Trading Profit and Loss Account.

*Remember:* The trial balance should always balance after our adjustments and this means that we need to do something else, because at the moment I have only added £3 000 to the debit side (shown below).

3 Make a note at the side of the asset being depreciated (i.e. the machinery), as this amount must also be deducted from the cost of the asset in the Balance Sheet.

*Trial Balance of L Peat as at 31.12.X9*

| | Dr £ | | Cr £ |
|---|---|---|---|
| Purchases and sales | 179 841 | | 200 000 |
| Stock as at 1.1.X9 | 21 679 | | |
| Capital | | | 75 000 |
| Creditors | | | 36 000 |
| Machinery (cost)* | 30 000 | (*– 3 000 Dep.) | |
| Premises | 60 000 | | |
| Debtors | 20 000 | | |
| Carriage inwards | 510 | | |
| Telephone | 216 | | |
| Loan | | | 2 328 |
| Electricity | 313 | | |
| Rates | 1 000 | | |
| Rent | 518 | | |
| Office expenses | 821 | | |
| Discounts | 1 000 | | 2 500 |
| Returns | 105 | | 175 |
| | 316 003 | | 316 003 |

*Depreciation of machinery £3 000

Notes:

1 Stock as at 31.12.X9 £29 887.
2 Electricity accrued £105.
3 Office expenses prepaid £300.
4 Create a provision for bad debts of 5 per cent of debtors.
5 Depreciation of machinery is 10 per cent on cost.

We have therefore made two adjustments:

(a) including the amount of depreciation as an expense at the foot of the trial balance;
(b) indicating the amount to be deducted from the cost of the asset in the Balance Sheet.

**PROGRESS TEST 2**

Produce a Trading Profit and Loss Account and Balance Sheet from the trial balance above, not forgetting to make adjustments for the notes relating to prepayments, accrual and provision for bad debts.

In the above question the depreciation charge was the first charge against the asset, but in some questions the asset may already have been depreciated in previous years. The trial balance under such circumstances would appear as follows:

*Trial Balance of V Sunderland as at 31.12.X9*

| | Dr £ | Cr £ |
|---|---|---|
| Purchases and sales | 71 059 | 92 100 |
| Capital | | 60 000 |
| Loan | | 30 000 |
| Stock as at 1.1.X9 | 10 000 | |
| Debtors and creditors | 16 100 | 10 000 |
| Premises | 75 000 | |
| **Motor van (at cost) (1)** | **10 000** | |
| **Provision for depreciation motor van (2)** | | **1 000** (*+900) |
| Bank | 3 000 | |
| Cash | 1 562 | |
| Wages | 5 000 | |
| Electricity | 369 | |
| Gas | 510 | |
| Insurance | 1 000 | |
| Provision for bad debts | | 500 |
| | 193 600 | 193 600 |

*Depreciation of motor van 900

*Notes*:

1 Stock as at 31.12.X9 £13 000.
2 Electricity owing £150.
3 Insurance prepaid £500.
4 Increase provision for bad debts to £750.
5 Depreciate motor vans on a reducing balance basis at the rate of 10 per cent per annum. (3)

The important points to note are:

1 The cost price of the motor van is given in the trial balance and should be shown in the Balance Sheet.

2 The provision for depreciation in the trial balance refers to depreciation which has been charged in previous years.

3 The *note* indicates *this year's depreciation charge which should be included as an expense in the Trading Profit and Loss Account.*

**Procedure**

1 Calculate the amount of depreciation for the year

| | £ |
|---|---|
| i.e. Cost | 10 000 |
| – Provision for depreciation | 1 000 |
| | 9 000 |

∴ 10% on a reducing balance basis
= 10% of £9 000 = 900

This amount is then posted to the ledger, which will now appear as follows:

*Provision for depreciation: motor van*

| | | | |
|---|---|---|---|
| | 31.12.X8 | Profit and loss | £1 000 |
| | 31.12.X9 | Profit and loss | £900 |

2 This year's depreciation charge of £900 is then included as an expense in the Trading Profit and Loss Account and I would therefore include the provision at the foot of the trial balance.

3 In the last example I made a note of the depreciation charge at the side of the asset to show the amount to be deducted in the Balance Sheet. In this case we can add the £900 to the previous year's depreciation of £1 000 as it is the total amount of the provision ledger which is deducted from the cost of the asset in the Balance Sheet.

**PROGRESS TEST 3**

Produce a Trading Profit and Loss Account and Balance Sheet from the trial balance below.

*Trial Balance of L Harris as at 31.12.X9*

| | Dr<br>£ | Cr<br>£ |
|---|---|---|
| Capital | | 100 000 |
| Sales | | 315 000 |
| Purchases | 201 591 | |
| Stock as at 1.1.X9 | 36 598 | |
| Premises | 84 000 | |
| Fixtures and fittings | 36 000 | |
| Motor vans (at cost) | 25 000 | |
| Provision for depreciation: Motor vans | | 5 000 |
| Debtors | 37 000 | |
| Creditors | | 12 689 |
| Wages | 30 100 | |
| Electricity | 3 000 | |
| Rates | 10 000 | |
| Office expenses | 5 000 | |
| Discounts | 700 | 550 |
| Carriage outwards | 250 | |
| Loan | | 36 000 |
| | 469 239 | 469 239 |

*Notes:*

1 Stock as at 31.12.X9 £42 000.
2 Prepaids: Wages £515, Rates £2 000.
3 Owing: Office expenses £700.
4 Create a provision for bad debts of £3 500.
5 Depreciation on motor vans is charged on a reducing balance basis at a rate of 20 per cent.

## ■ THE DISPOSAL OR SCRAPPING OF A FIXED ASSET

The calculation of depreciation is based on the cost of the asset, but you will recall, this requires an estimate to be made of the expected life of the asset and of the residual value.

Our first example was as follows:

| | |
|---|---|
| Van cost | £12 000 |
| Expected life | 3 years |
| Estimated residual value | £1 500 |

and the ledger at the end of Year 3 would therefore appear as follows, assuming the straight line method was adopted.

*Motor van*

| | | | | | |
|---|---|---|---|---|---|
| 1.1.X9 | Bank | £12 000 | | | |

*Provision for depreciation: motor van*

| | | | | | |
|---|---|---|---|---|---|
| | | | | | £ |
| | | | 31.12.X9 | Profit and loss | 3 500 |
| | | | 31.12.Y0 | Profit and loss | 3 500 |
| | | | 31.12.Y1 | Profit and loss | 3 500 |
| | | | | | 10 500 |

As a result the *book value*, appearing in the Balance Sheet at the end of Year 3, would be:

| | £ |
|---|---|
| Motor van (at cost) | 12 000 |
| less Provision for depreciation | 10 500 |
| | 1 500 |

i.e. according to *our books* the van is worth £1 500, but suppose we sold it for £2 000; how would we deal with this?

**Procedure**

1 Open a disposal ledger

As the name suggests, this ledger deals with the sale or disposal of the asset. If we have sold the motor van we no longer want it to appear in our accounts and we therefore need to close the motor van ledger and the provision for depreciation ledger which relates to the motor van.

This is done by transferring the balances of these ledgers to the disposal ledger:

*Motor van*

| | | | | | |
|---|---|---|---|---|---|
| 1.1.X9 | Bank | £12 000 | 31.12.X9 | Disposal | £12 000 |

*Prov. for depreciation: motor van*

| | | | | | |
|---|---|---|---|---|---|
| 31.12.X9 | Disposal | £10 500 | 21.12.Y1 | Balance | £10 500 |

*Disposal of motor van*

| | | | | | |
|---|---|---|---|---|---|
| 31.12.X9 | Motor van | £12 000 | 31.12.X9 | Prov. for dep. | £10 500 |

2 Enter the cash received from sale

Cash

| | | | | | |
|---|---|---|---|---|---|
| 31.12.X9 | Disposal | £2 000 | | | |

*Disposal of motor van*

| | | | | | |
|---|---|---|---|---|---|
| 31.12.X9 | Motor van | £12 000 | 31.12.X9 | Prov. for dep. | £10 500 |
| | | | 31.12.X9 | Cash | £2 000 |

3 Balance off the disposal ledger to reveal the profit or loss on sale by deduction

*Disposal of motor van*

| | | | | | |
|---|---|---|---|---|---|
| | | £ | | | £ |
| 31.12.X9 | Motor van | 12 000 | 31.12.X9 | Prov. for dep. | 10 500 |
| 31.12.X9 | Profit on sale | 500 | 31.12.X9 | Cash | 2 000 |
| | | 12 500 | | | 12 500 |

In our case there is a profit on disposal, but had the balancing figure appeared on the credit side of the disposal ledger then it would have been a loss.

4 Trading Profit and Loss Account
Profit on Sale: is added to gross profit
Loss of Sale: is included as an expense

The important thing to realise is that the profit or loss is only *book profits or losses*, which simply arise because the estimated residual value is different from the actual sale price and cash received.

## ■ DEALING WITH DISPOSALS IN THE TRIAL BALANCE

In the trial balance below we can see that motor vans at cost were £30 000, while the depreciation charged against these vans so far is £16 000.*

*Trial Balance as at 31.12.X9*

| | Dr £ | Cr £ |
|---|---|---|
| Purchases and sales | 50 000 | 100 000 |
| Stock at 1.1.X9 | 10 000 | |
| Premises | 80 000 | |
| Motor vans* | 30 000 | |
| Provision for depreciation: Motor vans* | | 16 000 |
| Fixtures and fittings | 11 500 | |
| Provision for depreciation: Fixtures | | 3 500 |
| Debtors | 21 000 | |
| Bank | 1 000 | |
| Cash | 500 | |
| Creditors | | 17 000 |
| Loan | | 15 000 |
| Capital | | 70 000 |
| Wages | 12 000 | |
| Office expenses | 3 903 | |
| Electricity | 397 | |
| Rates | 1 000 | |
| Insurance | 200 | |
| | 221 500 | 221 500 |

*Notes*:

1 Closing stock at 31.12.X9 £12 100.
2 Prepaids: Office expenses £100.
3 Accruals: Rates £200,
Insurance £50.
4 Depreciation has been and is to be charged on motor vans, at an annual rate of 20 per cent on cost. Depreciate fixtures and fittings £500.
5 On 1.1.X9 a motor van which originally cost £5 000 on 1.1.X6 was sold for £1 000. No entries have been made for this sale.

Before we can calculate the depreciation charge for the year (Note 4) we must deal with the sale of the van which took place on the 1.1.X9 (Note 5). Otherwise we would charge depreciation for the year on an asset which did not belong to the company that year.

**Procedure**

1 Open disposal ledger

Transfer to this ledger the cost of the van and the depreciation charged against *this van* to date.

| | |
|---|---|
| Cost 1.1.86 | £5 000 |
| Depreciation 20% on cost | £1 000* |
| Book value 1.1.X7 | £4 000 |
| Depreciation 20% on cost | £1 000* |
| Book value 1.1.X8 | £3 000 |
| Depreciation 20% on cost | £1 000* |
| Book value 1.1.X9 | £2 000 |

∴ Depreciation to date = £3 000

*Motor vans*

| | | | | | |
|---|---|---|---|---|---|
| 1.1.X9 | Balance | £30 000 | 1.1.X8 | Disposal | £5 000 |

*Prov. for depreciation: motor vans*

| | | | | | |
|---|---|---|---|---|---|
| 1.1.X9 | Disposal | £3 000 | 1.1.X9 | Balance | £16 000 |

*Disposal of motor van*

| | | | | | |
|---|---|---|---|---|---|
| 1.1.X9 | Motor van | £5 000 | 1.1.X9 | Prov. for dep. | £3 000 |

2 Enter the cash received from sale and calculate the book profit or loss by balancing off the disposal ledger

*Cash*

| | | | | | |
|---|---|---|---|---|---|
| 1.1.X9 | Disposal | £1 000 | | | |

*Disposal of motor van*

| | | | | | |
|---|---|---|---|---|---|
| | | £ | | | £ |
| 1.1.X9 | Motor van | 5 000 | 1.1.X9 | Prov. for dep. | 3 000 |
| | | | 1.1.X9 | Cash | 1 000 |
| | | | 1.1.X9 | *Loss on sale* | 1 000 |
| | | 5 000 | | | 5 000 |

3 Adjust the trial balance

You will therefore need to make the following notes to the trial balance, against the relevant items:

| | |
|---|---|
| (a) Motor vans (at cost) | – £5 000 |
| (b) Provision for depreciation: Motor vans | – £3 000 |
| (c) Cash | + £1 000 |
| and | |
| (d) Create a new expense, by making a note at the foot of the trial balance, for 'Loss on sale of van' | + £1 000 |

Each side should reduce by a net £3 000.

**PROGRESS TEST 4**

Prepare a Trading Profit and Loss Account and Balance Sheet from the trial balance above.

## ■ SUMMARY

1 SSAP 12 Accounting for Depreciation defines depreciation as:

'The measure of wearing out, consumption, other reduction in use of economic life of a fixed asset whether through use, effluxion of time or obsolescence through technological change'.

i.e. it is the amount by which the value of an asset is estimated to have reduced.

2 The matching concept requires the depreciation cost to be charged to the accounting periods which benefit from the use of the asset.

3 The most popular methods of calculating depreciation are:

(a) straight line;
(b) reducing balance;

4 The calculation is based on the historical cost of an asset and requires an estimate of the expected life and residual value of the asset.

5 Estimated Residual Value is the owner's estimate of the value of the asset at the end of its life with him.

6 Straight Line charges an equal amount of depreciation in each year of the asset's life.

7 Straight line rate

$$= \frac{\text{Cost} - \text{Estimated value}}{\text{Number of years of expected life}}$$

8 Reducing Balance applies a fixed percentage each year to the reducing value of the asset.

9 Reducing balance rate

$= 1 - \sqrt[n]{s/c}$

10 Trading Profit and Loss Account *includes only the charge for the year, as an expense.*

11 Balance Sheet shows

(a) The asset at *cost*
less
(b) The *total amount of depreciation charged over the life of the asset*, i.e. *net book value.*

12 Disposal Ledger is opened upon the sale/disposal of an asset in order to calculate the book profit or loss, and to remove details of the sold asset from the company's records.

13 Procedure upon disposal:

(a) Open a disposal ledger and transfer the cost and depreciation attributed to the sold asset to this ledger.
(b) Enter details of the cash received from sale.
(c) Balance off the disposal ledger to reveal the profit or loss on sale, by deduction.
(d) A profit on sale is added to gross profit while a loss on sale is included as an expense for the year.

14 The profit or loss on sale are *book profits or losses* which simply arise because the estimated residual value is different from the actual sale price and cash received.

## ■ SELF-ASSESSMENT QUESTIONS

Examination questions are normally concerned with:

(a) The general principles, i.e. what is depreciation and how is it calculated?
(b) Preparing Trading Profit and Loss Accounts and Balance Sheets.
(c) Dealing with the sale or disposal of a fixed asset.

1 Depreciation has been described as having an arbitrary basis of calculation, centred around a single fact and two estimates.

(a) What is arbitrary about the basis of calculation? (5)
(b) What is the single fact referred to? (2)
(c) What are the two estimates referred to? (4)
(d) What is done to make the whole subject of depreciation more meaningful to users of accounts? (5)
(e) In a Statement of Source and Application of Funds (i.e. a funds flow statement), why is depreciation added back to the net profit? (4)

(CIB November 1987)

2 (a) What is the purpose of charging depreciation on fixed assets? (3)
(b) 'The charging of depreciation does not provide funds for the replacement of worn-out or obsolete fixed assets.' Comment briefly on this statement. (2)
(c) Charles has bought a mobile compressor which he will use in his business. It cost £6 500 and he expects to use it for five years before he scraps it. He thinks its scrap value will be £500.

Describe *two* different methods by which he can charge depreciation. Show for each method the amounts of depreciation he would charge to his Profit and Loss Account for each of the five years. Work to the nearest £1. Provided one example arrives at the scrap value of £500, your second example need only approximate to this figure. (15)
(CIB Spring 1988)

3 'Some consideration of future events is inescapable even in the measurement of past income'.
(Professor R Sidebottom, *Introduction to the Theory and Context of Accounting.)*

*Required*:
Identify three future events which should be considered when preparing the Profit and Loss Account of a manufacturing business. Show how, in *each* case, such an event would or could affect the measurement of the past year's income. (20)
(CIB May 1989)

4 Supastores Ltd has been in existence for nearly four years. When it started it bought motor lorries and shop fittings. These assets are still held by the company.

It has now been discovered that in each of the last three years' accounts there has been an error in the depreciation calculations. It was intended that the motor lorries should be depreciated at 30 per cent and the shop fittings at 20 per cent, all depreciation being calculated on the reducing balance basis. In fact, these rates have inadvertently been transposed and the motor lorries have been depreciated at 20 per cent and the shop fittings at 30 per cent, both on the reducing balance basis.

In the Balance Sheet at the end of the third year the written down values are shows as:

| | |
|---|---|
| Motor lorries | £98 304 |
| Shop fittings | £43 218 |

*Required*:

(a) The entries which will appear in the company's Profit and Loss Account for Year 4 relating to depreciation. (10)

(b) The figures for aggregate cost and depreciation for motor lorries and shop fittings respectively which will appear in the company's Balance Sheet at the end of year 4. (10)

*Note:* You may assume that all motor lorries and shop fittings were purchased at the start of Year 1 and that no further purchases and no sales or scrappings have taken place.

(Total marks for question – 20)

(CIB May 1989)

5 The North Downs Bus Company Ltd has three buses in its fleet at 30 June 1988. Their cost and purchase dates were:

| | | |
|---|---|---|
| Bus No 22 | £15 200 | July 1976 |
| Bus No 23 | £25 600 | April 1984 |
| Bus No 24 | £52 000 | January 1987 |

The basis adopted for depreciation is that straight line depreciation is charged at 10 per cent of cost each year. A full year's depreciation is charged in the year of purchase and no depreciation is charged in the year of sale or scrapping. The company's accounting date is 30 June.

During the year ended 30 June 1989 the following transactions took place:

(i) Bus No 25 was bought for £58 000 in August 1988. In part payment of this cost, Bus No 22 was traded in for an allowance of £3 500.

(ii) Bus No 23 was involved in an accident in December 1988, as a result of which it was regarded as beyond repair. The insurance company paid £10 500 compensation to the bus company and arranged for the wrecked bus to be removed. Bus No 26 was bought as a replacement for £14 000. This was a second-hand vehicle which had originally been sold for £32 000 in July 1985, and although the North Downs Bus Company Ltd did not normally buy second-hand vehicles, this was the only vehicle which could be obtained at short notice to keep services running after the accident.

*Required:*

(a) The cost, accumulated depreciation, and net book value of each bus owned on 30 June 1988. (3)

(b) The cost, accumulated depreciation, and net book value of each bus owned on 30 June 1989. (5)

(c) The entries to be included in the company's Profit and Loss Account for the year ended 30 June 1989 based on the information given above. (7)

(d) Your views on whether you consider the company's depreciation policy

to be appropriate, having regard to the loss of Bus No 23. (5)
(Total marks for question – 20)
(CIB October 1989)

6 Hugh started a pet shop on 1 January 1986. The following trial balance has been extracted from his books at 31 December 1986.

| | £ | £ |
|---|---|---|
| Opening capital | | 5 000 |
| Lease of shop | 4 800 | |
| Purchase of livestock | 16 560 | |
| Purchases of other goods for sale | 19 209 | |
| Advertising | 1 863 | |
| Sales | | 48 100 |
| Rent | 5 000 | |
| Rates | 2 500 | |
| Wages | 6 220 | |
| Drawings | 5 200 | |
| Shop fittings and cages | 8 600 | |
| Vet's fees | 316 | |
| Heating and lighting | 417 | |
| Bank loan | | 8 000 |
| Bank interest and charges | 2 478 | |
| Other shop expenses | 3 143 | |
| Creditors | | 9 086 |
| Bank overdraft | | 6 120 |
| | 76 306 | 76 306 |

You are given the following additional information:

1 The lease of the shop expires on 31 December 1990.
2 Rent has been paid to 31 December 1986.
3 The last payment of rates was £1 100 and was in respect of the six months ended 31 March 1987.
4 The bank lent Hugh £10 000 on loan account when he opened the business: this was repayable £1 000 at the end of each six months, starting on 30 June 1986. An overdraft facility of £5 000 was also agreed.
5 Accrue £58 for electricity charges and £200 for accountancy fees.
6 At 31 December 1986 he valued his unsold livestock at £3 400 and other goods for cash at £1 750.
7 There are no debtors at 31 December 1986.
8 Depreciate shop fittings and cages 10 per cent on cost.

*Required*:
(a) A Trading and Profit and Loss Account for the year ended 31 December 1986 and a Balance Sheet at that date. (15)
(b) Comment on the position of the business as shown in the Balance Sheet. (5)
(CIB May 1987)

# 8 Sole trader revision

**OBJECTIVES**

**1 To provide you with a check list for dealing with adjustments.**

**2 To provide you with a specimen layout of a Trading Profit and Loss Account and Balance Sheet for a sole trader.**

## ■ DEALING WITH ADJUSTMENTS

### 1 Prepayments

(a) Deduct the amount from the expense in the trial balance and include the reduced figure as an expense in the Profit and Loss Account.

(b) Create a prepayment at the foot of the trial balance, which is included as a current asset in the Balance Sheet.

### 2 Accrual

(a) Add the amount to the expense in the trial balance, and include the increased figure as an expense in the Profit and Loss Account.

(b) Create an accrual at the foot for the trial balance, which is included as a current liability in the Balance Sheet.

### 3 Depreciation

***(a) Straight line or on cost***

| | |
|---|---|
| (i) Find cost price of asset (say) | £24 000 |
| (ii) Using percentage given (say) | 20% |
| Calculate 20% of £24 000 = | £4 800 |

*then*

(1) Charge £4 800 as an expense in the Profit and Loss Account.

(2) In the Balance Sheet deduct *total* depreciation (i.e. £4 800 from this year plus any depreciation deducted in previous years, see figure on credit side in trial balance) from cost price of asset (£24 000) to arrive at net book value.

***(b) Reducing balance or written down value***

| | |
|---|---|
| (i) Find cost price of asset (say) | £10 000 |
| (ii) Find total amount of depreciation deducted to date (see credit side of trial balance) say | £4 000 |
| (iii) Find the difference (i.e. the reduced balance) | £6 000 |
| (iv) Using percentage given (say) | 10% |
| calculate 10% of £6 000 = | £600 |

*then*

(1) Charge £600 as an expense in the Profit and Loss Account.

(2) In the Balance Sheet deduct *total* depreciation (i.e. £600 from this year plus any depreciation deducted in previous years), £4 000 from cost price.

### 4 Bad debts provision

#### *(A) Creation*

Decide on the amount of provision to be created (say 1% of debtors of £5 000 = £50)
*then*

(i) Charge the provision £50 to the Profit and Loss Account as an expense
(ii) Deduct £50 from debtors in the Balance Sheet

#### *(B) Increase in provision*

(i) Calculate the new provision (i.e. for this year)
(ii) Find out the old provision (i.e. for last year – look in trial balance – credit side)
(iii) Find the difference
*then*

(1) Charge the *difference* only to the Profit and Loss Account
(2) Deduct the *new total provision* from debtors in the Balance Sheet

#### *(C) Reduction in provision*

(i) Calculate the new provision (i.e. for this year)
(ii) Find out the old provision (i.e. for last year – look in trial balance – credit side)
(iii) Find the difference
*then*

(1) Add back the difference as *income* in the Profit and Loss Account
(2) Deduct the *new total provision* from debtor in the Balance Sheet

## ■ SPECIMEN LAYOUT OF A TRADING PROFIT AND LOSS ACCOUNT AND BALANCE SHEET OF A SOLE TRADER

The specimen layout and notes for dealing with adjustments are an important revision aid.

You must be familiar with this layout and know how to deal with all the adjustments before the examination.

**Sole trader**

*Trading Profit and Loss Account for Mr X Ample for the year ending 31 December 19X8*

| | £ | £ | £ |
|---|---|---|---|
| Sales | | | 35 000 |
| *less Returns in* | | | 150 |
| | | | 35 150 |
| *less Cost of goods sold* | | | |
| Opening stock | | 5 000 | |
| and purchases | 12 800 | | |
| *less* Returns out | 350 | | |
| | 12 450 | | |
| *plus* Carriage in | 200 | 12 650 | |
| | | 17 650 | |
| – Closing stock | | 7 500 | |
| Cost of goods sold | | | 10 150 |
| Gross profit on trading | | | 25 000 |
| *add Income* | | | |
| Discount received | | 1 000 | |
| Rent received | | 2 000 | |
| Interest received | | 2 000 | 5 000 |
| | | | 30 000 |
| *less Expenses* | | | |
| Rent | | 870 | |
| Rates | | 1 000 | |
| Lighting | 360 | | |
| + owing | 100 | 460 | |
| Heating | 540 | | |
| – Prepaid | 200 | 340 | |
| Discount allowed | | 180 | |
| Carriage out | | 362 | |
| Salaries | | 3 791 | |
| Provision for bad debt | | 584 | |
| Bad debts | | 300 | |
| Insurance | | 113 | |
| General expenses | | 2 000 | |
| Depreciation: | | | |
| fixtures | | 500 | |
| motor | | 500 | 11 000 |
| Net profit on trading | | | 19 000 |

*Balance Sheet of Mr X Ample as at 31 December 19X8*

| *Fixed assets (tangible assets)* | £ | £ | £ |
|---|---|---|---|
| Premises | | 35 000 | |
| Fixture and fittings | 10 000 | | |
| – Cumulative depreciation | 2 000 | 8 000 | |
| Motor vehicle | 6 000 | | |
| – Cumulative depreciation | 2 000 | 4 000 | 47 000 |
| *Current assets* | | | |
| Stock | | 7 500 | |
| Debtors | 10 000 | | |
| – Provision for Bad Debts | 2 000 | 8 000 | |
| Prepayment | | 200 | |
| Bank (No 1 Account) | | 2 000 | |
| Cash | | 1 000 | |
| | | 18 700 | |
| *less Current liabilities* | | | |
| Creditors | 7 700 | | |
| Accruals | 100 | | |
| Bank overdraft (No 2 Account) | 900 | 8 700 | |
| Working capital (CA-CL) | | | 10 000 |
| | | | 57 000 |
| Financed by: | | | |
| Capital | | | 45 000 |
| + Net profit | | | 19 000 |
| | | | 64 000 |
| – Drawings | | | 14 000 |
| | | | 50 000 |
| Long-term liability | | | |
| Loan (repayable in 5 years) | | | 7 000 |
| | | | 57 000 |

**PROGRESS TEST**

1 The following is the Trial Balance extracted from the ledger of Stamper, a sole trader who runs a shop, at 31 December 1989:

| | | £ | £ |
|---|---|---|---|
| Capital 1 January 1989 | | | 52 500 |
| Drawings | | 20 000 | |
| Sales | | | 150 750 |
| Purchases | | 112 800 | |
| Stock at 1 January 1989 | | 25 600 | |
| Wages | | 12 610 | |
| Rent | | 2 500 | |
| Motor expenses | | | 1 240 |
| Motor vehicle: | at cost | 17 000 | |
| | accumulated depreciation at 1 January 1989 | | 3 000 |
| Equipment: | at cost | 15 000 | |
| | accumulated depreciation at 1 January 1989 | | 4 500 |
| Bank | | 900 | |
| Debtors | | 9 950 | |
| Creditors | | | 8 100 |
| Cash float | | 250 | |
| Insurance | | 1 000 | |
| | | 218 850 | 218 850 |

You are given the following additional information:

1 Stock at 31 December 1989 was valued at £27 350.

2 Rent of £500 (included in the figure of £2 500 above) was prepaid at 31 December 1989.

3 Motor expenses of £140 are to be accrued at 31 December 1989.

4 A bad debt of £200 is to be written off.

5 An invoice for insurance of £450 was wrongly recorded as purchases, and is included under purchases in the trial balance.

6 The motor vehicle is depreciated on the straight line basis assuming a life of four years and a residual value of £5 000; the equipment is depreciated on the reducing balance basis using an annual rate of 30%.

*Required:*
Prepare the Trading and Profit and Loss Account for Stamper for the year to 31 December 1989 and the Balance Sheet at that date. (20)
(CIB May 1990)

2 Barry is a taxi driver who owns his taxi. It cost £10 500 new at the beginning of his financial year and he is taking depreciation into account at 25% per annum on the reducing balance basis.

At 30 April 1987, he had prepaid expenses of £453 in respect of the licence and insurance on his vehicle, he was owed £312 for fares incurred by regular customers (with whom he operates a monthly account) and in turn owed a garage £209 for servicing and petrol.

At 30 April 1988, his prepaid expenses on licence and insurance amount to £531, his regular customers owe him £587, and his debt to the garage is £319.

A summary of his bank account for the year ended 30 April 1988 is given below.

*Summary Bank Account*

| | £ | | £ |
|---|---|---|---|
| Balance b/fwd | 34 | Taxi operating expenses | 10 317 |
| Bankings | 16 013 | Hire of two-way radio | 540 |
| Advertising revenue from roof sign | 200 | Advertising in telephone directory | 192 |
| | | Trade subscription | 75 |
| | | Supply and fitting of illuminated roof sign to carry advertisements | 520 |
| | | Bank charges | 48 |
| | | Foreign currency (for Dutch holiday) | 427 |
| | | Personal expenses (including mortgage payments on house, income tax, rates) | 3 147 |
| | | Balance c/fwd | 981 |
| | 16 247 | | 16 247 |

The bankings represented all monies received for fares (including tips) after £75 per week for each of 50 weeks had been deducted: the latter sum he has retained in cash for housekeeping and personal expenses.

*Required*:

(i) A Balance Sheet at 30 April 1987. (6)

(ii) A Profit and Loss Account for the year ended 30 April 1988. (8)

(iii) A Balance Sheet at 30 April 1988. (6)

(Bankers Certificate May 1988)

3 David is a trainee accountant in a firm of chartered accountants. His manager has worked out all the individual figures relating to the accounts of a small mail order business for the year ended 31 March 1989. He has asked David to write out the Trading and Profit and Loss Accounts and the Balance Sheet. David's attempts are shown below. You will see that the Balance Sheet does not balance, by £23 470.

*Required*:

Rewrite the accounts in a proper format. All the individual figures are correct except for sub-totals, the net profit and the Balance Sheet difference.

*Trading and Profit and Loss Account as at 31 March 1989*

| | £ | £ | | £ | £ |
|---|---|---|---|---|---|
| Cash purchases | | 102 341 | Cash sales | | 217 820 |
| Credit purchases: | | | Credit sales: | | |
| Cash paid to suppliers | 98 317 | | Cash received from debtors | 210 021 | |
| *add* Debtors 31 March 1988 | 23 150 | | *add* Creditors 31 March 1988 | 10 316 | |
| | 121 467 | | | 220 337 | |
| *less* Debtors 31 March 1989 | 18 190 | 103 277 | *less* Creditors 31 March 1988 | 11 495 | 208 842 |
| Lighting and heating | | 8 170 | | | |
| Stock 31 March 1989 | | 96 217 | Stock 31 March 1988 | | 124 309 |
| Repairs | | 9 314 | | | |
| Gross profit c/d | | 231 652 | | | |
| | | 550 971 | | | 550 971 |
| Wages | | 40 000 | Gross profit b/d | | 231 652 |
| Rent and rates | | 21 047 | Discounts allowed | | 3 129 |
| Discounts received | | 13 092 | | | |
| Postage and telephone | | 15 203 | | | |
| Sundry trade expenses | | 10 305 | | | |
| Amortisation | | 800 | | | |
| Depreciation | | 750 | | | |
| Drawings | | 63 102 | | | |
| | | 164 299 | | | |
| Net profit for year | | 70 482 | | | |
| | | 234 781 | | | 234 781 |

*Balance Sheet for the year ended 31 March 1989*

| | £ | £ | | £ | £ |
|---|---|---|---|---|---|
| Capital account | | 62 940 | Leasehold premises at cost | 10 700 | |
| Profit and loss account | | 70 482 | Less aggregate depreciation | 3 900 | 6 800 |
| | | | Stock | | 124 309 |
| | | | Shop fittings at cost | 20 125 | |
| | | | Less aggregate amortisation | 7 680 | 12 445 |
| | | | | | 143 554 |
| Current liabilities | | | Current assets | | |
| Debtors | 23 150 | | Creditors | 11 495 | |
| Prepaid expenses | 4 298 | | Bank balance | 37 143 | |
| Advertising | 13 058 | 40 506 | Accrued expense | 5 206 | 53 844 |
| Difference on books? | | 23 470 | | | |
| | | 197 398 | | | 197 398 |

4 Malcolm Biskett is a grocer. From the following information you are required to:

(a) prepare a Trading and Profit and Loss Account for the year ended 30 September 1988; (7)

(b) prepare a Balance Sheet as at 30 September 1988; (8)

(c) calculate the percentage of gross profit on sales; (1)

(d) suggest two reasons which might explain why the gross profit is not the figure of 15 per cent on sales, the figure which was achieved last year. (4)

NB. *Wages should be shown in the Profit and Loss Account not the Trading Account.*

(Total marks for question – 20)

*Trial balance at 30 September 1988*

| | £ | £ |
|---|---|---|
| Aggregate depreciation on motor van to 30 September 1987 | | 3 776 |
| Aggregate depreciation on shop equipment to 30 September 1987 | | 6 430 |
| Bank charges | 214 | |
| Bank overdraft | | 3 042 |
| Capital | | 25 369 |
| Drawings | 19 302 | |
| General expenses | 779 | |
| Heating and lighting | 578 | |
| Interest on deposit account | | 34 |
| Motor van | 15 105 | |
| Post and telephone | 316 | |
| Print and stationery | 76 | |
| Printing and stationery | 179 124 | |
| Purchases | 143 | |
| Sales | | 205 982 |
| Shop equipment | 12 319 | |
| Stock, 30 September 1987 | 5 106 | |
| Travelling and van expenses | 1 257 | |
| Wages and National Insurance | 10 314 | |
| | 244 633 | 244 633 |

Stock at 30 September 1988 was valued at £7 564.

Depreciation is to be charged on the following basis:

Motor van 25 per cent of the reducing balance

Shop equipment 15 per cent on the reducing balance

At 30 September 1988, creditors for purchases amounted to £3 145 and debtors for sales to £758. The following accrued expenses are also to be taken into account:

Electricity £120

Accountancy £300

(CIB Autumn 1988)

# 9 Partnership accounts

**OBJECTIVES**

**After studying this chapter you should be able to:**

**1 Define a partnership;**
**2 Outline some of the agreements which may be made upon forming a partnership;**
**3 Appreciate how these agreements affect partnership accounts;**
**4 Produce final accounts for a partnership.**

## ■ INTRODUCTION

So far we have been mainly concerned only with the accounts of *sole traders* (someone who is the sole owner of a business, say a shopkeeper). There are a number of advantages and disadvantages associated with sole traders, e.g.

*Advantages*

1 All the profits are your own.
2 You make all the decisions.
3 Few formalities (i.e. accounts don't have to be published or audited as with PLCs)

*Disadvantages*

1 All the losses are yours alone.
2 Unlimited liability – you are liable not only to the extent of money involved in the business but also to the extent of your personal assets.
3 While you make all the decisions, you may lack expertise in certain areas, e.g. marketing.
4 Difficult to take holidays unless you have competent and trusted staff.
5 Finance is limited to what you can contribute in terms of capital and what you can borrow, which in itself costs money in terms of interest.

Forming a partnership is a way of overcoming some of the disadvantages outlined above. By asking someone to join you in business you can:

- share the risk;
- share the workload;
- bring new expertise to the business;
- raise further finance.

So, what is a partnership?

## ■ DEFINITION

'A partnership is the relation which subsists between persons carrying on a business in common with a view of profit': Partnership Act 1890, s.1.

**Example**

Bill and Ben decide to go into business together, as landscape gardeners, trading under the name of 'Greenfingers'.

Upon forming the partnership they make the following financial agreements:

1 Bill is to contribute £50 000 capital, whilst Ben will contribute £30 000.
2 In order to reward Bill for the extra capital he is contributing they decide that interest should be paid on capital at the rate of 10 per cent per annum.
3 As they realise that the first year of trading will be difficult they feel that drawing should be kept to a minimum. They therefore agree to pay interest on any drawings at the rate of 5 per cent.
4 Each partner will be paid a salary of £10 000 per annum.
5 Profits or losses will be shared equally.

Their trial balance at the end of their first year of trading appears as follows.

*Trial Balance of 'Greenfingers' as at 31.12.X9*

| | £ | £ |
|---|---|---|
| Sales | | 100 000 |
| Purchases | 50 000 | |
| Expenses | 10 000 | |
| Fixed assets | 80 000 | |
| Current assets | 30 000 | |
| Current liabilities | | 10 000 |
| Long-term liabilities | | 10 000 |
| Capital: | | |
| Bill | | 50 000 |
| Ben | | 30 000 |
| Drawings: | | |
| Bill | 20 000 | |
| Ben | 10 000 | |
| | 200 000 | 200 000 |

*Notes:*

1 Stock as at 31.12.X9 = Nil
2 Interest on capital: 10 per cent
3 Interest on drawings: 5 per cent
4 Salaries:
Bill £10 000
Ben £10 000
5 Profits or losses are to be shared equally.

As you can see details of the partnership agreements are given in the notes at the foot of the trial balance and we must therefore take these into consideration when constructing the final accounts, i.e:

1 *Capital* must indicate the amount contributed by each partner

2 *Interest on capital* must be calculated and given to each partner
3 *Interest on drawings* must be calculated and deducted from each partner
4 *Salaries* must be given to each partner
5 *Profits or losses* must be shared

While the capital contributed by each partner is revealed in the Balance Sheet, the other items which relate to the distribution of profits are shown in the *Appropriation Account*, at the foot of the Trading Profit and Loss Account.

The inclusion of an appropriation section is the only difference between a Trading Profit and Loss Account of a sole trader and that of a partnership.

## ■ PRODUCING THE FINAL ACCOUNTS OF A PARTNERSHIP

### 1 Trading Profit and Loss Account

The net profit or loss is calculated in *exactly* the same way as you did for sole traders.

### 2 Appropriation Account

This is then concerned with the partnership agreements to determine the profit or loss available for distribution:

(a) Amounts payable *by the partners* are then added to the net profit
i.e. Interest on drawing,
e.g. Bill 5 per cent of £20 000 = £1 000
(b) Amounts payable *to the partners* are then deducted,
i.e. interest on capital and salaries,
e.g. Bill 10 per cent of £50 000 = £5 000
(c) The resulting profit or loss is then available for distribution.

Look at the example below:

*Trading Profit and Loss Account of 'Greenfingers' for the year ending 31.12.X9*

| | | £ | £ | |
|---|---|---|---|---|
| Sales | | | 100 000 | As sole trader |
| *less* Cost of goods sold | | | 50 000 | |
| Gross profit | | | 50 000 | |
| *less* Expenses | | | 10 000 | |
| Net profit | | | 40 000 | |
| *Appropriation Account* | | | | |
| + Interest on drawings: | Bill | 1 000 | | |
| | Ben | 500 | 1 500 | |
| | | | 41 500 | |
| – Interest on capital: | Bill | 5 000 | | |
| | Ben | 3 000 | 8 000 | |
| | | | 33 500 | |
| – Salaries | Bill | 10 000 | | |
| | Ben | 10 000 | 20 000 | |
| Balance of profits | | | 13 500 | |
| shared as follows | Bill 50% | 6 750 | | |
| | Ben 50% | 6 750 | 13 500 | |

### 3 Balance sheet

From the previous chapters you will be aware that the Balance Sheet of a sole trader is shown as follows:

| | £ | £ |
|---|---|---|
| Fixed assets | | 200 000 |
| Current assets | 100 000 | |
| *less* Current liabilities | 20 000 | 80 000 |
| | | 280 000 |
| *Financed by* | | |
| Capital | | 180 000 |
| + Net profit | | 50 000 |
| | | 230 000 |
| – Drawings | | 30 000 |
| | | 200 000 |
| Long-term liabilities | | 80 000 |
| | | 280 000 |

The Balance Sheet of a partnership is exactly the same, except for the capital section highlighted above. This section is represented in one of two ways:

(a) Fixed capital plus current account;
(b) Fluctuating capital account.

#### *(a) Fixed capital plus current account*

This is where the capital is shown as the amount contributed by Bill and Ben. Profits, interest on capital and salaries less drawings and interest on drawings are then shown in a separate account known as the *current account.*

*Balance Sheet extract*

| | | £ | £ |
|---|---|---|---|
| Capital: | | | |
| Bill | | 50 000 | |
| Ben | | 30 000 | 80 000 |
| Current accounts | Bill | Ben | |
| | £ | £ | |
| Opening balance | nil | nil | |
| Share of profit | 6 750 | 6 750 | |
| Interest on capital | 5 000 | 3 000 | |
| Salary | 10 000 | 10 000 | |
| | 21 750 | 19 750 | |
| *less* Drawings | 20 000 | 10 000 | |
| | 1 750 | 9 750 | |
| *less* Interest on drawings | 1 000 | 500 | |
| | 750 | 9 250 | 10 000 |

***(b) Fluctuating capital account***

This is where the share of profits, interest on capital and salaries are added to the capital and the drawings and interest on drawings are deducted. The balance will therefore fluctuate/change each year.

*Balance Sheet extract*

| | *Bill* | *Ben* |
|---|---|---|
| | £ | £ |
| Capital | 50 000 | 30 000 |
| Share of profit | 6 750 | 6 750 |
| Interest on capital | 5 000 | 3 000 |
| Salary | 10 000 | 10 000 |
| | 71 750 | 49 750 |
| *less* Drawings | 20 000 | 10 000 |
| | 51 750 | 39 750 |
| *less* Interest on drawings | 1 000 | 500 |
| | 50 750 | 39 250 |

The *fixed capital plus current account* (method a) is preferred to the fluctuating capital accounts, which would conceal a situation where a partner was taking out more than his share of profits, salaries, etc. With separate accounts this is revealed by a debit balance on the current account.

## ■ SPECIMEN LAYOUT OF PARTNERSHIP ACCOUNTS

*Trading Profit and Loss Account of 'Greenfingers' for the year ending 31.12.X9*

| | | | £ |
|---|---|---|---|
| Sales | | | 100 000 |
| *less* Cost of goods sold | | | 50 000 |
| Gross profit | | | 50 000 |
| *less* Expenses | | | 10 000 |
| Net profit | | | 40 000 |
| + Interest on drawings: | Bill | 1 000 | |
| | Ben | 500 | 1 500 |
| | | | 41 500 |
| – Interest on capital: | Bill | 5 000 | |
| | Ben | 3 000 | 8 000 |
| | | | 33 500 |
| – Salaries: | Bill | 10 000 | |
| | Ben | 10 000 | 20 000 |
| Balance of profits | | | 13 500 |
| shared as follows: | Bill 50% | 6 750 | |
| | Ben 50% | 6 750 | 13 500 |

*Balance Sheet of 'Greenfingers' as at 31.12.X9*

| | £ | £ | £ |
|---|---|---|---|
| Fixed assets | | | 80 000 |
| Current assets | | 30 000 | |
| *less* Current liabilities | | 10 000 | 20 000 |
| | | | 100 000 |
| Capital: | | | |
| Bill | | 50 000 | |
| Ben | | 30 000 | 80 000 |
| Current accounts | *Bill* | *Ben* | |
| Opening balance | nil | nil | |
| Share of profit | 6 750 | 6 750 | |
| Interest on capital | 5 000 | 3 000 | |
| Salary | 10 000 | 10 000 | |
| | 21 750 | 19 750 | |
| *less* Drawings | 20 000 | 10 000 | |
| | 1 750 | 9 750 | |
| *less* Interest on drawings | 1 000 | 500 | |
| | 750 | 9 250 | 10 000 |
| | | | 90 000 |
| Long-term liabilities | | | |
| Loan | | | 10 000 |
| | | | 100 000 |

**PROGRESS TEST**

From the following information prepare an Appropriation Account for the year ending 31.12.Y0 and a Fixed Capital plus Current Account for Rowntree Makintosh Partners.

| | £ |
|---|---|
| Net profit | 100 000 |
| Capital: | |
| Rowntree | 100 000 |
| Makintosh | 100 000 |
| Opening current account balances | |
| Rowntree | 10 000 |
| Makintosh | (5 000) |
| Drawings: | |
| Rowntree | 25 000 |
| Makintosh | 5 000 |

*Notes*:

1 Interest on capital is paid at 10% per annum

2 Interest on drawings is charged at 20% per annum

3 Salaries:

| | |
|---|---|
| Makintosh | £20 000 |
| Rowntree | £11 000 |

4 Profits are shared between Rowntree and Makintosh in the ratio of 3:2 respectively

## ■ PARTNERSHIP AGREEMENTS

Partners can make any agreements they wish regarding the operation of their partnership.

For example, profits of say, £50 000 may be distributed between two partners:

(a) equally i.e. £25 000 each;
(b) in proportion to their contribution of capital, e.g.

| | | |
|---|---|---|
| Partner A: | Capital | £50 000 |
| Partner B: | Capital | £30 000 |
| | Total | £80 000 |

therefore A receives 5/8 of the profits as he contributes 5/8 of the capital, and B receives 3/8 of the profit.

*Distribution of profits*

| | |
|---|---|
| A 5/8 of £25 000 = | £15 625 |
| B 3/8 of £25 000 = | £9 375 |
| | £25 000 |

(c) in the ratio of 3:1
therefore A receives 3 of 4 parts or 3/4
B receives 1 of 4 parts or 1/4

*Distribution of profits*

| | |
|---|---|
| A = 3/4 of £25 000 = | £18 750 |
| B = 1/4 of £25 000 = | £6 250 |
| | £25 000 |

**Partnership Act 1890, s.24**

Where no agreements have been made either express or implied, section 24 of the Partnership Act 1890 will decide the outcome:

- profits and losses are to be shared equally;
- no interest is allowed on capital;
- no interest is charged on drawings;
- no salaries are allowed;
- any capital contributed in excess of the sum agreed will earn interest of 5 per cent per annum.

## ■ SUMMARY

1 A sole trader is someone who is the sole owner of a business, e.g. a shopkeeper.

2 A partnership is the relationship which subsists between persons carrying on a business in common with a view of profit (Partnership Act 1980, s.1).

3 Final accounts of partnerships are often effected by the following financial agreement:
   (a) amount of interest to be paid on capital;
   (b) amount of interest to be charged on drawings;
   (c) amount of salaries paid to each partner;
   (d) the amount of capital to be contributed by each partner;
   (e) the distribution of profits or losses.

4 Details of the partnership agreements are given in the notes to the trial balance.

5 Net profit is calculated in exactly the same way as for sole traders.

6 The appropriation account is concerned with the payment of interest by and to the partners and the payment of salaries to determine the amount of profit available for distribution.

7 The Balance Sheet is exactly the same as for a sole trader except for the capital section.

8 The preferred method for presenting the capital and profits, etc. is in the form of a Fixed Capital plus Current Account.

9 A Fixed Capital plus Current Account would clearly reveal a situation where a partner was withdrawing more than his balance of profits etc, with a debit balance on the current account.

10 Generally speaking, partners are left to make their own arrangements but where there are no agreements, Sec. 24 Partnership Act 1890 will decide the outcome.

## ■ SELF-ASSESSMENT QUESTIONS

1 What are the advantages and disadvantages of being in business as a sole trader and how can forming a partnership overcome some of the disadvantages?

2 What financial agreements may partners enter into when forming a partnership? How would the Partnership Act 1890 decide such matters if the partners did not come to any arrangements?

3 Horley, Horsham and Hayward are partners in a business which was established on 1 January 1990; they agreed that their capital account balances should remain fixed and all other transactions be put through each partner's current account. A profit, before any allocations to the partners, of £93 000 was made in the first year of trading. The partners are undecided as to how this profit should be shared between them and have provided you with the following information:

(i) At 31 December 1990 the following balances appear in the account:

| | Horley | Horsham | Hayward |
|---|---|---|---|
| | £ | £ | £ |
| Capital introduced 1 January | 75 000 | 65 000 | 50 000 |
| Drawings for 1990 | 19 000 | 21 000 | 23 000 |

(ii) The partners could have invested their capital outside the partnership to earn an annual return of 10%.
(iii) Horley could earn a salary of £20 000 per year if not working for the partnership, Horsham a salary of £17 000 and Hayward a salary of £16 000.

*Required*:
(a) Calculate how much profit would be credited to each partner in 1990 in the absence of any specific agreement, and show the balance on each partner's current account at 31 December 1990.
(b) Calculate the total amount of profit which would be credited to each partner in 1990 if due recognition is given to the alternative uses of their capital and labour, and any residue divided equally, and show the balance on each partner's current account at 31 December 1990.
(c) Discuss the alternative bases of profit division in (a) and (b). Explain which one you consider is fairer and the position if no formal agreement exists between the partners.
(CIB May 1991)

4 Wave and Trough run a shop together as partners. The following is the trial balance extracted from the firm's ledger at 30 June 1990:

| | £ | £ |
|---|---|---|
| Capital 30 June 1989: | | |
| Wave | | 90 000 |
| Trough | | 75 000 |
| Drawing: | | |
| Wave | 16 000 | |
| Trough | 15 800 | |
| Current account balances at 30 June 1989: | | |
| Wave | 1 000 | |
| Trough | | 10 600 |
| Sales | | 611 300 |
| Purchases | 426 100 | |
| Stock at 30 June 1989 | 35 500 | |
| Rates on premises | 15 000 | |
| Wages | 36 900 | |
| Motor expenses | 6 300 | |
| Land and buildings at cost | 134 000 | |
| Motor vehicle: | | |
| at cost | 20 000 | |
| accumulated depreciation at 30 June 1989 | | 3 000 |
| Fixtures and fittings: | | |
| at cost | 55 200 | |
| accumulated depreciation at 30 June 1989 | | 10 000 |
| Bank | | 15 100 |
| Debtors and creditors | 101 800 | 35 500 |
| Bank charges and interest | 3 600 | |
| Advertising | 21 200 | |
| Discounts allowed and received | 9 800 | 2 700 |
| Long-term loan at 10% | | 50 000 |
| Interest on long-term loan | 5 000 | |
| | 903 200 | 903 200 |

You are given the following additional information:

1 Stock at 30 June 1990 was valued at £42 700.

2 The rates account contains a payment of £8 000 made in April 1990 for the six months to 30 September 1990.

3 Some advertising was undertaken in April 1990, and the invoice for £4 300 was received in July. This is not included in the trial balance.

4 During the year to 30 June 1990, Wave took goods for his own use which cost £1 500. No record of this was made in the firm's books.

5 The motor vehicle is depreciated on the straight line basis assuming a life of six years and residual value of £2 000; the fixtures and fittings are also depreciated on the straight line basis assuming a life of 10 years and a residual value of £5 200.

6 The partners agree that profits and losses should be shared equally, after giving each partner interest on his capital account balance of 12% a year and an annual salary of £20 000 to Wave and £30 000 to Trough.

7 Capital account balances are to remain unchanged.

*Required:*
Prepare the Trading and Profit and Loss Account of Wave and Trough for the year to 30 June 1990 and the Balance Sheet at that date.
(CIB October 1990)

# 10 The admission or retirement of a partner

**OBJECTIVES**

**After studying this chapter you should be able to:**

1. **Understand what is meant by 'goodwill';**
2. **Outline reasons for goodwill and some of the methods of calculating goodwill;**
3. **Appreciate the need to make financial arrangements upon the admission, retirement or death of a partner, and following a change in the profit-sharing ratio;**
4. **Prepare final accounts for a partnership following the admission or retirement of a partner which calls for the revaluation of the business assets.**

## ■ INTRODUCTION

Bill and Ben have now been trading together for some years under the same agreements. They have decided to introduce a new partner, Mr A Pandy, who they hope will make a significant contribution to the firm's profitability.

Bill feels that profit should be shared equally. Ben is not sure. He agrees that Andy will add to the firm's *future profitability* but also feels that the firm's future profitability is due to the trade and reputation that Bill and Ben developed over the *past years*. 'If only we could place a value on the firm's trade and reputation developed over the past years.' This could then be said to be as a result of Bill's and Ben's efforts and therefore awarded to them in some way.

At a meeting with their accountant they explain their dilemma.

'You mean you need to value the *goodwill* of the business?' said the accountant.

'Goodwill what's that?' cried Bill and Ben.

## ■ GOODWILL

The easiest way to think of goodwill is to imagine you are buying a business, let us say a record shop. The assets are valued at:

| | £ |
|---|---|
| Premises | 40 000 |
| Equipment | 5 000 |
| Fittings | 3 000 |
| Stock | 2 000 |
| | 50 000 |

The owner, however, asks a price of £60 000 for the business, £10 000 being for goodwill.

**Reasons for goodwill**

You may be asked to pay in excess of the asset value for a number of reasons.

1 *Trade under the same name* – you therefore inherit the trade and reputation of the old company, provided they have a good name! This is something you would need to consider before paying for goodwill or trading under the same name.
2 *Inherit skilled/trained staff* – this will save recruitment and training costs as well as ensuring the business continues to operate smoothly.
3 *Location* – may be particularly advantageous and should therefore have a price as well as the individual assets of the business.
4 *Goodwill connections with suppliers.*
5 *Trade marks, patents and brands* – while the assets of Rowntrees and another less well known confectionery company may be the same, you would be asked to pay more for Rowntrees, simply due to the value attached to the brand names you would purchase.
6 *Monopoly position.*

All of the above features can make a significant contribution to a firm's profitability and as such are a valuable asset.

If you were buying a business as a going concern you would therefore have to pay for these features, which are not reflected in the asset values.

**Methods of valuing goodwill**

Placing a value on these features is very difficult and really depends on how much the purchaser is prepared to pay, based on how much he feels the goodwill will contribute to the future profitability of the business.

It is often calculated in accordance with the custom of the industry. For example:

1 negotiation between the buyer and seller;
2 sales × industry norm;
3 Profits × *x* years;
4 average profit for *x* years × industry norm;
5 super profits × *x* years;

i.e. net profit less the amount the owner could have earned had he not worked in the business – wages, e.g.

| | | £ |
|---|---|---|
| Net profit | | 20 000 |
| less Wages | 10 000 | |
| Interest (had capital been invested) | 2 000 | 12 000 |
| | | 8 000 |

6 Discounted momentum value method. While your first years' profits may owe much to the trade and reputation you have inherited, after say 5 years your customers will only be loyal because of your service and reputation, i.e. because of the goodwill you have put into the business. This method takes this into account by examining:

(a) estimated profits if the *existing business* is taken over, i.e. including inherited reputation;

(b) estimated profits if a new *identical business* starts (i.e. without the inherited reputation)

| Years | Estimated profits of existing firm *including goodwill* | Estimated profits of new firm *excluding goodwill* | Excess |
|---|---|---|---|
| £ | £ | £ | |
| 1 | 20 000 | 10 000 | 10 000 |
| 2 | 23 000 | 14 000 | 9 000 |
| 3 | 25 000 | 18 000 | 7 000 |
| 4 | 26 000 | 22 000 | 4 000 |
| 5 | 26 000 | 26 000 | — |
| | | | £30 000 |

The excess is therefore seen to be directly as a result of *goodwill*. So goodwill is the amount paid in excess of the asset value which, as we have seen, may be for a number of reasons and calculated in a number of ways.

Goodwill is the subject of SSSP 22 which is dealt with in greater depth in the Banking Diploma. For the Banking Certificate we need to concentrate on its effect on partnership accounts and in particular the admission and retirement of a partner.

## ■ THE ADMISSION OF A NEW PARTNER

Let us go back to Bill and Ben and assume that goodwill is valued at £30 000, i.e. *the value developed over the past years before Andy becomes a partner*. Subject to any contrary agreement each partner owns a share of goodwill in proportion to his share of profits.

If Andy was simply admitted as a partner with an equal share of the profits, then in the event of selling the business, and receiving £30 000 in respect to goodwill it would be shared:

| | |
|---|---|
| Bill 1/3 | £10 000 |
| Ben 1/3 | £10 000 |
| Andy 1/3 | £10 000 |

This is surely not fair to Bill and Ben, for had they sold the business before Andy became a partner they would each have received £15 000.

Arrangements must therefore be made to award the value of goodwill to Bill and Ben before Andy becomes a partner.

### Accounting procedure

| | *Old ratio* | *Amount* | *New ratio* | *Amount* | *Loss/gain* |
|---|---|---|---|---|---|
| Bill | 1/2 | £15 000 | 1/3 | £10 000 | (£5 000) |
| Ben | 1.2 | £15 000 | 1/3 | £10 000 | (£5 000) |
| Andy | — | — | 1/3 | £10 000 | £10 000 |
| | | £30 000 | | £30 000 | |

i.e. if Andy is simply admitted:

Bill and Ben will lose £5 000 each,
Andy will gain £10 000.

Therefore:

1 Andy could pay £5 000 cash, privately to Bill and Ben for the goodwill he will inherit.

Bill and Ben will each receive

| | |
|---|---|
| £5 000 | Cash now |
| £10 000 | From the sale of goodwill in the future (assuming it remains the same) |
| £15 000 | |

therefore their position has not been altered.

or

2 Andy could pay cash into the business which would be added to the Capital accounts of Bill and Ben, e.g.

*Bill: Capital*

| | | | |
|---|---|---|---|
| | | Balance | £50 000 |
| | | Cash | £5 000 |

*Ben: Capital*

| | | | |
|---|---|---|---|
| | | Balance | £30 000 |
| | | Cash | £5 000 |

*Cash*

| | | | |
|---|---|---|---|
| Capital | £10 000 | | |

Remember Bill and Ben still own a share of the goodwill (1/3 of £30 000 = £10 000). Therefore once again their position has not altered.

or

3 Open a goodwill account. If Andy has introduced £30 000 cash in the form of capital he may have insufficient cash to pay to Bill and Ben, or to pay into the business for this share of goodwill. Therefore a goodwill account is opened.

(a) *Open a goodwill account* – crediting the goodwill to the partners' capital account in the old profit sharing ratio.

(b) *Write off the goodwill account* – in the new profit sharing ratios.

*Goodwill*

| | £ | | £ |
|---|---|---|---|
| Capital (a) | 30 000 | Bill | 10 000 (b) |
| | | Ben | 10 000 (b) |
| | | Andy | 10 000 (b) |
| | 30 000 | | 30 000 |

*Bill: Capital*

| | £ | | £ | |
|---|---|---|---|---|
| Goodwill w/o (b) | 10 000 | Opening balance | 50 000 | |
| Closing balance | 55 000 | Goodwill | 15 000 | (a) |
| | 65 000 | | 65 000 | |
| | | Balance | 55 000 | |

*Ben: Capital*

| | £ | | £ | |
|---|---|---|---|---|
| Goodwill w/o (b) | 10 000 | Opening balance | 30 000 | |
| Closing balance | 35 000 | Goodwill | 15 000 | (a) |
| | 45 000 | | 45 000 | |
| | | Balance | 35 000 | |

*Andy: Capital*

| | £ | | £ |
|---|---|---|---|
| Goodwill w/o (b) | 10 000 | Opening balance | 30 000 |
| Closing balance | 20 000 | | |
| | 30 000 | | 30 000 |
| | | Balance | 20 000 |

Bill's and Ben's Capital amounts have increased by £5 000 to compensate them for their loss of goodwill.

| Bill and Ben will receive: | £5 000 | extra capital |
|---|---|---|
| | £10 000 | from the sale of goodwill in the future |
| | £15 000 | |

therefore their position has not altered.

Andy's capital has reduced by £10 000 in payment for his share of goodwill.

*Remember*

- While the goodwill account is closed, the trade and reputation of the business is still alive and could be sold in the future.
- Subject to contrary agreement a new partner must either pay for the goodwill he will inherit or reduce his capital by an equivalent amount, which is then distributed to the old partners to compensate for their loss.
- Subject to contrary agreement a change in the profit sharing ratio means a change in the goodwill sharing ratio and therefore similar accounting procedure must be followed.

**PROGRESS TEST 1**

(a) The following information has been presented to you by Matthew, Mark and Luke who are about to introduce John as a new partner.

They estimate that goodwill is valued at £60 000 and want to know how to account for this before admitting John as a new partner.

Complete the following table and then using a goodwill account show how each partner's capital account will be affected once goodwill is written off.

| | *Old ratio* | *Amount* | *new ratio* | *Amount* | *Loss/Gain* |
|---|---|---|---|---|---|
| Matthew | 3 | | 3 | | |
| Mark | 2 | | 2 | | |
| Luke | 1 | | 2 | | |
| John | — | | 1 | | |

(b) Luke is somewhat confused. He thought he was being awarded with his share of the goodwill, yet the results from (a) indicate a reduction in his capital account.

Explain to Luke how his position has not been affected by your accounting entries and John's introduction to the firm.

## ■ GOODWILL AS AN INTANGIBLE ASSET

If the goodwill account is not written off immediately (as shown above), then like all other ledgers/accounts it is balanced off at the end of the accounting period and transferred to the final accounts.

Goodwill is then shown as an intangible fixed asset, in the Balance Sheet. For example:

*Balance Sheet extract*

| Fixed assets | £ | £ |
|---|---|---|
| *Intangible* | | |
| Goodwill | | 30 000 |
| *Tangible* | | |
| Premises | 50 000 | |
| Fittings | 20 000 | |
| Van | 10 000 | 80 000 |
| | | 110 000 |
| Current assets | | |
| Stock | 30 000 | |

This increase in the assets is offset by the increase in the partners' capital account.

## ■ RETIREMENT OR DEATH OF A PARTNER

Let us suppose that after some years Bill decides to retire. By this time goodwill is valued at £45 000. Ben and Andy will continue in business sharing profits equally.

| | *Old ratio* | *Amount* | *New ratio* | *Amount* | *Loss/gain* |
|---|---|---|---|---|---|
| | | £ | | £ | £ |
| Bill | 1/3 | 15 000 | — | — | – 15 000 |
| Ben | 1/3 | 15 000 | 1/2 | 22 500 | +7 500 |
| Andy | 1/3 | 15 000 | 1/2 | 22 500 | +7 500 |
| | | 45 000 | | 45 000 | |

Bill will obviously wish to be paid for this share of goodwill, otherwise when the business is sold in the future, he will lose £15 000, and by this Ben and Andy will have gained an extra £7 500 each.

Ben and Andy will therefore have to pay Bill for the extra goodwill they will be able to sell at a later date.

1 Award each partner their share of goodwill in the old ratios.
2 Write off the goodwill in the new ratios.

*Bill: Capital*

| | £ | | £ |
|---|---|---|---|
| | | Opening balance | 55 000 |
| | | Goodwill | 15 000 (1) |
| Closing balance | 70 000 | | 70 000 |
| | | Balance | 70 000 |

*Ben: Capital*

| | £ | | £ |
|---|---|---|---|
| | | Opening balance | 35 000 |
| Goodwill w/o (2) | 22 500 | Goodwill | 15 000 (1) |
| Closing balance | 27 500 | | |
| | 50 000 | | 50 000 |
| | | Balance | 27 500 |

*Andy: Capital*

| | £ | | £ |
|---|---|---|---|
| | | Opening balance | 20 000 |
| Goodwill w/o (2) | 22 500 | Goodwill | 15 000 (1) |
| Closing balance | 12 500 | | |
| | 35 000 | | 35 000 |
| | | Balance | 12 500 |

*Goodwill*

| | £ | | £ |
|---|---|---|---|
| Bill | 15 000 | Ben | 22 500 |
| Ben | 15 000 | Andy | 22 500 |
| Andy | 15 000 | | |
| | 45 000 | | 45 000 |

as a result:

- Bill's and Andy's capital amounts have reduced by £7 500 each;
- *but* they now have a larger share of goodwill (i.e. £22 500, an increase of £7 500);
- therefore their positions have not altered;
- remember, while the goodwill account is closed in a sale situation, goodwill still exists.

3 Bill may wish to take his £70 000 in cash, or leave the money in the business in the form of a loan, in which case the balance would be transferred from his capital account to a loan account.

**PROGRESS TEST 2**

Matthew has now decided to retire from the partnership of Matthew, Mark, Luke and John (see Progress test 1).

Goodwill is now valued at £100 000 and the partners once again seek your assistance.

Using the information below, show the effect on their capital accounts if a goodwill account is used with goodwill then being written off immediately.

| | *Old ratio* | *New ratio* |
|---|---|---|
| Matthew | 3 | — |
| Mark | 2 | 2 |
| Luke | 2 | 2 |
| John | 1 | 1 |

## ■ REVALUATION OF ASSETS

As we have seen, adjustment for goodwill may be required:

(a) upon the admission of a new partner;
(b) upon a change in the profit sharing ratio;
(c) upon the retirement/death of a partner.

The assets may also need to be revalued on these occasions *as any increase in the value of assets is distributed between the partners in their profit sharing ratios* (subject to contrary agreement).

**Example**

Lake and Old are in partnership, sharing profits and losses equally. They are about to introduce Hurst who will also take an equal share of profits or losses.

Assets have a book value (balance sheet value) of £50 000 but upon revaluation, their value is found to be £80 000.

As increases in the value of assets are distributed between the partners in their profit sharing ratios, the increase of £30 000 would be distributed as follows:

| | *Prior to Hurst joining* | | *After Hurst joining* | |
|---|---|---|---|---|
| *Distribution* | *Ratio* | *Amount* | *Ratio* | *Amount* |
| | | £ | | £ |
| Lake | 1/2 | 15 000 | 1/3 | 10 000 |
| Old | 1/2 | 15 000 | 1/3 | 10 000 |
| Hurst | — | — | 1/3 | 10 000 |

As you can see, if action is not taken to account for the increase in value prior to Hurst being admitted as a partner, the old partners give up some of their share of the increase.

Clearly there is a need to revalue the assets upon a change in the profit sharing ratio which applies equally upon the retirement or death of a partner.

**Accounting procedure**

***Example***

A, B, C who share profits equally have decided to introduce D as a new partner. Before admitting D, who will take an equal share of the profits, they revalue the assets.

| | | *Balance Sheet value* | *Revaluation* | *Gain/loss* |
|---|---|---|---|---|
| | | £ | £ | £ |
| Premises | | 50 000 | 80 000 | + 30 000 |
| Machinery | | 20 000 | 30 000 | + 10 000 |
| Van | | 10 000 | 5 000 | – 5 000 |
| Stock | | 20 000 | 15 000 | – 5 000 |
| Debtors | | 10 000 | 7 000 | – 3 000 |
| Bank | | 10 000 | 10 000 | — |
| | | 120 000 | 147 000 | +27 000 |
| Capital | A | 40 000 | | |
| | B | 40 000 | | |
| | C | 40 000 | | |
| | | 120 000 | | |

*Step 1*

(a) Increase or decrease the ledger balance of each asset. The double entry being on entry in the *Revaluation Account*

*Premises*

| | | | |
|---|---|---|---|
| Opening balance | £50 000 | | |
| Revaluation increase | £30 000 (a) | | |

*Machinery*

| | | | |
|---|---|---|---|
| Opening balance | £20 000 | | |
| Revaluation increase | £30 000 (a) | | |

*Van*

| | | | |
|---|---|---|---|
| Opening balance | £10 000 | Revaluation decrease | £5 000 (a) |

*Stock*

| | | | |
|---|---|---|---|
| Opening balance | £20 000 | Revaluation decrease | £5 000 (a) |

*Debtor*

| | | | |
|---|---|---|---|
| Opening balance | £10 000 | Revaluation decrease | £3 000 (a) |

*Bank*

| | | | |
|---|---|---|---|
| Opening balance | £10 000 | | |

*Revaluation Account*

| *Decrease in assets* | | | *Increase in assets* | |
|---|---|---|---|---|
| Van | (a) | £5 000 | Premises | £30 000 (a) |
| Stock | (a) | £5 000 | Machinery | £10 000 (a) |
| Debtors | (a) | £3 000 | | |

*Step 2*

(b) The balance remaining on the revaluation account is then distributed to the partners in their profit sharing ratio.

*Capital: A*

| | | |
|---|---|---|
| | Opening balance | £40 000 |
| | Revaluation increase | £9 000 (b) |

*Capital: B*

| | | |
|---|---|---|
| | Opening balance | £40 000 |
| | Revaluation increase | £9 000 (b) |

*Capital: C*

| | | |
|---|---|---|
| | Opening balance | £40 000 |
| | Revaluation increase | £9 000 (b) |

*Revaluation Account*

| *Decrease in Assets* | | | *Increase in Assets* | |
|---|---|---|---|---|
| | | £ | | £ |
| Van | (a) | 5 000 | Premises | 30 000 |
| Stock | (a) | 5 000 | Machinery | 10 000 |
| Debtors | (a) | 3 000 | | |
| Capital A | (b) | 9 000 | | |
| Capital B | (b) | 9 000 | | |
| Capital C | (b) | 9 000 | | |
| | | 40 000 | | 40 000 |

## ■ SUMMARY

1 Goodwill is the amount paid by a purchaser of a business in excess of the asset values.

2 An amount is paid in excess of the asset values due to:

(a) the trade and custom you inherit;
(b) the skilled/trained staff you inherit;
(c) location of the business;
(d) good connections with suppliers;
(e) trade marks, patents, brands;
(f) monopoly position.

3 Goodwill can be valued in a number of ways according to the custom of the industry, e.g. based on sales or profits or the discounted momentum value method.

4 The discounted momentum value method of calculating goodwill is based on the fact that goodwill you inherit is replaced by your own goodwill as time passes.

5 Subject to any contrary agreement each partner owns a share of goodwill in proportion to their share of profits.

6 Goodwill must be distributed to the partners before:

(a) the admission of a new partner;
(b) retirement of an existing partner;

(c) a change in the profit sharing rate, otherwise the existing partners will give up some of their goodwill.

7 Admission of a new partner:

(a) the new partner pays cash privately to the existing partners for the goodwill he will inherit; or
(b) pays cash into the business which would be added to the capital accounts of the existing partners; or
(c) a goodwill account is opened.

8 Goodwill Account (where goodwill is to be written off immediately)

(a) credit the goodwill to the partner's capital account in the old profit sharing ratio;
(b) write off the goodwill in the new profit sharing ratios.

9 While the goodwill account is closed, the trade and reputation is still alive and therefore so, too, is the goodwill.

10 If the goodwill account is not written off immediately, goodwill appears as an intangible fixed asset in the Balance Sheet.

11 Revaluation of assets – must take place upon:

(a) admission of a new partner;
(b) retirement of an existing partner;
(c) a change in the profit sharing ratio.

12 An increase in the value of an asset is distributed between the partners in proportion to their profit sharing ratios (subject to contrary agreements).

13 Revaluation of assets – accounting procedure

(a) increase/decrease the ledger balance of each asset, the double entry being an entry in the revaluation account;
(b) the balance remaining on the revaluation account is then distributed to the partners in proportion to their profit sharing ratios.

## ■ SELF-ASSESSMENT QUESTIONS

1 What do you understand by the term goodwill?

2 Why might someone pay for goodwill?

3 How is goodwill calculated?

4 Why must goodwill be calculated and distributed to the existing partners of a firm before

(a) the admission of a new partner;
(b) the retirement of an existing partner;
(c) a change in the profit sharing ratio?

5 Using the information below, show the effect on each partner's capital account if goodwill were valued at £50 000 and

(a) cash were paid privately to the existing partners by Barley the new partner;
(b) cash were paid into the business by Barley;
(c) a goodwill account were opened, with goodwill being written off immediately.

| | *Old ratio* | *New ratio* |
|---|---|---|
| Rye | 3 | 3 |
| Wheat | 1 | 1 |
| Barley | — | 1 |

6 Some years later Wheat decides to retire. By this time the value of goodwill has increased to £75 000. Using a goodwill account, show the effect on each partner's capital account, if the following agreement is made about profit sharing.

| | *Old ratio* | *New ratio* |
|---|---|---|
| Rye | 3 | 2 |
| Wheat | 1 | — |
| Barley | 1 | 1 |

7 Simmons, Bond, Blackshaw and Allen share profits and losses in proportion to their capital. They are about to admit Wilshaw as a partner but before doing so they revalue their assets.

Complete the accounting entries and show the effect of the revaluation on the partners' capital accounts.

Once Wilshaw is admitted profits or losses will be shared equally.

| *Balance Sheet as at 31.12.Y0* | | | *Revaluation* |
|---|---|---|---|
| | £ | £ | £ |
| *Fixed assets* | | | |
| *Intangible assets* | | | |
| Goodwill | | — | 20 000 |
| *Tangible assets* | | | |
| Premises | | 70 000 | 110 000 |
| Equipment | | 30 000 | 25 000 |
| Fixtures and fittings | | 10 000 | 5 500 |
| | | 110 000 | |
| *Current assets* | | | |
| Stock | 20 000 | | 20 000 |
| Debtors | 15 000 | | 10 000 |
| Bank | 2 000 | | 2 000 |
| | 37 000 | | |
| *less Current liabilities* | | | |
| Creditors | 12 000 | | 12 000 |
| | | 25 000 | |
| | | 135 000 | |
| Capital: | | | |
| Simmons | | 50 625 | |
| Bold | | 33 750 | |
| Blackshaw | | 33 750 | |
| Allen | | 16 875 | |
| | | 135 000 | |

Goodwill should be written off immediately.

# 11 Limited company accounts

**OBJECTIVES**

**After studying this chapter you should be able to:**

**1 Outline the nature of a limited company;**
**2 Describe the essential differences between companies and partnerships;**
**3 Produce final accounts of a limited company.**

## ■ INTRODUCTION

So far we have examined the accounts of:

(a) sole trader;
(b) clubs and societies;
(c) partnerships.

In this chapter we will turn our attention to another type of business *limited companies*.

The nature of a limited company and the essential differences between a limited company and a partnership are highlighted in the table below. These differences are considered further in *Banking: the Legal Environment*, 2nd edition (David Palfreman, Pitman Publishing).

| | *Limited Companies* | *Partnerships* |
|---|---|---|
| Formation | Registered in accordance with the Companies Acts.<br>As a result they are bound by the rules of these Acts, e.g. company accounts must be drawn in accordance with the Companies Acts. Fortunately a detailed knowledge of their requirements is *not* required for your examination. | By agreement, express or implied.<br>This leaves partners to make any agreements they wish.<br>The Partnership Act 1890 will only be referred to where agreements have not been made. |
| Members (Owners) | These are the shareholders. Minimum 2, maximum unlimited.<br>This provides the opportunity to raise further capital by issuing more shares. | The partners. Minimum 2, maximum 20 except in special cases, e.g. solicitors.<br>The ability to raise further capital is therefore limited. |
| Separate Legal Entity | A company is a separate legal entity from its members (shareholders). | A partnership is not a separate legal entity, it is merely made up of the partners. |

| | *Limited companies* | *Partnerships* |
|---|---|---|
| Liability | Each member's liability is limited to the amount of shares he/she owns, i.e. in the event of liquidation the shareholders may lose the money they have invested in the company. | Partners have unlimited liability, i.e. in the event of the partnership going bankrupt they will be liable not only to the extent of money invested in the partnership but also to the extent of their personal assets. |
| Succession | A limited company continues independently unless it is wound up, i.e. the retirement of a director does not affect a company in the same way as the retirement of a partner affects the partnership. | Upon certain events the partnership will come to an end, e.g. if there are two partners and one retires. |
| Taxation | As a separate legal entity companies pay corporation tax on profits, which therefore appears in their accounts. | Partners pay income tax on the firm's net profit. |

## ■ ACCOUNTS

The accounts of a limited company are different from those of a partnership and sole trader. However, as you will see there are many common elements which makes your task of constructing such accounts that much easier.

Let us look at a specimen set of company accounts and in particular the differences between limited companies, partnerships and sole traders.

**Specimen layout**

*Trading Profit and Loss Account of Example Ltd for the year ending 31.12.X9*

| *Notes* | | £ | £ | £ |
|---|---|---|---|---|
| A: Trading Profit and Loss Account | Sales | | | 500 000 |
| | *Less cost of good sold* | | | |
| | Opening stock | | 50 000 | |
| | + Purchases | | 250 000 | |
| | | | 300 000 | |
| | – Closing stock | | 60 000 | 240 000 |
| | Gross profit | | | 260 000 |
| | *Less expenses* | | | |
| Same as sole trader and partnership | Rent and rates | | 5 000 | |
| | Provision less bad debts | | 3 000 | |
| | Light and heat | | 6 000 | |
| | Wages | | 50 000 | |
| | Motor expenses | | 20 000 | |
| However, note 1: | Directors' remuneration | | 40 000 | |
| 2: | Auditors' remuneration | | 3 000 | |
| 3: | Debenture interest | | 2 000 | |
| | Depreciation: | | | |
| | Equipment | | 5 000 | |
| | Fixtures and fittings | | 5 000 | 139 000 |
| B: Taxation | Net profit for the year before taxation | | | 121 000 |
| | *Less* corporation tax | | | 40 000 |
| | Net profit for the year after taxation | | | 81 000 |
| | Plus retained profits from previous year | | | 72 000 |
| | | | | 153 000 |
| C: Appropriation account | *Less appropriation* | | | |
| 1: Transfers | Transfer to general reserve | | 5 000 | |
| | Transfer to other reserves | | 6 000 | |
| | | | 11 000 | |
| 2: Write off | Goodwill written off | | 2 000 | |
| 3: Dividends | Preference dividends | | | |
| | Final proposed | | 3 000 | |
| | Ordinary dividends: | | | |
| | Interim paid | 2 000 | | |
| | Final proposed | 5 000 | 7 000 | 23 000 |
| D: Retained profits | | | | 130 000 |

*Notes*

**Trading Profit and Loss Account**

This is exactly the same as for partnerships and sole traders except that you may find some new expenses in the trial balance, such as:

1 Directors' remuneration – i.e. the directors' wages/salary;
2 Auditors' remuneration – the accounts of a limited company must be drawn in accordance with the Companies Act and check and certified as giving a true and a fair view of the company's affairs. The person/company who check the accounts are known as auditors, they will be paid for this service, and as such it is an expense to the company.
3 Debenture interest – A debenture is a loan received by the company and as a result the company may need to make interest payments.

**Taxation**

As stated earlier, companies are subject to corporation tax which must be deducted before any distribution of the profits can be made.

Questions may state 'ignore taxation', so don't simply include it, without being directed to in the notes, at the foot of the trial balance.

**Appropriation Account**

This section deals with the distribution of profits. After calculating the profit for the year, add the retained profits from previous years (given in the trial balance) and then make all the necessary distributions.

As with partnerships accounts, the need for such distribution will be revealed in the notes at the foot of the trial balance.

There are three types of distributions you need to be aware of:

1 Transfers to various reserves (see Balance Sheet notes);
2 Items written off, e.g. goodwill;
3 Dividends:

(a) paid;
(b) proposed.

Dividends are payments made by the company to their shareholders, in return for the shareholders investing money in the company.

That means in a sense that it represents the shareholder's interest on his investment, except that unlike interest on, say, bank investments, companies are not required to pay dividends.

The effect of the appropriations will also be seen in the Balance Sheet.

**Retained profits**

This is simply carried forward to the Balance Sheet.

**PROGRESS TEST 1**

Produce a Trading Profit and Loss Account for Davidsons Ltd for the year ending 31.12.X8, from the following table. A Balance Sheet is *not* required.

| | £ |
|---|---|
| Sales | 279 108 |
| Purchases | 87 107 |
| Stock at 1.1.X8 | 36 106 |
| Fixed assets | 310 000 |
| Debtors | 30 000 |
| Creditors | 50 000 |
| Wages | 16 091 |
| Rent | 5 000 |
| Rates | 3 000 |
| Motor expenses | 1 154 |
| Administration expenses | 2 189 |
| Directors' remuneration | 30 000 |
| Debenture interest | 1 000 |
| 10% Debenture | 10 000 |
| Ordinary dividend paid | 3 000 |
| Ordinary shares | 300 000 |

*Notes:*

1 Stock at 31.12.X8 £21 999

2 Wages owing £300
Motor expenses prepaid £159

3 Transfer to general reserve £5 000

4 Provide for corporation tax £10 000

5 Provide for a final ordinary dividend of 10 per cent

**Specimen layout**

*Balance Sheet of Example Ltd at 31.12.X8*

| *Notes* | £ | £ | £ |
|---|---|---|---|
| *Fixed Assets* | | | |
| 1 *Intangible:* | | | |
| Goodwill | | | 6 000 |
| *less* Goodwill written off | | | 2 000 |
| | | | 4 000 |
| *Tangible:* | | | |
| Premises | | 160 000 | |
| Equipment | 30 000 | | |
| – Depreciation | 10 000 | 20 000 | |
| Fixtures and fittings | 18 000 | | |
| – Depreciation | 5 000 | 13 000 | |
| Motor vehicles | | 21 000 | 214 000 |
| | | | 218 000 |
| *Current assets* | | | |
| Stock | | 60 000 | |
| Debtors | 20 000 | | |
| – Provision for bad debits | 5 000 | 15 000 | |
| Bank | | 20 000 | |
| Cash | | 1 000 | |
| *less* | | 96 000 | |
| 2 *Creditors: Amounts falling due* within one year | | | |
| Creditors | 10 000 | | |
| 3 Proposed dividends: | | | |
| Preference | 3 000 | | |
| Ordinary | 5 000 | | |
| 4 Taxation | 40 000 | 58 000 | |
| 5 Net current assets | | | 38 000 |
| | | | 256 000 |
| *less* | | | |
| 6 *Creditors: Amounts falling due* after more than one year | | | |
| 7 10% Debenture 1996 | | | 20 000 |
| | | | 236 000 |
| *Capital and reserves* | | | |
| 8 *Capital* | | *Authorised* | *Issued* |
| Ordinary shares of £1 each fully paid | | 70 000 | 50 000 |
| 10% Preference shares of £1 each | | 30 000 | 30 000 |
| | | 100 000 | 80 000 |
| 9 *Reserves* | | | |
| General reserves | | 10 000 | |
| Other reserves | | 16 000 | |
| Retained profits | | 130 000 | 156 000 |
| | | | 236 000 |

*Notes:*

Basically it is the same as sole traders and partnerships except for the following:

1 *Intangible assets.* These may well appear, with in our case £2 000 being written off the value of goodwill following the appropriation.
While goodwill is the most common intangible asset seen in examination questions, there are others such as patents, trade marks and research and development. All of which are an asset to the company but cannot be described as tangible, in that they are not clearly visible.
2 *Creditors: amounts falling due within one year.* This title simply replaces that of current liabilities.
3 *Proposed dividends.* As they are the dividends you *propose* to pay in the future, they have not yet been paid and as a result appear as amounts due within one year. *NB.* The dividends *paid* do *not* appear as they have actually been paid and are therefore *not due*. (Refer back to the Trading Profit and Loss Account.)
4 *Taxation.* Companies are liable for corporation tax based on the next profit. Therefore at the time of drawing the accounts the payment of tax is still outstanding. As a result taxation appears as a deduction from net profit in the Trading Profit and Loss Account and as an amount falling due within one year in the Balance Sheet.
5 *Net current assets.* That is the difference between current assets and accounts falling due within one year. This is the same therefore as *working capital.*
6 *Creditors: amount falling due after more than 1 year.* Simply another change of title, this time the title replaced in long-term creditors.
7 *Debentures.* These are loans received by the company, which are usually for long periods. In our case the loan is due to be repaid in 1996. The interest rate on the loan is 0 per cent (i.e. £2 000 pa), hence this amount appears in the *Trading Profit and Loss Account* as interest paid.
8 *Capital.* You must show:

(a) *Authorised share capital*, i.e. the amount of share capital the company is allowed to issued
(b) *Issued share capital*, i.e. the amount they have actually issued.
Shares may be in many forms, the most common being:
(i) *Ordinary shares* – these allow the shareholders a share of the profits after all other classes of shareholders;
(ii) *Preference shares* – such shareholders are entitled to a specified percentage rate of dividends. In our case 10 per cent;
(iii) *Cumulative preference shares* – the holders of these shares are entitled to a specified percentage rate of dividend, which is carried forward to future years if there are insufficient profits to pay the dividend in say Year 1.

9 *Reserves* These are shown as an addition to the share capital and represent retained profits – whether left as profit or transferred to a specific reserve, i.e.

(a) *Reserve reserves* – i.e. retained profits which can be distributed to shareholders in the form of dividends;
(b) *Capital reserves* – e.g. *general reserves*, which have been built up from the transfer of profits in the appropriation account. These reserves are not distributable, e.g. *share premium account*, where shares are issued at more than their normal value, for

example £1 ordinary shares, issued at £1.50 the amount in excess of the nominal value (i.e. 50p per share) is credited to a share premium account.

## ■ PRINCIPLES OF A BALANCE SHEET

Before progressing further it would be wise to reconsider the basic principles of a Balance Sheet as discussed in Chapter 2, namely that the Balance Sheet reflects a company's financial position at a given date by detailing:

(a) *Assets* – which the company own
(b) *Liabilities (Capital and creditors)* – which the business owes

More importantly and often confusing to students is that *'Liabilities indicate the source of finance'*.

In the Balance Sheet of Example Ltd, capital and reserves equal £236 000, i.e. this is a source of finance. *It does not mean* that the company has a drawer with £236 000 in cash just sitting there. This source of finance has been used to purchase the assets. The only cash available is £1 000 with an additional £20 000 available in the bank account; as indicated by the current assets.

The final Progress test indicates all the notes we have come across so far – if you can do this one, you can do any.

As it is the final test including all the complications so far, I have outlined the action to be taken; all you have to do is:

(i) make a note of the required action on the items in the trial balance. *Remember*, after you make the adjustment the trial balance should still balance. You may therefore need to insert a new item at the foot of the trial balance as we did before;
(ii) rearrange the items in the required order;
(iii) pay attention to neatness and headings.

## ■ CONCLUSION

While there are a number of new headings and items, I hope you will agree that basically the layout is the same as we have seen before.

It may seem a lot to take in, but if you just concentrate on the new items and try to learn the layouts, you will find constructing final accounts from a trial balance like doing a jigsaw – *get the right amounts in the right places and it will balance.* The only problem then, is to deal with the notes.

**PROGRESS TEST 2**

Construct a Trading Profit and Loss Account for the year ending 31.3.X9 and a Balance Sheet as at 31.3.X9 for Bernham Cars Ltd from the following Trial Balance.

*Trial Balance as at 31.3.X9*

| | Dr<br>£ | Cr<br>£ |
|---|---|---|
| £1 Ordinary shares – fully paid | | 92 000 |
| 7% Preference shares £1 each fully paid | | 50 000 |
| 10% Debenture | | 50 000 |
| Goodwill (at cost) | 1 000 | |
| Premises | 170 000 | |
| Equipment (at cost) | 70 000 | |
| Fixtures and fittings (at cost) | 5 000 | |
| Motor vehicles (at cost) | 20 000 | |
| Provision of depreciation: | | |
| Equipment | | 25 000 |
| Motor vehicles | | 14 000 |
| Stock at 1.4.X8 | 42 107 | |
| Debtors | 52 795 | |
| Bank | 7 508 | |
| Cash | 2 166 | |
| Creditors | | 31 704 |
| Debenture interest paid | 4 000 | |
| Dividends paid: ordinary | 500 | |
| General reserve | | 9 000 |
| Tax reserve | | 3 000 |
| Sales | | 207 284 |
| Purchases | 61 000 | |
| Returns in and out | 5 000 | 2 900 |
| Discounts received | | 3 109 |
| Interest received | | 4 000 |
| Wages | 13 521 | |
| Rent and rates | 5 000 | |
| Insurance | 2 500 | |
| Motor expenses | 2 000 | |
| Directors' remuneration | 27 500 | |
| Auditors' remuneration | 2 000 | |
| Provision for bad debts | | 1 600 |
| | 493 597 | 493 597 |

| *Notes* | *Action* |
|---|---|
| 1 Stock at 31.3.X9 = £36 987 | (a) Off cost of goods sold – TPL<br>(b) Current asset – BS |
| 2 Rent and rates owing = £1 500 | (a) Increase rent and rates – TPL<br>(b) Accrual (creditor) – BS i.e. Interest = 10% of £50 000 = £5 000 interest paid as per trial balance = £4 000 |
| 3 Debenture interest has not been fully paid for the year | (a) Increase – debenture interest – TPL<br>(b) Accrual (creditor) – BS |
| 4 Insurance prepaid = £300 | (a) Deduct off insurance – TPL<br>(b) Prepayment CA – BS i.e. Increase = £400 – Existing Provision = £1 600 as per Trial Balance |
| 5 Increase provision for bad debts to £2 000 | (a) £400 – expense TPL<br>(b) £2 000 off Debtors – BS<br>i.e. Cost £70 000<br>– Depreciation £25 000<br>Balance £45 000<br>therefore 10% of £45 000 = £4 500 |
| 6 Depreciate equipment 10% on a reducing balance basis | (a) £4 500 expenses TPL<br>(b) £25 000 + £4 500 off FA – BS |
| 7 Depreciate motor vehicles £1 000 | (a) £1 000 – expense – TPL<br>(b) 14 000 + £1 000 – off FA – BS |
| 8 Transfer £1 000 to general reserve | (a) £1 000 off profit – appropriation account<br>(b) Increase general reserve – BS |
| 9 Transfer £2 000 to tax reserve | (a) £2 000 off profit – appropriation account<br>(b) Increase Tax Reserve – BS |
| 10 £500 is to be written off goodwill | (a) £500 off profit – appropriation account<br>(b) Reduce goodwill (FA) – BS |
| 11 Proposed dividends ordinary £1 500 | (a) £1 500 off profit – appropriation account<br>(b) Creditors (within 12 months) i.e. 7% of £50 000 = £3 500 |
| 12 Proposed dividends – preference dividends are to be fully paid | (a) £3 500 off profit – appropriation account<br>(b) Creditors (within 12 months) – BS |
| 13 Corporation tax for the year = £24 000 | (a) Deduct £24 000 from profit before tax<br>(b) Include taxation as a current liability in the Balance Sheet |

## ■ SUMMARY

1 A limited company is registered in accordance with the Companies Acts and as a result is bound by these Acts. It is a separate legal entity from its members, with each member's liability being limited to the amount of shares he owns.

2 Trading Profit and Loss Account is exactly the same as that for a partnership and sole trader except that it may include new expenses such as directors' remuneration, auditors' remuneration and debenture interest.

3 Taxation. Limited companies are subject to corporation tax which may therefore appear as a deduction from net profit.

4 Appropriation Account. This outlines the distributions of profit which may be in the form of:

(a) transfers;
(b) write-offs;
(c) dividends.

5 Balance Sheet. Is basically the same as for sole traders except for the inclusion of new items and changes of heading.

6 Intangible Assets are items which cannot physically be seen, yet are considered of value to the company, e.g. goodwill, patents.

7 Proposed dividends are dividends you propose to pay in the future. As such they are still outstanding and appear as a creditor, due within 12 months.

8 Debentures are loans received by the Company, often for long periods.

9 Authorised Share Capital. This is the amount of shares the company is allowed to issue.

10 Issued Share Capital. This is the amount of shares the company have actually issued.

11 Ordinary Shares allow the shareholders a share of the profits after all other classes of shareholders.

12 Preference Shares allow shareholders a specified percentage rate of dividend.

13 Cumulative Preference Shares. Where the entitlement to a specified percentage rate is carried forward to future years if there are insufficient profits to pay the dividend in any particular year.

14 Reserves represent retained profits whether held as profits or transferred to a specific reserve.

15 Revenue Reserves are retained profits which can be distributed to shareholders as dividends.

16 Capital Reserves are non-distributable and are built up from transfers from retained profits. Reserves are *not* cash held in a drawer.

17 Share Premium Account. Where shares are issued at more than their nominal value the amount in excess of the nominal value is credited to a share premium account.

18 Liabilities (Capital, Reserves, Creditors) are sources of finances which the company has issued to purchase the assets.

## ■ SELF-ASSESSMENT QUESTIONS

1 What are the major differences between partnerships and limited companies?

2 Three of your bank's existing customers, all of good standing, have decided to set up in business together to develop and market a new product which one of them has invented. They are uncertain whether they should be organised as a partnership or a limited company.

*Required:*

Set out and explain for these three customers, from the *accounting* point of view, the different effects of organising as a partnership compared with organising as a limited company.

(CIB October 1990)

3 Write brief explanatory notes on the following:

(a) Goodwill
(b) Reserves
(c) Authorised share capital
(d) Dividends
(e) Corporation tax

4 Wendy runs a business as a home decorator and has just completed her third year, making a good profit. She writes to you as follows: 'In *Sound Business Management* magazine this month, I have read the enclosed article entitled "A Limited Company Is the Best Insurance Policy You Can Buy". This has made me wonder whether I should change my status from a sole trader to a limited company, but there are a few points I would like you to help me on before I make up my mind:

(a) Would I have to turn all my capital (£19 487 per last balance sheet) into share capital, or can some be left on a loan account so that I could draw it out later? (4)

(b) Does the title of the article mean that if I have a limited company I do not need to insure both with ordinary business insurance policies? (4)

(c) The balance sheet example shown in the article has 'Reserves' on it. Where would I get these? (4)

(d) What do you think I would find to be the two main advantages of being incorporated? And the two main disadvantages?' (4)

*Required:*

Write a letter to Wendy explaining the matters she has raised.

(CIB May 1988)

5 Starting with net profits before taxation, calculate the retained profit for the year ending 31.4.X9 and a Balance Sheet at that date for Sportsman Ltd.

| | £ |
|---|---|
| Net profit before taxation | 521 886 |
| General reserve | 10 000 |
| £1 Ordinary shares | 100 000 |
| 10% Preference shares | 200 000 |
| 12% Debenture 1999–2005 | 20 000 |
| Goodwill | 50 000 |
| Stock | 146 000 |
| Debtors | 120 000 |
| Creditors | 37 195 |
| Land and buildings (cost) | 460 000 |
| Equipment (cost) | 50 000 |
| Fixtures (cost) | 10 000 |
| Motor vehicles (cost) | 30 000 |
| Provision for depreciation: | |
| Fixtures | 1 000 |
| Motor vehicle | 3 000 |
| Bank (debit) | 30 000 |
| Provision for bad debts | 3 000 |
| Cash | 4 081 |

*Notes:*

1 Transfer £20 000 to general reserve

2 Authorised share capital:
   £1 ordinary shares £100 000
   10% Preference shares £200 000

3 Proposed dividends:
   Ordinary shares £100 000
   Preference shares – to be paid in full

4 Taxation for the year £150 000

5 Depreciation:
   Motor vehicles £2 000
   Fixtures £1 000

6 Increase provision for bad debts by £1 000

**6** Construct a Trading Profit and Loss Account of the year ending 31.8.Y0 and a Balance Sheet as at that date for Milestone PLC.

| | £ | £ |
|---|---|---|
| Purchases and sales | 79 104 | 196 666 |
| Stock at 1.9.X9 | 27 776 | |
| Carriage inwards | 205 | |
| Returns | 170 | 260 |
| Discounts | 3 000 | 5 100 |
| Wages | 11 790 | |
| Electricity | 2 407 | |
| Rates and rent | 5 000 | |
| Gas | 3 105 | |
| Office expenses | 2 198 | |
| Bad debts | 700 | |
| Provision for bad debts | | 3 000 |
| Retained profits | | 20 000 |
| Premises (cost) | 499 000 | |
| Equipment (cost) | 25 000 | |
| Provision for depreciation of equipment | | 5 000 |
| Motor vehicles (cost) | 10 000 | |
| Provision for depreciation: Motor vehicle | | 1 500 |
| Debtors and creditors | 36 166 | 41 095 |
| Bank | | 2 000 |
| General reserve | | 30 000 |
| Dividends paid: ordinary | 2 000 | |
| Auditors' remuneration | 2 000 | |
| Debenture interest paid | 3 000 | |
| 8% Debenture | | 40 000 |
| Goodwill | 12 000 | |
| £1 Ordinary shares | | 230 000 |
| 7% Preference shares | | 150 000 |
| | 724 621 | 724 621 |

*Notes:*

1. Stock as at 31.8.Y0 £30 000
2. Accrued wages £4 000
3. Prepayment:
   Electricity £500
   Office expenses £376
4. Reduce provision for bad debts to £2 500
5. Depreciate:
   Motor Vehicle 15% on a reducing balance basis
   Equipment 10% on cost
6. Debenture interest has not been fully paid for the year
7. Transfer £5 000 to general reserve
8. £2 000 is to be written off goodwill
9. Proposed dividends:
   Preference shares are to be paid in full
   Ordinary shares £7 500

10 Taxation 50%
11 Authorised share capital:
Ordinary shares £250 000
7% Preference shares £150 000

7 Nospe Ltd was established on 1 January 1990 to import computers and sell them to business customers. Its trial balance at the end of its first year of trading on 31 December 1990 was:

| | £000 | £000 |
|---|---|---|
| Ordinary shares of £1 each | | 150 |
| Loan at 12% annual interest repayable 1997 | | 100 |
| Sales | | 640 |
| Purchases | 410 | |
| Leasehold premises | 220 | |
| Fixtures and fittings | 50 | |
| Advertising | 32 | |
| Wages and salaries | 86 | |
| Rates on premises | 14 | |
| Light and heat | 8 | |
| Insurance for 1990 | 5 | |
| Delivery costs (outwards) | 21 | |
| Cash at bank and in hand | 15 | |
| General expenses | 27 | |
| Debtors and creditors | 34 | 32 |
| | 922 | 922 |

You are given the following additional information:

1 Trading stock at 31 December 1990 was valued at £42 000.
2 The long-term loan was taken out on 1 April 1990; the interest on it is payable each year on the anniversary of this date.
3 The lease of the premises had 20 years to run from 1 January 1990, the date when it was acquired. It will have a zero value at the end of this time, and its cost is to be written off on the straight line basis.
4 The fixtures and fittings are to be written off using the reducing balance method of depreciation. The annual rate of 30% will reduce them to approximately their expected residual value of £12 000 after four years.
5 The rates account contains the following entries:

| | £000 |
|---|---|
| 3 months to 31 March 1990 | 2 |
| 6 months to 30 September 1990 | 6 |
| 6 months to 31 March 1991 | 6 |
| As shown in the trial balance | 14 |

6 An invoice for £4 000 in respect of light and heat for the last three months of 1990 was received in January 1991; this is not included in the trial balance.
7 Nospe Ltd gives a one year guarantee with all the computers it sells. It is estimated that £7 000 will be spent in 1991 to carry out work under

guarantee on computers sold in 1990 and that provision should be made for this amount.

8 The directors consider that a dividend of 10 pence per share should be paid, and that provision for this should be made.

9 A provision for Corporation Tax at the rate of 25% of the trading profits is to be made.

*Required:*

Prepare the Trading and Profit and Loss Account and appropriation account of Nospe Ltd for the year 31 December 1990 and the Balance Sheet as at that date.

*Note:* Your answer should be presented in good form, but does not have to be in a form suitable for publication.

(CIB October 1991)

8 The following is the draft balance sheet of Driver Ltd as at 31 July 1990:

| | £000 | £000 | £000 |
|---|---|---|---|
| *Fixed assets:* | | | |
| Freehold premises at cost | | | 100 |
| Plant and machinery at cost | | 300 | |
| less: Accumulated depreciation | | 100 | |
| | | | 200 |
| | | | 300 |
| *Current assets:* | | | |
| Stocks | | 210 | |
| Goods out on sale or return | | 45 | |
| Debtors | | 250 | |
| | | 505 | |
| *Current liabilities:* | | | |
| Creditors | 142 | | |
| Overdraft | 110 | | |
| | | 252 | 253 |
| | | | 553 |
| Liabilities falling due in more than one year: | | | |
| less: Debentures | | | 50 |
| | | | 503 |
| Financed by: | | | |
| Ordinary shares of £1 each | | | 100 |
| Profit and Loss Account: | | | |
| Balance at 1 August 1989 | | 228 | |
| Trading profit for year to 31 July 1990 | | 125 | |
| | | | 353 |
| Capital reserve | | 50 | 503 |

It was discovered that the following matters had not been taken into account when preparing the balance sheet:

1 Additional plant and machinery was purchased on 1 August 1989, at a cost of £100 000. It was depreciated on the straight line basis assuming a life

of 6 years and a residual value of £10 000. The directors decide that, for this new plant, the reducing balance method of calculating depreciation, using an annual rate of 30% would be more appropriate and should be used for preparing the accounts.

2 The stock comprises two products, X and Y, valued as follows:

| | X | Y | Total |
|---|---|---|---|
| | £000 | £000 | £000 |
| Cost | 95 | 115 | 210 |
| Net realisable value | 75 | 180 | 255 |

*Let me help you with this note as it is something we have not yet covered. You will see that stock should be valued at the lower of cost and net realisable value*

| | | |
|---|---|---|
| X | = | 75 |
| Y | = | 115 |
| Total | | 190 |

3 The goods out on sale or return are valued at selling price; they cost £30 000.

4 The company made a bonus (capitalisation) issue of two new shares for each share already held on 31 July 1990.

*Once again this is something we have not yet covered. Basically a bonus issue is a free issue of shares to existing shareholders based on their existing holding. This issue will clearly increase shares from 100 to 300 (100+200). What else must you do in order to deal with this item and ensure the balance sheet balances?*

5 The freehold premises were professionally valued at 31 July 1990 and found to be worth £250 000. The directors consider that this value should be shown in the balance sheet. Depreciation is not charged on freehold premises.

6 On 31 July 1990 the company raised a loan through the issue of a debenture for £150 000. The cheque was paid into the bank account on the same day, but not entered in the cash book or shown on the bank statement until 1 August 1990.

7 No accrual had been made for the audit fee of £7 000.

8 A dividend of 5 pence per share is to be provided for on the entire share capital, including the bonus issue.

*Required:*

(a) Show your calculation of the company's trading profit for the year to 31 July 1990, taking into account any adjustments you consider necessary as a result of the information given in notes 1–8 above.

(b) Prepare theBalance Sheet of Driver Ltd at 31 July 1990 after making adjustments for all of the matters detailed in notes 1–8 above.
(CIB October 1990)

# 12 Manufacturing accounts

**OBJECTIVES**

**After studying this chapter you will be able to:**

**1 See the need for manufacturing accounts;**
**2 Calculate the *prime* cost of manufacture;**
**3 Calculate the total cost of manufacture;**
**4 Produce Trading Profit and Loss Accounts and Balance Sheets for manufacturing businesses.**

## ■ INTRODUCTION

So far we have looked at businesses which have simply bought and sold goods; as a result, their trading accounts have appeared as follows:

*Trading Account of Example Limited for the year ending 31.12.Y0*

| | £ | £ |
|---|---|---|
| Sales | | 100 000 |
| *less Cost of goods sold* | | |
| Opening stock | 30 000 | |
| and purchases | 80 000 | |
| | 110 000 | |
| – Closing stock | 20 000 | 90 000 |
| Gross profit | | 10 000 |

But suppose a company manufactured the goods they sold rather than purchased them. They would therefore need to calculate the cost of manufacture which would then replace the purchases figure in the Trading Account.

We therefore need to produce a Manufacturing Account before we can move on to the Trading Profit and Loss Account and Balance Sheet.

## ■ CALCULATING THE COST OF MANUFACTURE

A Manufacturing Account includes all costs related to the manufacture of goods and *only* these items.

The major costs, or *prime costs*, of manufacturing any items are materials and labour, but only the labour costs of those actually producing the goods, which would not, therefore, include the salesman's salary for example.

So we start the Manufacturing Account as follows:

*Manufacturing Account of Wonder Toys Limited for the year ending 31.12.Y0*

| | £ | £ |
|---|---|---|
| Opening stock of raw materials | | 30 000 |
| *add* Purchases of raw materials | 125 000 | |
| *add* Carriage in of raw materials | 5 000 | |
| | 130 000 | |
| *less* Returns out of raw materials | 2 000 | 128 000 |
| | | 158 000 |
| – Closing stock of raw materials | | 20 000 |
| 1 Direct material | | 138 000 |
| 2 Direct labour | | 30 000 |
| 3 Direct expenses | | |
| Prime cost of manufacture | | 168 000 |

*Notes:*

1 *Direct material* – must be calculated, but as you can see, this is exactly the same as we have seen before but using those items concerning direct material.

2 *Direct labour* – this is normally given in the trial balance, but remember, it refers to the labour costs of those actually manufacturing the goods and therefore may be referred to as manufacturers' wages, etc.

3 *Direct expenses* – this does *not* mean expenses such as light and heat etc., and I cannot stress that enough. It refers to expenses specifically relating to the product, such as royalties or patents.

So we have now got the prime cost of manufacture, but this is not the total cost. We must now add to this all the overhead costs such as light and heat, rent, rates etc., *but only the proportion of these costs which relate to the manufacture of the goods.*

**Example**

The rent for Wonder Toys' premises is £3 000 per annum. As the factory space (i.e. the area of manufacture) is twice as big as the office space they are able to say that £2 000 of the rent is a manufacturing overhead and £1 000 administrative expense.

**Examination**

You will either be given a list of items and asked to decide whether they are manufacturing overheads or not (as in Progress test 1a), or asked to apportion the cost in a particular manner as we did above.

**PROGRESS TEST 1**

(a) Which of the following are manufacturing overheads?
    Insurance of the factory
    Office expenses
    Depreciation of machinery
    Depreciation of motor vehicles
    Warehouse maintenance
    Factory rates
    Factory supervisors' wages

(b) Glassware Limited have premises made up of a factory of 50 000 square feet and offices of 20 000 square feet. They have decided to apportion the following expenses in relation to area.

Calculate the amount charged to the manufacturing account in each case.

| | £ |
|---|---|
| (i) Heat and light | 4 000 |
| (ii) Rent | 30 000 |
| (iii) Depreciation of premises | 8 000 |
| (iv) Insurance | 10 000 |

Check your answers before continuing

In the progress test above you should have discovered that any costs relating to the manufacture of goods, which includes supervisors' wages and depreciation of the machinery, are manufacturing overheads, because if the company didn't manufacture the goods, they wouldn't incur those costs.

The Manufacturing Account, therefore, appears as follows:

*Manufacturing Account of Wonder Toys Limited for the year ending 31.12.Y0*

| | £ | £ |
|---|---|---|
| Opening stock of raw materials | | 30 000 |
| and Purchases of raw materials | 125 000 | |
| + Carriage in of raw materials | 5 000 | |
| | 130 000 | |
| *less* Returns out of raw materials | 2 000 | 128 000 |
| | | 158 000 |
| *less* Closing stock of raw materials | | 20 000 |
| Direct material | | 138 000 |
| Direct labour | | 30 000 |
| Direct expenses | | — |
| Prime cost of manufacture | | 168 000 |
| *add factory overheads* (1) | | |
| Factory heat and light | 4 000 | |
| Factory rent | 5 000 | |
| Factory supervisors' wages | 15 000 | |
| Factory insurance | 7 000 | |
| Depreciation of machinery | 10 000 | 41 000 |
| | | 209 000 |
| *add* Opening stock of work in progress (2) | | 15 000 |
| | | 224 000 |
| *less* Closing stock of work in progress (2) | | 14 000 |
| Cost of manufacture | | 210 000 |

*Notes*

1 We are trying to calculate the total cost of manufacture, therefore *add* factory overheads to the prime cost of manufacture. Many students are so used to deducting expenses from gross profit that they deduct factory overheads. Do not make that mistake.

2 Having added the factory overheads we must then:
(a) add the opening stock of work in progress (i.e. half-finished toys); and

(b) deduct the closing stock of work in progress, for as you will see, the stock of these partly finished items is an asset belonging to the company and therefore not a cost.

**PROGRESS TEST 2**

Produce a Manufacturing Account for Clothing Manufacturers Limited for the year ending 31.12.Y0 from the following information. Be careful – not every item is needed in your solution.

| | £ |
|---|---|
| Stocks as at 1.1.Y0): | |
| Raw material | 30 000 |
| Work in progress | 41 000 |
| Stocks as at 31.12.Y0: | |
| Raw material | 26 000 |
| Work in progress | 31 500 |
| Wages: | |
| Manufacturing staff | 50 000 |
| Factory supervisors | 10 000 |
| Salesmen | 20 000 |
| Warehouse staff | 15 000 |
| Depreciation: | |
| Offices | 10 000 |
| Factory machinery | 12 000 |
| Rent | 12 500 |
| Insurance | 10 000 |
| Light and heat | 1 000 |
| Administrative expenses | 5 000 |
| Purchases of raw materials | 80 000 |
| Carriage in of raw materials | 2 000 |

The rent, insurance and light and heat are apportioned between the offices and the factory on a ratio of 1:1.

## ■ PRODUCING A TRADING PROFIT AND LOSS ACCOUNT FOR MANUFACTURING BUSINESSES

The format is exactly the same as we have seen for other limited companies except that:

1 the cost of manufacture now replaces cost of purchases;
2 the Trading Account, in which we calculate the gross profit on sales, includes the opening and closing stocks of *finished goods* as it is these items which have been traded and on which the gross profit is calculated;
3 the expenses are those expenses which relate to areas other than the manufacture of the goods, e.g.

- administration
- selling and distribution
- financial.

As you can see below, the Profit and Loss Account may show a sub-total for each of these categories rather than simply listing all the expenses.

*Trading Profit and Loss Account for Wonder Toys Limited for the year ending 31.12.Y0*

| | £ | £ | £ |
|---|---|---|---|
| Sales | | | 500 000 |
| *less cost of goods sold* | | | |
| Opening stock of *finished goods* (2) | | 50 000 | |
| and Cost of manufacture (1) | | 210 000 | |
| | | 260 000 | |
| – Closing stock of *finished goods* (2) | | 40 000 | 220 000 |
| Gross profit | | | 280 000 |
| *less Expenses* (3) | | | |
| *Administration* | | | |
| Office salaries | 60 000 | | |
| Office heat and light | 4 000 | | |
| Office expenses | 5 000 | | |
| Office rent | 5 000 | | |
| Office insurance | 7 000 | | |
| Depreciation of office equipment | 5 000 | 86 000 | |
| *Selling and distribution* | | | |
| Warehouse wages | 20 000 | | |
| Warehouse expenses | 4 000 | | |
| Selling expenses | 5 000 | | |
| Salesmen's salaries | 30 000 | 59 000 | |
| *Financial* | | | |
| Depreciation of premises | 2 000 | | |
| Discounts allowed | 3 000 | 5 000 | 150 000 |
| Net profit for the year before tax | | | 130 000 |
| *less* Taxation | | | 40 000 |
| Net profit for the year after tax | | | 90 000 |
| *less Appropriation* | | | |
| Transfer to reserves | | | 5 000 |
| | | | 85 000 |
| Proposed dividends – ordinary shares | | | 5 000 |
| Retained profits | | | 80 000 |

## ■ PRODUCING A BALANCE SHEET FOR MANUFACTURING BUSINESSES

Before looking at a question in which you are asked to produce a Trading Profit and Loss Account, can you think of the *one* thing that will be different in the Balance Sheet of a manufacturing business when compared with other limited companies?

The answer is the *stock*. While some limited companies simply have a closing stock of goods (which they have purchased), a manufacturing business has:

- closing stock of raw material;

- closing stock of work in progress;
- closing stock of finished goods;

all of which are current assets as they represent items owned by the company.

**PROGRESS TEST 3**

Produce a Manufacturing Trading Profit and Loss Account for the year ending 31.12.Y0 and a Balance Sheet as at that date for Doric Beds Limited from the following information.

*Trial Balance of Doric Beds Limited as at 31.12.Y0*

| | £ | £ |
|---|---|---|
| Stock as at 1.1.Y0: | | |
| Raw materials | 7 105 | |
| Work in progress | 7 721 | |
| Finished goods | 12 774 | |
| Purchases of raw materials | 21 908 | |
| Carriage in of raw materials | 700 | |
| Heat and light | 3 000 | |
| Rent | 7 500 | |
| Office expenses | 2 000 | |
| Factory expenses | 2 176 | |
| Bank charges | 485 | |
| Direct expenses (Patent) | 1 000 | |
| Warehouse expenses | 4 424 | |
| Discounts | 1 106 | 1 000 |
| Provision for bad debts | | 7 000 |
| Wages and salaries: | | |
| Manufacturing staff | 27 000 | |
| Administration staff | 37 000 | |
| Salesmen | 42 000 | |
| Foreman (factory) | 10 000 | |
| Salesmen's commission | 8 000 | |
| Land and building (cost) | 500 000 | |
| Equipment (cost) | 125 000 | |
| Provision for depreciation – equipment | | 35 000 |
| Motor vehicles (cost) | 20 000 | |
| Provision for depreciation – motor vehicles | | 11 000 |
| Fixtures and fittings | 12 000 | |
| Debtors | 80 000 | |
| Creditors | | 47 105 |
| Bank | 3 717 | |
| Cash | 162 | |
| 10% Debentures | | 96 500 |
| General reserve | | 3 000 |
| £1 Ordinary shares fully paid | | 300 000 |
| 9% Preference shares | | 60 000 |
| Sales | | 376 173 |
| | 936 778 | 936 778 |

*Notes:*

1 Closing stock:
Raw materials 17 177
Work in progress 6 433
Finished goods 10 616
2 Authorised share capital
£1 Ordinary shares £300 000
9% Preference shares £60 000
3 Office expenses owing £500
4 Depreciation:
Equipment £5 000
Motor vehicles £1 000
5 Increase provision for bad debts by £1 000
6 Proposed dividend:
Ordinary £10 000
Preference £2 000
7 Transfer £7 000 to general reserves
8 Apportion light and heat, and rent between the factory and offices on the ratio of 2:1 respectively
9 Taxation £60 000

## ■ SUMMARY

1 Where businesses manufacture goods they will need to produce a Manufacturing Account in order to calculate the cost of manufacture.

2 Prime cost of manufacture examines the major costs of manufacture which are:

- direct material;
- direct labour;
- direct expenses.

3 Direct labour refers to the wages of those actually manufacturing the goods.

4 Direct expenses are such things as patents or royalties relating to the particular goods.

5 Factory overheads are *added* to the prime cost of manufacture.

6 The cost of manufacture is transferred into the Trading Profit and Loss Account in order to calculate the cost of goods sold.

7 Work in progress – this refers to partly completed items.

8 The Trading Profit and Loss Account is exactly the same as for any other limited company except:

(a) cost of manufacture replaces purchases;
(b) the Trading Account features opening and closing stock of *finished* goods;
(c) expenses are often those which relate to areas other than the manufacture of goods, e.g. administration, selling, financial.

9 The only difference in the Balance Sheet of a manufacturing business is that it may include more than one closing stock, i.e.

- raw materials;
- work in progress;
- finished goods.

## SELF-ASSESSMENT QUESTIONS

1 Calculate the prime cost of manufacture for Wrenbury Gifts Limited for the year ending 31.12.Y0:

| | £ |
|---|---|
| Opening stock of: | |
| Raw material | 56 000 |
| Work in progress | 21 000 |
| Finished goods | 32 000 |
| Purchases of raw material | 117 119 |
| Direct expenses | 5 000 |
| Wages of foreman | 15 000 |
| Manufacturers' wages | 37 212 |
| Closing stock of: | |
| Work in progress | 19 818 |
| Raw materials | 41 000 |

2 Produce a Manufacturing Account for Alvanley Cabinet Makers Limited for the year ending 31.12.Y0 from the following information:

| | £ |
|---|---|
| Stocks as at 1.1.Y0: | |
| Raw material | 41 888 |
| Work in progress | 9 620 |
| Finished goods | 27 616 |
| Stocks as at 31.12.Y0: | |
| Raw material | 30 106 |
| Work in progress | 11 177 |
| Finished goods | 21 560 |
| Purchases of raw material | 46 166 |
| Returns out of raw material | 5 000 |
| Rent | 12 500 |
| Insurance | 8 444 |
| Light and heat | 7 000 |
| Office expenses | 5 000 |
| Warehouse expenses | 1 256 |
| Salesman's commission | 4 100 |
| Wages and salaries: | |
| Manufacturing | 32 166 |
| Salesman | 25 000 |
| Warehouse | 16 166 |
| Office staff | 41 818 |
| Foreman | 15 000 |

*Note:*
Rent, insurance and light and heat are apportioned between the factory and the offices on a ratio of 3:1 respectively.

3 Produce a Trading Profit and Loss Account for the year ending 31.12.Y0 and a Balance Sheet at that date for Siddington Limited.

*Trial Balance of Siddington Limited as at 31.12.Y0*

| | £ | £ |
|---|---|---|
| Sales | | 312 105 |
| Stock as at 1.1.Y0: | | |
| Raw material | 26 109 | |
| Work in progress | 11 717 | |
| Finished goods | 26 106 | |
| Purchases of raw materials | 86 111 | |
| Direct labour | 52 000 | |
| Land and buildings (cost) | 200 000 | |
| Machinery (cost) | 86 000 | |
| Provision for depreciation – machinery | | 16 340 |
| Motor vehicles (cost) | 31 000 | |
| Provision for depreciation – motor vehicles | | 6 000 |
| Fixtures and fittings (cost) | 26 000 | |
| Provision for depreciation fixtures and fittings | | 11 000 |
| Rent | 11 000 | |
| Electricity | 15 000 | |
| Motor expenses | 2 000 | |
| Gas | 3 000 | |
| Telephone expenses | 1 560 | |
| Bad debts | 2 000 | |
| Office salaries | 76 000 | |
| Office expenses | 4 176 | |
| Discounts allowed and received | 2 000 | 3 100 |
| Debtors and creditors | 57 100 | 36 161 |
| Bank | | 65 580 |
| Cash | 407 | |
| Dividends paid – ordinary shareholders | 1 000 | |
| General reserve | | 20 000 |
| Profit and loss account | | 100 000 |
| £1 Ordinary shares fully paid | | 150 000 |
| | 720 286 | 720 286 |

*Notes:*

1 Stock as at 31.1.Y0:

| | |
|---|---|
| Raw materials | £17 777 |
| Work in progress | £12 616 |
| Finished goods | £31 777 |

2 Authorised share capital ordinary shares £150 000:

3 Depreciation:
Machinery is depreciated on a reducing balance basis at 10 per cent per annum.
Motor vehicles are depreciated on a straight line basis, 10 per cent on cost.
Depreciate fixtures and fittings £2 000.
4 Rent, electricity and gas are apportioned between the factory and the office equally.
5 Telephone expenses: prepaid £150.
6 A bill of £300 is outstanding in respect of motor expenses.
7 Create a provision for bad debts of 10% of debtors.
8 A dividend of £10 000 has been proposed.
9 Taxation for the year equals £10 000.

4 The following is the trial balance of Reigate, a sole trader and manufacturer, at 31 December 1990:

| | £000 | £000 |
|---|---|---|
| Sales | | 500 |
| Capital at 31 December 1989 | | 110 |
| Purchases of raw materials | 126 | |
| Loan interest | 12 | |
| Manufacturing wages | 73 | |
| Manufacturing plant at cost | 164 | |
| Accumulated depreciation on manufacturing plant at 31 December 1989 | | 75 |
| Sales delivery vehicles at cost | 100 | |
| Accumulated depreciation on delivery vehicles at 31 December 1989 | | 25 |
| Rent | 24 | |
| Manufacturing expenses | 34 | |
| Administration salaries | 28 | |
| Stock of raw materials at 31 December 1989 | 13 | |
| Stock of finished goods at 31 December 1989 | 28 | |
| General administration expenses | 11 | |
| Rates | 15 | |
| Debtors | 56 | |
| Cash at bank | 24 | |
| Creditors | | 32 |
| Wages of sales delivery van drivers | 30 | |
| Drawings | 36 | |
| Long-term loan at 12% | | 100 |
| Light, heat and power | 28 | |
| Vehicle running expenses | 13 | |
| Advertising | 23 | |
| Bad debts | 4 | |
| | 842 | 842 |

The following information is relevant:

1 Stock at 31 December 1990 comprised:

| | £000 |
|---|---|
| Raw materials | 15 |
| Finished goods | 33 |

2 Depreciation on the manufacturing plant is calculated on the straight line basis, assuming a life of 10 years and a residual value of £14 000.
3 The delivery vehicles are depreciated on the straight line basis, assuming a life of 3 years and a residual value of £25 000.
4 The balance on the rent account is for the 9 months to 30 September 1990.
5 A payment of £6 000 was made in October 1990 for the rates to 31 March 1991.
6 Seventy-five per cent of the cost of rent, rates and heat, light and power relate to manufacturing activity; the balance is for administration.
7 The long-term loan is repayable in one amount in 1998.

*Required:*
(a) Prepare the manufacturing account of Reigate for the year to 31 December 1990 showing clearly the cost of goods manufactured.
(b) Prepare the Trading and Profit and Loss Account of Reigate for the year to 31 December 1990 and the Balance Sheet at that date.
(CIB May 1991)

# 13 Statements of Standard Accounting Practice (SSAPs) and Financial Reporting Standards (FRSs)

**OBJECTIVES**

**After studying this chapter you should be able to:**

**1 Outline what is meant by SSAPs and FRSs and Accounting Policies;**

**2 Outline the aims and objectives of SSAPs and FRSs and in particular SSAP 2 – Disclosure of Accounting Policies;**

**3 Explain and illustrate the effect of:**

- **SSAP 6 – Extraordinary items and prior year adjustments**
- **SSAP 9 – Stocks and work in progress**
- **SSAP 8 and 15 – Taxation**

**on the final accounts of limited companies;**

**4 Be aware of the problems caused by inflation and the limitations of preparing accounts on an 'historical cost' basis.**

## ■ INTRODUCTION – SYLLABUS AND EXAMINATION REQUIREMENTS

(A) *Syllabus*: You are required to have an understanding of the following matters:

1 The nature of SSAPs and accounting policies;
2 SSAP 2 – Disclosure of Accounting Policies (*see* Chapter 6);
3 SSAP 6 – Extraordinary Items and Prior Year Adjustments;
4 SSAP 9 – Stock and Work in Progress;
5 SSAP 12 – Accounting for Depreciation (*see* Chapter 7);
6 SSAPs 8 and 15 – relating to taxation.
7 FRS 1 – Cash flow Statements, which is the subject of Chapter 16.

(B) *Examination questions* will be concerned with the following:

1 an understanding of SSAPs, FRSs and accounting policies;
2 discussion of their importance;
3 an ability to illustrate the impact of the above standards and policies on final accounts, in particular the reported profit.

## ■ WHAT ARE STATEMENTS OF STANDARD ACCOUNTING PRACTICE (SSAPs) AND FINANCIAL REPORTING STANDARDS (FRSs)?

SSAPs and FRSs outline the recommended accounting practice to be followed when producing the final accounts of a business. The objectives of these rules or standards are to:

1 recommend disclosure of accounting bases;
2 narrow the areas of difference and variety in accounts;
3 require disclosure of departure from standards;
4 introduce a system of wide standard setting;
5 seek improvements in existing disclosure requirements of Company Law and Stock Exchange regulations.

SSAPs *were* issued by the Accounting Standards Committee (ASC) whilst FRSs are *now* issued by the Accounting Standards Board (ASB) which replaced the ASC in August 1990, in order to restore credibility to the standard setting process following earlier problems.

So far we have one FRS: FRS 1 *Cash Flow Statements* which replaced SSAP 10 and is the subject of Chapter 16.

While we will now see future FRSs and not SSAPs, companies must still adhere to the existing SSAPs until replaced or amended, together with the new FRSs.

## ■ WHY DO WE NEED SSAPs AND FRSs?

Without them companies would be free to draw up their final accounts in any manner they desired.

### Example

The two companies below are both clothes retailers. Their accounts are identical, except that they have adopted different accounting policies relating to depreciation and the provision for bad debts.

Let us look at how this will affect their accounts.

| *Accounting Policies* | | *Company A* | | *Company B* |
|---|---|---|---|---|
| Depreciation policy | | Straight line | | No charge |
| Provision for bad debt policy | | 5% of Debtors | | No charge |
| Profit and Loss Account | | | | |
| | £ | £ | £ | £ |
| Gross profit on trading | | 20 000 | | 20 000 |
| *less Expenses* | | | | |
| Provision for depreciation | 2 000 | | Nil | |
| Provision for bad debts | 500 | | Nil | |
| Trading expenses | 10 000 | 12 500 | 10 000 | 10 000 |
| Net profit on trading | | 7 500 | | 10 000 |

Both companies have achieved the same gross profit and incurred the same trading expenses, but Company B appears more profitable, *not* because they trade more effectively, but simply because they have adopted different accounting policies.

Comparison and evaluation of a company's performance is therefore difficult if companies are free to adopt any policy they desire. *SSAPs were therefore developed with their primary aim being to narrow and regularise the range of permissible accounting treatments applicable to transactions or situations* following the outcry against the lack of uniformity in the late 1960s.

## ■ HOW DO SSAPs AND FRSs SOLVE THE PROBLEM?

The standards could simply state that all companies must adopt exactly the same policies, e.g.

- account for depreciation using straight line;
- provide for bad debts at a rate of 5 per cent of debtors.

The Accounting Standards Board (ASB) responsible for drafting the new Financial Report Standards (FRSs) and their predecessors the Accounting Standards Committee who were responsible for drafting Statements of Standard Accounting Practice (SSAPs) recognise that not all companies or industries are the same and therefore not all companies can adopt exactly the same policies, e.g.

- It may be more realistic for one company to adopt the reducing balance method of calculating depreciation due to the nature of their assets.
- Bad debts may be higher in one industry than another and hence their provision for bad debts should be higher.

Therefore:

- SSAPs outline the recommended practice to be followed in the case of certain transactions or situations, while allowing companies a degree of flexibility to interpret the standards in a way most suitable for their company and industry;
- this still allows two companies to report different profit figures, simply because of the way they have interpreted the accounting policies.

However, SSAP 2 – Disclosure of Accounting Policies imposes an obligation to disclose;

(a) any departure from the four fundamental concepts, namely:

- the *going concern* concept;
- the *consistency* concept;
- the *accruals* or matching concept;
- the *prudence* concept; and

(b) the accounting policies followed for items judged material or critical.

These concepts have been fully considered in Chapter 6.

Companies are also free to follow a different policy / practice from that recommended by the relevant standard, *but* they must *state why they have not adopted the recommended policy*.

## ■ WHAT AUTHORITY DO SSAPs AND FRSs HAVE?

Many of the standards, for example SSAPs 2, 6, 9 and 12, are incorporated into the Companies Act 1985 and therefore carry legal backing.

Generally speaking, however, the standards' power comes from the requirements imposed by the accounting bodies on their members. Any departure from the standards should be reported by a qualified auditor, who, you will recall, is responsible for checking that company accounts represent a 'true and fair' view of their financial position.

Let us examine each SSAP in turn and consider its effects on a company's final accounts (remember FRS 1: Cash Flow Statements will be dealt with in Chapter 16).

**SSAP 6 – Extraordinary Items and Prior Year Adjustments**

***Extraordinary items***

Here are two furniture companies:

| | *Better Homes PLC* | *The Furniture Factory PLC* |
|---|---|---|
| | £ | £ |
| Net profit | 100 000 | 150 000 |

From this you might easily conclude that The Furniture Factory trades more efficiently than Better Homes PLC, but how were those profits achieved?

Closer examination may reveal:

| | *Better Homes PLC* | *The Furniture Factory PLC* |
|---|---|---|
| | £ | £ |
| Profit from trading | 100 000 | 50 000 |
| Profit from sale of properties | — | 100 000 |
| Total profit | 100 000 | 150 000 |

While The Furniture Factory has a higher total profit figure, we can see most of this comes from the sale of one of their properties and *not* from the buying and selling of furniture.

Therefore SSAP 6 requires companies to disclose:

1 *Profit/loss from ordinary activities*: those usually, frequently and regularly undertaken and any related activities incidental or arising therefrom.
2 *Profit/loss from extraordinary items*: derived from events outside ordinary activities, e.g. sale of property – as the ordinary activity of this business is the buying and selling of furniture.

***Presentation***

*Profit and Loss Account Extract of The Furniture Factory PLC for the year ending 31.12.X8*

| | £ |
|---|---|
| Gross profit | 100 000 |
| *less* Expenses | 10 000 |
| Net profit on *ordinary activities* before taxation | 90 000 |
| *less* Taxation | 40 000 |
| Net profit on *ordinary activities* after taxation | 50 000 |
| *Extraordinary profit* | 100 000 |
| Net profit for the year | 150 000 |
| *less* Dividends | 20 000 |
| Retained profit | 130 000 |

Anyone examining the company's accounts will therefore be able to see how the profit for the year of £150 000 has been achieved.

The published accounts of the company would also indicate that the extraordinary profit was derived from the sale of property.

### *Exceptional or abnormal items*

Exceptional items are those items which are derived from the ordinary activities of the business but are exceptional by virtue of their size or incidence, e.g.

- redundancy costs
- exceptionally high bad debts.

The standard recommends that such items should be reflected in the calculation of profit or loss on ordinary activities, as it is derived from the ordinary activities of the business, but should be disclosed separately to give a true and fair view of the company's financial affairs.

| *Profit and Loss Account Extract* | £ |
|---|---|
| Profit before exceptional items | 150 000 |
| *Exceptional items (redundancy costs) | 20 000 |
| Profit on ordinary activities before taxation | 130 000 |
| Taxation | 40 000 |
| Profit on ordinary activities after taxation | 90 000 |
| *Extraordinary items (profit on sale of property) | 30 000 |
| Profit for the financial year | 120 000 |
| Dividends | 20 000 |
| Retained profit for the year | 100 000 |

### *Prior year adjustments*

SSAP 6 is also concerned with prior year adjustments, which, as the name suggests, are adjustments to the previous year's Profit and Loss Account and the retained profits brought forward.

The reason for making such adjustments are:

(a) following a change in accounting policy, or
(b) to correct fundamental errors which have a material effect on the profit for the current year.

When we looked at prepayments and accruals you will remember that sometimes estimates of the expenditure incurred have to be used in the accounting period where the actual bill is not due for some time. While such estimates may prove to be inaccurate they are not considered to be 'prior year adjustments' unless considered material.

***Presentation***

| *Profit and Loss Account Extract* | £ | £ |
|---|---|---|
| Gross profit | | 200 000 |
| *less* Expenses | | 50 000 |
| Net profit before exceptional items | | 150 000 |
| * *less Exceptional items* | | 30 000 |
| Profit on ordinary activities before taxation | | 120 000 |
| Taxation | | 40 000 |
| Profit on ordinary activities after taxation | | 80 000 |
| * *plus Extraordinary items* | | 1 000 |
| Profit for the year before dividends | | 81 000 |
| *less* Dividends | | 20 000 |
| Profit for the year | | 61 000 |
| +Retained profit brought forward | 50 000 | |
| * *less prior year adjustment* | 10 000 | 40 000 |
| | | 101 000 |

As a result of the prior year adjustment the reserves will be different and therefore a statement must also be included showing the movements on reserves.

**PROGRESS TEST 1**

SSAP 6 'Extraordinary items and prior year adjustments' contained the following terms:

- exceptional items
- extraordinary items
- prior year adjustments

*Required:*

(a) Define *each* of these terms.

(b) Give *one* example of *each* of these terms.

(c) Explain how *each* term is to be disclosed in the published accounts of limited companies.

(d) Discuss why it is important to distinguish between these three types of entry.

(CIB October 1990)

## SSAP 9 – Stock and Work in Progress

***Stock***

SSAP 9 states that:

The 'normal basis for stock valuation is the lower of *cost* and *net realisable value*'

(A) *'Cost'* is defined by SSAP 9 as being 'expenditure which *has been* incurred in the normal course on business in bringing the product or service *to its present location and condition*'.

A manufacturer may therefore calculate his cost of stock in the following manner:

| | |
|---|---|
| Raw materials | £500 |
| Wages of manufacturing staff | £1 000 |
| | £1 500 |

i.e. he has added together those costs involved in the items manufactured, which is known as *marginal cost basis*.

Alternatively, the manufacturer may add to this an amount in respect of overheads incurred in manufacturing the items, e.g. factory light and heat, but not salesman's salary. This is known as *total cost basis*.

(B) *'Net realisable value'* means the estimated selling price less any *further costs to be* incurred, on completion of product, e.g. advertising, selling or delivery costs.

The difference in calculating the *cost* and the *net realisable value* can be represented as follows. As you will see it relies on your knowledge of their definitions.

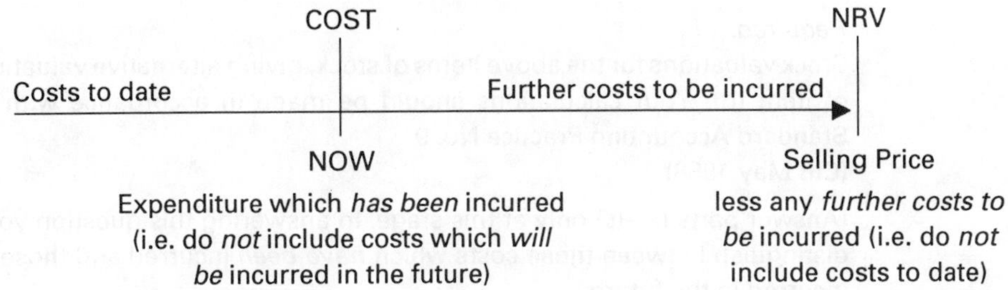


Having calculated both the 'Cost' and 'Net realisable value' the basis for valuing your stock is the lower of cost and net realisable value.

Therefore, where the stock of a clothes shop consisted of platform shoes and flares which cost £5 000 but could only realise £2 000, they should be valued at the lower figure of £2 000.

This is because the higher figure would overstate the asset figure and overstate the profit. We shall examine the effect on profit more clearly later, but for now, think about the relationship between closing stock and profit – how does a higher closing stock result in a higher profit figure?

**PROGRESS TEST 2**

The Great Clearance Stores plc, who specialise in the disposal of bankrupt and liquidation stocks, have the following items in their stock at 31 March 1988.

(a) *Second-hand timber sleepers from British Rail.* These cost £2 each, and are being sawn into gate posts of which four can be obtained from each sleeper. It is usually found that 10 per cent of the sleepers are too rotted to be used: these are readily identified by inspection prior to sawing, and are disposed of without cost by giving them to Boy Scouts for their camp fires. The sawing costs are £1.78 per sleeper and the finished gate posts can be sold for £1.85 each, which includes 50p for delivery costs incurred by Great Clearance Stores plc. At stock taking, there are 4 100 unexamined sleepers and 6 120 finished gate posts.

(b) *Army berets.* 3 185 surplus army berets were bought for £2 000. They have since been dyed at a cost of £680 and will have tassels sewn on to them at a later date, costing £1.20 per beret. It is expected that they will then be sold at £2.75 each, post paid, by mail order. The postage and packing is expected to cost 65p each and advertising costs of £550 will be incurred.

(c) *Plastic knives.* A batch of 10 000 plastic knives was bought for £100. The batch was made from a defective mould which failed to provide a cutting edge and the only way to make these knives usable will be to grind them to provide a cutting edge. This will cost 2p per knife but it is likely that 20 per cent of the knives will break in the grinding process. The sub-contractor who will undertake the grinding states that he will charge 2p each, irrespective of whether or not the knife breaks, as his time in handling them will be the same. It is expected that the sharpened knives will be sold at 5p each, without incurring any advertising or selling costs.

(d) *Ladders.* The company bought 600 ladders at £15 each and sold 325 of them at £29 each. The company then bought a further 400 identical ladders but had to pay £19 each for these. It therefore increased its selling price to £35 and sold a further 150 ladders.

Assume:

(i) The company uses First In First Out method for valuing these ladders.

(ii) The company uses Average Cost method.

*Required:*

Stock valuations for the above items of stock, giving alternative valuations in the case of item (d). Your calculations should be made in accordance with Statement of Standard Accounting Practice No. 9.

(CIB May 1988)

(Answer parts (a)–(c) only at this stage. In answering this question you will need to distinguish between those costs which *have been* incurred and those which *will be* incurred in the future.)

***Calculating the cost of closing stock***

A shopkeeper will need to add up the number of items left on the shelves and then multiply this by the cost price. This is known as stocktaking, and in many larger companies is done with the help of a computer.

It sounds very simple, but what is the valuation of the closing stock in this example?

*DIY Stores Ltd*

| | | | |
|---|---|---|---|
| January 1 | Purchased | 10 units at £15 each | = £150 |
| 10 | Purchased | 20 units at £18 each | = £360 |
| 12 | Sold | 22 units at £25 each | = £550 |
| 15 | Purchased | 10 units at £20 each | = £200 |
| 26 | Sold | 6 units at £25 each | = £150 |

*Step 1* – Calculate the closing stock

| | |
|---|---|
| Purchases | 40 units |
| less Sales | 28 units |
| Closing stock | 12 units |

*Step 2* – Calculate the value of the closing stock.

But which 12 units are left in stock? There are a number of methods which assist us in this matter, (a) FIFO, (b) LIFO, (c) AVCO.

(a) FIFO (First In First Out), i.e. we assume that the first items purchased are the first to be sold. We are therefore left with the latest purchases. As a result the 12 units left are:

| | |
|---|---|
| 10 purchased on 15 January at £20 each | = £200 |
| and | |
| 2 of those purchased on 10 January at £18 each | = £36 |
| | £236 |

(b) LIFO (Last In First Out), i.e. we assume that the last items purchased are the first sold. As a result the 12 units left in stock are:

| | | |
|---|---|---|
| 10 purchased on 1 January at £15 each | = | £150 |
| and | | |
| 2 of those purchased on 10 January at £18 each | = | £36 |
| | | £185 |

(c) AVCO (Average Cost) – as the name suggests we calculate the average price per unit purchased.

| | | | |
|---|---|---|---|
| January | 1 | 10 at £15 each = | £150 |
| | 10 | 20 at £18 each = | £360 |
| | 15 | 10 at £20 each = | £200 |
| | | 40 | £710 |

$\frac{£710}{40}$ = £17.75 average price per unit

Average price per unit × number in stock
£17.75 × 12 = £213

**PROGRESS TEST 3**

DIY Stores' sales for the month were £700 (22 units at £25 each on 12 January, plus 6 units at £25 each on 26 January). Purchases were £710.

If this was their first month's trading, and hence opening stock was *nil*, what would be their gross profit for the month using the above stock valuations?

From the progress test above you should have discovered different profit figures for each stock valuation. We can, therefore, conclude that the method of stock valuation has a bearing on the profit calculated. The higher the closing stock, the higher the profit.

The stock valuations above are known as *periodic valuations*, as they view the period as a whole, examining total purchases during the accounting period.

Where companies are able to maintain detailed stock records they may choose to value stock on a *perpetual inventory basis*, where purchases and sales are matched on a transaction basis.

**(a) FIFO (Perpetual inventory basis)**

| Date | Receipts Quantity | Receipts Price | Receipts Value | Issues Quantity | Issues Price | Issues Value | Stock Quantity | Stock Price | Stock Value |
|---|---|---|---|---|---|---|---|---|---|
| Jan 1 | 10 | £15 | £150 | | | | 10 | £15 | £150 |
| Jan 10 | 20 | £18 | £180 | | | | 10 | £15 | £150 |
| | | | | | | | 20 | £18 | £360 |
| | | | | | | | 30 | | £510 |
| Jan 12 | | | | 10 | £15 | £150 | 8 | £18 | £144 |
| | | | | 12 | £18 | £216 | | | |
| | | | | 22 | | £366 | | | |
| Jan 15 | 10 | £20 | £200 | | | | 8 | £18 | £144 |
| | | | | | | | 10 | £20 | £200 |
| | | | | | | | 18 | | £344 |
| Jan 26 | | | | 6 | £18 | £108 | 2 | £18 | £36 |
| | | | | | | | 10 | £20 | £200 |
| | | | | | | | 12 | | £236 |

*Notes:*

1 *Stock* – always list the items which make up the stock, making sure you keep them in date order.

2 *Issues* – by listing the stock in order of purchase it is a simple matter of looking at the list and under FIFO taking the *first (top)* items (see 12 January).

3 After each issue we can check we are correct.
e.g. Stock 10 January = £510
less Issues 12 January = £366
Stock 12 January £144

4 *Sale price £25* is *not* part of the cost calculation.

5 Using FIFO the *perpetual* valuation is always the same as the *periodic* valuation. Therefore, if the examiner asks you to calculate the closing stock using FIFO under the PERPETUAL basis, you will be able to check your answer.

The examiner will, however, expect to see a table similar to that above and not just the final figure, so use it only to check your result.

**(b) LIFO (Perpetual inventory basis)**

| Date | Receipts Quantity | Receipts Price | Receipts Value | Issues Quantity | Issues Price | Issues Value | Stock Quantity | Stock Price | Stock Value |
|---|---|---|---|---|---|---|---|---|---|
| Jan 1 | 10 | £15 | £150 | | | | 10 | £15 | £150 |
| Jan 10 | 20 | £18 | £180 | | | | 10 | £15 | £150 |
| | | | | | | | 20 | £18 | £360 |
| | | | | | | | 30 | | £510 |
| Jan 12 | | | | 20 | £18 | £360 | 8 | £15 | £120 |
| | | | | 2 | £15 | £30 | 8 | | £120 |
| | | | | | | £390 | | | |
| Jan 15 | 10 | £20 | £200 | | | | 8 | £15 | £120 |
| | | | | | | | 10 | £20 | £200 |
| | | | | | | | 18 | | £320 |
| Jan 26 | | | | 6 | £20 | £120 | 8 | £15 | £120 |
| | | | | | | | 4 | £20 | £80 |
| | | | | | | | 12 | | £200 |

*Note:*
Unlike FIFO, LIFO can produce different results for *periodic* and *perpetual* basis.

As LIFO assumes that the last items in are the first out, the stock valuation may be based on items purchased a long time ago. The cost of these items may not reflect the current position as prices tend to increase over a period of time.

While LIFO is acceptable under the Companies Act 1985, SSAP 9 prefers this method not to be adopted.

### (c) AVCO (average cost)

| | Receipts | | | Issues | | | Stock | Average | |
|---|---|---|---|---|---|---|---|---|---|
| *Date* | *Quantity* | *Price* | *Value* | *Quantity* | *Price* | *Value* | *Quantity* | *Price* | *Value* |
| Jan 1 | 10 | £15 | £150 | | | | 10 | £15 | £150 |
| Jan 10 | 20 | £18 | £360 | | | | 10 | | £150 |
| | | | | | | | 20 | | £360 |
| | | | | | | | 30 | | £510 |
| | | | | | | | Av. price = $\frac{£510}{30}$ | | |
| | | | | | | | 30 | £17 | £510 |
| Jan 12 | | | | 22 | £17 | £374 | 8 | £17 | £136 |
| Jan 15 | 10 | £20 | £200 | | | | 8 | | £136 |
| | | | | | | | 10 | | £200 |
| | | | | | | | 18 | | £336 |
| | | | | | | | Av. price = $\frac{£336}{18}$ | | |
| | | | | | | | 18 | £18.66 | £336 |
| Jan 26 | | | | 6 | £18.66 | £112 | 12 | £18.66 | £224 |

*Note:*
AVCO involves calculating the average price per unit after each transaction and issuing stock at the average price ruling at that time.

**PROGRESS TEST 4**

(a) Now that we have looked at FIFO and AVCO, have a go at Part (d) of Progress test 2 – Great Clearance Stores plc.
(b) (i) Calculate the closing stock of Stockport Stores Ltd who started in business on 1 September with no stock, using:

(i) FIFO
(ii) LIFO
(iii) AVCO

on both *periodic* and *perpetual* basis.

Sept 1 Purchased 100 units at £25
Sept 11 Purchased 50 units at £27
Sept 12 Sold 65 units at £50
Sept 16 Purchased 30 units at £28
Sept 17 Sold 30 units at £52
Sept 27 Purchased 10 units at £29

(ii) Calculate the gross profit for Stockport Stores Ltd in each of the above cases.

***Long-term contracts***

The valuation of long-term contracts is:

| | £ |
|---|---|
| Cost (including production overheads) | x |
| + any attributable profit (1) | x |
| | x |
| less any foreseeable losses (2) | (x) |
| | x |
| less progress payments received or to be received | (x) |
| | X |

1 *Attributable profit* can be added as the contract progresses in accordance with the *'matching concept'*. To wait until the contract is complete may well result in many years of losses followed by a year of high profit when the contract was complete. This would therefore give a misleading view of the company's progress.
2 *Foreseeable losses* must be deducted in line with the need to be *'prudent'*. If the contract is expected to result in a loss, then the whole loss should be recognised.

**SSAP 12 – Accounting for Depreciation**

SSAP 12 recommends which assets should be depreciated *not* which method of calculation should be used. Therefore two companies who have traded exactly the same but adopted a different method of calculating depreciation could arrive at a different profit figure.

| | Company X | Company Y |
|---|---|---|
| *Depreciation policy* | *Straight line* | *Reducing balance* |
| | £ | £ |
| Net profit before depreciation | 50 000 | 50 000 |
| *less* Depreciation | 5 000 | 10 000 |
| Net profit after depreciation | 45 000 | 40 000 |

*But* they are required to disclose details of the method they have adopted.

Therefore, those with a vested interest in these or any other companies (i.e. shareholders, creditors, banks, etc.) can examine the accounting policies in order to understand how the profit has been determined and to appreciate the effect of the policies on the final accounts. Reference should also be made to Chapter 7.

## ■ TAXATION

(a) SSAP 8 – The Treatment of Taxation under the Imputation System
(b) SSAP 15 – Accounting for Deferred Taxation

### (a) SSAP 8 – The Treatment of Taxation under the Imputation System

***Corporation tax***

Corporation tax was introduced by the 1965 Finance Act. It is a charge on the company's profits which is payable some time after the end of the accounting period, e.g.

(i) *Companies formed after 1.4.65* pay corporation tax 9 months after the company's financial year end;
(ii) *Companies formed before 1.4.65* pay corporation tax on 1 January following 6 April following the end of the company's financial year.

| i.e. *Year end* | *Next 6 April* | *Date payable* | *Delay period* |
|---|---|---|---|
| 31 March 92 | 6 April 92 | 1 January 93 | 9 months |
| 30 April 92 | 6 April 93 | 1 January 94 | 20 months |

Where the delay period exceeds 12 months there may be two years of tax outstanding in the Balance Sheet: the present year's liability which will appear as a creditor (amounts falling due after more than one year) and the previous year's, which will appear as a creditor (amount falling due within one year).

***Advance corporation tax (ACT)***

When a company *pays* a dividend to its shareholders they are required to make an advance payment of corporation tax (ACT) within 14 days of the end of the quarter in which the dividend was paid.

ACT is not payable on proposed dividends until they are actually paid to the shareholders.

The amount of ACT is based on the basic rate of tax, e.g.

Basic rate 30%
Dividend paid £75 000

$$\text{ACT payable} = £75\,000 \times \frac{30}{100-30} = £32\,143$$

Therefore

| | |
|---|---|
| Dividend paid | £75 000 |
| ACT payable | £32 143 |
| Franked payment | £107 143 |

If the tax rate were 25% the formula would be:

$$£75\,000 \times \frac{25}{100-25} = £25\,000$$

The ACT payment can, however, be offset against the company's corporation tax, e.g.

| | |
|---|---|
| Corporation tax liability | £100 000 |
| Less ACT | £32 143 |
| Corporation tax payable | £67 857 |

**PROGRESS TEST 5**

1 World Wide PLC was formed on 1.1.80.
Corporation tax on 1993 profits = £100 000
Dividend paid = £20 000
Dividends proposed = £25 000

Basic rate tax = 25%

Calculate the ACT and corporation tax payable.

2 If the following companies were formed prior to 1.4.65, when is their corporation tax due and what is the delay period.

| | *Financial year end* |
|---|---|
| (a) Dunstable PLC | 31 May 93 |
| (b) Winchester PLC | 30 November 93 |
| (c) Gem PLC | 28 February 93 |

***Franked investment income***

Companies not only pay dividends to shareholders but receive dividends in respect of shares they hold in other companies.

SSAP 8 requires that 'incoming dividends from UK resident companies should be included at the amount of cash received or receivable *plus* the tax credit, e.g.

Basic rate tax = 25%
Dividend received = £7 500 (net of tax)

$$\text{Tax paid} = £7\,500 \times \frac{25}{100 - 25} = £2\,500$$

i.e. the company receive a *'tax credit'* of £2 500

Therefore:

| | |
|---|---|
| Dividend received | £7 500 |
| Tax credit | £ 2 500 |
| Franked income | £10 000 |

Profits on ordinary activities before taxation will include a dividend income of £10 000 and the tax credit of £2 500 will be written off as part of the tax charge.

**(b) SSAP 15 – Accounting for Deferred Taxation**

The profit for tax purposes may be different from that for accounting purposes. This may be because of *'timing differences'*, i.e. tax charges or allowances which occur in a different period from the accounting entries which gave rise to them. Such differences are capable of reversing in later periods.

***Example***

Davidson PLC has profits of £200 000 after charging depreciation of £40 000 on machinery which cost £160 000 and has a 100 per cent capital allowance, i.e. its cost can be offset against the company's tax liability.

| | |
|---|---|
| *Profit for accounting purposes* | = £200 000 |
| *Profit for tax purposes* | £ |
| Trading profit | 200 000 |
| Add back depreciation (bookkeeping entry) | 40 000 |
| | 240 000 |
| *less* Capital allowances | 160 000 |
| | 80 000 |

Corporation tax liability = £80 000 × Tax Rate (e.g. 50%)
£80 000 × 50% = £40 000

*Year 1 Trading Profit and Loss Extract*

| | |
|---|---|
| Trading profit | £200 000 |
| *less* Corporation tax | £40 000 |
| Profit after tax | £160 000 |

**The purpose of deferred tax**

***Example***

Suppose Davidson PLC achieved the same profit and incurred the same depreciation charge the following year but had no capital allowances.

*Profit for tax purposes*

| | £ |
|---|---|
| Trading profit | 200 000 |
| Add back depreciation | 40 000 |
| | 240 000 |
| *less* Capital allowances | Nil |
| | 240 000 |

£240 000 × 50% = £120 000

*Year 2 Trading Profit and Loss Extract*

| | £ |
|---|---|
| Trading profit | 200 000 |
| *less* Corporation tax | 120 000 |
| Profit after tax | 80 000 |

While the profit before tax in Years 1 and 2 is the same, profit after tax is £160 000 in Year 1 but only £80 000 in Year 2. A deferred tax account is used to adjust for such differences by transferring to or from the account.

***Example***

*Year 1 Trading Profit and Loss Extract*

| | £ | £ |
|---|---|---|
| Trading profit | | 200 000 |
| *less* Corporation tax 50% | 40 000 | |
| Transfer to deferred tax account | 60 000 | 100 000 |
| Profit after tax | | 100 000 |

*Year 2 Trading Profit and Loss Extract*

| | | |
|---|---|---|
| Trading profit | | 200 000 |
| *less* Corporation tax 50% | 120 000 | |
| *less* Transferred from deferred tax account | 20 000 | 100 000 |
| | | 100 000 |

*Deferred tax account*

| | | £ | | | £ |
|---|---|---|---|---|---|
| | | | Year 1 | Profit and Loss | 60 000 |
| Year 2 | Profit and Loss | 20 000 | | | |
| Balance | | 40 000 | | | |
| | | 60 000 | | | 60 000 |
| | | | Year 3 | Balance c/o | 40 000 |

The credit balance of £40 000 will then be shown separately in the Balance Sheet as a liability. Had there been a debit balance it should only be carried forward as an asset if there is reasonable certainty that it will be recovered.

## ■ INFLATION

### Introduction

The Profit and Loss Account and Balance Sheet are based on actual cost (historical cost) with little or no recognition of the effects of inflation.

As a result assets may appear in the Balance Sheet at their original cost when prices were much lower. It is therefore necessary to revalue the assets to reflect a more accurate position. This is done using a *revaluation reserve*, e.g.

*Balance Sheet Extract*

| | £ |
|---|---|
| Fixed assets (at cost 1980) | 20 000 |
| *less* accumulated depreciation | 10 000 |
| | 10 000 |

A more realistic valuation of the assets is believed to be £50 000.

*Fixed asset*

| | £ | | £ |
|---|---|---|---|
| 1980 Cost | 20 000 | (1) Revaluation account | 20 000 |
| (3) 1990 Valuation | 50 000 | | |

*Depreciation*

| | £ | | £ |
|---|---|---|---|
| (2) Revaluation account | 10 000 | 1989 Balance | 10 000 |

*Revaluation account*

| | £ | | £ |
|---|---|---|---|
| (1) Fixed asset at cost | 20 000 | (2) Accumulated depreciation | 10 000 |
| 1990 Balance c/o | 40 000 | (3) 1990 Valuation | 50 000 |
| | 60 000 | | 60 000 |
| | | (4) Balance c/o | 40 000 |

(1) Dr Revaluation account with historical cost
Cr Fixed asset account with historical cost

(2) Dr Revaluation account with accumulated depreciation
Cr Depreciation account with accumulated depreciation

(3) Dr Fixed asset account with new valuation
Cr Revaluation account with new valuation

(4) Dr Revaluation account with balance on revaluation
Cr Revaluation reserves with balance on revaluation

(i.e. as shown in the Balance Sheet below).

*Balance sheet extracts*

| | |
|---|---|
| Fixed assets | £50 000 |
| Capital | |
| + *reserves* | |
| Revaluation reserve | £40 000 |

i.e. both sides of the Balance Sheet have been increased by £40 000.

**SSAP 16 Current Cost Accounting**

SSAP 16 has been suspended but remains 'an authoritative reference'. When in force, companies were required to publish final accounts on both historical and current cost basis, i.e. adjusted to account for price changes. Knowledge of SSAP 16 is not, however, required for the Banking Certificate.

## ■ SUMMARY

1 SSAPs and FRSs outline the recommended practice to be followed when producing the final accounts of a business.

2 Their main objective is to narrow the areas of difference and variety in accounts.

3 While recommending practice to be followed they allow companies a degree of flexibility. Companies can therefore interpret the standard as they see fit or in some cases ignore the standard.

4 SSAP 2 – Disclosure of Accounting Policies imposes an obligation to disclose any departure from the four fundamental concepts and the accounting policies followed for items judged material or critical.

**SSAP 6**

5 Extraordinary Items – profit or loss derived from events outside the ordinary activities of the company.

6 Ordinary Activities – those usually, regularly and frequently undertaken and any related activities incidental or arising therefrom.

7 Exceptional or Abnormal Items – derived from the ordinary activities but are exceptional by virtue of the size of the incidence.

8 Prior Year Adjustments – adjustments to the previous year's Profit and Loss Account and the retained profit brought forward.

**SSAP 9**

9 Stock valuation – lower of cost and net realisable value.

10 Cost – expenditure which has been incurred in the normal course of business in bringing the product or service to its present location and condition.

11 Net Realisable Value – the estimated selling price less any further costs to be incurred.

12 The cost of stock may be valued using

(a) FIFO
(b) LIFO
(c) AVCO

on both *periodic* or *perpetual* basis.

13 A higher stock valuation will result in a higher profit figure.

**SSAP 12**

14 While companies are free to select their method of depreciation they must disclose the method used.

**SSAP 8**

15 Companies formed after 1.4.65 pay corporation tax nine months after the end of their financial year.

16 Companies formed before 1.4.65 pay corporation tax on 1 January following the 6 April following the end of their financial year.

17 Advanced Corporation Tax is payable when a company pays a dividend, within 14 days of the end of the quarter in which the dividend was paid.

18 ACT is calculated:

$$\text{Dividend paid} \times \frac{\text{Basic tax rate}}{100 - \text{Basic tax rate}}$$

19 ACT can be offset against corporation tax.

20 Franked Investment Income is the dividends received grossed up.

**SSAP 15**

21 Deferred Tax Accounts are used to adjust for timing differences.

22 Timing Differences are tax charges or allowances which occur in a different period to the accounting entries which gave rise to them.

23 As accounts are based on historical cost, the assets may not represent their true value due to inflation; as a result companies should revalue their assets and adjust their accounts using a valuation reserve.

## ■ SELF-ASSESSMENT QUESTIONS

1 Define the term 'accounting policies' and discuss why it is important to disclose them.

2 'In circumstances where more than one accounting basis is acceptable in principle, the accounting policy followed can significantly affect a concern's reported results and financial position and the view presented can be properly appreciated only if the policies followed in dealing with material items are also explained. For this reason, adequate disclosure of the accounting policies is essential to the fair presentation of financial accounts.'

*Statement of Standard Accounting Practice No. 2.*

*Required:*

(a) Explain how an accounting policy can significantly affect a concern's reported results and financial position. (6)
(b) Give examples of two matters which can be affected by variations in accounting policy. Illustrate your examples by giving a profit figure under each matter and explaining how a change of accounting policy can affect it. (2 × 7 = 14)
(CIB Spring 1987)

3 SSAP 6 distinguishes between *exceptional* and *extraordinary* items in the Profit and Loss Account.

(a) Explain the difference between such items. (6)
(b) Give *two* examples of each in relation to a manufacturing company. (8)
(c) Why is it desirable to give exceptional and extraordinary items different treatment in a company's profit and loss account, and what treatment is specified for each? (6)
(CIB November 1987)

Look at Progress test 1 – notice anything similar to the above question? As you can see practising past examination questions can be most helpful.

4 Stock is usually valued at the lower of cost or net realisable value.

(a) What is meant by 'cost'. (6)
(b) What is meant by 'net realisable value'? (6)
(c) When, if at all, could interest be included as part of the cost? (4)
(d) Give two examples where you might find net realisable value to be below cost. (4)
(Specimen CIB question)

5 The following questions should be answered in accordance with SSAPs 8 and 15.

(a) What are 'tax credits' in connection with dividend payments? (2)
(b) What is 'franked investment income' received by a company? (2)
(c) What treatment is required for franked investment income by SSAP 8? (1)
(d) Why does a company provide for deferred taxation? (2)
(e) When a company does provide for deferred taxation, where is the provision debited in the company's Profit and Loss Account? (2)

(f) A company is proposing to pay a dividend to its shareholders. In the Profit and Loss Account, will the debit for this be merely the cash amount going to the shareholders, or will it include the advance corporation tax which the company will be required to pay to the Inland Revenue? (2)
(g) On what date will the ACT be due for payment to the Inland Revenue? (2)
(h) What are 'timing differences'? (Give an example in your answer.) (2)
(i) How does the receipt of franked investment income by a company help to minimise the payment of any ACT? (2)
(j) What factors should be considered when assessing the size of an intended provision for deferred taxation? (3)

(Total marks for question – 20)

(CIB November 1988)

6 Accounts prepared under the normal (historical cost) convention are said to be misleading because they give too little, if any, recognition of the effects of inflation.

(a) Consider the case of a company manufacturing wooden furniture. In what ways do you think the declared figure might be misleading? (10)
(b) In what ways, if any, might such shortcomings be the subject of an adjustment? (10)
(CIB November 1988)

# 14 Cash flow forecasts

**OBJECTIVES**

**After studying this chapter you should be able to:**

1. **Outline what is meant by a cash flow forecast;**
2. **Appreciate the importance of such forecasts;**
3. **Understand why profit and cash are not the same thing;**
4. **Produce a cash flow forecast which deals with the giving and receiving of credit;**
5. **Produce forecast Trading Profit and Loss Accounts and Balance Sheets from a cash flow forecast;**
6. **Explain how business plans can be adapted to provide an acceptable cash flow, having regard to resources.**

## ■ INTRODUCTION – WHAT IS A CASH FLOW FORECAST?

As the name suggests it is a forecast of the cash which will flow into and out of the business in the future.

## ■ WHAT IS THE PURPOSE OF PRODUCING SUCH FORECASTS?

Cash flow forecasts have a number of uses:

1 They act as an early warning system and enable companies to determine whether or not the business will be able to meet its financial commitments as they fall due. Just because a company can buy goods at £5 000 and sell them for £10 000 does not mean it is destined for success. If it can only sell the goods on three months' credit, it must have sufficient cash to initially purchase the goods and also finance wages, light, heat, etc. until cash comes in from sales.

2 Companies are able to assess whether or not they will need assistance, and, if so, how much. If companies do need assistance, banks will wish to see their cash flow forecast for the next year. It is therefore important that you understand these statements.

3 They enable companies to assess whether or not the company will be profitable.

4 Companies are able to measure their performance by comparing the actual results to the budget and analysing significant variances.

5 Forecasts act as a guide for management decisions.

6 They provide financial discipline and targets to be reached.

***Specimen layout***

*Cash flow forecast of Expectations Ltd for the 12 months ending 31.12.Y0*

| | 1 | 2 | 3 | 4 | 5 | 6 | 7 | 8 | 9 | 10 | 11 | 12 | Dr/Cr | Total |
|---|---|---|---|---|---|---|---|---|---|---|---|---|---|---|
| *Income* | | | | | | | | | | | | | | |
| Sales: Cash | | | | | | | | | | | | | | |
| 1 month credit | | | | | | | | | | | | | | |
| 2 month credit | | | | | | | | | | | | | | |
| *Total income* | | | | | | | | | | | | | | |
| *Expenditure* | | | | | | | | | | | | | | |
| Initial stock | | | | | | | | | | | | | | |
| Purchases | | | | | | | | | | | | | | |
| Wages | | | | | | | | | | | | | | |
| Electricity | | | | | | | | | | | | | | |
| Insurance | | | | | | | | | | | | | | |
| Premises | | | | | | | | | | | | | | |
| Motor vans | | | | | | | | | | | | | | |
| Equipment | | | | | | | | | | | | | | |
| Interest charges etc. | | | | | | | | | | | | | | |
| *Total expenditure* | | | | | | | | | | | | | | |
| *Income – expenditure* | | | | | | | | | | | | | | |
| *Opening balance (capital)* | | | | | | | | | | | | | | |
| *Other injections (e.g. loans)* | | | | | | | | | | | | | | |
| *Cumulative balance* | | | | | | | | | | | | | | |

## ■ HOW ARE THEY CONSTRUCTED?

The cash flow forecast is a financial summary of the sales and production budgets together with all other financial data, e.g. interest charges. The marketing/sales director will need to examine the economic and market trends and predict his sales turnover for the year ahead, based on past performance and recent events. Similarly the production director will forecast the expected production levels, together with the associated costs, e.g. wages, electricity etc.

The bringing together of these two budgets is not as easy as it sounds. It is not uncommon for a sales director to be forecasting sales far in excess of what the production director feels can be produced.

**Example**

***Specimen CIB Question***

Susan is starting a dress shop. She has £15 000 capital in her bank account and her bank have agreed to grant her a £5 000 loan which shall be repayable over two years by quarterly instalments of £625 starting in March, her third month of business. Her manager also agrees an overdraft facility of £1 000.

She obtains a leasehold shop without premium, the rent on which is £4 000 per annum payable quarterly in advance. Rates are £600 per annum which she elects to pay by twelve monthly instalments. She buys a motor car for £3 000 which she thinks will depreciate to £1 800 over the next year. She also buys £6 000 worth of carpets and shop fittings: these she expects to last for five years, after which she will discard them and refurbish the shop.

She purchases an initial stock of £10 000. On this, as with all her purchases, she imposes a mark-up of 100 per cent. As stock is sold, she replaces it in the same month. For the first six months she has to pay cash on delivery for her stock. After that, she gets one month's credit.

All her sales are for cash or on credit card. Her monthly operating expenses (other than any identified above) are £500 per month for the first four months and £750 per month thereafter.

She expects her sales in her first year to be:

| | | | |
|---|---|---|---|
| January | £2 000 | July | £ 6 000 |
| February | £2 000 | August | £ 8 000 |
| March | £3 000 | September | £ 9 000 |
| April | £3 500 | October | £12 000 |
| May | £4 000 | November | £10 000 |
| June | £6 000 | December | £12 000 |

The June sales figure includes £3 000 for goods sold at cost in a summer sale. The October sales figure included £4 000 for goods sold at cost in an autumn sale.

She will draw £500 per month for personal living expenses.

***Required:***

(a) A cash flow forecast for Susan's first year. Ignore bank interest, credit card charges and taxation. (16)

(b) In the light of this forecast, can you offer any advice to Susan? (4)

(See specimen cash flow forecast on page 170.)

*Cash flow forecast for Susan's first year*

| | Jan | Feb | Mar | Apr | May | Jun | Jul | Aug | Sep | Oct | Nov | Dec | Dr/Cr | Total |
|---|---|---|---|---|---|---|---|---|---|---|---|---|---|---|
| | £ | £ | £ | £ | £ | £ | £ | £ | £ | £ | £ | £ | £ | (6) |
| *Income* | | | | | | | | | | | | | | |
| Sales | 2 000 | 2 000 | 3 000 | 3 500 | 4 000 | 6 000 | 6 000 | 8 000 | 9 000 | 12 000 | 10 000 | 12 000 | | 77 500 |
| *Total income* | 2 000 | 2 000 | 3 000 | 3 500 | 4 000 | 6 000 | 6 000 | 8 000 | 9 000 | 12 000 | 10 000 | 12 000 | | 77 500 |
| *Expenditure* | | | | | | | | | | | | | | |
| Bank loan | | | 625 | | | 625 | | | 625 | | | 625 | | 2 500 |
| Rent | 1 000 | | | 1 000 | | | 1 000 | | | 1 000 | | | | 4 000 |
| Rates | 50 | 50 | 50 | 50 | 50 | 50 | 50 | 50 | 50 | 50 | 50 | 50 | | 600 |
| Motor car (1) | 3 000 | | | | | | | | | | | | | 3 000 |
| Carpets and shop fittings (1) | 6 000 | | | | | | | | | | | | | 6 000 |
| Initial stock | 10 000 | | | | | | | | | | | | | 10 000 |
| Purchases (2, 3, 4, 5) | 1 000 | 1 000 | 1 500 | 1 750 | 2 000 | 4 500 | | 3 000 | 4 000 | 4 500 | 8 000 | 5 000 | 6 000 | 42 250 |
| Operating expenses | 500 | 500 | 500 | 500 | 750 | 750 | 750 | 750 | 750 | 750 | 750 | 750 | | 8 000 |
| Personal living expenses | 500 | 500 | 500 | 500 | 500 | 500 | 500 | 500 | 500 | 500 | 500 | 500 | | 6 000 |
| *Total expenditure* | 22 050 | 2 050 | 3 175 | 3 800 | 3 300 | 6 425 | 2 300 | 4 300 | 5 925 | 6 800 | 9 300 | 6 925 | 6 000 | 82 350 |
| *Income expenditure* | (20 050) | (50) | (175) | (300) | 700 | (425) | 3 700 | 3 700 | 3 075 | 5 200 | 700 | 5 075 | | |
| *Opening balance (capital)* | 15 000 | (50) | (100) | (275) | (575) | 125 | (300) | 3 400 | 7 100 | 10 175 | 15 375 | 16 075 | | |
| *Other injections (loan)* | 5 000 | | | | | | | | | | | | | |
| *Cumulative balance* | (50) | (100) | (275) | (575) | 125 | (300) | 3 400 | 7 100 | 10 175 | 15 375 | 16 075 | 21 150 (7) | | |

***Notes to cash flow forecast on page 172.***

1 Cash flow forecasts are concerned only with *cash*. Therefore depreciation does not appear as this is merely a bookkeeping entry.

2 The cash flow forecast is concerned with *when* cash is received or paid, *not* the date of sale or purchase, e.g. after the first six months Susan received one month's credit in respect of purchases. Therefore while purchasing goods in July she did not actually pay for them until August, hence the cash flow forecast does not include a payment in July for purchases.

3 Cash to be received after the final month represents a *debtor*, while cash to be paid after the final month represents a *creditor*, e.g. the goods Susan purchased in December will not be paid for until January of next year, hence we have a *creditor*.

4 Questions often include a note that stock will remain at the same level, as in Susan's case. This means that Susan will have to purchase enough stock each month to replace the units sold, though hopefully at a reduced price. This is a point which escapes some people – they see that £6 000 of stock has been sold and therefore purchase £6 000 of stock.

5 This last point is linked with the need to consider mark-up and margins.

(a) *Mark-up* = amount by which purchases are increased to arrive at the selling price.

| | |
|---|---|
| e.g. Purchases per unit | = £100 |
| Mark-up | = 50%, i.e. £50 |
| ∴ Selling price per unit | = £100 + 50% = £150 |

(b) *Margin* = amount by which selling price exceeds the purchasing cost.

| | |
|---|---|
| e.g. Selling price per unit | = £150 |
| Margin | = 50% = £75 |
| ∴ Purchasing price per unit | = £150 − 50% = £75 |

*Note:*

Despite the same selling price a mark-up and margin of 50 per cent arrive at different purchasing costs, as we have taken 50 per cent of different items.

In Susan's case she has imposed a mark-up of 100 per cent, i.e. purchasing costs are half the selling price. There is also an additional problem built in to this particular question – the goods sold at cost in the summer and autumn sales.

| | | *Replacement cost* | |
|---|---|---|---|
| June | £ | | |
| Total sales | £6 000 | | |
| Sales at cost | £3 000 | 3 000 | |
| ∴ Sales at mark-up | £3 000 | 1 500 | i.e. 50% |
| | | 4 500 | |
| October | | | |
| Total sales | £12 000 | | |
| Sales at cost | £4 000 | 4 000 | |
| ∴ Sales at mark-up | £8 000 | 4 000 | i.e. 50% |
| | | 8 000 | *payable in November* |

6 Always total the budget both across (including any debtors or creditors) and down; it both acts as a check and forms the role of a trial balance when one is asked to produce a Forecast Trading Profit and Loss Account and Balance Sheet from a cash flow forecast.

7 Past questions have asked students to consider whether or not they would provide overdraft or loan facilities. Remember profit does not equal cash. In this case we are asked to advise Susan. The forecast tells us that:

(a) Susan will have a credit balance of £21 150 by the end of the year;
(b) she will only need overdraft facilities January–April and for June;
(c) her maximum overdraft will be £575.

Provided we can rely on Susan's estimates (i.e. that sales are not over-estimated and that items of expenditure have not been overlooked) we can safely assist Susan.

With such a large credit balance building up she should be advised to consider the investment of these funds, or consider paying off the loan in order to avoid further interest charges.

**PROGRESS TEST 1**

Louise is proposing to open a restaurant. She is buying the lease of suitable premises for £10 000. The lease has five years to run and the rent is £6 000 a year, payable quarterly in advance, £1 500 per quarter. She will also spend £8 000 on catering equipment which she expects to have a ten-year life.

Her initial stock of china and cutlery will cost £2 000. This is expected to last her only two years, after which she will need to start buying replacements at £1 000 each year. In the first three months she expects to spend £2 000 a month on wages (including her share of National Insurance contributions): for the rest of the year she expects her cost of wages to rise to £2 800 each month. Her own drawings will remain constant at £500 each month.

The cost of food and other consumables will be a constant one-third of her takings, and after the first three months she expects her suppliers to give her one month's credit on all supplies. Her takings she forecasts as follows:

| | |
|---|---|
| Month 1 | £3 600 |
| Months 2 and 3 | £6 000 each month |
| Months 4, 5, 6 and 7 | £7 500 each month |
| Months 8, 9, 10, 11 and 12 | £8 400 each month |

She will require an initial stock of food and wines costing £1 000; this level of stock will not increase in amount throughout the year.

She will have to pay rates on the restaurant as follows:

Month 1 £800; Month 4 £2 000; Month 10 £2 200

All other expenses will amount to £300 per month, excluding only an accountancy fee of £250 which will not be payable until after the end of her first year.

Her opening capital is £15 000, which she is just transferring to her current account from a deposit account. Her uncle has promised to lend her £3 000 free of interest, but will not be able to pay her this until Month 3, when he receives the proceeds of a life assurance policy due to mature.

*Required:*

(a) A cash flow forecast for Louise for her first twelve months, indicating the maximum bank overdraft she will need to see the above programme through. (16)
(b) On the basis of your cash flow forecast, and if you were her banker and had suitable

security for any possible overdraft, would you consider the business proposition viable? Give reasons for your decision. (4)

*Note:* Ignore interest
(CIB September 1987)

## ■ PRODUCING A FORECAST TRADING PROFIT AND LOSS ACCOUNT AND BALANCE SHEET FROM A CASH FLOW FORECAST

Once you have produced a cash flow forecast, producing forecast accounts is very simple. Let us look back at Susan's cash flow forecast and see exactly how it is done.

As I stated earlier, the *total column* forms the basis of a *trial balance.* It is therefore a case of rearranging these items and including:

(a) The cash balance as at the end of the period, as a current asset, i.e. £21 150
(b) The capital amount = £15 000
(c) The outstanding loan as a current or long-term liability, i.e.

| | | |
|---|---|---|
| Loan | £5 000 | |
| – Repayments | £2 500 | (4 × £625) |
| | £2 500 | |

(d) *Depreciation* which you will recall was not included in the cash flow forecast as it is a *non-cash item*, i.e.

| | | | |
|---|---|---|---|
| Motor car | = | £1 800 | |
| Fittings | = | Cost | £6 000 |
| | | Life | 5 years |
| | | Residual value value | Nil |
| | = | $\frac{£6\,000}{5}$ = | £1 200 p.a. |

*Note:* Be careful if the cash flow forecast is only for a six-month period, as in some questions, then you should only include depreciation for six months.

You should use every item in the total column plus those mentioned above, therefore if your Balance Sheet does not balance, quickly check that you have not missed an item.

Also, remember, if stock has remained constant, the closing stock will be the same as the opening stock.

*Forecast Trading Profit and Loss Account of Susan for the year ending – –*

| | £ | £ |
|---|---|---|
| Sales | | 77 500 |
| *less Cost of goods sold* | | |
| Opening stock | 10 000 | |
| + Purchases | 42 250 | |
| | 52 250 | |
| – Closing stock | 10 000 | 42 250 |
| *Gross profit* | | 35 250 |
| *less Expenses* | | |
| Rent | 4 000 | |
| Rates | 600 | |
| Operating expenses | 8 000 | |
| Depreciation: Motor car (d) | 1 800 | |
| Fittings | 1 200 | 15 600 |
| *Net profit* | | 19 650 |

*Forecast Balance Sheet of Susan as at – –*

| | | |
|---|---|---|
| *Fixed assets* | | |
| Motor car | | 3 000 |
| – Depreciation (d) | | 1 800 |
| | | 1 200 |
| Fittings | 6 000 | |
| – Depreciation (d) | 1 200 | 4 800 |
| | | 6 000 |
| *Current assets* | | |
| Stock | 10 000 | |
| Debtors | | |
| Bank/Cash (a) | 21 150 | |
| | 31 150 | |
| *less Current liabilities* | | |
| Creditors (b) | 6 000 | 25 150 |
| | | 31 150 |
| *Financed by* | | |
| Capital | | 15 000 |
| and Net profit | | 19 650 |
| | | 34 650 |
| – Drawings | | 6 000 |
| | | 28 650 |
| *Long-term liabilities* | | |
| Loan (c) | | 2 500 |
| | | 31 150 |

## ■ SUMMARY

1 A cash flow forecast is a forecast of the cash which will flow into and out of the business in the future.

2 It enables companies to determine whether or not the business will be able to meet its financial commitments as they fall due.

3 Other uses are:

(a) it allows you to assess whether or not you will need assistance, and if so, how much and for how long;
(b) it enables you to assess your profitability;
(c) it enables you to measure performance by comparing actual results with forecast results and analysing significant variances;
(d) it acts as a guide for management decisions;
(e) it provides financial discipline and targets.

4 Cash flow forecasts are constructed from the sales and production budgets, together with all other financial data, e.g. interest charges.

5 Cash flow forecasts are concerned only with *cash*; therefore do *not include* depreciation.

6 Cash flow forecasts reflect *when* cash is received and paid, *not* the date of sale or purchase.

7 Cash to be received after the final month represents a *debtor*, while cash to be paid after the third month represents a *creditor*.

8 If stock is to be kept at the same level, purchases must replace stock sold.

9 Mark-up is the amount by which purchases are increased to arrive at the selling price.

10 Margin is the amount by which selling price exceeds the purchasing costs.

11 Cash flow forecasts reveal:

- the forecast cash balance at the end of the accounting period;
- the maximum overdraft requirement;
- the period over which overdraft facilities are required.

12 Forecast Trading Profit and Loss Accounts and Balance Sheets can be drawn from cash flow forecasts. *But* you must include:

- depreciation;
- closing cash balance;
- capital.

## ■ SELF-ASSESSMENT QUESTIONS

1 Explain how a firm's overdraft can increase at the same time as it makes a profit. (Your explanation should include examples/illustrations.)

2 'A shopkeeper does not need to keep books to know whether he is making a profit or a loss – he has only got to look at his bank balance. If it keeps falling, there is no way he can be making a profit.'

Discuss this statement and give *four* possible explanations of how a business might be making a profit, yet have the balance of its cash at bank reducing. (20)

Both questions 3 and 4 are based on the information given below.

Mr and Mrs Deepan are about to start a 'Telephone Pizza' service. They will advertise locally so that customers may order a pizza by phone which will be freshly cooked and delivered to their door.

They realise that, starting such a business from scratch, they will inevitably make a loss and will need bank support until they have become established, but they feel that once they have got their turnover up to £1 000 per month they will have no further problems. Advertising will need to be heavy in the early months, but can be reduced as they become known and build up a regular clientele.

They provide the following estimates:

| | | Sales | Advertising |
|---|---|---|---|
| Month | 1 | £300 | £200 |
| | 2 | £500 | £200 |
| | 3 | £600 | £150 |
| | 4 | £700 | £150 |
| | 5 | £800 | £50 |
| | 6 | £1 000 | £50 |

All sales will be for cash and all expenses will be paid in cash.

Ingredients (including packaging) are expected to cost 20 per cent of the sales price. They will buy an initial stock of ingredients costing £200, to enable them to offer a wide variety of pizza fillings. The stock will be maintained at this figure for the first two months, but in Month 3 will be increased to £300, and further increased to £400 in Month 5.

They are taking a lease on a small shop for three years: this requires a premium of £1 000, followed by a rental of £2 000 per year payable quarterly in advance with the first payment in Month 1. Legal fees of £200 will also have to be paid in the first month.

In Month 6 they expect to hire an assistant cook (part-time) at £100 per month. General shop expenses will cost £150 per month.

Comprehensive insurance (covering both the food supplied and the motor cycle Mr Deepan will use for deliveries) will be taken out and the first year's premium will cost £350; this will have to be paid in Month 1.

Catering equipment will be bought on hire-purchase terms. The cash price would have been £820, but under the hire-purchase agreement the Deepans will pay an initial deposit in Month 1 of £180, followed by 24 monthly instalments of £35 (which will start in Month 2).

Mr Deepan already owns his motor cycle, which he values at £1 200. He estimates his running expenses will be £30 per month and the motor cycle will be used for business purposes.

Drawings for the couple will amount to £300 per month. Mr and Mrs Deepan have £900 in the bank to start the business.

3 (a) Using the information given above, prepare a cash flow forecast for the first six months of the business showing the cash surplus or deficit at the end of each month. (15)

(b) If suitable security were available, would you be willing, as their banker, to provide the overdraft facilities required in the first six months? Give reasons for your answer. (5)

(Total marks for question – 20)

**4** Take the information provided above and construct:

(a) a forecast Trading and Profit and Loss Account for the first six months of Mr and Mrs Deepan's business; (10)
(b) a forecast Balance Sheet at the end of that period. (10)

Notes to Question 4:
(i) Interest charges included in the hire-purchase payments for the six months amount to £86.
(ii) The closing bank balance may be taken as the balancing figure in the Balance Sheet prepared in (b).
(iii) Depreciate the lease by one sixth of the cost in this period and depreciate both the equipment and the motor cycle at the rate of 20 per cent per annum on the straight line method, assuming a zero residual value in both cases.
(Total marks for question – 20)
(CIB November 1989)

**5** Mr Merstham is considering starting a business on 1 June 1991. He is able to introduce cash of £7 000 as capital, but is wondering whether this will be enough to stop him running into cash problems. He has approached his bank and has been asked to prepare a cash forecast for the first six months of business operations. His assumptions are:

1 On 1 June fixtures and fittings will be purchased on credit for £4 500; payment will be made in July. These will have a life of five years and a zero residual value.
2 During June £4 300 will be paid for rent and £1 650 for insurance; both of these are for a full year.
3 Sales will be made on both cash and credit terms: 40% will be for cash and the remaining 60% on credit. Credit customers will pay the amount due in the month following the one in which the sale is made, i.e. the cash for credit sales made in June will be received in July.
4 Sales in each of the first three months of trading will be £10 000, and in the second three months £16 000 per month.
5 Suppliers will expect to be paid in cash for the purchases made in the first three months but, after that, one month's credit is expected.
6 An initial stock of goods for resale costing £4 000 will be purchased on 1 June; the level of stock will be raised to £8 000 on 1 September in response to the anticipated increase in sales. Each month sufficient purchases will be made, in addition to those needed to provide stock, to replace items sold. Merstham expects to be able to sell goods at twice the price he pays for them, i.e. an item which costs £100 will be sold for £200.
7 Monthly cash payments will be made in respect of: wages £1 000; general expenses £750; and drawings £1 250.

*Required:*
Prepare a monthly cash flow forecast for the first six months of Merstham's business showing clearly the cash balance at the end of each month. (20)
(CIB May 1991)

6 Ivor Shop is proposing to open a shop on 1 July 1988 to sell micro-computers and associated software. He has £10 000 in his bank account for opening capital.

He is obtaining the shop premises on a lease and the rent will be £8 000 per annum, payable quarterly in advance in July, October, January and April. No premium is being paid for the lease but Ivor will have to pay both his own and the landlord's legal costs as soon as he takes the lease and these are expected to amount to £400 in total.

Ivor will have to fit the shop out. He expects to acquire the shop fittings on hire-purchase terms: this will involve a down payment of £2 500 in July and a monthly payment of £215 for each of the next 24 months. He will depreciate the shop fittings at the rate of £1 200 each year.

He expects to pay rates of £360 in August, £960 in October and £980 in April.

For the first two months, while trading is building up, he will not employ any staff, but starting 1 September he expects to employ a sales assistant who will receive £500 per month salary. He estimates his sales will be as follows:

| 1988 | | 1989 | |
|---|---|---|---|
| | £ | | £ |
| July | 3 000 | January | 7 500 |
| August | 3 600 | February | 7 500 |
| September | 4 500 | March | 9 000 |
| October | 4 500 | April | 9 000 |
| November | 6 000 | May | 12 000 |
| December | 6 000 | June | 12 000 |

All sales will be made for cash.

His selling prices will be set at 50 per cent above his cost price. He will replace all stock sold in the same month that the sale takes place. For the first six months he expects to pay cash for his purchases, but for all purchases thereafter he confidently expects to be able to get a month's credit from his suppliers. He will purchase an initial stock costing £15 000 on 1 July 1988. Other business expenses are estimated at £250 per month.

An aunt is lending Ivor £5 000 as an interest-free loan from 1 July but insists that she must be repaid this loan in January 1989 when she has a large income tax bill to pay.

Ivor will draw £400 a month from the business for personal living expenses.

Ignore any bank charges or interest on the overdraft.

*Required*:

(a) A cash flow forecast for the twelve months ending 30 June 1989. (16)

(b) A note of the biggest overdraft he will need and the month in which he will need it. (2)

(c) A note of the biggest overdraft he will need and the month in which he will need it *if his suppliers will grant him a month's credit after his first three months' trading*. (2)

(CIB May 1988)

# 15 Cash and working capital

**OBJECTIVES**

**After studying this chapter you should be able to:**

1. **Define working capital;**
2. **Appreciate the importance of working capital;**
3. **Describe the flow of funds cycle;**
4. **Calculate working capital and the flow of funds cycle;**
5. **State ways in which working capital can be kept to a minimum.**

## ■ INTRODUCTION – WHAT IS WORKING CAPITAL?

You should by now be aware that working capital is calculated in the following manner:

| *Current assets* | less | *Current liabilities* |
|---|---|---|
| (Cash or items which can be converted into cash) | | (Amounts owed and due for repayment within 12 months) |

This is often expressed in the form of a ratio, e.g.

| *Current assets* | – | *Current liabilities* | = | *Working capital* |
|---|---|---|---|---|
| £10 000 | – | £5 000 | = | £5 000 |

Ratio = 2:1

You should always indicate how many times current liabilities are covered. In the last example they were covered twice. However, the situation may be as follows:

| *Current assets* | – | *Current liabilities* | = | *Working capital* |
|---|---|---|---|---|
| £5 000 | – | £10 000 | = | (£5 000) |

Current assets cover only half of the current liabilities and the ratio will, therefore, be expressed as:

0.5:1

Have a go at the Progress test. We shall refer to your answers throughout the chapter.

**PROGRESS TEST 1**

(a) Calculate the working capital ratio in the following examples:

| | *Current assets* | *Current liabilities* |
|---|---|---|
| | £ | £ |
| Hi-Fi Equipment Ltd | 212 579 | 79 298 |
| Stores UK plc | 41 085 | 63 287 |
| Engineering Co Ltd | 310 000 | 150 000 |
| Office Suppliers Inc. | 289 761 | 162 049 |
| Doncasters Ltd | 20 000 | 20 000 |

(b) From the following details, extracted from the Balance Sheet of a trading company, calculate the working capital and the working capital ratio.

| *Assets* | £ |
|---|---|
| Freehold premises | 250 000 |
| Office equipment | 225 065 |
| Work-in-progress | 24 107 |
| Stock | 85 391 |
| Debtors | 25 024 |
| Prepaid expenses | 3 197 |
| Cash at bank, deposit account | 15 000 |
| Cash at bank, current account | 8 124 |
| *Capital and liabilities* | |
| Share capital | 150 000 |
| General reserve | 300 000 |
| Profit and loss account | 37 097 |
| Debentures | 100 000 |
| Provision for corporation tax | 20 750 |
| Creditors | 31 923 |
| Accrued expenses | 5 072 |

(CIB May 1989)

## ■ ASSESSING A COMPANY'S WORKING CAPITAL POSITION

You should have discovered that the working capital ratio is found by simply dividing current assets by current liabilities.

*But which company has the best working capital situation?*

Unfortunately, it is not just a simple matter of saying it is Hi-Fi Equipment Ltd because theirs is the highest. We must consider:

(a) the components of the calculation;
(b) the nature of the company's industry.

**(a) The components of the calculation**

*Balance Sheet extract of Hi-Fi Equipment Ltd as at 31.12.Y0*

| | £ | £ |
|---|---|---|
| *Fixed assets* | | |
| *Current assets* | | |
| Stock | | 100 000 |
| Debtors | | 100 000 |
| Bank | | 12 000 |
| Cash | | 579 |
| | | 212 579 |
| *less Current liabilities* | | |
| Taxation | 9 000 | |
| Creditors | 70 000 | |
| Accrued expenses | 298 | 79 298 |
| Working capital | | 133 281 |

On the face of it Hi-Fi Equipment would appear to be in a satisfactory position, with cash or items which can be converted into cash covering amounts due for repayment within 12 months almost 2.7 times.

But what if:

(a) *Stock* included bad stock of £80 000 which needed to be written off;
(b) *Debtors* included bad debts of £70 000 which, once again, needed to be written off and other debtors who were not due to pay for over 3 months; and
(c) *Creditors* were all pressing for payment in the next day or so.

As you can see, the Balance Sheet can be misleading and we must, therefore, consider the components of the working capital calculations and, in particular, when payments and receipts are due.

**(b) The nature of the company's industry**

As we have seen, Hi-Fi's apparently satisfactory ratio of 2.7:1 can, in reality, be worse. Does this mean that Stores UK plc with a ratio of only 0.65:1 will, in reality, be in an even worse position, if in fact 0.65:1 is a bad position?

The answer is *'No, not necessarily'*. An examination of the component parts may not reveal the problems encountered by Hi-Fi Equipment Ltd. It may even reveal that 0.65:1, for a Superstore, is quite satisfactory due to the nature of their industry, e.g.

(a) *Stock* must be low otherwise goods will go off;
(b) *Debtors* will be low as customers do not receive credit, they pay by cheque or cash;
(c) *Creditors* – payment may not be due for some time, therefore 0.65:1 *can be* satisfactory.

However, it is important to remember that many expenses need to be paid in advance, such as rent and rates. Therefore, even if a customer sells on cash terms and is able to secure long credit terms for suppliers, they will still need to pay these items in advance. Similarly, they will also need to maintain a cash float for day-to-day use.

As a result, working capital may still be required by food retailers, though the published accounts of the large superstores (e.g. Tesco) demonstrate their ability to operate profitably on working capital ratios of less than 1:1.

Let us take a closer look at a company's working capital position by examining their *cash cycle/flow of funds*.

## ■ CASH CYCLE/FLOW OF FUNDS

The cash cycle of many companies follows the pattern below (*see* Fig. 3):

- they buy goods or material or credit;
- they manufacture stock;
- they make sales on credit to debtors;
- they receive cash from their debtors at a later date; which
- enables them to repay their creditors.

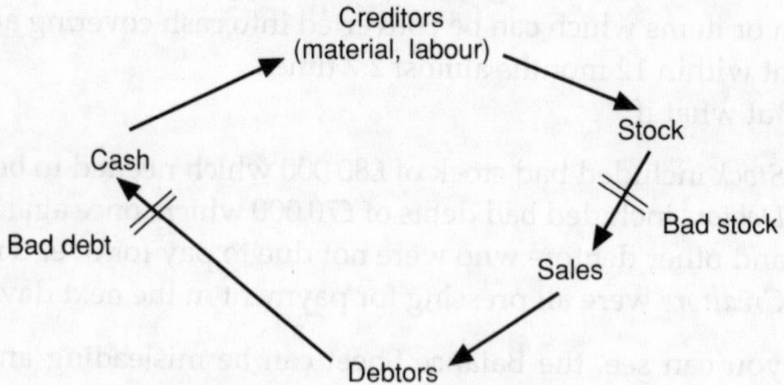


**Figure 3 Cash cycle/flow of funds**

We can calculate the company's cash cycle using the following ratios:

(a) *Average stock turnover*

$$\frac{\text{Average stock}}{\text{Cost of goods sold}} \times 365 = \text{Number of days to turn stock}$$

$$\text{NB: Average stock} = \frac{\text{Opening stock + Closing stock}}{2}$$

If you are not given sufficient information to calculate average stock, it is quite acceptable to use the stock figure you have been given.

(b) *Average debtors' settlement period*

$$\frac{\text{Debtors}}{\text{Sales}} \times 365 = \text{Number of days before debtors settle their debt}$$

(c) *Average creditors' settlement period*

$$\frac{\text{Creditors}}{\text{Purchases}} \times 365 = \text{Number of days before we pay our creditors}$$

**PROGRESS TEST 2**

The following forecasts are provided in respect of Grassington Ltd, a company trading in a single product for 1984:

| | £ |
|---|---|
| Sales | 2 700 |
| Purchases | 1 800 |
| Cost of goods sold | 1 830 |
| Average trade debtors outstanding | 300 |
| Average trade creditors outstanding | 160 |
| Average stocks held | 305 |

All purchases and sales are made on credit, and trading transactions are expected to occur at an even rate throughout the year.

*Required*:

(a) Calculations of the rate of payment of creditors, the rate of collection of debtors and the rate of stock turnover. (9)

(b) A calculation of the expected cash operating cycle (i.e. the time lag between making payment to suppliers and collecting cash from customers in respect of goods purchased and sold) for 1984. (5)

*NB:* Assume a 360-day year for the purpose of your calculations

Check your answers before continuing.

Assuming Grassington Ltd has no other current assets or current liabilities, its working capital is, on average, 3.78:1

| | £ |
|---|---|
| *Current assets* | |
| Stock | 305 |
| Debtors | 300 |
| | 605 |
| *less Current liabilities* | |
| Creditors | 160 |
| **Working capital** | **445** |

It cannot be allowed to reach a position where current assets only equal current liabilities, as its creditors (suppliers) are paid 32 days after purchase while Grassington only collect the cash after 100 days (*see* Progress Test answer).

If current assets were only equal to current liabilities it would, therefore, be unable to pay its creditors when requested to do so, and do not forget, it will also need to pay certain expenses in advance.

Grassington must, therefore, maintain a level of working capital.

## ■ THE COST OF MAINTAINING WORKING CAPITAL

Having money tied up in working capital is expensive, e.g.

- *Stock.* This will have cost money to buy or produce and earns the company nothing 'sitting on the shelf'. It may even cost the company money storing it – warehouse costs, staff etc.

- *Debtors.* If you allow your debtors too much credit, you may need to turn to the bank for an overdraft.
- *Bank.* Balances should be kept to a minimum. While it can earn you interest, the return is likely to be less than if it were invested in new machinery which could improve your business.
- *Cash.* Once again, your cash float should be kept to a minimum. Cash will not give you a return.

Companies should, therefore, keep working capital to a minimum.

## ■ HOW DO YOU KEEP WORKING CAPITAL TO A MINIMUM?

1 Monitor *stock* levels and try to predict future demand so that stock is kept to a minimum.
2 Chase *debtors* who fail to pay on time. Obviously, you could demand payment in cash but this may lose you sales.
3 Keep *bank* and *cash* balances to a minimum.
4 Take advantage of *credit* offered.

i.e. let your creditors finance your operations though, obviously, you will need to be able to pay them when payment is due.

### PROGRESS TEST 3

1 Using the information provided in Progress test 2, explain any one method by which the directors *might* achieve a reduction of £20 000 in the company's bank overdraft requirement at 31 December, 1984, and demonstrate the effect on the cash operating cycle. (6)
*Note:* Assume a 360-day year for the purpose of your calculations.
2 Would increasing turnover reduce your need for working capital? If not, why not?
3 If working capital is so expensive, why maintain working capital?

## ■ CONCLUSION – THE IMPORTANCE OF WORKING CAPITAL

Working capital could be described as the 'blood' of the business; once it stops *flowing* the business is dead.

Should a company wish to expand they will need to purchase/manufacture more stock, all of which requires money. The additional sales may need to be on credit terms, which will increase debtors and, therefore, investment in working capital may be vital.

Similarly, companies may need to invest in working capital simply to maintain existing levels of operations, i.e. to meet bills, operate a cash float, or simply due to their cash cycle, as in the case of Grassington Ltd.

## ■ SUMMARY

1 Working capital = Current assets – Current liabilities.

2 It is often expressed as a ratio, in order to reflect how many times current assets cover current liabilities, e.g. 2:1 or 0.5:1.

3 Many companies can operate on ratios of less than 1:1.

4 Where the ratio is less than 1:1 it means that, on the face of it, cash or items which can be easily converted into cash do not cover amounts owing and due for repayment within 12 months. This can, obviously, be a problem.

5 In assessing a company's working capital position we must consider:

(a) the components of the calculation;
(b) the nature of the company's industry.

6 Even where current assets cover current liabilities companies can be in difficulty if current assets include bad stock/bad debts and/or if creditors are pressing for payment.

7 While Superstores can operate on ratios of less than 1:1 we must not forget that some bills must be paid in advance.

8 $$\text{Stock turnover} = \frac{\text{Stock}}{\text{Cost of goods sold}} \times 365$$

9 $$\text{Debtors' settlement period} = \frac{\text{Debtors}}{\text{Sales}} \times 365$$

10 $$\text{Creditors' settlement period} = \frac{\text{Creditors}}{\text{Purchases}} \times 365$$

11 The cash operating cycle examines how quickly a company turns its stock, receives payment from debtors and pays creditors.

12 Working capital is expensive and should be kept to a workable minimum.

13 In order to keep working capital to a minimum we must:

- monitor stock levels and predict future demand;
- chase debtors;
- keep cash and bank balances to a minimum;
- take advantage of credit.

14 Working capital is vital for the operation of a business, and particularly, if the company decides to expand.

## ■ SELF-ASSESSMENT QUESTIONS

1 Calculate the working capital ratio in the following examples:

| | *Current Assets* | *Current Liabilities* |
|---|---|---|
| | £ | £ |
| (a) Smithfield Ltd | 150 000 | 50 000 |
| (b) Daubrey PLC | 317 290 | 116 209 |
| (c) Hoverblast Ltd | 20 000 | 36 000 |
| (d) Evident Ltd | 51 000 | 47 000 |

2 From the following details, calculate the working capital and the working capital ratio:

| | £ |
|---|---|
| Stock | 215 000 |
| Cash | 10 000 |
| Creditors | 60 000 |
| Debtors | 100 000 |
| Debentures | 200 000 |
| Prepaid expenses | 7 500 |
| Accrued expenses | 10 000 |
| Bank investment account | 20 000 |
| Bank overdraft | 16 000 |
| Office furniture | 56 000 |

3 From the following information, calculate the cash operating cycle of Dewhurst Dynamics Ltd:

| | £ |
|---|---|
| Sales | 10 000 |
| Purchases | 7 700 |
| Cost of goods sold | 1 750 |
| Stock | 150 |
| Debtors | 850 |
| Creditors | 1 960 |

4 Winstanly Ltd have sales of £200 000 and purchases of £150 000. If its debtors settlement period is, on average, 72 days, and its creditors settlement period on average 30 days, what are its average outstanding debtors and creditors?

5 Working capital is expensive. If you were the managing director of a wholesale electrical store, state with reasons, *four* practical steps you would take to ensure that the need for working capital was kept to a minimum. (4 × 5 marks = 20)

6 (a) Henry is about to set up in business as the proprietor of a take-away food shop. He says, 'I shall sell only for cash, my stock will never exceed a week's supply, and my suppliers are granting me a month's credit on all supplies of food: therefore, I shall not need any working capital'. State, with reasons, whether or not you agree with this view. (4)
(b) Specify *two* ways in which management decisions can impose a need for more working capital in a business, and *two* ways in which such a need might be met. (4)
(CIB May 1988)

7 The directors of Sevoaks Ltd, which prepares its published accounts for the year to 30 September, are reviewing the company's draft balance sheet which shows the firm's position at 31 March 1991. The balance sheet shows the working capital position as follows:

| | £ | £ | £ |
|---|---|---|---|
| Stock | | 65 000 | |
| Debtors | | 88 000 | |
| | | | 153 000 |
| Creditors | 55 000 | | |
| Overdraft | 110 000 | | |
| | | | 165 000 |
| Working capital | | | (12 000) |

The directors are not satisfied with this, and want to improve the working capital position before 30 September 1991 as they consider that the firm's credit position may be badly affected if a negative capital working position is shown. The following possibilities have been suggested, all of which could be implemented in time for their full effect to be shown in the balance sheet at 30 September 1991:

1 At the moment, debtors take two months to settle their debts; this could be cut to one month.
2 A secured long-term loan of £50 000 could be raised.
3 One of the directors has pointed out that, in the funds flow statement, depreciation is added to profit to find the funds generated from operations. He went on to suggest that, to increase the funds flow, the depreciation charge for the second half of the financial year could be increased by £60 000.
4 Payment could be delayed with the result that creditors would be increased by £20 000.
5 A fixed asset with a written down value of £17 000 could be sold for cash of £30 000.

*Required:*
(a) Show the separate effect, i.e. the amount of increase (+) or decrease (–), of each of the above suggestions on the company's overdraft, working capital and working capital ratio at 30 September 1991. Present your answer in the form of a table:

| *Suggestion* | *Overdraft* £ | *Working Capital* £ | *Working Capital Ratio* |
|---|---|---|---|
| 1 | | | |
| 2 | | | |
| 3 | | | |
| 4 | | | |
| 5 | | | |

(10)

(b) Discuss each of the suggestions separately, indicating the extent to which it achieves the objectives of the directors and mentioning any other factors which should be taken into consideration before implementing it. (10)
(Total—20 marks)

*Notes:*
1 Ignore interest when answering part (a) of this question.
2 Work to two decimal places when calculating the working capital ratio.
(CIB May 1991)

# 16 Cash flow statements

**OBJECTIVES**

**After studying this chapter you should be able to:**

**1 Outline the purpose of a cash flow statement;**

**2 Identify inflows (sources) and outflows (applications) of cash;**

**3 Produce cash flow statements which deal with the sale or purchase of assets.**

## ■ INTRODUCTION

In the last two chapters we have discovered that cash flow is as important as profit. Without cash flowing through the business, a company will be unable to pay its debts as they fall due, even if they are able to sell goods at a profit.

As a result the published Trading Profit and Loss Account and Balance Sheet of a company may show a profit but to the majority of readers hide a cash flow problem.

FRS 1 makes it obligatory for all businesses to publish what is known as a cash flow statement which shows where funds have come from and where they have gone and, therefore, provides the reader with an indication of the financial policy adopted by the company and effect on the company's financial position.

## ■ CASH FLOWS: IN AND OUT

The objective of the statement is to show:

- where funds have come from
- where funds have gone.

FRS 1 calls for this information to be presented under the following five headings, each of which is explained below.

1 *Operating activities*. Under this heading, you must show:
   - *net profit* before tax and interest
     - *add back* depreciation for the year (as this is a non-cash item)
     - *plus/minus* changes in working capital items, excluding cash – in other words, stock, debtors and creditors.

2 *Returns on investment and servicing*. Under this heading, you must show:
   - interest paid or received; and
   - dividends paid or received.

Those *paid* are *outflows*; those *received* are *inflows*.

3 *Taxation*. Under this heading, you must show:

- corporation tax (including advance corporation tax) paid during the year.

4 *Investing activities*. Under this heading, you must show:

- purchase of fixed assets (outflow)
- sale of fixed assets (inflow).

5 *Financing*. Under this heading, you must show:

- amounts paid and received in respect of the raising of finance
- share issues
- long-term loans paid/received.

The total of the five sections is then matched by the changes in cash/bank during the year – if you have done it correctly! After all, the company must have got the money to buy or pay for the items listed under the five headings either from its cash holding or from its bank account.

## ■ EXAMPLE PRESENTATION

Look at the example of a cash flow statement on the next page. The important things to note are:

- which items fall under each heading
- an *increase* in stock obviously resulted in an *outflow* of funds – hence it appears as (1 400); a *decrease* in stock would have been (+)1 400
  (Notice how the same can be said for every item in the statement: items *paid* are *outflows* – e.g. tax paid is (6 000) – and items resulting in cash being *received* are *inflows* – e.g. sale of fixed assets is (+1 400).)
- the total of the five sections – i.e. the decrease in cash/bank of 1 000 in this example – equals the analysis of changes in cash/bank during the year.

When you are asked to provide a cash flow statement, I would suggest that you do the analysis of changes in cash/bank first, as this is easy and gives you something to aim at. However, you should present your final answer with the analysis at the bottom of your statement as shown in the example.

*Cash flow statement for year ended 31 March 19X3*

| | £ | £ |
|---|---|---|
| ***Operating activities*** | | |
| Net profit before tax and interest | 11 600 | |
| Depreciation for year | 3 800 | |
| Gain on sale of equipment | (400) | |
| Increase in stock | (1 400) | |
| Increase in debtors | (400) | |
| Increase in creditors | 1 000 | |
| Net cash inflow from operating activities | | 14 200 |
| **Returns on investments and servicing of finance** | | |
| Interest paid | (1 600) | |
| Interest received | NIL | |
| Dividends paid | NIL | |
| Dividends and interest received | NIL | |
| Net cash outflow from returns on investments and servicing of finance | | (1 600) |
| **Taxation** | | |
| Tax paid | | (6 000) |
| ***Investing activities*** | | |
| Purchase of fixed assets | (9 000) | |
| Sale of fixed assets | 1 400 | |
| Net cash outflow from investment activities | | (7 600) |
| Net cash outflow before financing | | (1 000) |
| ***Financing*** | | |
| New capital/issue of shares/loans | NIL | |
| Repayment of shares/loans | NIL | |
| Net cash inflow/outflow from financing | | NIL |
| ***Decrease in cash/bank*** | | (1 000) |
| **Analysis of changes in cash/bank during year** | | |
| Balance at start of year | | 2 000 |
| Net cash outflow | | (1 000) |
| ***Balance at end of year*** | | 1 000 |

*Note:* the items marked 'NIL' are shown here for illustrative purposes, and would not be shown as such in an examination answer.

## ■ PREPARING A CASH FLOW STATEMENT

Having used some examples of inflows and outflows, and looked at a specimen cash flow statement, see if you can prepare such a statement for Ranpgill Ltd.

*Balance sheet for Ranpgill Ltd*

| | 31.12.X0 | 31.12.X1 | | 31.12.X0 | 31.12.X1 |
|---|---|---|---|---|---|
| | £ | £ | | £ | £ |
| Fixed assets at cost | 390 000 | 426 000 | Share capital | 200 000 | 220 000 |
| *less* Depreciation | 52 000 | 62 000 | General reserve | 5 000 | 10 000 |
| Net book value | 338 000 | 364 000 | Profit and loss a/c | 175 000 | 200 000 |
| | | | | 380 000 | 430 000 |
| | | | 10% Debenture | 30 000 | 15 000 |
| | | | | 410 000 | 445 000 |
| *Current assets* | | | *Current liabilities* | | |
| Stock | 80 000 | 100 000 | Taxation | 20 000 | 30 000 |
| Debtors | 30 000 | 50 000 | Creditors | 20 000 | 30 000 |
| Bank | 15 000 | 10 000 | Proposed dividend | 15 000 | 20 000 |
| Cash | 2 000 | 1 000 | | | |
| | 465 000 | 525 000 | | 465 00 | 525 000 |

*Profit before taxation = £80 000

**Answer**

*Cash flow statement of Ranpgill Ltd for year ended 19X1*

| | £ | £ |
|---|---|---|
| **Operating activities** | | |
| *Note* | | |
| (a) Net profit before tax and interest | 80 000 | |
| (b) Depreciation for year | 10 000 | |
| (c) Increase in stock | (20 000) | |
| (c) Increase in debtors | (20 000) | |
| (c) Increase in creditors | 10 000 | |
| Net cash inflow from operating activities | | 60 000 |
| **Returns on investments and servicing of finance** | | |
| (d) Dividend paid | (15 000) | |
| | | (15 000) |
| **Taxation** | | |
| (e) Taxation paid | (20 000) | |
| | | (20 000) |
| **Investing activities** | | |
| (f) Purchase of fixed assets | (36 000) | |
| | | (36 000) |
| Net cash outflow before financing | | (11 000) |
| **Financing** | | |
| (g) Issue of shares (i.e. cash received from issue) | 20 000 | |
| Repayment of debenture | (15 000) | |
| Net cash inflow from financing | | 5 000 |
| **Decrease in cash/bank** | | (6 000) |

**Analysis of changes in cash/bank during year**

| | | |
|---|---|---|
| *Balance at start of year* | | |
| Cash | 2 000 | |
| Bank | 15 000 | |
| | | 17 000 |
| *Balance at end of year* | | |
| Cash | 1 000 | |
| Bank | 10 000 | |
| | | 11 000 |
| ***Net cash outflow*** | | 6 000 |

*Notes*

**Operating activities**

1 *Profit before taxation.* You must always start with profit before taxation, as this is the major source of funds. In this question this figure was given as a note, but in other questions you will need to calculate it from the balance sheets. The easiest way to do this is to think of your limited company layout and work backwards, filling in the figures until you arrive back at profit before taxation. In the example above, we would have done this as follows.

*Trading profit and loss account extract of Ranpgill Ltd for the year ending 31.12.X1*

| | £ | |
|---|---|---|
| Profit before taxation | 80 000 | ↑ |
| *less* Taxation | 30 000 | |
| Profit after taxation | 50 000 | |
| *less* Proposed dividend | 20 000 | *work* |
| | 30 000 | *backwards* |
| *less* Transfer to general reserve | 5 000 | |
| Retained profit for the year | 25 000 | |
| Retained profit c/d | 175 000 | |
| Balance of profits | 200 000 | |

Many students find this difficult, so let us just look at what happened by referring to Ranpgill's balance sheets for 19X0 and 19X1.

The retained profit as at 31.12.X1 is £200 000, whereas it was only £175 000 as at 31.12.X0. We can, therefore, conclude that this year's trading has achieved a profit of £25 000. But remember, this is after making certain appropriations. In our example, these are:

- *Transfer to reserves.* In our case this is £5 000 as general reserves have grown from £5 000 (19X0) to £10 000 (19X1)
- *Proposed dividend and taxation.* You will note that I have added back the amount outstanding as at 31.12.X1 and *not* the difference between the two years.

2 You must then add items not involving the flow of funds, i.e. cash which, as you know, includes depreciation (since this is a bookkeeping entry and not a cash item). The depreciation for the year is £10 000 (£52 000 in Year 1 to £62 000 in Year 2). As this amount has previously been deducted from profit we must now add it back.

**Increases and decreases in working capital: items excluding cash**

3 The figures are obtained by looking at the movements in the items of working capital over the two years. But remember: in doing so you must ask yourself, has this caused an increase or decrease in working capital? Do not simply list all increases and deduct all decreases.

For example, while creditors have increased by £20 000 (£10 000 to £30 000), this represents a decrease in working capital.

**Returns on investments and servicing of finance**

4 *Dividends*. The amount which has been *paid* is £10 000, the amount outstanding as at 31.12.X0. The proposed dividend of £20 000 as at 31.12.X1 has not yet been paid.

**Taxation**

5 As we are trying to identify the amount which has been *paid*, the figure we use is £20 000 – the amount outstanding as at 31.12.X0. You will recall that the amount outstanding at 31.12.X1 is still outstanding and, if the company was incorporated after 1.4.65, not due for payment until nine months after the end of its accounting period.

**Investing activities**

6 We can see from the difference between the two balance sheets that £36 000 of fixed assets have been purchased.

**Financing**

7 These items are found simply by looking at differences between the two balance sheets.

**PROGRESS TEST 1**

Draw up a Cash Flow Statement for Sandersons PLC for the year ending 31.12.Y2.

*Balance Sheet of Sandersons PLC as at:*

| | 31.12.Y1 | 31.12.Y2 | | 31.12.Y1 | 31.12.Y2 |
|---|---|---|---|---|---|
| | £ | £ | | £ | £ |
| *Fixed assets* (Cost) | 212 000 | 365 000 | Share capital | 150 000 | 175 000 |
| – Depreciation | 10 000 | 20 000 | General reserve | 20 000 | 25 000 |
| | 202 000 | 345 000 | | | |
| | | | Profit and loss a/c | 36 127 | 50 200 |
| | | | | 206 127 | 250 200 |
| *Current assets* | | | | | |
| Stock | 36 105 | 40 000 | 10% Debenture | 10 000 | 30 000 |
| Debtors | 29 761 | 17 000 | | 216 127 | 280 200 |
| Prepayments | 361 | 200 | Taxation | 12 000 | 21 000 |
| Cash | 100 | 1 000 | Creditors | 30 000 | 40 000 |
| | | | Accrual | 200 | 2 000 |
| | | | Proposed dividend | 8 000 | 15 000 |
| | | | Bank overdraft | 2 000 | 45 000 |
| | 268 327 | 403 200 | | 268 327 | 403 200 |

## ■ THE PURCHASE AND SALE OF FIXED ASSETS DURING THE YEAR

So far we have ignored the situation where a company both buys and sells assets during the year, e.g.

*Balance Sheet of Wire Mesh Ltd as at 31.12.X7 and X8*

| | 19X7 | 19X8 | | 19X7 | 19X8 |
|---|---|---|---|---|---|
| | £ | £ | | £ | £ |
| *Fixed assets* | | | | | |
| *(cost)* | 40 000 | 70 000 | Share capital | 20 000 | 25 000 |
| – Depreciation | 10 000 | 15 000 | Profit and loss a/c | 8 000 | 5 000 |
| | 30 000 | 55 000 | | 28 000 | 30 000 |
| *Current assets* | | | Loan | 5 000 | 10 000 |
| Stock | 10 000 | 20 000 | | 33 000 | 40 000 |
| Debtors | 5 000 | 1 000 | | | |
| Bank | 6 000 | 1 000 | Creditors | 8 000 | 32 000 |
| | | | Proposed dividend | 10 000 | 5 000 |
| | 51 000 | 77 000 | | 51 000 | 77 000 |

*Notes:*

1 Profit before taxation £2 000

2 Fixed assets which had cost £3 000, and which had been depreciated by £1 000, were sold during the year for £2 500.

**Procedure**

1 *Calculate the profit or loss on sale.*

| | £ |
|---|---|
| Cost | 3 000 |
| – Depreciation | 1 000 |
| Book value | 2 000 |
| Sale proceeds | 2 500 |
| – Book value | 2 000 |
| Book profit | 500 |

NB: This is only a bookkeeping profit (i.e. the amount we received over the book value). It is, therefore, an item which does not involve the flow of funds and will be deducted from profit before tax under our calculation of net cash inflow/outflow from 'operating activities'.

The actual proceeds received (and, therefore, an inflow) are included under the heading 'investing activities'.

2 *Calculate the movement in fixed assets.*

| | Cost | Depreciation | Book value |
|---|---|---|---|
| | £ | £ | £ |
| Balance sheet 19X7 (see above) | 40 000 | 10 000 | 30 000 |
| *less* Sale (see note 2) | 3 000 | 1 000 | 2 000 |
| | 37 000 | 9 000 | 28 000 |
| *add* Additions | 33 000 | 6 000 | 27 000 |
| Balance sheet 19X8 (see above) | 70 000 | 15 000 | 55 000 |

By deduction, we can see that Wire Mesh Ltd purchased £33 000 of fixed assets and charged depreciation of £6 000 during the year.

3 *Construct the cash flow statement using the information calculated in stages 1 and 2 above.*

*Cash flow statement of Wire Mesh Ltd for year ended 31.12.X8*

| | £ | £ |
|---|---|---|
| **Operating activities** | | |
| Net profit before tax and interest | 2 000 | |
| Depreciation for year | 6 000 | |
| Profit on sale of fixed asset | (500) | |
| Increase in stock | (10 000) | |
| Decrease in debtors | 4 000 | |
| Increase in creditors | 24 000 | |
| Net cash inflow from operating activities | | 25 500 |
| **Returns on investments and servicing of finance** | | |
| Dividend paid | (10 000) | |
| | | (10 000) |
| **Taxation** | | |
| Taxation | NIL | |
| | | NIL |
| **Investing activities** | | |
| Purchase of fixed assets | (33 000) | |
| Sale of fixed assets | 2 500 | |
| Net outflow from investing activities | | (30 500) |
| **Financing** | | |
| Cash received from issue of shares | 5 000 | |
| Cash received from loan | 5 000 | |
| Net inflow from financing | | 10 000 |
| **Decrease in cash/bank** | | (5 000) |
| **Analysis of changes in cash/bank during year** | | |
| *Balance at start of year* | | |
| Cash | — | |
| Bank | 6 000 | |
| | | 6 000 |
| *Balance at end of year* | | |
| Cash | — | |
| Bank | 1 000 | |
| | | 1 000 |
| ***Net cash outflow*** | | (5 000) |

## ■ ANALYSIS OF THE CASH FLOW STATEMENT

### Financial policy

As we have stated, the Cash Flow Statement provides the reader with an indication of the financial policy adopted by the company and its effect on the company's financial position, e.g. financing long-term investments and overtrading.

#### *Financing long-term investments*

Analysis of the Cash Flow Statement will reveal how the company have financed their long-term investments, such as the purchase of fixed assets.

The purchase of long-term investments should be financed by the raising of long-term finance, such as share issues, retained profits or loans.

In the case of Wire Mesh Ltd above, we can clearly see that the purchase of £33 000 fixed assets has *not* been financed by the raising of long-term finance (profits, share issues and loans only equal £17 500 when added together).

The purchase has, obviously, been achieved by reducing the period available to debtors, reducing the bank balance and, in particular, by increasing the credit from suppliers.

This situation can only continue for so long, as debtors may begin to look elsewhere, the bank may refuse to extend the overdraft and creditors may demand repayment.

#### *Overtrading*

Many companies, and this may go for Wire Mesh Ltd, suffer from overtrading, i.e. from attempting to expand too quickly by accepting large, or additional, orders which require additional working capital and leave little resources for the day-to-day business.

For example, suppose the level of production in Year 1 was 1 000 bed mattresses per week, which they sold to bed manufacturers on cash terms. In Year 2, however, they accepted an order for 2 000 mattresses per week from one of the brand leaders, with payment on credit terms of 2 months. The acceptance of this order has resulted in:

(a) the need for new machinery;
(b) an increase in stock;
(c) a reduction in the bank balance, and
(d) an increase in the supply of raw materials (creditors).

What also tends to happen in such situations is that the normal business is neglected in an attempt to satisfy the large order, which may then lead to the loss of 'bread and butter' business making the company dependent on the large contract.

## ■ SUMMARY

1 FRS 1 makes it obligatory for all businesses to publish a Cash Flow Statement.

2 This statement shows where funds have come from and where they have gone.

3 Examples of sources are:

- profits;
- sale of fixed assets;
- issue of shares;
- borrowing long term.

4 Applications include:

- losses
- purchase of fixed assets
- repaying loans
- paying taxation
- paying dividends

5 Adjustments must be made for items not involving the flow of funds, e.g. depreciation, which is merely a bookkeeping entry and book profits.

6 In working back towards profit before taxation, add back the taxation and proposed dividends of Year 2.

7 The tax and dividends which have been paid are an outflow of funds, and are the amounts in the Balance Sheet for Year 1.

8 Where the company has purchased and sold assets during the year you will need to:

(a) calculate the profit on sale (which is a book profit);
(b) calculate the movements in fixed assets.

9 The Cash Flow Statement provides an indication of the financial policy adopted by the company and its effects on the company's financial position.

10 Analysis will reveal how the company finance their long-term investments.

11 The purchase of long-term investments should be financed by the raising of long-term finance, such as share issues, retained profits or loans, otherwise the company may be short of working capital for their day-to-day business.

12 Overtrading is where companies attempt to expand too quickly.

13 Overtrading may result in:

(a) an increase in fixed assets;
(b) an increase in stock;
(c) reduction in credit given to debtors;
(d) reduction in the bank balance;
(e) increase in credit taken from suppliers.

14 You are advised to read the 'Signpost' article 'Cash Flow Statements: make sure you are ready' which is reproduced in Chapter 20.

## SELF-ASSESSMENT QUESTIONS

1 From the following information, prepare a Cash Flow Statement (funds flow statement) for the year ended 30 April 1989.

The company deals in television sets, both selling and hiring them.

*Profit and Loss Accounts years ended 30 April*

| | 1989 | | 1988 | |
|---|---|---|---|---|
| | £ | £ | £ | £ |
| Net profit for the year after charging: | | 21 871 | | 13 550 |
| Depreciation on shop fittings | 5 942 | | 4 102 | |
| Depreciation on TV sets for rental | 10 537 | | 8 275 | |
| Depreciation on motor vehicles | 5 070 | | 4 510 | |
| Directors' remuneration | 25 000 | | 24 000 | |
| Bank charges | 691 | | 1 209 | |
| Provision for bad debts | 1 340 | | 696 | |
| *less* Provision for corporation tax on the profits of the year | | 5 100 | | 4 300 |
| | | 16 771 | | 9 250 |
| Profit on sale of motor vehicles | | 285 | | — |
| Loss on sale of TV sets for rental | | — | | 205 |
| | | 17 056 | | 9 045 |
| *less* Dividends proposed | | 1 500 | | 1 000 |
| | | 15 556 | | 8 045 |
| Retained profits brought forward | | 25 142 | | 17 097 |
| | | 40 698 | | 25 142 |
| Transfer to general reserve | | 10 000 | | — |
| Retained profits carried forward | | 30 698 | | 25 142 |

*Note:*
In the year ended 30 April 1988, TV sets for rental were sold for £750. These had originally cost £8 200 and had been written down to £955.

In the year ended 30 April 1989, motor vehicles were sold for £4 250. These had originally cost £10 500 and had been written down to £3 965.

*Balance sheets at 30 April*

| | 1989 | | 1988 | |
|---|---|---|---|---|
| | £ | £ | £ | £ |
| *Fixed assets* | | | | |
| Shop fittings at cost | 38 189 | | 33 189 | |
| *less* Aggregate depreciation | 15 362 | 22 827 | 9 420 | 23 769 |
| TV sets for rental at cost | 39 250 | | 39 250 | |
| *less* Aggregate depreciation | 28 712 | 10 538 | 18 175 | 21 075 |
| Motor vehicles at cost | 38 200 | | 27 200 | |
| *less* Aggregate depreciation | 6 670 | 31 530 | 8 135 | 19 065 |
| | | 64 895 | | 63 909 |
| *Current assets* | | | | |
| Stock of TV sets for sale | 24 107 | | 19 206 | |
| Debtors | 10 134 | | 12 101 | |
| Prepaid expenses | 1 786 | | 952 | |
| Cash at bank | 11 200 | | — | |
| | 47 227 | | 32 259 | |
| *less Current liabilities* | | | | |
| Creditors | 14 019 | | 17 803 | |
| Accrued expenses | 805 | | 737 | |
| Bank overdraft | — | | 7 186 | |
| Provisions for corporation tax | 5 100 | | 4 300 | |
| Proposed dividends | 1 500 | | 1 000 | |
| | 21 424 | 25 803 | 31 026 | 1 233 |
| | | 90 698 | | 65 142 |
| *Share capital and reserves* | | | | |
| Issued share capital | 30 000 | | 25 000 | |
| Share premium account | 10 000 | | 5 000 | |
| General reserve | 20 000 | | 10 000 | |
| Profit and loss account | 30 698 | 90 698 | 25 142 | 65 142 |

(CIB May 1989)

2 The balance sheets of Trapper, a trader, at 30 June 1990 and 1991 were as follows:

*Balance sheets at 30 June 1990 and 1991*

| | 30 June 1990 £000 | 30 June 1990 £000 | 30 June 1991 £000 | 30 June 1991 £000 |
|---|---|---|---|---|
| *Fixed assets* | | | | |
| Fixed assets at cost | | 200 | | 300 |
| *Less:* accumulated depreciation | | 100 | | 130 |
| | | 100 | | 170 |
| *Current assets* | | | | |
| Stock | 90 | | 120 | |
| Debtors | 110 | | 150 | |
| Cash | 50 | | — | |
| | 250 | | 270 | |
| *Current liabilities* (due within 1 year) | | | | |
| Trade creditors | 70 | | 95 | |
| Overdraft | — | | 20 | |
| | 70 | | 115 | |
| | | 180 | | 155 |
| | | 280 | | 325 |
| Debenture repayable 1999 | | — | | 40 |
| | | 280 | | 285 |
| *Financed by:* | | | | |
| Capital at 1 July | | 275 | | 280 |
| Profit for year | | 35 | | 50 |
| Drawings | | (30) | | (45) |
| | | 280 | | 285 |

You are given the following additional information:

1 The company did not dispose of any fixed assets during the year to 30 June 1991.
2 It is not expected to invest in extra capacity in the foreseeable future.
3 It is anticipated that the trading results of the year to 30 June 1991 will be repeated in future years.

*Required:*
(a) Prepare a funds flow statement (Cash Flow Statement) for Trapper for the year to 30 June 1991. (8)
(b) Calculate Trapper's working capital ratio and liquidity ratio at 30 June 1990 and 30 June 1991. (3)
(c) Discuss the financial progress of Trapper during the year to 30 June 1991 and comment on the firm's likely future prospects. (10)
*Note:* Work to one decimal place.
(Total – 20 marks)
(CIB October 1991)

3 Mr Schooner, a shopkeeper, is a customer of the bank for which you work. He is worried because the shop's current account has become overdrawn, despite the fact that he is sure that profits are being made. He supplies you with the following balance sheets and information.

*Balance sheets at 31 March 1989 and 1990*

| | *31 March 1989* | | *31 March 1990* | |
|---|---|---|---|---|
| | £000 | £000 | £000 | £000 |
| Fixed assets at cost | | 25 000 | | 50 000 |
| *Less* accumulated depreciation | | 15 000 | | 20 000 |
| | | 10 000 | | 30 000 |
| Stock | 14 600 | | 21 100 | |
| Debtors | 12 900 | | 15 030 | |
| Cash | 2 310 | | — | |
| | 29 810 | | 36 130 | |
| Trade creditors | 9 280 | | 12 830 | |
| Bank overdraft | — | | 16 200 | |
| | 9 280 | | 29 030 | |
| | | 20 530 | | 7 100 |
| | | 30 530 | | 37 100 |
| *Less* loan | | 5 000 | | — |
| | | 25 530 | | 37 100 |
| Financed by: | | | | |
| Capital account balance | | 25 530 | | 37 100 |

Other information relating to the year to 31 March 1990:

1 Schooner's cash drawings for the year were £13 000.
2 In January 1990 Schooner won a Premium Bond prize of £1 000 and paid this into the shop's bank account.
3 During the year he purchased a new delivery van and made improvements to the shop. He reports that these changes have led to a significant increase in turnover.
4 There were no disposals of fixed assets during the year.

*Required:*
(a) Calculate Schooner's trading profit for the year to 31 March 1990. (4)
(b) Prepare a funds flow statement (cash flow statement) for Schooner for the year to 31 March 1990. (10)
(c) Prepare a brief explanation for Schooner of why the shop's cash balance has declined despite the fact that a profit was made. (6)
(Total – 20 marks)
(CIB May 1990)

# 17 Reconciliation statements

**OBJECTIVES**

**After studying this chapter you should be able to:**

1. **Explain the nature and purpose of reconciliation statements;**
2. **Produce reconciliation statements;**
3. **Outline what action, if any, should be taken following the production of such statements.**

## ■ INTRODUCTION – WHAT ARE RECONCILIATION STATEMENTS?

Reconciliation statements are statements drawn up to confirm whether or not the entries in two separate records, which relate to the same transaction, are compatible, for example:

- is the cash book kept by the company compatible with the bank statement?
- is the purchase ledger relating to an amount owed to a supplier compatible with the statement of account received from the supplier?

A reconciliation statement could also be used to indicate the movements in, say the bank account, by reconciling the opening balance and the closing balance.

Let us have a closer look at these statements and consider how they are produced.

## ■ BANK RECONCILIATION STATEMENTS

If you are like me, you may well have received a bank statement which informs you that your account is in credit when you know that if all the cheques you had written were presented your account would be overdrawn. A bank reconciliation statement will indicate why the two records do not agree and indicate any items which have been forgotten by the account holder or which have been entered in error by the bank.

**Example**

Hughes Supplies Ltd has, today, received its bank statement which shows the balance at the close of business on 31.1.Y0 as £4 290. It cannot understand this as its own records indicate the balance should be only £2 700.

Draw a bank reconciliation statement to explain the difference:

*Cash book*

| | | | | | |
|---|---|---|---|---|---|
| 01.1.Y0 | Balance b/f | £2 000 | 02.1.Y0 | Purchases | £400 |
| 08.1.Y0 | V Brown | £1 000 | 06.1.Y0 | Purchases | £200 |
| 11.1.Y0 | D Firth | £750 | 10.1.Y0 | Wages | £500 |
| 28.1.Y0 | I Hardy (a) | £600 | | | |
| | | | 30.1.Y0 | Electricity DD | £200 |
| | | | 30.1.Y0 | Purchases | £350 (b) |
| | | | 31.1.Y0 | Balance c/d | £2 700 |
| | | £4 350 | | | £4 350 |

*Bank statement*

| *Date* | | | *Payments* | *Receipts* | *Balance* |
|---|---|---|---|---|---|
| 01.1.Y0 | Opening balance | | | | 2 000 Cr |
| 08.1.Y0 | Cheque 01234 | | 200 | | 1 800 Cr |
| 10.1.Y0 | Cash | (c) | 500 | | 1 300 Cr |
| 12.1.Y0 | Direct debit Pacific Ins Co | (c) | 300 | | 1 000 Cr |
| 13.1.Y0 | Credit | | | 1 750 | 2 750 Cr |
| 15.1.Y0 | Cheque 01233 | | 400 | | 2 350 Cr |
| 25.1.Y0 | Credit | | | 2 150 (d) | 4 500 Cr |
| 30.1.Y0 | Direct debit: electricity | | 200 | | 4 300 Cr |
| 31.1.Y0 | Charges | (c) | 10 | | 4 290 Cr |

**Procedure**

1 Check that the opening balance of both the cash book and the bank statement agree. In our examples they do and we can, therefore, proceed but we shall look at an example where the balances do not agree later.

2 Tick off the entries which are common to both records.

*Note*: A credit on the bank statement may be made up of a number of cheques received from various customers, e.g. 13.1.Y0. Credit £1 750 was made up of cheques received from:

| | |
|---|---|
| V Brown | £1 000 |
| A Firth | £750 |
| | £1 750 |

Also note that cheques are not necessarily presented in the order they were issued so you may have to search for common entries.

3 At most, you will be left with four sets of unmatched items.

(a) Items recorded as receipts by the company in its cash book but not credited in the bank statement, e.g. cheques received from suppliers but which the company has yet to pay in at the bank or, alternatively, bank giro credits still in the bank's clearing.

(b) Items recorded as payments by the company in its cash book but not deducted in the bank statement, e.g. cheques issued to supplier which have not been presented for payment.

(c) Items deducted in the bank statement but not recorded in the cash book by the company, e.g. standing orders and bank charges which the company may easily forget.
(d) Items credited in the bank statement but not recorded in the cash book by the company.

Items (c) and (d) may, therefore, need entering in the cash book to bring it up to date which we shall consider later.

It is also possible, however, that (c) and (d) represent items credited or debited in error by the bank, which would need to be brought to the bank's attention.

4 Draw up a bank reconciliation statement, i.e. start with the bank statement balance and work towards the cash book balance (or vice versa) by entering the unmatched items.

*Note*: Be careful when dealing with overdrawn accounts.

*Bank Reconciliation Statement as at 31.1.Y0*

| | £ | £ |
|---|---|---|
| Balance as per bank statement | | 4 290 |
| (a) *add* banking/lodgements not credited | | 600 |
| | | 4 890 |
| (b) *less* unpresented charges | | 350 |
| | | 4 540 |
| (c) *add* outgoings not entered in the cash book | | |
| Direct Debit: Pacific Ins Co | 300 | |
| Charges | 10 | 310 |
| | | 4 850 |
| (d) *less* receipts not entered in the cash book | | |
| balance as per bank statement | | 2 150 |
| | | 2 700 |

(a) and (b) are straightforward – they have been entered in the cash book but not in the statement, therefore, add or deduct them from the bank balance as if they were presented at the bank.

(c) and (d) are more difficult. The statement balance which we are working from already includes these items so we must *cancel out their effect*, hence outgoings are added back and receipts are deducted.

As stated earlier, you could start with the cash book balance and work towards the bank statement balance, both are acceptable, but be careful the additions and subtractions are not the same.

*Bank Reconciliation Statement as at 31.1.Y0*

| | £ | £ |
|---|---|---|
| Balance as per cash book | | 2 700 |
| *less* Outgoings not entered in the cash book | | |
| Direct Debit Pacific Ins Co | 300 | |
| Bank charges | 10 | 310 |
| | | 2 390 |
| *add* receipts not entered in the cash book | 2 150 | |
| | | 4 540 |
| *less* Banking/lodgements not credited | | 600 |
| | | 3 940 |
| *add* Unpresented cheques | | 350 |
| Balance as per bank statement | | 4 290 |

**PROGRESS TEST 1**

Mr Brown calls at your bank and complains that some errors have occurred on his account. He shows you the bank statement he has received recently, which closes with an overdrawn balance of £72.68. He also shows you his cash book which has a closing overdraft of £266.87. 'I'm not complaining', he says, 'but I thought I ought to point out your mistakes to you, because your auditors will no doubt catch up on them eventually. You were all right only a month ago.'

*Cash Book*

| | | | | | |
|---|---|---|---|---|---|
| March | 1 Balance | 1 027.34 | March | 10 Car road tax | 100.00 |
| | 2 Wood & Co | 32.65 | | 11 PAYE | 352.96 |
| | 4 Green Ltd | 125.46 | | 11 Brown | 82.37 |
| | 5 John Bull | 86.33 | | 11 Smith | 41.87 |
| | 10 Downs Ltd | 13.41 | | 11 Major Stores | 125.42 |
| | 11 J Parker | 37.84 | | 11 Ajax Garage | 91.35 |
| | 11 M Lees | 23.15 | | 20 The Stores | 21.37 |
| | 11 D Orton | 129.37 | | 20 Petty Cash | 50.00 |
| | 15 Broomhead Ltd | 241.65 | | 26 British Rail | 32.15 |
| | 15 Lesser & Co | 123.92 | | 30 J Saunders | 159.27 |
| | 16 Alexander | 351.27 | | 30 John Benson | 34.27 |
| | 18 John Bull | 86.33 | | 30 H Burgess | 85.16 |
| | 20 M Sanger | 13.26 | | 20 Wages | 2 150.62 |
| | 20 B Bollins | 135.82 | | | |
| | 20 Best Bookshops | 21.85 | | | |
| | 22 Trading Centre | 81.37 | | | |
| | 22 Town Council | 21.39 | | | |
| | 22 M Parker | 144.18 | | | |
| | 26 H Johnson | 31.42 | | | |
| | 26 J Charles | 113.24 | | | |
| | 31 M Higgins | 93.27 | | | |
| | 31 J Brown | 125.42 | | | |
| | | 3 059.94 | | | |
| | Balance c/d | 266.87 | | | |
| | | 3 326.81 | | | 3 326.81 |

*Bank Statement*

| | | | *Dr* | *Cr* | *Balance* |
|---|---|---|---|---|---|
| March | 1 | Balance | | | 1 027.34 Cr |
| | 2 | Sundries | | 32.65 | 1 059.99 Cr |
| | 5 | Sundries | | 211.79 | 1 271.78 Cr |
| | 12 | Sundries | | 203.77 | 1 475.55 Cr |
| | 13 | 015 | 352.96 | | 1 122.59 Cr |
| | 14 | 019 | 91.35 | | 1 031.24 Cr |
| | 14 | Standing Order | 13.10 | | 1 018.14 Cr |
| | 16 | 014 | 100 00 | | 918.14 Cr |
| | 16 | Sundries | | 716.84 | 1 634.98 Cr |
| | 18 | 016 | 82.37 | | 1 552.61 Cr |
| | 18 | 018 | 125.42 | | 1 427.19 Cr |
| | 20 | Sundries | | 257.26 | 1 684.45 Cr |
| | | VAT refund | | 137.81 | 1 822.26 Cr |
| | | Bank Charges | 25.70 | | 1 796.56 Cr |
| | | Interest | 18.35 | | 1 778.21 Cr |
| | | 021 | 50.00 | | 1 728.21 Cr |
| | 23 | 017 | 41.87 | | 1 686.34 Cr |
| | | Sundries | | 246.94 | 1 933.28 Cr |
| | 30 | 026 | 2 150.62 | | 217. 34 o/d |
| | | Sundries | | 144.66 | 72.68 o/d |

*Required:*

(a) A reconciliation statement as at 31 March.

(b) A note of the action, if any, which Mr Brown needs to take.

*(Specimen question (CIB))*

## ■ UPDATING THE CASH BOOK

Let us go back to Hughes Supplies Ltd. Should the items entered on the bank statement belong to the company, the cash book will need bringing up to date, e.g.

*Cash Book*

| | £ | | £ |
|---|---|---|---|
| Balance b/f | 2 700 | Direct debit | |
| | | Pacific Ins Co | 300 |
| Credit | 2 150 | Bank charges | 10 |
| | | Balance c/d | 4 540 |
| | 4 850 | | 4 850 |

We can then produce a bank reconciliation statement using the updated cash book balance.

*Bank Reconciliation Statement as at 31.1.Y0*

| | £ |
|---|---|
| Balance as per cash book | 4 540 |
| *less* Bankings (lodgements) not credited | 600 |
| | 3 940 |
| *add* Unpresented cheques | 350 |
| Balance as per bank statement | 4 290 |

*Examination*: Unless asked to do so I would not bring the cash book up to date as the unmatched items may not belong to the company.

## ■ DIFFERENT OPENING BALANCES

**Example**

West Bank Ltd have received their bank statement for the month ending 28.2.Y0 but cannot reconcile this with their cash book.

*Bank Statement*

| | | | *Payments* | *Receipts* | *Balance* |
|---|---|---|---|---|---|
| Feb | 1 | Opening Balance | | | 2 551.88 Cr |
| | 2 | Credit | | 136.79 | 2 688.67 Cr |
| | 5 | Credit | | 121.10 | 2 809.77 Cr |
| | 6 | Cheque 1042 | 50.00 | | 2 759.77 Cr |
| | 15 | Bank giro credit | | 400.00 | 3 159.77 Cr |
| | 17 | Direct debit. Water | 40.00 | | 3 119.77 Cr |
| | 20 | Cheque 1047 | 51.11 | | 3 068.66 Cr |
| | 22 | Standing order. Rent | 30.00 | | 3 038.66 Cr |
| | 27 | Credit | | 360.00 | 3 398.66 Cr |
| | 28 | Credit | | 120.00 | 3 518.66 Cr |
| | 28 | Cheque 1051 | 20.00 | | 3 498.66 Cr |

*Cash Book*

| | | £ | | | | £ | |
|---|---|---|---|---|---|---|---|
| Feb | 1 | Balance c/f | 2 638.67 | Feb | 6 | Electricity | 50.00 |
| | 2 | Sales B Black | 121.10 | | 17 | Purchases | 51.11 |
| | 10 | Sales K Allan | 200.00 | | 22 | Rent | 30.00 |
| | 12 | Sales A Burke | 175.00 | | 28 | Cash | 20.00 |
| | 14 | Sales P Platt | 25.00 | | 28 | Fixtures | 1 500.00 |
| | 22 | Sales V Gardner | 120.00 | | | | |
| | 26 | Sales J Mannion | 240.00 | | | | |
| | | | | | 28 | Balance c/d | 1 868.66 |
| | | | 3 519.77 | | | | 3 519.77 |

At first sight we cannot tick off the opening balances as they do not agree.

When faced with this problem, find the difference – in our case £86.79. Then look to see if there are any items on the bank statement which might have appeared in the cash book for the previous period and, therefore, be part of the opening balance of £2 638.67. Alternatively, items may appear on the cash book and relate to past bank statements.

In this example it would seem that the following entries appeared in the cash book in the previous period.

| | | |
|---|---|---|
| Feb 2 | Credit | £136.79 |
| Feb 6 | Cheque | – £50.00 |
| Net | | £86.79 |

We can, therefore tick off the opening bank statement balance and these items against the opening cash bank balance and proceed as normal.

**PROGRESS TEST 2**

Prepare a bank reconciliation statement for West Bank Ltd from the information above.

A reconciliation statement could also be drawn up in a similar manner to reconcile the purchase ledger of the company with the statement of account received from their supplier.

## ■ RECONCILING THE OPENING AND CLOSING BANK/CASH BALANCE

Rather than asking you to draw up a Statement of Sources and Applications of Funds, the examiner may simply ask you to reconcile the opening bank balance with the closing bank balance. You will, therefore, need to identify:

(a) *Items increasing the balance such as:*

- Net profit
- Depreciation for the year (remember this must be added to profit as it is only a bookkeeping entry
- Proceeds from the sale of fixed assets
- Taking out a loan
- Reduction in stock or debtors (if stock is sold or debtors pay their debts the bank balance will obviously improve); and

(b) *Items decreasing the balance such as:*

- Losses
- Drawings
- Purchase of fixed assets
- Repaying a loan
- Increase in stock or debtors

Such a reconciliation statement may, therefore appear as:

| | £ |
|---|---|
| Opening balance | 1 000 |
| + items increasing the balance | 500 |
| | 1 500 |
| – items reducing the balance | 200 |
| Closing balance | 1 300 |

## ■ SUMMARY

1 Reconciliation statements are statements drawn up to confirm whether or not the entries in two separate records which relate to the same transactions are compatible.

2 Bank reconciliation statements are used to reconcile the cash book maintained by the company and the bank statement produced by the bank.

3 In drawing a reconciliation statement you should:

(a) check that the opening balances agree. If they do not, find the difference and look to see if there are any items on the bank statement which might have appeared in the cash book for the previous period, or vice versa;
(b) tick off all common items (remember a credit on the bank statement may be made up of many entries in the cash book;
(c) identify those items not ticked off;
(d) draw up the reconciliation statement.

4 If requested to do so, the cash book should be brought up to date by inserting the entries which appear on the statement but not in the cash book.

5 Reconciliation statements are also used to reconcile purchase ledger and statements of accounts and opening and closing bank balances.

## ■ SELF-ASSESSMENT QUESTIONS

1 Shown on the next page is the cash book of General Traders Ltd for the month of September 1987, together with the bank statement for that month on the opposite page.

As the company's bookkeeper you are required:

(a) to prepare a bank reconciliation statement as at 30 September; (10)
(b) to state what action (if any) you would take in respect of each item appearing in the reconciliation statement. (10)

*Cash Book*

| | | | £ | | | | £ |
|---|---|---|---|---|---|---|---|
| Sept | 1 | Balance brought forward | 281 | Sept | 1 | Borough Treasurer | 703 |
| | 1 | Ajax | 517 | | 4 | Export Agency | 152 |
| | 1 | Bertram | 72 | | 5 | Publishers Assoc | 55 |
| | 2 | Chorlton | 314 | | 9 | Petty Cash | 50 |
| | 3 | Dennis | 25 | | 9 | British Road | 172 |
| | 4 | Ebury | 152 | | 9 | Customs & Excise | 795 |
| | 5 | Franks | 31 | | 11 | Smithers & Sons | 23 |
| | 8 | Gordons | 234 | | 11 | Blackburn Brothers | 118 |
| | 9 | Hastings | 87 | | 11 | Johnson & Co | 257 |
| | 10 | Ironside | 125 | | 17 | Petty Cash | 80 |
| | 11 | Jolly | 10 | | 17 | Office Services Ltd | 37 |
| | 12 | Kingfisher | 782 | | 17 | Higgins Supplies | 179 |
| | 15 | Leonard | 87 | | 26 | Orb Construction | 217 |
| | 16 | Masters | 131 | | 26 | Thames Water Auth'y | 110 |
| | 17 | Newton | 252 | | 26 | Wages | 752 |
| | 18 | Oliver | 304 | | 30 | Balance c/f | 293 |
| | 19 | Parsons | 57 | | | | |
| | 22 | Quinton | 92 | | | | |
| | 23 | Rogers | 12 | | | | |
| | 24 | Stavely | 15 | | | | |
| | 25 | Thompson | 108 | | | | |
| | 26 | Ullyses | 92 | | | | |
| | 29 | Victor | 178 | | | | |
| | 30 | Watson | 35 | | | | |
| | | | 3 993 | | | | 3 993 |

*Bank Statement*

| *Date* | | *Particulars* | *Debits* | *Credits* | *Balance* |
|---|---|---|---|---|---|
| Sept | 1 | Balance forward | | | 281 |
| | 2 | Paid in | | 903 | 1 184 |
| | 5 | 081 | 703 | | |
| | | Paid in | | 208 | 689 |
| | 7 | 084 | 50 | | |
| | | Paid in | | 321 | |
| | | Bank giro credit – Jones | | 825 | 1 785 |
| | 10 | 083 | 55 | | |
| | | Paid in | | 125 | 1 855 |
| | 12 | 082 | 152 | | |
| | | 087 | 795 | | |
| | | Paid in | | 792 | 1 700 |
| | 17 | 085 | 117 | | |
| | | 086 | 172 | | |
| | | 091 | 80 | | |
| | | Paid in | | 218 | 1 549 |
| | 18 | Returned cheque | 782 | | 767 |
| | 19 | 089 | 118 | | |
| | | Paid in | | 613 | 1 262 |
| | 23 | Direct debit – Moon Ins Co | 375 | | |
| | | 088 | 23 | | |
| | | Dividend – Excelsior Tdg plc | | 35 | 899 |
| | 26 | 093 | 179 | | |
| | | Paid in | | 319 | 1 039 |
| | 30 | Bank charges | 97 | | |
| | | 092 | 37 | | |
| | | 094 | 217 | | |
| | | 096 | 752 | | 64 o/d |

(CIB November 1987)

2 Ken owns a hardware store. He gives you a copy of his 1987 accounts (reproduced below) and says: 'I do not understand what has gone wrong. My turnover this last year has been the best ever, and my customers owe me less money than before, but despite cutting my drawings to a minimum I have ended the year with an overdraft'.

*Required*:

(a) A short report for Ken explaining why his cash position has worsened in the year. (10)

(b) A statement reconciling his bank balance on 30 June 1987 with the balance a year earlier. (10)

*Balance sheets as at 30 June*

| | 1987 | | 1986 | |
|---|---|---|---|---|
| | £ | £ | £ | £ |
| *Fixed assets* | | | | |
| Shop fittings and equipment at cost | 8 781 | | 7 206 | |
| *less* Depreciation | 3 829 | 4 952 | 3 109 | 4 097 |
| Motor car – at cost | 6 250 | | 2 510 | |
| *less* Depreciation | 500 | 5 750 | 1 960 | 550 |
| | | 10 702 | | 4 647 |
| *Current assets* | | | | |
| Stock | 31 159 | | 22 015 | |
| Debtors | 351 | | 724 | |
| Bank | — | | 3 417 | |
| | 31 510 | | 26 156 | |
| *Current liabilities* | | | | |
| Sundry creditors and accrued expenses | 15 079 | | 13 215 | |
| Bank overdraft | 3 442 | | — | |
| | 18 521 | 12 989 | 13 215 | 12 941 |
| | | 23 691 | | 17 588 |
| *Capital account* | | | | |
| Balance brought forward | 17 588 | | 17 202 | |
| *add* Net profit for year | 19 871 | | 16 309 | |
| | 37 459 | | 33 511 | |
| *less* Drawings | 13 768 | 23 691 | 15 923 | 17 588 |

*Extracts from Profit and Loss Accounts*

| | *Year to 30/6/87* | *Year to 30/6/86* |
|---|---|---|
| Sales | 170 452 | 143 219 |
| Gross profit | 50 795 | 45 257 |
| Net profit | 19 871 | 16 309 |
| after charging: | | |
| depreciation | 1 200 | 874 |
| advertising | 4 500 | 3 700 |
| bank interest | 216 | — |
| and crediting: | | |
| profit on sale of car | 400 | — |

(CIB November 1987)

3 The cashier of Wrecker Ltd balanced the company's cash book at the end of July 1990 and found that it showed an overdraft of £27 392. The balance on the company's bank statement of the same date was an overdraft of £23 570.

Investigations showed the difference between these two balances to be caused by the following:

1 A standing order for rates of £1 700 was charged in the bank statement on 2 July 1990.
2 An entry on the bank statement dated 31 July showed that Buyit Ltd, a debtor of Wrecker Ltd, has settled its outstanding balance of £3 400 by direct credit of £3 200; the difference was due to a prompt payment discount.
3 A cheque for £532 had been wrongly charged to Wrecker Ltd's bank account; it should have been charged to the account of Wretched Ltd, a company which banks at the same branch.
4 Bank charges of £1 853 for the three months to 30 June 1990 were charged to the account on 2 July 1990.
5 At 31 July 1990 cheques drawn by Wrecker Ltd but not yet presented amounted to £15 326.
6 The cashier had entered the firm's receipts of £10 619 for 31 July 1990 in the cash book on that date and taken them to the bank, but they did not appear on the statement until 1 August.

*Required*:
(a) Complete the cash book of Wrecker Ltd for the period to 31 July 1990, starting with the overdrawn balance of £27 392. (8)
(b) Reconcile the balance on Wrecker Ltd's bank statement with the corrected cash book balance computed for part (a). (6)
(c) State what action should be taken in respect of the items which appear in the bank reconciliation at 31 July 1990. (4)
(d) State *two* general benefits to be derived from the regular preparation of bank reconciliation statements. (2)
(Total – 20 marks)
(CIB October 1990)

**4** Mr Matrix set up a business on 1 July 1990 as a window cleaner, and on that day opened a bank account into which he paid £7 000 as capital. During the year to 30 June 1991 the following took place:

1 On 1 July 1990 he bought a second-hand van for £6 000 and a set of ladders for £550.
2 On 2 July 1990 he paid £450 to have a sign painted on the sides of the van, which would last for the life of the van.
3 During the year to 30 June 1991 he received cash from customers of £15 000, and he paid by cheque: £1 025 for sundry materials; £1 500 for motor expenses; and £2 500 for casual labour. He withdrew £750 per month for his own use.
4 At 30 June 1991 he was owed £750 by industrial customers. He himself owed £75 for sundry materials and £85 for motor expenses. He valued the van and ladders at £5 310 and £405 respectively after charging depreciation for the year.
5 All cash receipts were immediately paid into the bank, and all payments were made by cheque. On 30 June 1991 he had issued cheques totalling £890 which had not yet appeared on the bank statement. The last day's takings of £50 (included in the total takings for the year), although banked immediately and entered in the cash book, did not appear on the bank statement until 1 July 1991.

*Required*:
(a) Prepare the cash account of Mr Matrix's business for the year to 30 June 1991. (4)
(b) Calculate the balance which appears on the firm's bank statement at 30 June 1991, and reconcile it with the balance on the cash account prepared in answer to part (a) of this question. (2)
(c) Mr Matrix estimates that the van will last 5 years and have a residual value at the end of that time of £750. Identify and explain which depreciation policy Mr Matrix is using. (2)
(d) Prepare Mr Matrix's profit and loss account for the year to 30 June 1991 and the balance sheet as at that date. (12)
(Total – 20 marks)
(CIB October 1991)

# 18 Ratio analysis

**OBJECTIVES**

**After studying this chapter you should be able to:**

1. **Explain the use of accounting ratios;**
2. **Calculate the various accounting ratios;**
3. **Analyse a company's performance using ratio analysis;**
4. **Outline the limitations of ratios and consider such limitations when analysing company performance.**

## ■ INTRODUCTION – WHAT IS RATIO ANALYSIS?

Ratio analysis is a method of analysing a company's performance over a period of time and can be extremely useful to both the management of the company and bank managers when faced with loan requests.

In the future you may be asked by your manager to calculate various ratios in respect of a customer's account and to discuss your findings with him before he meets the customer.

So let us see how we calculate accounting ratios.

## ■ CALCULATING ACCOUNTING RATIOS

*Trading Profit and Loss Account of Poynton Limited for the years ending 31.12.Y0 and 31.12.Y1*

| | 31.12.Y0 | | 31.12.Y1 | |
|---|---|---|---|---|
| | £ | £ | £ | £ |
| Sales | | 200 000 | | 400 000 |
| *less Cost of goods sold* | | | | |
| Opening stock | 30 000 | | 15 000 | |
| + Purchases | 85 000 | | 165 000 | |
| | 115 000 | | 180 000 | |
| – Closing stock | 15 000 | 100 000 | 30 000 | 150 000 |
| Gross profit | | 100 000 | | 250 000 |
| *less* Expenses | | 80 000 | | 215 000 |
| Net profit before tax | | 20 000 | | 35 000 |
| *less* Taxation | | 7 000 | | 12 000 |
| Retained profit for the year | | 13 000 | | 27 000 |
| +Balance of profits | | 27 000 | | 40 000 |
| Retained profits | | 40 000 | | 67 000 |

*Balance Sheet of Poynton Limited as at 31.12.Y0 and 31.12.Y1*

| | 31.12.Y0 | | 31.12.Y1 | |
|---|---|---|---|---|
| | £ | £ | £ | £ |
| Fixed assets | | 250 000 | | 250 000 |
| *Current assets* | | | | |
| Stock | 15 000 | | 30 000 | |
| Debtors | 30 000 | | 65 000 | |
| Bank | 1 000 | | 4 000 | |
| Cash | 1 000 | | – | |
| *less* | 47 000 | | 99 000 | |
| *Current liabilities* | | | | |
| Taxation | 7 000 | | 12 000 | |
| Creditors | 30 000 | | 50 000 | |
| | 37 000 | 10 000 | 62 000 | 37 000 |
| | | 260 000 | | 287 000 |
| Share capital | | 200 000 | | 200 000 |
| and retained profits | | 40 000 | | 67 000 |
| | | 240 000 | | 267 000 |
| *Long-term liabilities* | | | | |
| Loan | | 20 000 | | 20 000 |
| Capital employed | | 260 000 | | 287 000 |

| | *Ratio* | *Formula* | *19Y0* | *19Y1* |
|---|---|---|---|---|
| A | *Profitability* | | | |
| 1 | Return on capital employed | $\frac{\text{Net profit before tax}}{\text{Capital employed}} \times 100$ | $\frac{20\ 000}{260\ 000} \times 100$ = 7.69% | |
| 2 | Gross profit margin | $\frac{\text{Gross profit}}{\text{Sales}} \times 100$ | $\frac{100\ 000}{200\ 000} \times 100$ = 50% | |
| 3 | Net profit margin | $\frac{\text{Net profit before tax}}{\text{Sales}} \times 100$ | $\frac{20\ 000}{200\ 000} \times 100$ = 10% | |
| B | *Operating performance* | | | |
| 4 | Rate of stock turnover | $\frac{\text{Stock}}{\text{Cost of goods sold}} \times 365$ | $\frac{15\ 000}{100\ 000} \times 365$ = 55 days | |
| 5 | Debtor settlement period | $\frac{\text{Debtors}}{\text{Sales}} \times 365$ | $\frac{30\ 000}{200\ 000} \times 365$ = 55 days | |
| 6 | Creditor settlement period | $\frac{\text{Creditors}}{\text{Purchases}} \times 365$ | $\frac{30\ 000}{85\ 000} \times 365$ = 129 days | |

| | | |
|---|---|---|
| C *Liquidity* | | |
| 7 Working capital ratio | Current assets: current liabilities | 47 000 : 37 000<br>1.27 : 1 |
| 8 Liquidity ratio | Liquid assets: current liabilities<br>(Liquid assets = current assets less stock) | 32 000 : 37 000<br>0.86 : 1 |
| D *Capital adequacy* | | |
| 9 Gearing | $\frac{\text{Long-term liabilities}}{\text{Capital employed}} \times 100$ | $\frac{20\,000}{260\,000} \times 100$ |
| 10 Debt : Equity | Long-term liabilities: shareholders' capital employed | 20 000 : 240 000<br>0.08 : 1 |

**PROGRESS TEST 1**

In the table above I have calculated the ratios for 19Y0. Using the formulae given calculate the ratios for 19Y1.

## ■ INTERPRETATION OF ACCOUNT RATIOS

Having calculated the ratios we must now look at the results and consider what they mean.

In analysing the results we are concerned with the *trend*, i.e. the direction in which the company is going, by comparing the results of 19Y0 with those of 19Y1.

Alternatively, we could use ratio analysis to compare the performance of two companies, but in doing so we must consider the nature of each company's industry, e.g. the ratios of a supermarket will be significantly different from those of an engineering company, simply because of the nature of their business.

### A Profitability

1 *Return on capital employed* – this measures the return on the long-term funds employed in the business and is an indication of whether the company have successfully utilised their assets during the period.

2 *Gross profit margin* – this measures gross profit as a percentage of sales and indicates how effectively the company have controlled the cost of goods sold, e.g.

| | | *19Y0* | | *19Y1* | |
|---|---|---|---|---|---|
| | Sales | £200 | 100% | £400 | 100% |
| *less* | Cost of goods sold | £100 | 50% | £150 | 37.5% |
| | Gross Profit | £100 | 50% | £250 | 62.5% |

Gross profit margin has increased as a result of their ability to control their cost of goods sold.

An increase may also be due to the company's ability to raise the selling price without a corresponding increase in the cost of goods sold. Alternatively, a decrease in the gross margin may be due to a reduction in the selling price against stable costs, though one would hope that the reduced price would bring greater volume sales.

3 *Net profit margin* – this measures net profit as a percentage of sales and indicates how effectively the company have controlled *all* their costs (purchasing/manufacturing and expenses).

| | | *19Y0* | | *19Y1* | |
|---|---|---|---|---|---|
| | | £ | | £ | |
| | ▶ Sales | 200 000 | 100% | 400 000 | 100% |
| *less* | Cost of goods sold | 100 000 | 50% | 150 000 | 37.5% |
| | Gross Profit | 100 000 | 50% | 250 000 | 62.5% |
| *less* | Expenses | 80 000 | 40% | 215 000 | 53.75% |
| | ▶ Net Profit | 20 000 | 10% | 35 000 | 8.75% |

By comparing the gross margin and net margin we can see that the reason for the reduction in net margin was due to the company's failure to control their expenses.

**B Operating performance (*see* Chapter 14, Cash Flow Forecasts)**

4 *Average rate of stock turnover* – this measures how quickly a company is turning its stock. The quicker the turnover the better, as this would speed up the cash flow cycle and ensure that expensive stock is not sat idle on the shelves.

5 *Average debtors settlement period* – how long it takes for debtors to settle their debts.

If the period is increasing companies may need to chase their debtors, but they must be careful not to chase them away. An increased settlement period may be the reason for increased sales.

You must remember that this only indicates the average settlement period (e.g. 55 days, 19Y0). If some of the sales are on cash terms, then some debtors are outstanding for longer than 55 days and the debtors' figure may even include bad debts.

As a result an Aged Analysis of Debtors would prove useful.

Aged Analysis of Debtors

| | Period | Amount |
|---|---|---|
| | 0–7 days | |
| over | 7–14 days | |
| over | 14–21 days | |
| over | 21–28 days | |
| etc. | | |

6 *Average creditors settlement period* – how long it takes the company to pay its creditors.

If the period is getting longer it may be because management are taking full advantage of credit facilities, or it could be that they have a cash flow problem. We should therefore compare this result with our liquidity ratios.

**C Liquidity**

7 *Working capital* (*see* Chapter 15) – whether cash and items which can be converted into cash adequately cover amounts due for repayment.

8 *Liquidity ratio* – by deducting stock from the current assets we are able to compare the most liquid current assets with current liabilities to gain a more critical assessment of liquidity.

You will no doubt recall from our look at the cash flow cycle that stock can take some time before being converted into cash (e.g. stock sold on credit may take 7 months – stock turnover 2 months, debtors settlement period 5 months).

### D Capital adequacy

9 *Gearing* – this examines the extent to which the company rely on borrowed funds. Where companies are highly geared (e.g. above, say, 55%) they are relying heavily on borrowed funds and will be faced with high interest charges and may find it difficult to raise further finance.
10 *Debt : Equity* – this also examines the extent to which the company rely on borrowed funds by comparing debt (funds borrowed long term) with equity (shareholders' funds).

#### PROGRESS TEST 2

Prepare a report on the performance of Poynton Limited during the period 19Y0/Y1.

In commenting upon their performance you are advised to take each ratio in turn and write a sentence on:

(a) what the ratio is designed to show;
(b) the result;
(c) your assessment of the result.

## ■ LIMITATION OF RATIO ANALYSIS

1 The Balance Sheet is only like a photograph of the business at a particular date. It may not be typical of the business. The ratios are therefore only an average.
2 Ratios are taken over the whole business, which may hide certain areas of business which are performing badly.
3 A ratio of 10 per cent can be good or bad. In isolation ratios mean nothing; we must compare either the *trend* or with other companies of a similar nature.
4 Companies may distort the true picture.
5 Reference should be made to the SSAPs adopted, e.g. different methods of valuing stock will produce different profit figures.
6 Inflation must also be considered. An increase in sales may not be an improvement in real terms.
7 Balance Sheet values are based on historical cost which may be out of date and therefore unrealistic.
8 If we only have one set of accounts, i.e. for one year, we are not able to examine the direction in which the company is going.

## ■ CONCLUSION

Ratio analysis is an aid to assessing a company's performance, by examining the *trend* or comparing the company with similar companies.

There are, however, limitations and one should consider other things, e.g.

- cash flow forecasts;
- forecast trading profit and loss account;

- source and application of funds;
- trading outlook;
- management capabilities;

and also consider *why* the trend is increasing or decreasing.

In many ways, ratios point to questions rather than providing answers.

**PROGRESS TEST 3**

A long-established company has approached your bank for a loan, and has supported its request with a copy of its last set of published accounts. Explain the limitations of using *these accounts alone* in this situation. What additional information will you require as the lending banker? (20)
(CIB October 1991)

## ■ SUMMARY

1 Ratio analysis is a method of analysing a company's performance.

2 The most important thing is to examine the *trend.*

3 You will be expected to know the following ratios and I would therefore suggest you learn this table.

| *Ratio* | *Formula* | *Analysis* |
|---|---|---|
| *Profitability* | | |
| 1 Return on capital employed | $\frac{\text{Net profit before tax}}{\text{Capital employed}} \times 100$ | • the return on long-term funds employed in the business<br>• how effectively the company have utilised their assets |
| 2 Gross margin | $\frac{\text{Gross profit}}{\text{Sales}} \times 100$ | • gross profit as a percentage of sales<br>• how effectively the company have controlled their cost of goods sold |
| 3 Net margin | $\frac{\text{Net profit before tax}}{\text{Sales}} \times 100$ | • net profit as a percentage of sales<br>• how effectively the company have controlled *all* their costs |
| *Operating performance* | | |
| 4 Rate of stock turn | $\frac{\text{Stock}}{\text{Costs of goods sold}} \times 365$ | • how quickly the company are turning their stock |
| 5 Debtors' settle-ment period | $\frac{\text{Debtors}}{\text{Sales}} \times 365$ | • how long it takes debtors to settle their debts |
| 6 Creditors' settle-ment period | $\frac{\text{Creditors}}{\text{Purchases}} \times 365$ | • how long it takes the company to pay their creditors |

| | | | |
|---|---|---|---|
| *Liquidity* | | | |
| 7 Working capital | Current assets: Current liabilities | • | whether cash and items which can be converted into cash adequately cover amounts due for repayment |
| 8 Liquidity ratio | Liquid assets: Current liabilities | • | by deducting stock we gain a more critical assessment of liquidity |
| *Capital adequacy* | | | |
| 9 Gearing | $\frac{\text{Long-term liabilities}}{\text{Capital employed}} \times 100$ | • | the extent to which the company rely on borrow funds. |
| 10 Debt: Equity | Long-term liabilities: Shareholders' capital employed | | |

4 Ratio analysis has a number of limitations, e.g.

- balance sheet values may not be representative or typical of the business
- ratios are taken over the whole business
- in isolation ratios mean nothing
- companies may distort the true picture
- reference must be made to the SSAPs adopted
- inflation must also be considered.

5 When analysing a company's performance reference should be made to other sources, e.g. cash flow budget, and consider the management potential and trading outlook.

6 Always consider *why* ratios are increasing or decreasing as there may be either a good or a bad reason.

## ■ SELF-ASSESSMENT QUESTIONS

1 The summarised accounts of Gee-Whiz Electronics Ltd for the last two years are shown below. The company is a wholesaler in the electrical trade.

*Profit and Loss Accounts*

| | 1986 | 1987 |
|---|---|---|
| | £ | £ |
| Sales | 2 154 203 | 3 196 124 |
| *less* Cost of sales | 1 421 774 | 2 301 209 |
| Gross profit | 732 429 | 894 915 |
| *less* Expenses | 581 635 | 627 819 |
| Net profit | 150 794 | 267 096 |
| *less* Taxation | 52 778 | 93 484 |
| Retained profit for year | 98 016 | 173 612 |
| Retained profit brought forward | 151 079 | 249 095 |
| Retained profit carried forward | 249 095 | 422 707 |

*Balance Sheets*

| | 31 December 1986 | | 31 December 1987 | |
|---|---|---|---|---|
| | £ | £ | £ | £ |
| Fixed assets | | 174 917 | | 368 512 |
| *Current assets* | | | | |
| Stock | 125 217 | | 148 217 | |
| Debtors | 317 412 | | 352 140 | |
| Cash | 109 120 | | 99 146 | |
| | 551 749 | | 599 503 | |
| *less* Creditors | 77 571 | 474 178 | 145 308 | 454 195 |
| | | 649 095 | | 822 707 |
| Share capital | | 400 000 | | 400 000 |
| Retained profits | | 249 095 | | 422 707 |
| | | 649 095 | | 822 707 |

*Required:*
Comment upon the changes you can see between the 1986 and 1987 results, calculating and using at least *five* accounting ratios in your review.
(CIB May 1988)

2 Changes have been made in the way each of the following four businesses (A, B, C and D) operate. Suggest (with reasons), for each business, what you think these changes were. Use only the information supplied below.

*Business A*
Gross profit has increased from 25 per cent to 30 per cent. The debtors at the year-end represent 62 days' sales, against 29 days last year. (5)

*Business B*
Gross profit has increased from 40 per cent to 43 per cent. The creditors at the year-end represent 4 days' purchases, against 30 days last year. (5)

*Business C*
The gross profit percentage has remained constant, but the amount of it has doubled. The net profit percentage has doubled. (5)

*Business D*
Sales have increased by 350 per cent. Gross profit percentage has fallen from 50 per cent to 25 per cent. Net profit has increased in amount by 60 per cent. (5)
(CIB November 1987)

3 Consider each of the following statements carefully and say whether you agree or disagree with the statement, giving reasons for your decision.

(a) If sales increase, gross profit must also increase.
(b) If gross profit increases, net profit must also increase.
(c) If depreciation is not charged, there will be no funds for the purchase of a replacement asset.
(d) If debtors take longer to pay it will reduce working capital.
(e) If net profit exceeds drawings, working capital will always increase.

# 19 Break even analysis

**OBJECTIVES**

**After studying this chapter you should be able to:**

**1 Explain the meaning and purpose of break even analysis;**
**2 Distinguish between fixed and variable costs;**
**3 Calculate the break even point;**
**4 Use break even analysis as a decision making tool and planning aid;**
**5 Outline the assumptions on which break even analysis is based.**

## ■ INTRODUCTION – WHAT IS BREAK EVEN ANALYSIS?

Break even analysis is a method of identifying the volume of sales required at a given sales price in order to break even, i.e. in order to cover total costs.

The analysis is based on a number of assumptions which I shall outline in greater depth later. The main assumption on which the analysis is based is that costs can be identified as being either fixed or variable.

## ■ FIXED AND VARIABLE COSTS

### Fixed costs

These are costs which are unaffected by changes in the volume of output, e.g. rates. A company with a rates bill of £1 000 must pay £100 whether they manufacture one item or thousands.

This does not mean that fixed costs will not alter, e.g. next year the rates bill may increase to £1 200 but this is not as a result of increase in output.

Other examples of fixed costs include rent, insurance and administration expenses.

### Variable costs

These are costs which vary in proportion to the level of output, e.g.

(a) *Direct material*. A table manufacturer who needs one piece of wood to manufacture one table, will need two pieces to manufacture two tables and three pieces to manufacture three tables, etc. (assuming no wastage).
(b) *Direct labour*. If employees are paid so much for every table they manufacture (i.e. piece rate) this is a variable cost.

In reality many costs are *semi-variable* (an element of both fixed and variable costs), e.g.

*Electricity*. The lights and heating will be on whether tables are being produced or whether the workers are sat idle (fixed cost element), but the electricity used to power the cutting machines will only be used when production takes place (variable cost element).

*NB. Examinations.* While you will not be asked to split the costs in this manner you will need to be aware of what is meant by semi-variable costs.

## ■ CALCULATING THE BREAK EVEN POINT

**Example**

Lighting Limited manufacture table lamps. They present you with the following information and ask you to calculate their break even point.

| | |
|---|---|
| Selling price per unit | £50 |
| Direct material per unit | £20 |
| Direct labour per unit | £10 |
| Variable overheads per unit | £5 |
| Fixed costs per annum | £15 000 |

*Step 1 – Calculate the contribution per unit,* i.e. how much the sale of each unit contributes towards eliminating fixed costs. In order to calculate the contribution we must deduct all costs directly associated with the product (variable costs).

CONTRIBUTION = Sales
less Variable costs
Contribution

*Lighting Limited*

| | | *Per Unit* |
|---|---|---|
| | £ | £ |
| Sales | | 50 |
| *less Variable costs* | | |
| Direct material | 20 | |
| Direct labour | 10 | |
| Variable overheads | 5 | 35 |
| *Contribution per unit* | | 15 |

*Step 2 – Calculate the break even point.* So every table lamp we sell will contribute £15 towards eliminating the fixed costs of £15 000. Therefore:

$$\text{Break even point (units)} = \frac{\text{Total fixed costs}}{\text{Contribution per unit}}$$

$$= \frac{£15\,000}{15} = \underline{\underline{1\,000 \text{ units}}}$$

Which in terms of revenue equals *sales* of
1 000 units × £50 selling price = £50 000

**PROGRESS TEST 1**

Complete the following table.

| | *Selling price per unit* | *Variable costs per unit* | *Fixed cost* | *Break even point units* |
|---|---|---|---|---|
| (a) | £20 | £10 | £175 000 | |
| (b) | £11 | £6.50 | £18 000 | |
| (c) | £8.50 | £4.50 | | 5 000 |
| (d) | £22.75 | £14.25 | | 10 000 |
| (e) | £9.50 | | £5 000 | 7 500 |
| (f) | £0.60 | | £9 000 | 30 000 |
| (g) | | £1.25 | £13 000 | 10 000 |
| (h) | | £0.40 | £3 000 | 6 000 |

## ■ CONTRIBUTION/SALES RATIO

Contribution can also be expressed as a percentage to sales, e.g.

| | | |
|---|---|---|
| Sales | £50 | 100% |
| *less* Variable cost | £35 | 70% |
| Contribution | £15 | 30% |

$$\text{CONTRIBUTION/SALES RATIO} = \frac{\text{Contribution}}{\text{Sales}} \times 100$$

$$= \frac{15}{50} \times 100 = 30\%$$

i.e. every £1 of sales will provide 30p contribution.

We can then use this to calculate the break even point in terms of revenue by calculating how many 30ps, and hence £1 of sales, are required to cover fixed costs of £15 000 and therefore break even.

$$\text{Break even point (£)} = \frac{\text{Total fixed costs}}{\text{Contribution/sales ratio}}$$

$$\frac{15\,000}{0.30} = \underline{\underline{£50\,000}}$$

$$\text{Therefore, break even points (units)} = \frac{£50\,000}{£50} = \underline{\underline{1\,000 \text{ units}}}$$

## ■ BREAK EVEN CHARTS

The break even point can be presented, or even found, by means of a break even chart or graph (Fig. 4).

**Procedure/hints**

(a) Label each axis – horizontal axis – units of production
– vertical axis – amount (£)

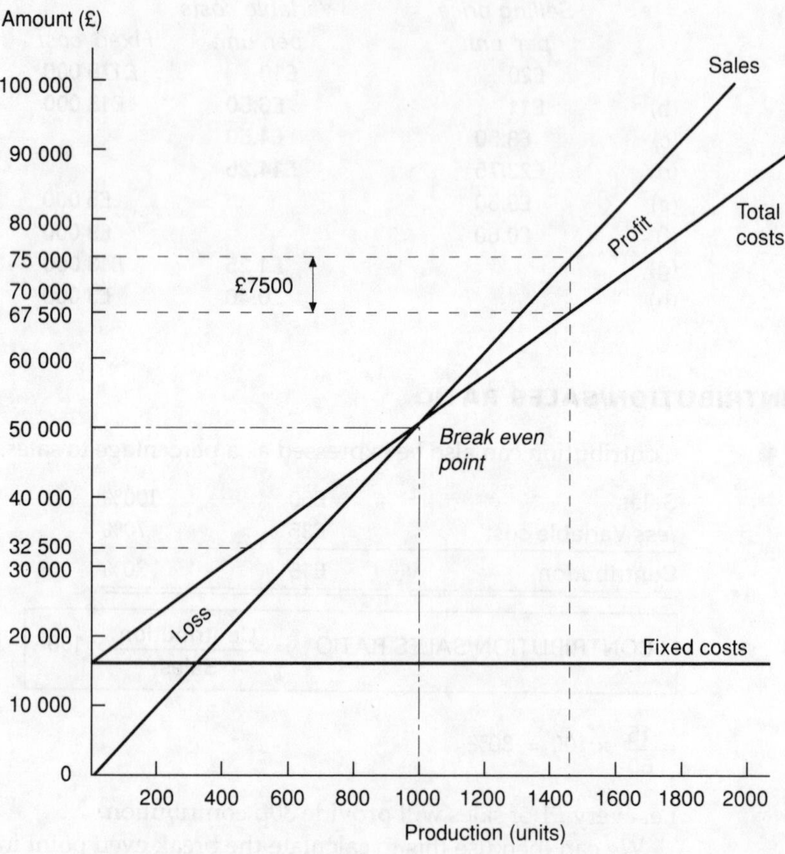


**Figure 4 Break even chart of Lighting Limited**

(b) As fixed costs are £15 000 whatever the level of production, we can draw this as a straight line.

(c) The variable costs are then built on the fixed cost line to form the *total cost line*, e.g.

| | | | |
|---|---|---|---|
| Production 0 units | Fixed cost | = £15 000 | |
| | Variable cost | = 0 | |
| | *Plot at* | £15 000 | |
| Production 500 units | Fixed cost | = £15 000 | |
| | Variable cost | = £17 500 | (500 × £35) |
| | *Plot at* | £32 500 | |
| Production 1 500 units | Fixed cost | = £15 000 | |
| | Variable cost | = £52 500 | (1 500 × £35) |
| | *Plot at* | £67 500 | |

As variable costs vary in proportion to output you will only need to work out two points.

(d) Plot the sales revenue line.

(e) The point where the sales revenue and the total cost lines cross is the break even point, which you can then read off in terms of units or £.

(f) *Do not forget* a title.

The chart can also be used to calculate the profit or loss at various levels of sales, e.g.

| | | |
|---|---|---|
| At sales of 1 500 units – | Sales | £75 000 |
| | Total costs = | £67 500 |
| | | £7 500 |

## ■ MARGIN OF SAFETY

This is the amount by which forecast sales exceed the break even point, e.g.

*Lighting Limited*

| | | |
|---|---|---|
| Forecast sales | 2 000 units | 100% |
| Break even point | 1 000 units | 50% |
| Margin of safety | 1 000 units | 50% |

or alternatively.

$$\frac{\text{Margin of safety}}{\text{Forecast sales}} \times 100$$

$$\frac{1\,000}{2\,000} \times 100 = 50\%$$

It allows the company to assess their degree of risk, for example, a margin of safety of only 1 per cent would indicate that if sales fell by more than 1 per cent of the budgeted figure a loss would result.

In the case of Lighting Limited sales can drop by 50 per cent before a loss will result.

## ■ THE EFFECT OF CHANGES IN SALES VOLUME AND COSTS

A reduction in sales volume will affect every business unless they are able to reduce their costs proportionately.

Unfortunately, a company may not be able to reduce their fixed costs, e.g.

*High Fixed Limited*

| | 10 000 Units | 8 000 Units |
|---|---|---|
| Sales (at £10 per unit) | £100 000 | £80 000 |
| *less* | | |
| Variable costs (£5 per unit) | £50 000 | £40 000 |
| Contribution | £50 000 | £40 000 |
| *less* | | |
| Fixed costs | £40 000 | £40 000 |
| Net profit | £10 000 | Nil |

As a result companies with a high proportion of fixed costs will be badly affected by a reduction in volume, while those with mainly variable costs will be less affected.

The opposite, however, is also true, i.e. where a company has a high proportion of fixed costs they will benefit more than those with high variable costs if sales volume can be increased, e.g.

*High Fixed Limited*

| | 10 000 Units | 12 000 Units |
|---|---|---|
| Sales (at £10 per unit) | £100 000 | £120 000 |
| *less* | | |
| Variable costs (at £5 per unit) | £50 000 | £60 000 |
| Contribution | £50 000 | £60 000 |
| *less* | | |
| Fixed costs | £40 000 | £40 000 |
| | £10 000 | £20 000 |

*High Variable Limited*

| | 10 000 Units | 12 000 Units |
|---|---|---|
| Sales (at £10 per unit) | £100 000 | £120 000 |
| *less* | | |
| Variable costs (at £7 per unit) | £70 000 | £84 000 |
| Contribution | £30 000 | £36 000 |
| *less* | | |
| Fixed costs | £20 000 | £20 000 |
| | £10 000 | £16 000 |

## ■ THE USE OF BREAK EVEN ANALYSIS AS A DECISION MAKING TOOL AND PLANNING AID

### A Deciding whether or not to accept new orders at reduced rates

***Example***

Lighting Limited have been asked to supply one of the top hotel groups, Mansion plc, with 500 table lamps. While management feel this order may lead to further business, they are not sure whether to accept it, as Mansion plc are only prepared to pay £40 per lamp (£10 less than normal selling price).

Provided that there is spare capacity and that the only additional costs to be incurred from accepting this order are variable costs, the order can be accepted as it will still produce a positive contribution:

| | |
|---|---|
| Selling price | £40 |
| *less* Variable costs | £35 |
| | £ 5 |

Fixed costs are covered by the normal production.

**PROGRESS TEST 2**

Arean manufacture leather footballs and provide you with the following information.

| | £ | £ |
|---|---|---|
| Revenue Sales (£14) | | 1 400 000 |
| *Costs* | | |
| Direct materials (100% variable) | 400 000 | |
| Direct labour (30% variable) | 200 000 | |
| *Overheads* | | |
| Variable | 140 000 | |
| Fixed | 300 000 | 1 040 000 |
| Profit | | 360 000 |

Calculate:

(a) Break even point.
(b) Contribution to sales ratio.
(c) Margin of safety.
(d) Draw a break even chart and calculate the profit or loss if:

(i) 120 000 units are sold, and
(ii) £250 000 worth of goods are sold.

(e) If the maximum capacity is 150 000 units, would an extra order of 5 000 units at £7 per unit be profitable, or would it be better to sell 150 000 units at £10 per unit?

## B Achieving maximum profit with limited resources

***Example***

Lighting have now developed a range of products, all of which use the same basic materials but vary slightly in design and quantity of material.

Unfortunately, Lighting have insufficient material to manufacture budgeted sales of all products and ask your help in deciding the optimum level of production.

| | *Traditional* | | *European* | | *High Tech* | | *Total* |
|---|---|---|---|---|---|---|---|
| Sales (units) | | 50 | | 60 | | 65 | 175 |
| *less Variable costs* (units) | | | | | | | |
| Direct material | 20 | | 30 | | 30 | | |
| Direct labour | 15 | 35 | 10 | 40 | 18 | 48 | 123 |
| Contribution | | 15 | | 20 | | 17 | 52 |
| Budgeted sales (units) | 2 000 | | 2 000 | | 2 000 | | 6 000 |

Raw material is limited to £120 000 worth (i.e. this is the *limiting factor*; other items such as cash or labour could be the limiting factor).
Total fixed costs = £50 000

*Step 1 – Calculate the contribution for each product*

| | *Traditional* | *European* | *High Tech* |
|---|---|---|---|
| Contribution | 15 | 20 | 17 |

If there were no limiting factors we could say that the European designs are more valuable to the company as they contribute more.

*But* they also use more of the limiting factor (raw material).

*Step 2 – Calculate the contribution per £1 of limiting factor*

| | *Traditional* | *European* | *High Tech* |
|---|---|---|---|
| Contribution | 15 | 20 | 17 |
| Raw material | 20 | 30 | 30 |
| Contribution per £1 of limiting factor | $\frac{15}{20}$ | $\frac{20}{30}$ | $\frac{17}{30}$ |
| | 0.75 | 0.66 | 0.56 |

We can now see that for every £1 of raw material used, Traditional lamps will provide £0.75p of contribution, whereas European lamps will provide only £0.66p of contribution.

Therefore, Traditional makes best use of the scarce resource or limiting factor as it is known, and we should therefore use the raw material to first produce Traditional lamps, then European and finally, if we have any left, High Tech lamps.

*Step 3 – Calculate the production levels*
(a) *Traditional:*

Material required = Budgeted sales × Raw material per unit
= 2 000 × £20
= £40 000

this leaves £80 000 of raw material to produce European and High Tech (£120 000 – £40 000)
(b) *European:*

Material required = Budgeted sales × Raw material per unit
= 2 000 × £30
= £60 000

We now have only £20 000 of material left with which to produce High Tech lamps (£80 000 – £60 000)
(c) *High Tech:*

$$\text{Production} = \frac{\text{Stock of raw material}}{\text{Raw material per unit}}$$

$$\frac{£20\,000}{£30} = 666.66 \text{ units}$$

*Step 4 – Calculate the profit*

| | *Traditional* | *European* | *High Tech* | *Total* |
|---|---|---|---|---|
| Contribution (unit) | £15 | £20 | £17 | |
| Production | 2 000 | 2 000 | 666 | |
| Total contribution | £30 000 | £40 000 | £11 322 | £81 322 |
| *less* | | | | |
| Fixed costs | | | | £20 000 |
| Profit | | | | £61 322 |

You may be wondering why I have not started with sales, e.g.

| | | *Traditional* | |
|---|---|---|---|
| Sales | (2 000 × £50) | | £100 000 |
| *less Variable costs* | | | |
| Direct material | (2 000 × £20) | £40 000 | |
| Direct labour | (2 000 × £15) | £30 000 | £70 000 |
| Contribution | | | £30 000 |

But as you can see, you can arrive at the same answer simply by starting with the contribution.

If you still find this difficult to accept and feel that a greater profit could be achieved by producing in order of the highest contribution, consider the next example.

| | *Product A* | *Product B* |
|---|---|---|
| Contribution per unit | £20 | £200 |

On the face of it, Product B is of greater benefit to the company, but imagine if the total stock of material was 1 000 kg and Product A took 1 kg to produce, whereas B took the full 1 000 kg. Calculate the total contribution if you produced either all of Product A or all of Product B.
The answer is quite simply:

| | *Product A* | *Product B* |
|---|---|---|
| Contribution per unit | £20 | £200 |
| Kg required per unit | 1 kg | 1 000 kg |
| Maximum production | 1000 units | 1 unit |
| Total contribution at maximum production | £20 000 | £200 |

**PROGRESS TEST 3**

Howards Limited manufacture fibreglass dinghies which are made from a mould. They have three sizes of dinghy, each taking a different quantity of material.

As material is in short supply they seek your help and ask you to identify their optimum level of production based on the following information.

| | *Junior* | *Standard* | *Double* |
|---|---|---|---|
| | £ | £ | £ |
| Sales (per unit) | 120 | 200 | 450 |
| Direct material (per unit) | 40 | 60 | 80 |
| Direct labour (per unit) | 20 | 25 | 30 |
| Variable overheads (per unit) | 5 | 7 | 10 |
| Budgeted sales | 3000 | 5000 | 1000 |

Total fixed cost £300 000
Supply of raw material 80 000 kg
Cost of raw material £5 per kg
Labour hours available 50 000
Cost of labour per hour £5

*NB.* You are advised to identify the *limiting factor first.*

### C Calculating the sales necessary to achieve target profits

If we were asked to calculate the number of units required to achieve a profit of say £300 000, this could be found as follows:

$$\text{Sales (units)} = \frac{\text{Fixed costs} + \text{Required profit}}{\text{Contribution per unit}}$$

In other words, there needs to be sufficient contribution in order to:

- cover the fixed costs, and
- to achieve the required profit.

***Example***

| | |
|---|---|
| Sales per unit | 20 |
| Variable costs per unit | 10 |
| Contribution per unit | 10 |

Fixed costs = £200 000
Required profit = £300 000

$$\text{Sales required units} = \frac{£200\,000 + £300\,000}{£10}$$

$$= \underline{\underline{50\,000 \text{ units}}}$$

### D Make or buy decisions

Companies may be faced with a decision of whether to continue making certain components or to buy them in.

Break even analysis can assist this decision by analysing the costs saved as a result of stopping production compared with the extra costs incurred resulting from buying the components.

Apart from purely financial considerations the company would need to consider whether they can be sure of delivery, quality and continued supply if they decide to purchase the components.

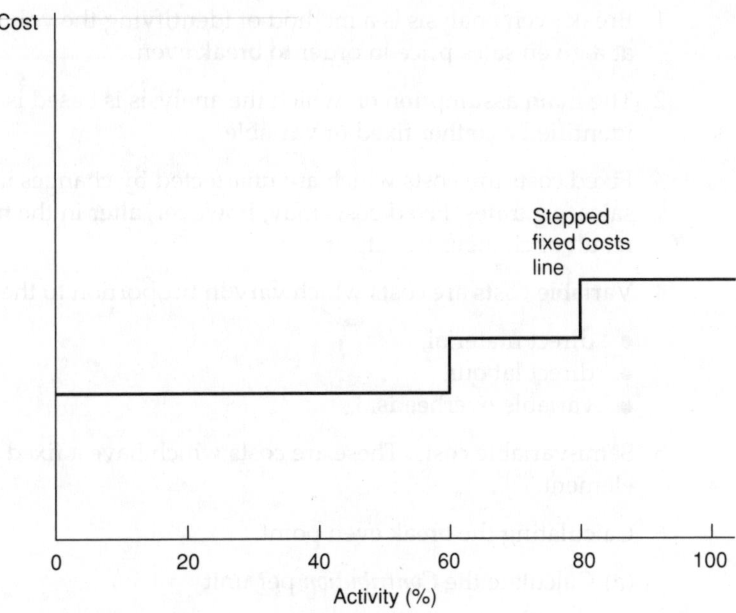


**Figure 5 Increase of fixed costs at different levels of activity**

## ■ ASSUMPTIONS/LIMITATIONS

Break even analysis is based on the following assumptions which must be considered when assessing its value:

(a) Costs can be defined as fixed or variable, but as we have seen, some costs are semi-variable and management will therefore need to assess the fixed and variable elements.
(b) Fixed costs will remain constant and variable costs vary proportionally with output. Fixed costs may, in fact, increase at certain levels of output, e.g. at 80 per cent capacity more factory space may be required. This can, however, be built into the break even analysis, giving a stepped fixed cost line (Fig. 5).
(c) The only factor affecting costs and reserve is volume. In practice managerial decisions can alter costs, e.g. they can replace a small labour team (variable cost) with an automatic machine (fixed cost).
(d) Technology and production methods remain unchanged.
(e) Price stability.
(f) The analysis relates to one particular product or a constant product mix.
(g) No stock level changes.

## ■ SUMMARY

1 Break even analysis is a method of identifying the volume of sales required at a given sales price in order to break even.

2 The main assumption on which the analysis is based is that costs can be identified as either fixed or variable.

3 Fixed costs are costs which are unaffected by changes in the volume of sales, e.g. rates. Fixed costs may, however, alter in the future, but not as a result of changes in output.

4 Variable costs are costs which vary in proportion to the level of output, e.g.

- direct material,
- direct labour,
- variable overheads.

5 Semi-variable costs. These are costs which have a fixed and variable element.

6 Calculating the break even point

(a) Calculate the *Contribution* per unit

$$\text{Contribution} = \text{Sales} - \text{Variable costs}$$

(b) Calculate the break even point

$$\text{Break even point} = \frac{\text{Total fixed costs}}{\text{Contribution per unit}}$$

7 Contribution indicates how much the sale of each unit contributes towards eliminating fixed costs.

$$\text{Contribution/Sales ratio} = \frac{\text{Contribution}}{\text{Sales}} \times 100$$

This indicates the amount of contribution for every £1 of sales.

9

$$\text{Break even point (£)} = \frac{\text{Total fixed costs}}{\text{Contribution/sales ratio}}$$

10 Break even charts can also be used to find or represent the break even point.
*Procedure*

(a) Label axis;
(b) Plot fixed cost line;
(c) Build the variable cost line on to the fixed cost line to form *total costs;*
(d) Plot the sales revenue;
(e) Where the sales reserve and total cost lines cross is the break even point;
(f) Do not forget a title.

11 Margin of safety is the amount by which forecast sales exceed the break even point which allows the company to assess their degree of risk

$$\frac{\text{Margin of safety}}{\text{Forecast sales}} \times 100$$

12 Use of break even analysis as a decision making tool and planning aid;

(a) deciding whether or not to accept new orders at reduced rates;
(b) achieving maximum profit with unlimited resources;
*Step 1* – calculate the contribution for each product;
*Step 2* – calculate the contribution per £1 of limiting factor;
*Step 3* – calculate the production levels, producing those with the highest contribution per £1 of limiting factor first;
*Step 4* – calculate the profit.
(c) Calculating the sales necessary to achieve target profits;

$$\text{Sales (units)} = \frac{\text{Fixed costs + Required profit}}{\text{Contribution per unit}}$$

(d) make or buy decisions.

13 Assumption of break even analysis

(a) cost can be defined as fixed or variable;
(b) fixed cost will remain constant and variable costs vary proportionally with output;
(c) the only factor affecting costs and revenue is volume;
(d) technology and production methods remain unchanged;
(e) price stability;
(f) the analysis relates to one particular product or a constant product mix;
(g) no stock level changes.

## ■ SELF-ASSESSMENT QUESTIONS

1 Complete the following table.

| | *Selling price per unit* | *Variable cost per unit* | *Fixed cost* | *Break even point units* |
|---|---|---|---|---|
| (a) | £17.25 | £8.50 | £20 000 | |
| (b) | £11.79 | £10.20 | £5 000 | |
| (c) | £36.12 | £20.00 | | 2 000 |
| (d) | £11.00 | £5.00 | | 60 000 |
| (e) | £0.50 | | £10 000 | 40 000 |
| (f) | £110.00 | | £160 000 | 3 200 |
| (g) | | £2.30 | £20 000 | 9 000 |
| (h) | | £180.00 | £100 000 | 5 000 |

2 Dennis is starting a double-glazing business. He will buy the windows, made to measure, from an established manufacturer and his operations will be restricted to selling, measuring and fitting.

His plan is to spend £2 000 a month on press advertising to provide 'leads' for his salesman. His salesman will be paid a flat £100 per week for 52 weeks as basic salary and expenses, out of which the salesman will have to provide and run his own car. The salesman will, in addition, be paid 7.5 per cent commission on all sales resulting from his work.

Dennis himself will undertake the actual measuring work, since it is vital that accurate specifications be passed to the factory.

The fitting operation is an expensive element. Dennis will need a specially fitted van which he will rent for £200 per week. He will employ a craftsman and a labourer and their labour costs (including National Insurance contributions) will be £200 and £150 per week respectively. The men will be paid for 52 weeks a year and will be expected to work the equivalent of 47 weeks a year after allowing for bank holidays and sickness, but Dennis will have to pay 52 weeks' rent for the van. He expects to spend £50 a week on van running costs for each week his fitting team works.

The fitting team are expected to be able to fit windows to an aggregate value of £4 000 each week.

If business booms, Dennis is satisfied that the salesman would work overtime on the same commission basis, that he himself could cope with all the measuring work, and that the factory would be able to handle all orders. The difficulty in coping with the fitting would be resolved by hiring a further van and employing another fitting team, all at the same costs as detailed above.

Dennis requires earnings of £10 000 per year for himself. Bank charges and interest are expected to amount to £1 000 per year, office expenses (including insurance and accountancy) to £1 500, and his selling price will be fixed by doubling the factory cost of the windows.

*Required*:
(a) The level of sales at which Dennis will achieve break even point, allowing for the £10 000 earnings he requires for himself. (18)
(b) Will Dennis need to employ a second fitting team to achieve the sales you specify in your answer to part (a)? (2)
(Total marks for question – 20)
(CIB November 1987)

3 The directors of Presbury Limited have under consideration two alternative schemes for manufacturing a new product for which they believe there exists a strong demand. The details relating to the two schemes are as follows:

*Scheme A*
The company will acquire plant costing £280 000. Fixed expenses (other than depreciation) would amount to £130 000 per annum and variable expenses per unit would be £150.

*Scheme B*
The company will acquire plant costing £400 000. Fixed expenses (other than depreciation) would amount to £300 000 per annum and variable expenses per unit would be £120.

In both cases the plant is expected to last four years and then be worthless. The straight line method of depreciation is considered appropriate. The finished product will be marketed for £200 per unit irrespective of the level of sales. The forecast level of demand is 7 000 units per annum. The working capital requirement amounts to £60 000 under each scheme.

*Required*:

(a) For each scheme, A and B, calculate:

(i) the number of units which must be produced and sold each year to break even (i.e. where total revenues exactly cover total costs);

(ii) the forecast profit per annum;

(iii) the margin of safety. (11)

(b) Calculate the annual level of sales at which the same profit arises under each scheme. (3)

(c) A discussion of these two alternative schemes of production indicating the main factors to be taken into account when choosing between scheme A and scheme B. (6)

(Total marks for question – 20)

(Banking Diploma (amended))

4 The market research department of Brigton Ltd has carried out a survey which suggests that the following quantities of a new product called 'Letroc' could be sold, at a price of £10 per unit, in the next five years:

| | *Units* *000* |
|---|---|
| 1992 | 50 |
| 1993 | 60 |
| 1994 | 70 |
| 1995 | 80 |
| 1996 | 90 |

The company's directors are interested in entering the market for this product, but are undecided about how it should obtain supplies. Three options are under consideration, only one of which can be selected:

*Option 1*

(i) Buy fixed assets for £1 000 000; these have a five-year life, a zero residual value, and a maximum annual capacity of 90 000 units.

(ii) The variable cost per unit would be £5.

(iii) Annual fixed costs, excluding depreciation, would be £75 000.

*Option 2*

(i) Buy fixed assets for £2 000 000; these have a five-year life, a residual value of £250 000, and a maximum annual capacity of 90 000 units.

(ii) The variable cost per unit would be £3.

(iii) Annual fixed costs, excluding depreciation, would be £60 000.

*Option 3*

Buy 'Letroc' from another manufacturer at a cost of £9 per unit. Annual fixed costs of £10 000 would be incurred.

*Required*:

(a) Prepare in column form, for each of three options separately, a statement of the forecast profit for each of the five years 1992 to 1996 inclusive. (12)

(b) Advise management on which option you would recommend they adopt, and give your reasons. (8)
(Total – 20 marks)

*Notes*:
1 Discounting techniques are not to be used in answering this question.
2 The fixed assets acquired under options 1 and 2 are to be depreciated using the straight line basis.
(CIB May 1991)

5 The directors of Barque Ltd, a manufacturing company, are considering the introduction of a new product to their range. This product can be made by either of two methods, and the production director has supplied the following information about these alternatives:

| | *Method 1* | *Method 2* |
|---|---|---|
| Investment in plant | £3 000 000 | £1 000 000 |
| Annual fixed costs | | |
| (excluding depreciation) | £420 000 | £370 000 |
| Variable cost per unit | £0.5 | £1.0 |

In both cases the plant has a maximum output of 250 000 units per annum, an expected life of 10 years and a zero residual value. The selling price per unit is £5.

The sales director says that the market for the new product is very unpredictable, but he expects sales to be between 100 000 and 250 000 units a year. However, he is sure that if, in addition to the fixed costs identified by the production director, an advertising campaign costing £135 000 each year is undertaken, then annual sales would be at least 200 000 units while the maximum sales would remain at 250 000 units.

*Required*:
(a) For *each* production method, assuming that the advertising campaign *is* undertaken, calculate:
(i) the break even point in units; and
(ii) the maximum possible profit. (8)
(b) For *each* production method, assuming that the advertising campaign *is not* undertaken, calculate:
(i) the break even point in units; and
(ii) the maximum possible profit. (8)
(c) Explain to the management the course of action which you would recommend, on the assumption that the directors wish to take the minimum possible risk. (4)
(Total – 20 marks)
*Note*: Ignore the time value of money when answering this question.
(CIB May 1990)

6 The managing directors of Thin Ltd and Stout Ltd met at a convention and found that their companies manufactured and sold the same product. Chickles, which sells at £10 per unit. They agreed to exchange details of revenues and costs, which were as follows for the year to 30 June 1990:

| | Thin Ltd | | Stout Ltd | |
|---|---|---|---|---|
| | £000 | £000 | £000 | £000 |
| Sales (100 000 units) | | 1 000 | | 1 000 |
| Materials | 300 | | 300 | |
| Direct labour | 200 | | 50 | |
| Depreciation | 100 | | 250 | |
| Manufacturing costs | | 600 | | 600 |
| Gross profit | | 400 | | 400 |
| Other expenses: | | | | |
| Fixed | 150 | | 20 | |
| Variable | 150 | | 100 | |
| | | 300 | | 300 |
| Net profit | | 100 | | 100 |

The managing directors agreed that output and sales for the year to 30 June 1991 were likely to be 40% higher than those for the previous year.

*Required*:
(a) Prepare statements, in the same format as those given above, to show the expected profit of each company for the year to 30 June 1991 if the assumption about the expected level of sales turns out to be correct. (6)
(b) State and discuss the assumptions which you have made when preparing your answer to part (a) of this question. (8)
(c) Explain the differences between the level of expected profits of the two companies for the year to 30 June 1991. (6)
(Total – 20 marks)
(CIB Ocotber 1990)

# 20 Examination preparation/revision

**OBJECTIVES**

**After studying this chapter you should be:**

1. **Aware of the examination format;**
2. **Able to appreciate what the Chief Examiner is looking for;**
3. **Able to enter the examination, having practised a mock examination and therefore feel more confident and prepared for your final examination.**

## ■ INTRODUCTION – EXAMINATION FORMAT

A total of *five questions* must be answered.
*Section A contains one compulsory question.*

- This will involve the preparation or use of final accounts, i.e. Trading and/or Profit and Loss Account and/or Balance Sheet.
- You must satisfy the examiner in this question in order to pass the examination.

*Section B* contains two questions; you must *answer at least one of these questions.*

- They will be of a more academic or theoretical nature and will be biased towards essay-style questions, although some numerical aspects may be included or required as explanation or examples.

*Section C* contains four questions; you must *answer at least two of these questions.*

- a variety of questions will appear in this section.

A *fifth question* must then be answered from either Section B or Section C.

So that is

| | | | |
|---|---|---|---|
| Section A | – | answer | 1 compulsory question |
| Section B | – | answer | 1 of 2 questions |
| Section C | – | answer | 2 of 4 questions |
| and | – | answer | 1 other question from Sections B or C. |
| | | | 5 |

Each question carries *20 marks* and you are therefore advised to spend *36 minutes* on each.

Be careful not to spend too long on any one question. It is so easy to go over the 36 minutes by trying to see why your Balance Sheet does not balance. If the 36 minutes are up and you cannot find why it does not balance, leave it; it may simply be that you have added a column up incorrectly, in which case the layout and adjustments will be correct and you will have passed on that question anyway. It is also comforting to note that credit is always given for the subsequent correct use of wrong figures.

## ■ EXAMINATION TIPS

### Section A

It is important that you are competent in the following areas:

(a) adjusting profit and loss account items for prepayments and accruals,
(b) depreciation,
(c) the layout and content, which includes the heading.

You are also advised to show all workings in order to gain full credit.

### Section B

(a) Read the question carefully; do not simply write all you know about a topic, apply it to the question, e.g. 'What is depreciation?' does not mean 'Why is it charged?' or 'How is it calculated?'

(b) Do not be too brief.

(c) Although questions may not be sub-divided they may contain more than one section, e.g. 'Define the term "accounting policies" and discuss why it is important to disclose them'.

(d) When a question asks for examples or illustrations these should be given, on a numbered basis if appropriate.

(e) While questions in this section are biased towards essay-style, note-form answers are acceptable, *but remember*, you may need to support essays or notes with numerical explanations/examples, e.g. discuss the impact on profit measurement of LIFO and FIFO.

### Section C

In this section questions will range from purely numerical to those requiring discussion or interpretation of the results calculated.

In view of the importance of Question 1, which is compulsory and which you *must pass* in order to pass overall and the relevance of FRS 1 'Cash Flow Statements' at the time of writing, I have reproduced in full two 'Signpost' articles from *Banking World* of July 1992 and November 1992, written by your Chief Examiner, Howard Mellett, and by Dick Edwards, to whom I would like to express thanks for their kind permission to reproduce these articles.

I would also advise you to watch out for further articles of this kind which appear in *Banking World* and usually indicate future exam questions – so it is well worth taking the cellophane off your copy!

## ■ FROM TRIAL BALANCE TO FINAL ACCOUNTS

### Introduction

Question 1 of the Introduction to Accounting paper of the Banking Certificate has a number of special features. One obvious benefit to the candidate is that the topic is known, it being the preparation of final accounts. However, this has to be set against the facts that the question is compulsory and, to pass the paper as a whole, a minimum of 10 marks must be achieved. Well-prepared candidates should be able to achieve a good mark on this question, and so approach the rest of the paper with confidence. However, candidates aware of having made a poor attempt are likely to face the rest of the paper in a pessimistic frame of mind and so perhaps not perform to their full ability. This article provides guidance on the preparation of answers to this type of question, starting from the trial balance, together with some useful background information.

### The Trial Balance

Double-entry bookkeeping involves making two entries in the books of account, one a debit and the other a credit, to record each transaction. It follows from this that the debit and credit entries made during a period of time must be equal in total value. At regular intervals, at least annually, the balances from the individual accounts are listed in the trial balance, which consists of two columns of figures having the same total value, together with a description of each item. The debit balances are in the left-hand column, and the right-hand column contains the credits.

The compulsory question 1 requires students to convert the figures set out in the trial balance, together with any additional information provided, into a set of final accounts. The main elements in this process are now considered.

### Final Accounts

Candidates should know the contents and layout of a 'normal' set of final accounts, namely a Manufacturing Account (if appropriate), a Trading Account, a Profit and Loss Account, an Appropriation Account (if appropriate), and a Balance Sheet. Summaries of these statements, their contents and purpose are given here. You should be familiar with all the terms used, and, if you are not, some revision is needed. While there is a large degree of latitude as to what represents an acceptable layout, certain unconventional presentation, such as the inclusion of accumulated depreciation as a current liability, will result in the loss of marks awarded, for example, for showing the written-down value of fixed assets.

### The Adjustments

The debit entries in the trial balance represent either assets (for inclusion in the balance sheet) or expenses (for use in calculating the profit or loss), while the credit entries are liabilities (for inclusion in the balance sheet) or income (for use in calculating the profit or loss). Some of the values can be transferred from the trial balance to the final accounts without any alteration, while others have to be adjusted in the light of additional information given in the question. Remember that the debit and credit effect of each adjustment must be included in order to keep the total values of debits and credits in the trial balance equal. Remember also that the underlying objectives are:

1 To charge against revenue for an accounting period the expenditure incurred in order to enable the company to carry on business during that period.
2 To carry forward in the balance sheet, as assets, payments made during the accounting period, which will provide benefits in a future accounting period and, as liabilities, amounts owing in respect of benefits received during the current accounting period.

A great variety of adjustments may have to be made on the basis of information provided; the main ones likely to be required are now considered individually:

*Closing stock* Taking the case of the trader who buys goods and sells them without further processing, the trial balance contains debit entries for the opening stock and purchases made during the year; the value of closing stock is usually given as part of the additional information. The cost of goods sold is found in the trading account by arranging these items in the following manner:

Opening stock ........................ Debit
plus: Purchases ...................... Debit
less: Closing stock ................. Credit
= Cost of goods sold

***Manufacturing, Trading, Profit and Loss and Appropriation Accounts***

| | |
|---|---|
| Manufacturing account * | Used by manufacturing companies to calculate the cost of producing goods for sale. The total manufacturing cost of goods completed during the year is transferred to the trading account. |
| Trading account | The cost of goods sold is deducted from the value of sales to find the gross profit. The gross profit is transferred to the profit and loss account. |
| Profit and loss account | All other costs of running the firm are deducted from the gross profit to find the net profit. The net profit is transferred to the appropriation account (partnerships and limited companies) or the capital account (sole trader). |
| Appropriation account ** | Contains: for limited companies, the balance of profit brought forward, taxation, dividends, transfers to reserve, and balance carried forward; for partnerships, the division of profit between partners. |

* Required only in the case of a manufacturing company
** Not required in the case of a sole trader

***The Balance Sheet***

| | | |
|---|---|---|
| A | *Fixed Assets* | Show each type of asset at cost less accumulated depreciation at the year end |
| B | *Current Assets* | |
| | Stock | Raw materials, work in progress and finished goods |
| | Debtors | Amounts owed to the firm |
| | Prepayments | Expenses paid in advance |
| | Cash | |
| C | *Current Liabilities* | |
| | Trade Creditors | Amounts owed to suppliers |
| | Overdraft | |
| | Accruals | Expenses unpaid at the accounting date, including taxation and dividends |
| D | *Working Capital* | Total B less Total C |
| E | *Total Assets Less Current Liabilities* | Total A plus Total D |
| F | *Loans due after 12 months or more* | |
| G | *Total Net Assets* | Total E less Total F |
| | financed by | |
| H | *Capital* | Equal in value to Total G |

The corresponding debit entry for closing stock is entered in the balance sheet under current assets. It becomes the opening balance for the following accounting period.

Where a business is that of manufacturer, it is likely to have two additional categories of stock, namely raw materials and work in progress. The amount of raw materials consumed during the year is part of the cost of producing goods for resale. The calculation in the manufacturing account, together with the source from which the relevant information is derived, is set out below:

| *Entry in the Manufacturing Account* | *Source of Information* |
|---|---|
| Opening stock of raw materials .................... | Debit from trial balance |
| plus: Purchase of raw materials .................... | Debit from trial balance |
| less: Closing raw material stocks .................. | Credit from additional information |
| = Cost of raw materials consumed. | |

Again, the corresponding debit entry for the closing value of the stock of raw materials is entered in the balance sheet.

Work in progress consists of units of output which are partly completed at the balance sheet date, and its value is used to adjust the total manufacturing cost to give the cost of completed production. Closing work in progress is carried forward to the next period in the balance sheet in the same way as the other categories of stock:

| | |
|---|---|
| Opening Work in Progress ............................ | Debit from trial balance |
| plus: Total production cost ............................ | Manufacturing Account |
| less: Closing Work in progress ...................... | Credit from additional information |
| = Cost of completed output | |

The cost of the completed output is transferred to the Trading Account, where it is adjusted for opening and closing stock of finished goods, in the same way as purchases are dealt with for a trader (see above).

*Depreciation* The depreciation charge for the year has to be calculated, on the basis of information provided, and entered in the accounts as both a debit entry and a credit entry. The debit entry represents the charge for the period which is taken into account when calculating profit. However, care must be taken when deciding where to enter this annual charge. The depreciation related to manufacturing plant and machinery is entered in the manufacturing account, while that of other fixed assets goes in the profit and loss account. In some cases a depreciation charge may relate to both manufacturing and other activities, in which case it can be apportioned. For example, 60 per cent of a building may be used for manufacturing and the remaining 40 per cent as offices; in this case, 60 per cent of the annual charge would be put in the manufacturing account and the remaining 40 per cent in the profit and loss account.

Having dealt with the debit side of the entry for depreciation, we can now turn to the credit. This is used to calculate the written down value of fixed assets in the balance sheet. The first step is to enter the cost of fixed assets (a debit balance in the trial balance) in the balance sheet. The second step is to take the credit balance called depreciation from the trial balance; this is the accumulated amount of depreciation brought forward at the start of the accounting period. Thirdly, the charge debited when calculating profit is credited, that is added, to give the value of accumulated depreciation at the *end* of the period. This amount must then be deducted from the original cost of fixed assets to find the net book value. This procedure should be carried out separately for each category of fixed asset, so that if a firm owns three types of fixed assets, say, land and buildings, plant and machinery and vehicles, the written down value of each type should be shown.

*Prepayments* Sometimes a service is paid for before it is consumed. For example, a business has to pay the rates on its premises in advance. The payment is entered in the accounts, and therefore included in the trial balance, immediately it takes place. However, the profit for a period is computed by charging against sales only those goods or services consumed during the period under review. Therefore, any amounts paid in advance should be excluded when calculating profit, and instead carried forward as a prepayment in the balance sheet.

In examination questions, the value of any prepayment will either be given in the notes to the question, or must be calculated. For example, a prepayment covering six months may be paid in advance so that, if the accounting date falls three months into the period, half of it is charged when calculating profit and the other half carried forward in the balance sheet as a prepayment.

*Accruals* It is possible for an expense to be incurred during an accounting period, but remain unrecorded in the books at the date the trial balance is extracted. This may happen, for example, in the case of electricity and gas, where the bills are received *after* consumption has taken place. To ensure that all the resources used are recorded in the correct accounting period, an accrual has to be made. This involves charging the amount due in the current period, as a debit, and inserting the credit in the balance sheet as a current liability.

*Bad and doubtful debts* It is to be expected that, when a firm makes sales on credit, not all of its customers will settle the amounts due, and this gives rise to bad debts. There are two possibilities when these arise; (a) they have already been identified and removed from debtors, in which case a debit entry appears in the trial balance and is transferred to the profit and loss account; or (b) it is known that some of the amounts included in the value of debtors in the trial balance are bad and will never be collected. In the latter instance, the figure for debtors has to be reduced by means of a credit entry, and the related debit is entered in the profit and loss account as part of the charge for bad debts.

Doubtful debts arise where it is known from experience that a proportion of debtors will not pay, but their precise identity is not known. In these circumstances a provision for doubtful debts is created by debiting a charge to the profit and loss account, and reducing the reported value of debtors in the balance sheet. If a credit balance called something like 'provision for doubtful debts' appears in the trial balance, this represents the amount provided at the start of the year. In such a case it is necessary, in the current year, only to make an entry to re-state the opening balance at its closing amount. To do this, the difference between the opening and the required closing balance is entered in the profit and loss account as a debit, if the provision is increased, or as a credit if it is decreased. The provision existing at the accounting date is deducted from the value of debtors.

*Transfers* Sometimes details are given of amounts which have been charged to the wrong accounts. This error does not affect the balancing of the trial balance, and both a debit and credit entry have to be made to correct it. For example, the purchase of a fixed asset may have been recorded as the purchase of goods for resale, and so the value of purchases has to be reduced by a credit entry, and fixed assets are increased by the debit. Also remember that extra fixed assets may result in an additional depreciation charge.

### Possible Scenarios

Care should be taken, before starting the question, to find out what type of organisation is being dealt with as this has some effect on the accounts to be produced. The alternatives, and the accounting consequences are:

*Sole trader* The profit is calculated in the normal way, but no amounts should be charged in the profit and loss account which relate to payments to the owner. Once the profit is found, it is transferred to the capital account in the balance sheet and added to the opening value of capital; the drawings, that is amounts taken from the business by the owner, are then deducted to give the value of closing capital.

*Partnerships* Profit is found in the same way as for the sole trader, i.e. payments made to the partners are excluded. The profit is transferred to the appropriation account where it is shared out on the basis of the agreement between the partners. This may involve allocating interest on capital and salaries to each partner before the residue is split between them in the profit or loss sharing ratio.

In the balance sheet, there may be a fixed capital account for each partner, which is left unchanged, and current accounts which are used to record each one's share of profit and drawings. The important point to note is to calculate separately each partner's account balance. This starts with the balance brought forward, has interest, salaries and shares of profit added to it, and drawings deducted.

*Limited company* The net profit is again transferred to the appropriation account, but, in this case, it is added to the balance at the start of the year. Taxation and dividends are charged against it by debit entries; the corresponding credit entries being entered in the balance sheet as current liabilities. The remaining amount, of retained profit, is part of the shareholders' investment in the business and is included in the equity section of the balance sheet.

### Conclusion

In this article we have intentionally not included numerical examples; there are plenty of these available, and you are specifically referred to the *Examiners' Reports* produced by the Institute, where past papers, solutions and examiners' comments can be found. What we have done is to highlight the areas of knowledge which you should have when tackling question 1 of the Introduction to Accounting paper so that you can identify aspects which need further work. Finally, the usual advice which always bears repeating is given: read the question before attempting it so that you know what is expected, and show your workings so that all due credit can be given.

## ■ CASH FLOW STATEMENTS: MAKE SURE YOU ARE READY

As students will be aware, the Accounting Standards Committee was replaced by the Accounting Standards Board (ASB) in August 1990 as part of a shake-up designed to restore credibility to the standard-setting process following the problems of the 1980s. Another new name which we must get used to is Financial Reporting Standards (FRS), which are issued by the ASB as compared with Statements of Standard Accounting Practice issued by its predecessor body. The first standard, FRS1, entitled Cash Flow Statements was issued in September 1991 and came into effect for accounting periods ending on or at 23 March 1992.

FRS1 replaces SSAP10 (Statements of Source and Application of Funds) which proved to have a shelf life of 17 years from its initial introduction in 1975. In making this change the UK is following the path trodden by the United States, which changed from funds flow accounting to cash flow accounting with the issue, in November 1987, of Statement of Financial Accounting Standards 95 – Statements of Cash Flow.

The survival and success of the business entity is determined by its ability to generate cash inflows in excess of cash outflows, and the published Cash Flow Statement, although historical in its orientation, is intended to help in that direction. The change from funds flow to cash flow is more than a matter of mere window dressing. It reflects a basic conviction that cash flows are a more useful basis for analysing corporate progress than movements in working capital. An important virtue of the Cash Flow Statement is that even the layman clearly understands what is meant by cash, whereas the term working capital is meaningless except to the financially aware.

FRS1 requires businesses to analyse their cash flows into five separate categories. The new standard does not specify a standard layout, but a number of illustrative formats are contained in the explanatory section which presents the items, although in greater detail, in the order shown in Figure 1.

It is thought that the information contained in the Cash Flow Statement, when used in conjunction with other information in the corporate report, will help bankers and other users to:

- assess an enterprise's ability to generate positive future net cash flows;
- assess its ability to meet its financial obligations, such as the payment of dividends and the need to repay external funding;
- assess the effect on the enterprise's financial position of investments undertaken during the accounting period;
- explain the reasons for differences between profits and cash flows arising from normal operating activity; and
- provide a useful input for business valuation models which are based on estimates of likely future cash flows.

**Figure 1 Skeleton Cash Flow Statement**

| *Net cash flow from operating activities* | *£000* |
|---|---|
| Returns on investment and servicing of finance | X |
| Taxation | X |
| Investing activities | X |
| Financing | X |
| Increase (decrease) in cash and cash equivalents | X |

**Preparation**

When preparing financial statements, an orderly presentation is required so as to improve the clarity of the message intended to be conveyed. It is for this reason that assets reported in the balance sheet are listed in order of permanence (starting with fixed assets and finishing with cash) with like items grouped together under the headings tangible assets, intangible assets and current assets. A particular virtue of this presentation is that it enables the investment in particular areas to be identified and facilitates comparison with other years and other business entities. A similar philosophy underpins the preparation of the Cash Flow Statements with FRS1 identifying the following five categories previously summarised in Figure 1.

**1 Operating activities**

This is the cash generated from business operations and may be calculated in either of two ways:

*Direct method.* The calculation starts with cash received from customers, from which is deducted payments to suppliers and employees for goods and services required to carry on business activity.

It will help if we use an example to illustrate the preparation of a Cash Flow Statement (advance corporation tax ignored). Figure 2 contains the Profit and Loss Account of Lisvane Ltd, for the year to 31 December 1991, together with a balance sheet at that date and corresponding figures for 12 months previous. Using the information contained in Figure 2, we are able to calculate net cash flow from operating activities as follows.

| | £000 | |
|---|---|---|
| Cash from sales | 3 519 | W1 |
| Cash paid for: | | |
| purchases | (1 735) | W2 |
| administrative expenses | (1 136) | |
| distribution costs | (275) | |
| Net cash flow from operating activities | 373 | |

W1 £3 620 000 + £407 000 (opening debtors ) – £508 000 (closing debtors)

W2 £1 760 000 + £156 000 (opening creditors) – £181 000 (closing creditors)

*Indirect method:* The calculation starts with operating profit and makes the adjustments necessary to arrive at the net cash flow from operating activities. Adjustments are required for items of revenue and expenditure which have been taken into account in calculating operating profit but which do not result in cash flows during the current accounting period. The calculation may be made as follows:

| | £000 |
|---|---|
| Operating profit | 389 |
| Depreciation charge | 104 |
| Loss on sale of tangible fixed assets | 25 |
| Increase in stocks | (69) |
| Increase in debtors | (101) |
| Increase in trade creditors | 25 |
| | 373 |

The ASB gave careful consideration to the question of which method should be preferred – direct or indirect. The principal advantage of the direct method is its clarity, while the indirect method helps to highlight the reasons for differences between operating profit and operating cash flow. The conclusion reached was to require companies to publish:

- a single figure for net cash flow from operating activities on the face of the Cash Flow Statement
- a reconciliation employing the indirect method of way of note.

In addition businesses are given the freedom to publish information complying with the direct method if they so wish.

## 2 Returns on investments and servicing of finance

The comprises interest and dividends received and paid and is a straightforward calculation. The relevant items, from Figure 1, are as follows:

| | £000 | |
|---|---|---|
| Interest received | 26 | |
| Interest paid | (10) | |
| Dividends paid | (165) | W3 |
| Net cash flow from returns on investment and servicing of finance | (149) | |

W3 £45 000 (Interim dividend for 1991) + £120 000 (final dividend for 1990)

## 3 Taxation

This consists of payments in respect of mainstream corporation tax on both revenue and capital profits, and payments in respect of advance corporation tax, net of any tax rebates. Receipts or payments in respect of VAT should not normally appear as operating cash flows, as cash flows must be shown net of VAT to the extent that VAT is irrecoverable. The relevant item, from Figure 2, is as follows:

| | £000 |
|---|---|
| Mainstream corporation tax | (117) |

Note that the mainstream corporation tax payment is the amount outstanding at the end of 1990 which will have been paid on 30 September 1991. The transfer to the deferred tax account is not a cash transaction and does not appear in the Cash Flow Statement.

**Figure 2**

The following information is provided for Lisvane Ltd in respect of the year to 31 December 1991:

*Profit and Loss Account for the year to 31 December 1991*

| | £000 | £000 |
|---|---|---|
| Sales | | 3 620 |
| Less: Opening stock | 224 | |
| Purchases | 1 760 | |
| Closing stock | (293) | |
| Cost of goods sold | | 1 691 |
| Gross profit | | 1 929 |
| less Depreciation | 104 | |
| Loss on sale of fixed assets | 25 | |
| Administration expenses | 1 136 | |
| Distribution costs | 275 | |
| | | 1 540 |
| Operating profit | | 389 |
| Interest received | 26 | |
| Interest paid | (10) | 16 |
| Profit on ordinary activities before tax | | 405 |
| Tax on profits on ordinary activities | 90 | |
| Transfer to deferred taxation account | 30 | 120 |
| | | 285 |
| Dividends: Paid | 45 | |
| Proposed | 180 | 225 |
| Retained profit for the year | | 60 |

*Balance Sheet as at 31 December 1991*

| | 1991<br>£000 | 1990<br>£000 |
|---|---|---|
| *Fixed assets* | | |
| Plant and machinery at book value, 1 January | 945 | 1 000 |
| Additions | 530 | 20 |
| Disposals at book value (cash proceeds £15 000) | (40) | — |
| Depreciation charged | (104) | (75) |
| | 1 331 | 945 |
| *Current assets* | | |
| Stocks | 293 | 224 |
| Debtors | 508 | 407 |
| Investments | 78 | 142 |
| Cash at bank and in hand | — | 53 |
| | 879 | 826 |
| *Creditors: Amounts falling due within one year* | | |
| Bank overdraft | 171 | — |
| Trade creditors | 181 | 156 |
| Proposed dividend | 180 | 120 |
| Mainstream corporation tax | 90 | 117 |
| | 622 | 393 |
| Net current assets | | |
| Total assets less current liabilities | 1 588 | 1 378 |
| *Creditors: amounts falling due after more than one year* | | |
| Debentures | — | (200) |
| *Provision for liabilities and charges* | | |
| Deferred taxation | (90) | (60) |
| *Net assets* | 1 498 | 1 118 |
| *Capital and Reserves* | | |
| Called up share capital | 1 200 | 1 000 |
| Share premium account | 120 | — |
| Profit and loss account | 178 | 118 |
| | 1 498 | 1 118 |

## 4 Investing activities

This covers the cost of acquiring fixed assets and investments (other than investments included as cash equivalents, see below), and cash inflows from the disposal of these items:

The relevant entries for Lisvane Ltd are:

| | £000 |
|---|---|
| Payments to acquire tangible fixed assets | (530) |
| Receipts from the sale of tangible fixed assets | 15 |
| Net cash outflow from investing activities | (515) |

## 5 Financing

Financing cash flows are made up of receipts and repayments of share capital, loan capital and short-term borrowings (other than those included within cash equivalents), together with any payments of expenses or commission in relation to their issue. The relevant amounts are as follows:

| | £000 | |
|---|---|---|
| Issue of shares | 320 | W4 |
| Repayment of debentures | (200) | |
| Net cash flow from financing | 120 | |

W4 £200 000 (increase in share capital) + £120 000 (increase in share premium)

Companies are also required to provide, as a note to the accounts, a detailed reconciliation of opening and closing figures for share capital and loans. This demonstrates the effect of the increase or decrease in financing detailed above.

| | Share capital £000 | Debenture loan £000 |
|---|---|---|
| Balance at 31 December 1990 | 1 000 | 200 |
| Cash inflow (outflow from financing) | 320 | (200) |
| Balance at 31 December 1991 | 1 320 | — |

We are now in a position to assemble the above calculations in the form of a comprehensive Cash Flow Statement for Lisvane Ltd, together with related notes. This information is set out in Figure 3.

Students should note the following two further points regarding the presentation.

- Figure 3 contains a total at the foot of the Cash Flow Statement captioned 'Decrease in cash and cash equivalents' and, under note 2, there appears an 'Analysis of changes in cash and cash equivalents during the year'. The reason for these disclosures is that the ADB believes it is important not only to report cash flows but also the impact of cash flows on the reporting entity's cash position, helping to demonstrate the ways in which it has improved or deteriorated.
- Figure 3 contains a sub-total in the main Cash Flow Statement captioned 'Net cash outflow before financing (408)'. This helps to distinguish the extent to which operations have been financed from internal or external sources.

### Further Technical Points

- The definition of cash used for the purpose of FRS1 includes what are described as 'cash equivalents'. These are near cash items, defined by the ASV as investments with no more than three months to maturity and borrowings falling due within a similar time scale. The justification for regarding these as cash is the high level of liquidity associated with them.

**Figure 3**

*Lisvane Ltd: Cash flow Statement for the year ended 31 December 1991*

| | £000 | £000 |
|---|---|---|
| *Net cash flows from operating activities* | | 373 |
| *Returns on investment and servicing of finance* | | |
| Interest received | 26 | |
| Interest paid | (10) | |
| Dividend paid | (165) | |
| Net cash flow from returns on investment and servicing of finance | | (149) |
| *Taxation* | | |
| Mainstream corporation tax | (117) | |
| Tax paid | | (117) |
| *Investing activities* | | |
| Payments to acquire tangible fixed assets | (530) | |
| Receipts from sale of tangible fixed assets | 15 | |
| Net cash outflow from investing activities | | (515) |
| *Net cash outflow before financing* | | (408) |
| Financing | | |
| Issue of shares | 320 | |
| Repayment of debentures | (200) | |
| Net cash flow from financing | | 120 |
| *Decrease in cash and cash equivalents* | | (288) |

**Notes to the cash flow statement**

1 Reconciliation of operating profit to net cash inflow from operating activities

| | £000 |
|---|---|
| Operating profit | 389 |
| Depreciation charges | 104 |
| Loss on sale of tangible fixed assets | 25 |
| Increase in stocks | (69) |
| Increase in debtors | (101) |
| Increase in trade creditors | 25 |
| | 373 |

2 Analysis of changes in cash and cash equivalents during the year

| | 1991 | 1990 | Change |
|---|---|---|---|
| | £000 | £000 | £000 |
| Investments | 78 | 142 | (64) |
| Cash at bank and in hand | — | 53 | (53) |
| Bank overdraft | (171) | — | (171) |
| | (93) | 195 | (288) |

3 Analysis of changes in financing during the year

| | Share capital | Debenture loan |
|---|---|---|
| | £000 | £000 |
| Balance at 31 December 1990 | 1 000 | 200 |
| Cash inflow (outflow from financing) | 320 | (200) |
| Balance at 31 December 1991 | 1 320 | — |

- Where cash flows relate to exceptional items or extraordinary items, they should be allocated to the appropriate heading within the Cash Flow Statement. Exceptional items relate to normal activities and will be included under 'Net cash flow from operating activities' with an indication of the nature of the cash flow relating to the exceptional item given in a note. The treatment of an extraordinary item would depend upon its precise form but, for example, proceeds from the sale of a fixed asset or from the discontinuance of a significant part of the company's business, of sufficient magnitude, would be separately listed under 'Investing activities'.
- The format used in Figure 3 is similar to illustrative example 1 contained in the explanatory section attached to FRS1. Companies are not required to use precisely this form, but one might expect that the recommended format will be fairly closely followed by the majority of companies.

### Scope and Coverage

It is intended that FRS1 should apply to the financial statements published by most business entities, but there are some important exceptions. The main ones are wholly-owned subsidiaries and small reporting entities. The latter are defined as entities (companies, businesses and not for profit organisations) which come within the size specifications identified by the Companies Act 1985 for small companies, i.e. an entity where at least two of the following three criteria are not exceeded: turnover, £2m; gross assets at year end, £0.975m; average number of employees per week, 50. The justification for this exemption is that the cost of preparing the Cash Flow Statement for entities which are often owner managed is likely to be disproportionate to the benefits received. In particular, the owner is in close touch with the business operations and does not require a Cash Flow Statement to highlight business developments. Alternatively, if the owner does feel that the information would be useful, he/she is in a position to ensure appropriate arrangements are made. In other words, the matter is left to the individuals concerned.

This rationalisation overlooks the fact that the owners are not the only users of financial reports. In particular, such information might be useful to banks and other creditors. The ASB has chosen not to make publication an obligation, however, on the grounds that the abbreviated accounts, which small companies are required to file with the Registrar, and thus enter the public domain, do not have to include a Cash Flow Statement. It is therefore up to the bank and other creditors to put pressure on customers and clients in order to ensure that a Cash Flow Statement is prepared for their examination.

### Interpretation

The preparation of a Cash Flow Statement is not, of course, an end in itself. The justification for this reporting requirement depends upon its usefulness as a basis for assessing business development. It is therefore relevant to review the information contained in Figure 3 to see what messages it contains.

- The company has a substantial net cash flow from operations, and note 1 helps to explain the extent to which this differs from operating profit. We can see that *funds* from operations (represented by operating profit, depreciation charge, loss on sale of tangible fixed assets) are mainly responsible for cash generation, some of which has been used to finance the increase in stocks and debtors, to the extent that this has not been covered by the increase in trade creditors, leaving a residual of £373 000 which appears in the main statement.
- The entry for 'Returns on investment and servicing of finance' shows that the main outflow is dividends paid which absorbs about nearly one half of net cash flow from operating activities.
- Taxation. This shows that approximately 40 per cent of net cash flow has been absorbed in the form of corporation tax payments.

- Investing activities. A substantial outlay has been made during the current accounting period. This is the single largest item in the Cash Flow Statement and is mainly responsible for a net cash *outflow* before financing of £408 000.
- Financing. The company has made a significant share issue which has been substantially absorbed in meeting the cost of repaying the debentures, leaving a balance of only £120 000 to help defray net investment during the current accounting period.
- The outcome is a substantial decrease in cash and cash equivalents of £288 000, with the analysis in note 2 highlighting the fact that a liquid balance of £195 000, at the beginning of the year, has been converted into a deficit of £93 000 at the year end as the result of these developments.

The overall impression is of a significant expansion which appears to have put a considerable strain on the company's liquidity position. It would of course be necessary to examine the company's profitability and financial position in greater depth based on other information in the accounts – an appraisal which would call for the calculation of relevant accounting ratios – before reaching any balanced conclusions concerning the performance of Lisvane Ltd during 1991.

## ■ MOCK EXAMINATION – CIB MAY 1992

1 Read the instructions carefully.
2 Answer *five questions in total.*
Answer Question 1 from Section A.
Answer at least 1 question from Section B.
Answer at least 2 questions from Section C, and
answer 1 other question from either Section B or C.
3 The number in brackets after each question, or part of question, shows the marks allocated.
All questions carry a total of 20 marks each.
4 Answers in listed note form are acceptable, provided they are presented in a clear and logical manner, the points made are adequately developed, and no other format is specified in the question.
5 Silent non-programmable pocket calculators may be used in this examination. *Whether candidates use them or not, it is essential to show the basic figures from which the calculations are made.*
6 Candidates are reminded that orderly presentation and clear handwriting are essential in their answers.
7 Taxation, in all forms, should be ignored.
8 Time allowed: *three hours.*

### Section A

*Answer Question 1*

1 Tower is a sole trader who owns a retail shop. The trial balance extracted from the firm's ledger at 31 December 1991 is:

| | £000 | £000 |
|---|---|---|
| Capital at 1 January 1991 | | 148 |
| Loan from the finance company | | 50 |
| Freehold premises at cost | 108 | |
| Fixtures and fittings at cost | 25 | |
| Accumulated depreciation on fixtures and fittings at 1 January 1991 | | 10 |
| Stock at 1 January 1991 | 125 | |
| Purchases | 620 | |
| Wages and salaries | 31 | |
| Rates | 16 | |
| Debtors | 64 | |
| Sales | | 800 |
| Creditors | | 38 |
| Delivery expenses | 7 | |
| Bank | | 7 |
| Bank interest | 1 | |
| Bank charges | 2 | |
| Heat, light and power | 9 | |
| Drawings | 24 | |
| General expenses | 21 | |
| | 1 053 | 1 053 |

The following information is relevant:

1 During the year to 31 December 1991, Tower withdrew stock which had cost £3 000 for his personal use. This is not reflected in the above trial balance.

2 No depreciation is charged on freehold property.

3 Stock at 31 December 1991 was valued at £136 000.

4 During the year to 31 December 1991 additional fixtures and fittings were purchased at a cost of £5 000. This was, in error, entered in the purchases account.

5 Fixtures and fittings are to be depreciated on the reducing balance basis using an annual rate of 40%.

6 On 31 December 1991, by agreement with Tower, a customer, who had purchased goods on credit and not yet paid for them, returned the goods. Their selling price was £16 000 and they had cost Tower £10 000. Their return is not reflected in the above trial balance, but they have been included in closing stock at a value of £16 000.

7 Bad debts of £4 000 are to be written off, and a general provision for doubtful debts of £9 000 created.

8 At 31 December 1991 bank interest and bank charges outstanding, and not yet accrued, amounted to £1 000 and £2 000 respectively, and £200 of rates had been paid in advance.

9 The loan from the finance company was taken out in 1987 and carries an annual interest charge of 12%, which is paid on 1 January each year in respect of the previous year.

*Required*:
Prepare the trading and profit and loss account of Tower for the year to 31

December 1991 and the balance sheet at that date. The balance sheet should disclose the values of fixed assets, current assets, current liabilities, working capital and Tower's capital at 31 December 1991. (20)

## Section B

*Answer at least* ONE *question but not more than TWO questions from this section*

2 (a) Define the term 'goodwill'. Explain how it comes into existence and the benefit which a firm derives if it possesses goodwill. (6)
(b) Define the terms 'capital expenditure' and 'revenue expenditure'. (4)
(c) On 31 March 1992 General Ltd acquired as a going concern the business of Trainer, a sole trader, for a cash payment of £450 000. The assets taken over were valued at the following amounts:

| | £000 |
|---|---|
| Debtors | 74 |
| Freehold land and buildings | 200 |
| Stock | 216 |
| Goodwill | 80 |
| Motor vehicles | 65 |
| Cash | 5 |
| | 450 |

Using the information set out above, identify those assets which represent capital expenditure. Describe *two* alternative methods by which the goodwill acquired could be treated in the accounts of General Ltd and explain their impact on the balance sheet of General Ltd. (10)
(Total – 20 marks)

3 (a) Describe *three* types of long-term finance which may be found in the balance sheet of a business. (6)
(b) Define the term 'over-trading' and describe *four* symptoms of over-trading which may be found in a set of annual accounts of a limited company. Explain why these indicate that over-trading might have occurred. (10)
(c) Explain why it is important for a business to fund long-term applications of funds from long-term sources of funds. (4)
(Total – 20 marks)

## Section C

*Answer at least* TWO *but not more than* THREE *questions*

4 The directors of Martin Ltd, a manufacturing company, are considering the introduction of a new product, called 'Wheely' into their range. There are two alternative ways in which this can be manufactured, one of which uses a partly automated production line (Method 1) while the other is reliant on labour intensive techniques (Method 2). It is expected that sales will be 100 000 units per annum irrespective of which production method is used.

The sales director and production director have produced the following data in respect of Wheely, based on an output of 100 000 units.

| | Method 1 | Method 2 |
|---|---|---|
| Selling price per unit | £33 | £33 |
| Direct material cost per unit | £13 | £15 |
| Direct labour cost per unit | £8 | £14 |
| Average fixed cost per unit (excluding depreciation) | £7 | £2 |
| Purchase of fixed assets | £1 200 000 | £200 000 |
| Life of fixed assets | 5 years | 5 years |
| Residual value of fixed assets | £200 000 | Zero |
| Maximum annual output | 150 000 units | 120 000 units |

Depreciation is to be calculated using the straight line basis.

*Required*:

(a) Calculate, for each method of production:

(i) the contribution per unit

(ii) the break even point, in units and in value

(iii) the maximum annual profit which may be earned if sales exceed the forecast

(iv) the maximum annual loss which may be incurred

(v) the annual profit at the expected level of sales.

(b) Comment on the relative merits/drawbacks of the two alternative methods of production, and indicate any other factors which management should take into consideration when deciding which method to adopt. (5)

(Total – 20 marks)

5 The following are the summarised balance sheet of Maurice Ltd at 1 January 1991 and its trading and profit and loss account for the twelve months commencing 1 January 1991:

*Balance Sheet at 1 January 1991*

| | £000 | £000 |
|---|---|---|
| Freehold premises at cost | | 500 |
| Plant at cost | 1 500 | |
| less: Accumulated depreciation | 750 | |
| | | 750 |
| | | 1 250 |
| Stock | 190 | |
| Debtors for sales | 225 | |
| Bank account | 25 | |
| | 440 | |
| Trade creditors | 115 | |
| Proposed dividend for 1990 | 100 | |
| Corporation tax due for 1990 | 135 | |
| | | 350 |
| | | 90 |
| | | 1 340 |
| Financed by: | | |
| Ordinary shares of £1 each | | 400 |
| Share premium | | 200 |
| Profit and loss account | | 740 |
| | | 1 340 |

*Trading and Profit and Loss Account for the year to 31 December 1991*

| | £000 | £000 |
|---|---|---|
| Sales | | 4 800 |
| Opening stock | 190 | |
| Purchases | 3 000 | |
| Closing stock | (210) | |
| | | 2 980 |
| | | 1 820 |
| Depreciation of plant | 250 | |
| Salaries and wages | 760 | |
| Delivery costs | 125 | |
| Other expenses | 105 | |
| Debenture interest | 50 | |
| | | 1 290 |
| Trading profit | | 530 |

The proposed dividend and corporation tax for 1990 were both paid in 1991.

On 1 January 1991 the company purchased for cash additional plant at a cost of £1 000 000. This purchase was mostly financed by the issue of 200 000 ordinary shares of £1 each at a premium of £1 per share and a debenture of £500 000 carrying interest at an annual rate of 10% payable on 31 December.

The directors had the freehold premises valued at 31 December 1991, and found that its value at that date was £2 000 000. They decided that this value should be incorporated in the company's balance sheet at 31 December 1991.

The corporation tax for 1991 is estimated at £195 000 and the directors think that a dividend of 25 pence per ordinary share in issue at 31 December 1991 should be recommended.

At 31 December 1991, debtors for sales were £250 000 and trade creditors were £120 000.

*Required*:
(a) Prepare the profit and loss appropriation account of Maurice Ltd for the year to 31 December 1991, showing the balance to be carried forward to 1992. (4)
(b) Prepare the balance sheet of Maurice Ltd as at 31 December 1991. (The balance of the account is to be found by preparing the appropriate ledger account in the books of Maurice Ltd for 1991.) (16)
(Total – 20 marks)

6 The following are the summarised balance sheets and trading and profit and loss accounts of Relay and Baton for the year to 31 March 1992:

*Trading and Profit and Loss Account*

| | Relay | Baton |
|---|---|---|
| | £000 | £000 |
| Sales | 200 | 150 |
| Cost of goods sold | 100 | 100 |
| | 100 | 50 |
| Expenses | 80 | 30 |
| | 20 | 20 |

*Balance Sheet*

| | Relay | | Baton | |
|---|---|---|---|---|
| | £000 | £000 | £000 | £000 |
| Fixed assets at cost less depreciation | | 300 | | 220 |
| Stock | 50 | | 60 | |
| Debtors | 16 | | 11 | |
| Cash | — | | 3 | |
| | 66 | | 74 | |
| Trade creditors | 59 | | 11 | |
| Overdraft | 10 | | — | |
| | 69 | | 11 | |
| | | (3) | | 63 |
| | | 297 | | 283 |
| Loan at 12% interest per annum, secured on fixed assets | | 100 | | – |
| | | 197 | | 283 |
| Financed by: | | | | |
| Capital | | 197 | | 283 |

*Required:*
Write a report which compares and contrasts the financial performance and position of Relay and Baton. You should indicate any limitations of your analysis and use the following accounting ratios, calculated to two places of decimals, to support your discussion: gross profit to sales; net profit to sales; return on capital employed; working capital ratio; liquidity ratio; and the debt/equity (gearing) ratio. (20)

7 Mr Sutol rented a shop and started trading on 1 January 1991 under the name 'Sutol & Co'. He did not keep any accounting records, and has asked you to help him calculate the firm's profit for 1991 and its position at the year end. You have asked him to provide you with details of assets and liabilities, and, in response, he has given you the following items of information:

(a) I opened a business bank account on 1 January and transferred into it £10 000 from my personal current account which I had won as a premium bond prize. This left a balance of £530 on my personal account.

(b) On 1 January I purchased a delivery van for £8 000; the value of this on 31 December was about £6 000. I have kept my car for personal use; this was worth £3 000 on 1 January and, at that time, had about three years' life left.

(c) During the year I had to arrange an overdraft for the business, and used my house as security. As I bought my house some time ago for £45 000 the bank asked me to have it valued, and I was pleased to find that it is now worth £125 000, although I still owe the building society £12 000 on its mortgage.
(d) I managed to reduce the firm's overdraft on 1 July as my rich uncle lent the firm £4 000 which was paid into the business bank account. We agreed that he will be paid 6% annual interest on the loan, with the first payment being made on 30 June 1992.
(e) 1991 must have been my lucky year as I won another premium bond prize, although this time it was only £1 000, which I paid into the business bank account.
(f) During 1991 I took £15 000 in cash from the business for living expenses.
(g) At 31 December 1991 I reckon that the assets and liabilities not mentioned above were:

| | £ |
|---|---|
| Bank overdraft | 2 700 |
| Cash in personal bank account | 450 |
| Trading stock | 3 300 |
| Electricity due on business premises | 70 |
| Electricity due on house | 50 |
| Rates prepaid on business premises | 260 |
| Creditors for trading purchases | 1 125 |
| Debtors for sales | 2 500 |
| Bank interest on overdraft and charges due | 110 |

*Required*:
(a) Define the term 'entity concept' and explain its effect on the preparation of accounting reports. Illustrate your answer using the information in (a)–(f) above. (10)
(b) Prepare the balance sheet of Sutol & Co at 31 December 1991, showing clearly the firm's profit for 1991. (10)
(Total – 20 marks)

# Appendix A: Answers to progress tests

## ■ CHAPTER 2: THE BALANCE SHEET

**1(a)**

| | Assets | Capital | Liabilities |
|---|---|---|---|
| | £ | £ | £ |
| (a) | 7 500 | 5 000 | 2 500 |
| (b) | 37 500 | 26 500 | 11 000 |
| (c) | 15 000 | 12 500 | 2 500 |
| (d) | 25 000 | 15 750 | 9 250 |

**(b)**

*Balance Sheet of Costa's Bakery at 30.9.Y0*

| | £ | £ | £ | | |
|---|---|---|---|---|---|
| *Fixed assets* | | | | | |
| Premises | 56 500 | | | Capital | 60 500 |
| Fixtures | 7 000 | | | | |
| Equipment | 5 000 | 68 500 | | *Liabilities* | |
| | | | | Loan | 12 000 |
| *Current assets* | | | | | |
| Stock | 2 000 | | | | |
| Cash | 2 000 | 4 000 | | | |
| | | 72 500 | | | 72 500 |

**2**

Effect upon:

| | Assets | Capital | Liabilities |
|---|---|---|---|
| (a) Purchased stock for £3 000 cash | Stock + £3 000<br>Cash – £3 000 | | |
| (b) Paid a creditor by cheque £5 000 | Bank – £5 000 | | Creditor – £5 000 |
| (c) Obtained a loan for £1 000 | Cash + £1 000 | | Loan + £1 000 |
| (d) The owner injected a further £5 000 into the business | Cash + £5 000 | Capital + £5 000 | |

## ■ CHAPTER 3: DOUBLE ENTRY BOOKKEEPING

**1**

*Capital*

| | | | | | |
|---|---|---|---|---|---|
| | | | Oct 1 | Cash | £20 000 |

*Cash*

| | | | | | |
|---|---|---|---|---|---|
| Oct 1 | Capital | £20 000 | Oct 2 | Van | £10 000 |
| | | | | Equipment | £2 000 |
| | | | | Fittings | £2 000 |
| | | | Oct 4 | Bank | £3 000 |

*Van*

| | | | | | |
|---|---|---|---|---|---|
| Oct 2 | Cash | £10 000 | | | |

*Equipment*

| | | | | | |
|---|---|---|---|---|---|
| Oct 2 | Cash | £2 000 | | | |

*Fittings*

| | | | | | |
|---|---|---|---|---|---|
| Oct 2 | Cash | £2 000 | | | |

*Loan*

| | | | | | |
|---|---|---|---|---|---|
| | | | Oct 3 | Bank | £10 000 |

*Bank*

| | | | | | |
|---|---|---|---|---|---|
| Oct 3 | Loan | £10 000 | | | |
| Oct 4 | | £3 000 | | | |

*Note*: A new ledger is opened for each different item – for every debit there is a credit.

**2**

| | Account debited | Account credited |
|---|---|---|
| (a) Sold goods for £1 000 cash | Cash | Sales |
| (b) Bought fixtures by cheque for £3 000 | Fixtures | Bank |
| (c) Paid wages of £200 cash | Wages | Cash |
| (d) Returned goods to Miss B Jones for £150 | B Jones | Returns out |
| (e) Received rent of £100 in cash in respect of premises sub-let | Cash | Rent received |
| (f) Paid electricity £200 by cheque | Electricity | Bank |

(g) Allowed Mr Hussain £50 discount | Discount allowed | Mr Hussain

*Note*: Rent received is entered on the credit side as the double/outside entry to the cash received.

**3**

*Bank*

| | £ | | £ |
|---|---|---|---|
| Nov 1 Capital | 2 000 | Nov 3 | 1 000 |
| Nov 30 Loan | 5 000 | Nov 12 Rent | 50 |
| | | Nov 20 M Lowe | 105 |
| | | Nov 30 Balance | 5 845 |
| | 7 000 | | 7 000 |
| Dec 1 | 5 845 | | |

*Capital*

| | £ | | £ |
|---|---|---|---|
| | | Nov 1 Bank | 2 000 |
| Nov 30 Balance | 2 000 | | |
| | 2 000 | | 2 000 |
| | | Dec 1 Balance | 2 000 |

*Purchases*

| | £ | | £ |
|---|---|---|---|
| Nov 2 M Lowe | 175 | | |
| Nov 19 N Rose | 1 000 | | |
| | | Nov 30 Balance | 1 175 |
| | 1 175 | | 1 175 |
| Dec 1 Balance | 1 175 | | |

*M Lowe*

| | £ | | £ |
|---|---|---|---|
| Nov 5 Returns Out | 50 | Nov 2 Purchases | 175 |
| Nov 20 Discount rec'd | 20 | | |
| Nov 20 Bank | 105 | | |
| | 175 | | 175 |

*Van*

| | £ | | £ |
|---|---|---|---|
| Nov 3 Bank | 1 000 | | |
| | | Nov 31 Balance | 1 000 |
| | 1 000 | | 1 000 |
| Dec 1 | 1 000 | | |

*Sales*

| | £ | | £ |
|---|---|---|---|
| | | Nov 4 Cash | 1 000 |
| | | Nov 8 P Daubney | 500 |
| | | Nov 26 Cash | 300 |
| Nov 31 Balance | 1 800 | | |
| | 1 800 | | 1 800 |
| | | Dec 1 Balance | 1 800 |

*Cash*

| | £ | | £ |
|---|---|---|---|
| Nov 4 Sales | 1 000 | Nov 10 Drawings | 500 |
| Nov 26 Sales | 300 | Nov 12 Electricity | 36 |
| | | | 764 |
| | 1 300 | | 1 300 |
| Dec 1 Balance | 764 | | |

*Returns out*

| | £ | | £ |
|---|---|---|---|
| | | Nov 5 M Lowe | 50 |
| Nov 31 Balance | 50 | | |
| | 50 | | 50 |
| | | Dec 1 Balance | 50 |

*P Daubney*

| | £ | | £ |
|---|---|---|---|
| Nov 8 Sales | 500 | Nov 29 Returns In | 100 |
| | | Nov 31 Balance | 400 |
| | 500 | | 500 |
| Dec 1 Balance | 400 | | |

*Drawings*

| | £ | | £ |
|---|---|---|---|
| Nov 10 Cash | 500 | | |
| | | Nov 31 Balance | 500 |
| | 500 | | 500 |
| Dec 1 Balance | 500 | | |

*Electricity*

| | £ | | £ |
|---|---|---|---|
| Nov 12 Cash | 36 | Nov 31 Balance | 36 |
| | 36 | | 36 |
| Dec 1 Balance | 36 | | |

*Rent*

| | £ | | £ |
|---|---|---|---|
| Nov 16 Bank | 50 | Nov 31 Balance | 50 |
| | 50 | | 50 |
| Dec 1 Balance | 50 | | |

*N Rose*

| | £ | | £ |
|---|---|---|---|
| Nov 31 Balance | 1 000 | Nov 19 Purchases | 1 000 |
| | 1 000 | | 1 000 |
| | | Dec 1 Balance | 1 000 |

*Discount received*

| | £ | | £ |
|---|---|---|---|
| Nov 31 Balance | 20 | Nov 20 M Lowe | 20 |
| | 20 | | 20 |
| | | Dec 1 Balance | 20 |

*Returns in*

| | £ | | £ |
|---|---|---|---|
| Nov 29 P Daubney | 100 | Nov 31 Balance | 100 |
| | 100 | | 100 |
| Dec 1 Balance | 100 | | |

*Loan*

| | £ | | £ |
|---|---|---|---|
| Nov 31 Balance | 5 000 | Nov 30 Bank | 5 000 |
| | 5 000 | | 5 000 |
| | | Dec 1 Balance | 5 000 |

*Note*: Drawings are noted on the debit side as the double entry to cash paid out.

*Trial Balance as at 31.11.X9*

| | Debit £ | Credit £ |
|---|---|---|
| Bank | 5 845 | |
| Capital | | 2 000 |
| Purchases | 1 175 | |
| M Lowe (Creditor) | — | — |
| Van | 1 000 | |
| Sales | | 1 800 |
| Cash | 764 | |
| Returns out | | 50 |
| P Daubney (Debtor) | 400 | |
| Drawings | 500 | |
| Electricity | 36 | |
| Rent | 50 | |
| N Rose (Creditor) | | 1 000 |
| Discounts received | | 20 |
| Returns in | 100 | |
| Loan | | 5 000 |
| | 9 870 | 9 870 |

## ■ CHAPTER 4: ERRORS AND CONTROL ACCOUNTS

**1**

*Suspense account*

| | £ | | £ |
|---|---|---|---|
| Purchases | 1 000 | Difference as per trial balance | 5 000 |
| Creditors | 300 | | |
| B Brown | 1 400 | Returns In | 700 |
| Suspense | 3 000 | | |
| | 5 700 | | 5 700 |

*Purchases*

| | | | |
|---|---|---|---|
| | | Suspense | £1 000 |

*Creditors*

| | | | |
|---|---|---|---|
| | | Suspense | £300 |

*B Brown*

| | | | |
|---|---|---|---|
| | | Suspense | £1 400 |

*Bank*

| | | | |
|---|---|---|---|
| | | Suspense | £3 000 |

*Returns in*

| | | |
|---|---|---|
| Suspense | £700 | |

*Journal*

| | Dr | Cr |
|---|---|---|
| Purchases | | 1 000 |
| Suspense | 1 000 | |
| Purchases overcast by £1000 | | |
| Creditors | | 300 |
| Suspense | 300 | |
| Creditor undercast by £300 | | |
| B Brown | | 1 400 |
| Suspense | 1 400 | |
| £1 400 received not entered in B Brown's ledger | | |
| Bank | | 3 000 |
| Suspense | 3 000 | |
| Purchase of a van not entered in the bank ledger | | |
| Returns in | 700 | |
| Suspense | | 700 |
| goods returned not entered | | |

**2**

*Sales ledger control account*

| | £ | | £ |
|---|---|---|---|
| Opening balance | 3 705 | Cash received | 7 468 |
| Sales | 150 000 | Cheques received | 120 000 |
| Interest | 5 000 | Returns in | 5 000 |
| Unpaid cheques | 576 | Bad debts written off | 3 107 |
| | | Discounts allowed | 2 000 |
| | | Balance c/d | 21 706 |
| | 159 281 | | 159 281 |

*Purchase ledger control account*

| | £ | | £ |
|---|---|---|---|
| Cash paid | 3 441 | Opening balance | 21 000 |
| Cheques paid | 190 000 | Purchases | 200 000 |
| Discount received | 1 000 | Interest charged by suppliers | 4 000 |
| Returns out | 500 | | |
| Balance | 30 059 | | |
| | 225 000 | | 225 000 |

i.e. there is an error of £1 000

## ■ CHAPTER 5: TRADING PROFIT AND LOSS ACCOUNT

**1(1)**

| | (a) | | (b) | | (c) | | (d) | |
|---|---|---|---|---|---|---|---|---|
| | £ | £ | £ | £ | £ | £ | £ | £ |
| Sales | | 100 000 | | 50 000 | | 135 950 | | 80 000 |
| *less Cost of goods sold* | | | | | | | | |
| Opening stock | 30 000 | | 25 000 | | 52 105 | | 40 000 | |
| + Purchases | 50 000 | | 10 000 | | 87 769 | | 60 000 | |
| | 80 000 | | 35 000 | | 139 874 | | 100 000 | |
| – Closing stock | 40 000 | 40 000 | 10 000 | 25 000 | 47 950 | 91 924 | 10 000 | 90 000 |
| Gross profit | | 60 000 | | 25 000 | | 44 026 | | (10 000) |

**1(2)**

*Trading Profit and Loss Account of M Reid for the year ending 31.10.X9*

| | £ | £ |
|---|---|---|
| Sales | | 20 959 |
| *less Cost of goods sold* | | |
| Opening stock | 7 815 | |
| + Purchases | 12 107 | |
| | 19 922 | |
| – Closing stock | 4 810 | 15 112 |
| Gross profit | | 5 847 |
| *less Expenses* | | |
| Rent | 105 | |
| Electricity | 205 | |
| Insurance | 75 | 385 |
| Net profit | | 5 462 |

**2**

*Trading Profit and Loss Account of B West for the year ending 31.10.X9*

| | £ | £ | £ |
|---|---|---|---|
| Sales | | | 73 955 |
| *less* Returns In | | | 515 |
| | | | 73 440 |
| *less* Cost of goods sold | | | |
| Opening stock | | 11 518 | |
| + Purchases | 2 108 | | |
| *less* Returns out | 205 | | |
| | 26 903 | | |
| + Carriage in | 70 | 26 973 | |
| | | 38 491 | |
| – Closing stock | | 5 809 | 32 682 |
| Gross profit | | | 40 758 |
| *less Expenses* | | | |
| Rent | | 200 | |
| Rates | | 800 | |
| Wages | | 5 801 | |
| Carriage out | | 175 | 6 976 |
| Net profit | | | 33 782 |

**3**

*Trading Profit and Loss Account of E Loughlan for the year ending 31.10.X8*

| | £ | £ | £ |
|---|---|---|---|
| Sales | | | 55 950 |
| *less* Returns in | | | 210 |
| | | | 55 740 |
| *less Cost of goods sold* | | | |
| Opening stock | | 17 105 | |
| + Purchases | 41 807 | | |
| *less* Returns out | 108 | | |
| | 41 699 | | |
| + Carriage in | 309 | 42 008 | |
| | | 59 113 | |
| – Closing stock | | 15 000 | 44 113 |
| Gross profit | | | 11 627 |
| *add Income* | | | |
| Interest received | | | 250 |
| | | | 11 877 |
| *less Expenses* | | | |
| Rates | | 1 000 | |
| Discount allowed | | 410 | |
| Electricity | | 300 | |
| Wages | | 6 000 | |
| Insurance | | 500 | 8 210 |
| Net profit | | | 3 667 |

*Balance Sheet of E Loughlan as at 31.10.X8*

| | £ | £ | | £ | £ |
|---|---|---|---|---|---|
| *Fixed assets* | | | Capital | | 60 000 |
| Premises | 50 000 | | + Net profit | | 3 667 |
| Fixtures | 15 000 | | | | 63 667 |
| Van | 5 000 | 70 000 | – Drawings | | 5 000 |
| | | | | | 58 667 |
| *Current assets* | | | | | |
| Stock | 15 000 | | *Long-term liabilities* | | |
| Debtors | 3 105 | | Loan | | 20 000 |
| Cash | 1 895 | 20 000 | | | |
| | | | *Current liabilities* | | |
| | | | Creditors | 8 410 | |
| | | | Bank overdraft | 2 923 | 11 333 |
| | | 90 000 | | | 90 000 |

*Note*: A Trading Profit and Loss Account is always 'for the year ending ...' or 'for the month ending ...' etc, as you are calculating the profit achieved over that period.

A Balance Sheet being a photograph of a company's assets and liabilities is always 'as at' a particular date and will change the following day.

The question will normally reveal this by asking for a Trading Profit and Loss Account for the year ending... and a Balance Sheet as at a particular date, but try to remember this, it is important and often worth a mark in the examination.

## ■ CHAPTER 6: TRADING PROFIT AND LOSS ACCOUNT AND BALANCE SHEET – EXTRA MATTERS

**1**

*Trading Profit and Loss Account for the year ending 31.11.X9 for N Cunningham*

| | £ | £ | £ |
|---|---|---|---|
| Sales | | | 31 705 |
| *less Cost of goods sold* | | | |
| Opening stock | | 13 201 | |
| + Purchases | 9 959 | | |
| *less* Returns out | 100 | | |
| | 9 850 | | |
| – Carriage in | 200 | 10 059 | |
| | | 23 260 | |
| *less* Closing stock | | 7 500 | 15 760 |
| Gross profit | | | 15 945 |
| *less Expenses* | | | |
| Wages | | 5 000 | |
| Carriage out | | 317 | |
| Discounts allowed | | 250 | |
| Electricity | | 700 | |
| Rates | | 500 | |
| Insurance | | 1 049 | 7 816 |
| Net profit | | | 8 129 |

*Balance Sheet of N Cunningham as at 31.11.X9*

| | £ | £ |
|---|---|---|
| *Fixed assets* | | |
| Premises | | 30 000 |
| Machinery | | 5 000 |
| Motor vehicles | | 10 000 |
| Fixtures and fittings | | 7 000 |
| | | 52 000 |
| *Current assets* | | |
| Stock | 7 500 | |
| Debtors | 12 109 | |
| Bank | 754 | |
| Cash | 121 | |
| | 20 484 | |
| *less Current liabilities* | | |
| Creditors | 6 755 | |
| Working capital | | 13 729 |
| | | 63 729 |
| Financed by: | | |
| Capital | | 50 000 |
| + Net profit | | 8 129 |
| | | 58 129 |
| – Drawings | | 11 400 |
| | | 46 729 |
| Long-term liabilities | | |
| Loan | | 19 000 |
| | | 65 729 |

**2(a)**

*Trading Profit and Loss Account of A Johnson for the year ending 31.12.X9*

| | £ | £ | £ |
|---|---|---|---|
| Sales | | | 150 000 |
| *less Cost of goods sold* | | | |
| Opening stock | | — | |
| + Purchases | | 95 000 | |
| | | 95 000 | |
| – Closing stock | | 20 000 | 75 000 |
| Gross profit | | | 75 000 |
| *less Expenses* | | | |
| Rent | | 1 100 | |
| Rates | 3 000 | | |
| – prepaid | 100 | 2 900 | |
| Electricity | | 200 | |
| Gas | | 100 | |
| Telephone | 50 | | |
| + owing | 20 | 70 | 4 370 |
| | | | 70 630 |

*Balance Sheet of A Johnson as at 31.12.X9*

| | £ | £ | £ |
|---|---|---|---|
| *Fixed assets* | | | |
| Premises | | | 60 000 |
| Fixtures | | | 20 000 |
| Vehicles | | | 19 360 |
| | | | 99 360 |
| *Current assets* | | | |
| Stock | 20 000 | | |
| Debtors | 12 170 | | |
| Prepayments | 100 | 32 270 | |
| less Current liabilities | | | |
| Creditors | 10 980 | | |
| Accruals | 20 | 11 000 | 21 270 |
| | | | 120 630 |
| Capital | | | 50 000 |
| + Net profit | | | 70 630 |
| | | | 120 630 |

**(b)**

*Trading Profit and Loss Account of S Smith for the year ending 31.12.X9*

| | £ | £ | £ |
|---|---|---|---|
| Sales | | | 150 295 |
| *less* Returns in | | | 210 |
| *less* Cost of goods sold | | | 150 085 |
| Opening stock | | — | |
| + Purchases | | 81 400 | |
| *less* Returns out | | 518 | |
| | | 80 882 | |
| + Carriage inwards | | 298 | |
| | | 81 180 | |
| – Closing stock | | 21 598 | 59 582 |
| Gross profit | | | 90 503 |
| *less Expenses* | | | |
| Rent | 215 | | |
| + owing | 410 | 625 | |
| Rates | | 1 009 | |
| Motor expenses | | 109 | |
| Insurance | 75 | | |
| – prepaid | 10 | | |
| Office expenses | 510 | | |
| + owing | 218 | 728 | |
| Carriage out | | 109 | |
| Wages and salaries | 3 176 | | |
| – prepaid | 300 | 2 876 | 5 521 |
| | | | 84 982 |

*Balance Sheet of S Smith as at 31.12.X9*

| | £ | £ | £ |
|---|---|---|---|
| *Fixed assets* | | | |
| Land and building | | | 84 889 |
| Office equipment | | | 21 095 |
| Motor van | | | 5 298 |
| | | | 111 282 |
| *Current assets* | | | |
| Stock | | 21 598 | |
| Debtors | | 2 105 | |
| Prepayments | | | |
| Insurance | 10 | | |
| Wages | 300 | 310 | |
| | | 24 013 | |
| *less Current liabilities* | | | |
| Creditors | 3 095 | | |
| Accruals | | | |
| Rent | 410 | | |
| Office expenses | 218 | 3 723 | 20 290 |
| | | | 131 572 |
| Capital | | | 50 000 |
| + Net profit | | | 84 982 |
| | | | 134 982 |
| – Drawings | | | 8 410 |
| | | | 126 572 |
| *Long-term liabilities* | | | |
| Loan | | | 5 000 |
| | | | 131 572 |

**3**

*Trading Profit and Loss Account of Mrs A Bowden for the year ending 31.3.X9*

| | £ | £ | £ |
|---|---|---|---|
| Sales | | | 100 000 |
| *less Cost of goods sold* | | | |
| Opening stock | | 40 109 | |
| + Purchases | | 60 297 | |
| | | 100 406 | |
| – Closing stock | | 61 206 | 39 200 |
| Gross profit | | | 60 800 |
| *less Expenses* | | | |
| Wages | | 20 105 | |
| Rent and rates | 4 000 | | |
| less prepaid | 700 | 3 300 | |
| Insurance | 1 500 | | |
| plus owing | 500 | 2 000 | |
| Electricity | | 715 | |
| Office expenses | | 951 | |
| Bad debts | | 700 | |
| Provision for bad debts | | 500 | 28 271 |
| Net profit | | | 32 529 |

*Balance Sheet of Mrs A Bowden as at 31.3.X9*

| | £ | £ | £ |
|---|---|---|---|
| *Fixed assets* | | | |
| Premises | | | 70 000 |
| Equipment | | | 21 000 |
| | | | 91 000 |
| *Current assets* | | | |
| Stock | | 61 206 | |
| Debtors | 20 109 | | |
| *less* Provision for bad debts | 2 000 | 18 109 | |
| Prepayments | | 700 | |
| Cash | | 170 | |
| | | 80 185 | |
| *less Current liabilities* | | | |
| Creditors | 17 109 | | |
| Accruals | 500 | | |
| Bank overdraft | 2 700 | 20 309 | 59 876 |
| | | | 150 876 |
| *Financed by:* | | | |
| Capital | | | 140 115 |
| + Net profit | | | 32 529 |
| | | | 172 644 |
| – Drawings | | | 21 768 |
| | | | 150 876 |

## ■ CHAPTER 7: DEPRECIATION

**1(a)**

(i) See text
(ii) See text
(iii) Cost £10 000
Useful life 5 years
Estimated residual value £3 000
(i) Straight line
Total depreciation = (£10 000 – £3 000) = £7 000
Depreciation p.a. = £7 000/5 = £1 400 p.a.
(ii) Reducing balance

$$r = 1 - \sqrt[5]{\frac{3\,000}{10\,000}} = \text{Approx } 22\%$$

| | Straight line £ | Reducing balance £ |
|---|---|---|
| Cost | 10 000 | 10 000 |
| Depreciation Year 1 | 1 400 | 2 200 |
| | 8 600 | 7 800 |
| Depreciation Year 2 | 1 400 | 1 716 |
| | 7 200 | 6 084 |
| Depreciation Year 3 | 1 400 | 1 338 |
| | 5 800 | 4 746 |
| Depreciation Year 4 | 1 400 | 1 044 |
| | 4 400 | 3 702 |
| Depreciation Year 5 | 1 400 | 676 |
| Book value end in Year 5 | 3 000 | 3 026 |

**(b)**

(a) See text
(b) See text
(c) *Straight line*

| | |
|---|---|
| Cost of asset | 10 000 |
| Residual value | 1 681 |
| Total depreciation | 8 319 |
| ÷ Life | 5 yrs |
| Annual charge | 1 661 |
| *Reducing balance* | |
| Cost | 10 000 |
| Yr 1 at 30% | 3 000 |
| | 7 000 |
| Yr 2 at 30% | 2 100 |
| | 4 900 |
| Yr 3 at 30% | 1 470 |
| | 3 430 |
| Yr 4 at 30% | 1 029 |
| | 2 401 |
| Yr 5 at 30% | 720 |
| | 1 681 |

- Reducing balance gives a larger charge in the initial years but lower in later years.
- As depreciation is an expense this will directly effect the reported profit figures.
- Straight line gives a constant charge but may not be realistic, e.g. cars depreciate heavily in year 1.
- Over the 5 years both methods charge nearly the same amount of depreciation.

**2**

*Trading Profit and Loss Account of L Peat for the year ending 31.12.X9*

| | £ | £ | £ |
|---|---|---|---|
| Sales | | | 200 000 |
| *less* Returns in | | | 105 |
| | | | 199 895 |
| *less* Cost of goods sold | | | |
| Opening stock | | 21 679 | |
| Purchases | 179 841 | | |
| + Carriage in | 510 | | |
| | 180 351 | | |
| – Returns out | 175 | 180 176 | |
| | | 201 855 | |
| – Closing stock | | 29 887 | 171 968 |
| Gross profit | | | 27 927 |
| *add Income* | | | |
| Discounts received | | | 2 500 |
| | | | 30 427 |
| *less Expenses* | | | |
| Telephone | | 216 | |
| Electricity | 313 | | |
| + owing | 105 | 418 | |
| Rates | | 1 000 | |
| Rent | | 518 | |
| Office expenses | 821 | | |
| – prepaid | 300 | 521 | |
| Discounts allowed | | 1 000 | |
| Provision for bad debts | | 1 000 | |
| Provision for depreciation machinery | | 3 000 | 7 673 |
| Net profit | | | 22 754 |

*Balance Sheet of L Peat as at 31.12.X9*

| | £ | £ | £ |
|---|---|---|---|
| *Fixed assets* | | | |
| Premises (cost) | | | 60 000 |
| Machinery (cost) | | 30 000 | |
| – Depreciation | | 3 000 | 27 000 |
| | | | 87 000 |
| *Current assets* | | | |
| Stock | | 29 887 | |
| Debtors | 20 000 | | |
| – Provision for bad debts | 1 000 | 19 000 | |
| Prepaid office expenses | | 300 | |
| | | 49 187 | |
| *– Current liabilities* | | | |
| Creditors | 36 000 | | |
| Accruals – Electricity | 105 | 36 105 | 13 082 |
| | | | 100 082 |
| Capital | | | 75 000 |
| + Net profit | | | 22 754 |
| | | | 97 754 |
| *Long-term liabilities* | | | |
| Loan | | | 2 328 |
| | | | 100 082 |

**3**

*Trading Profit and Loss Account for L Harris for the year ending 31.12.X9*

| | £ | £ | £ |
|---|---|---|---|
| Sales | | | 315 000 |
| *less Cost of goods sold* | | | |
| Opening stock | | 36 598 | |
| + Purchases | | 201 591 | |
| | | 238 189 | |
| – Closing stock | | 42 000 | 196 189 |
| Gross profit | | | 118 811 |
| *add Income* | | | |
| Discounts received | | | 550 |
| | | | 119 361 |
| *less Expenses* | | | |
| Wages | 30 100 | | |
| – Prepaid | 515 | 29 585 | |
| Electricity | | 3 000 | |
| Rates | 10 000 | | |
| – Prepaid | 2 000 | 8 000 | |
| Office expenses | 5 000 | | |
| + owing | 700 | 5 700 | |
| Discounts allowed | | 700 | |
| Carriage outwards | | 250 | |
| Provision for bad debts | | 3 500 | |
| Provision for depreciation: Motor vehicles | | 4 000 | 54 735 |
| | | | 64 626 |

*Balance Sheet of L Harris as at 31.12.X9*

| | £ | £ | £ |
|---|---|---|---|
| *Fixed assets* | | | |
| Premises | | | 84 000 |
| Fixtures and fittings | | | 36 000 |
| Motor vehicles (cost) | | 25 000 | |
| – Depreciation | | 9 000 | 16 000 |
| | | | 136 000 |
| *Current assets* | | | |
| Stock | | 42 000 | |
| Debtors | 37 000 | | |
| – Provision for bad debts | 3 500 | 33 500 | |
| Prepayments: | | | |
| Wages | 515 | | |
| Rates | 2 000 | 2 515 | |
| | | 78 015 | |
| *less Current liabilities* | | | |
| Creditors | 12 689 | | |
| Accruals – Office expenses | 700 | 13 389 | 64 626 |
| | | | 200 626 |
| Capital | | | 100 000 |
| + Net profit | | | 64 626 |
| | | | 164 626 |
| *Long-term liabilities* | | | |
| Loan | | | 36 000 |
| | | | 200 626 |

**4**

*Trading Profit and Loss Account for the year ending 31.12.X9*

| | £ | £ | £ |
|---|---|---|---|
| Sales | | | 100 000 |
| *less Cost of goods sold* | | | |
| Opening stock | | 10 000 | |
| + Purchases | | 50 000 | |
| | | 60 000 | |
| – Closing stock | | 12 100 | 47 900 |
| Gross profit | | | 52 100 |
| *less Expenses* | | | |
| Wages | | 12 000 | |
| Office expenses | 3 903 | | |
| – Prepaid | 100 | 3 803 | |
| Electricity | | 397 | |
| Rates | 1 000 | | |
| + owing | 200 | 1 200 | |
| Insurance | 200 | | |
| + owing | 50 | 250 | |
| Depreciation: Fixtures and fittings | | 500 | |
| Motor vehicles | | 5 000 | |
| Loss of sale of van | | 1 000 | 24 150 |
| Net profit | | | 27 950 |

*Balance Sheet as at 31.12.X9*

| | £ | £ | £ |
|---|---|---|---|
| *Fixed assets* | | | |
| Premises | | | 80 000 |
| Motor vehicles | | 25 000 | |
| – Depreciation | | 18 000 | 7 000 |
| Fixtures and fittings | | 11 500 | |
| – Depreciation | | 4 000 | 7 500 |
| | | | 94 500 |
| *Current assets* | | | |
| Stock | | 12 100 | |
| Debtors | | 21 000 | |
| Prepaid office expenses | | 100 | |
| Bank | | 1 000 | |
| Cash | | 1 500 | |
| | | 35 700 | |
| *less Current liabilities* | | | |
| Creditors | 17 000 | | |
| Accruals: | | | |
| Rent | 200 | | |
| Insurance | 50 | 17 250 | 18 450 |
| | | | 112 950 |
| Capital | | | 70 000 |
| + Net profit | | | 27 950 |
| | | | 97 950 |
| *Long-term liabilities* | | | |
| Loan | | | 15 000 |
| | | | 112 950 |

## ■ CHAPTER 8: SOLE TRADER REVISION

**1**

*Trading Profit and Loss Account*

| | | |
|---|---|---|
| Sales | | 150 750 |
| Opening stock | 25 600 | |
| Purchases (112 800 – 450) | 112 350 | |
| Closing stock | – 27 350 | |
| Cost of goods sold | | 110 600 |
| Gross profit | | 40 150 |
| Wages | 12 610 | |
| Rent (2 500 – 500) | 2 000 | |
| Motor expenses (1 240 + 140) | 1 380 | |
| Depreciation: | | |
| Motor vehicle (17 000 – 5 000)/4 | 3 000 | |
| Equipment (15 000 – 4 500) × 30% | 3 150 | |
| Bad debt | 200 | |
| Insurance (1 000 + 450) | 1 450 | 23 790 |
| Net profit | | 16 360 |

*Balance Sheet*

| | | |
|---|---|---|
| *Fixed assets* | | |
| Motor vehicle at cost | 17 000 | |
| *less* Accumulated depreciation (3 000 + 3 000) | 6 000 | |
| | | 11 000 |
| Equipment at cost | 15 000 | |
| *less* Accumulated depreciation (4 500 + 3 150) | 7 650 | |
| | | 7 350 |
| | | 18 350 |
| *Current assets* | | |
| Stock | 27 350 | |
| Debtors (9 950 – 200) | 9 750 | |
| Cash and bank (900 + 250) | 1 150 | |
| Prepayment | 500 | |
| | 38 750 | |
| *Current liabilities* | | |
| Creditors | 8 100 | |
| Accrual | 140 | |
| | 8 240 | |
| Working capital | | 30 510 |
| | | 48 860 |
| Financed by: | | |
| Capital 1 January 1989 | | 52 500 |
| *add* Profit | | 16 360 |
| | | 68 860 |
| *less* Drawings | | 20 000 |
| | | 48 860 |

**2(i)**

*Balance Sheet as at 30th April 19X7*

| | £ | £ |
|---|---|---|
| *Fixed assets:* | | |
| Taxi | 10 500 | |
| *less* Depreciation | 2 625 | 7 875 |
| *Current assets:* | | |
| Debtors | 312 | |
| Prepayments | 453 | |
| Bank | 34 | |
| | 799 | |
| *less Current liabilities:* | | |
| Creditors | 209 | |
| Working capital | | 590 |
| | | 8 465 |
| *Financed by:* | | |
| Capital | | 8 465 |
| | | 8 465 |

**(ii)**

*Profit and Loss Account for year ended 30th April X8*

| | £ | £ |
|---|---|---|
| Income from customers (*Note 1*) | | 20 038 |
| Advertising revenue | | 200 |
| | | 20 238 |
| *less:* | | |
| Operating expenses (*Note 2*) | 10 349 | |
| Hire of radio | 540 | |
| Advertising | 192 | |
| Trade subscriptions | 75 | |
| Bank charges | 48 | |
| Depreciation (*Note 3*) | 2 099 | |
| | | 13 303 |
| Net profit | | 6 935 |

*Notes:*

| 1 *Income* | £ |
|---|---|
| Bankings | 16 013 |
| *add* Drawings | 3 750 |
| | 19 763 |
| *less* Opening debtors | 312 |
| | 19 451 |
| *add* Closing debtors | 587 |
| | 20 038 |

| 2 *Operating expenses:* | £ |
|---|---|
| Amount paid | 10 317 |
| Beginning of year: | |
| *add* Prepaid | 453 |
| *less* Owing | (209) |
| | 10 561 |
| End of year: | |
| *add* Owing | 319 |
| *less* Prepaid | (531) |
| | 10 349 |

| 3 *Depreciation* | £ |
|---|---|
| Book value as at 30.4.87 | 10 500 |
| – Depreciation 25% | 2 625 |
| Book value as at 30.4.88 | 7 875 |
| + Illuminated roof sign | 520 |
| | 8 395 |
| Depreciation = 25% of 8 395 | 2 099 |

**(iii)**

*Balance Sheet as at 30th April 19X8*

| | £ | £ |
|---|---|---|
| *Fixed assets:* | | |
| Taxi | 11 020 | |
| *less* Depreciation | 4 724 | 6 296 |
| *Current assets:* | | |
| Debtors | 587 | |
| Prepayments | 531 | |
| Bank | 981 | |
| | 2 099 | |
| *less Current liabilities:* | | |
| Creditors | 319 | |
| Working capital | | 1 780 |
| | | 8 076 |
| *Financed by:* | | |
| Capital | 8 465 | |
| *add* Net profit | 6 935 | |
| | 15 400 | |
| *less* Drawings (*Note 4*) | 7 324 | 8 076 |
| | | 8 076 |

| 4 Personal expenses | 3 147 | |
|---|---|---|
| Drawings | 3 750 | (taken from fares) |
| Currency for holiday | 427 | |
| | 7 324 | |

**3**

*Trading Profit and Loss Account for the year ending 31.3.X9*

| | £ | £ |
|---|---|---|
| Sales (*Note 1*) | | 422 881 |
| *less Cost of sales*: | | |
| Opening stock | 124 309 | |
| Purchases (*Note 2*) | 201 837 | |
| | 326 146 | |
| Closing stock | 96 217 | 229 929 |
| Gross profit | | 192 952 |
| Discount received | | 13 092 |
| | | 206 044 |
| Discount allowed | 3 129 | |
| Repaid | 9 314 | |
| Lighting and heating | 8 170 | |
| Wages | 40 000 | |
| Rent and rates | 21 047 | |
| Post and telephone | 15 203 | |
| Sundry expenses | 10 305 | |
| Amortisation | 800 | |
| Depreciation | 750 | |
| Advertising | 13 058 | 121 776 |
| Net profit | | 84 268 |

*Notes*:

| | £ |
|---|---|
| 1 *Sales* | |
| Cash received | 210 021 |
| – Opening debtors | 23 150 |
| | 186 871 |
| *add* Closing discount | 18 190 |
| | 205 061 |
| + Cash | 217 820 |
| | 422 881 |

| | |
|---|---|
| 2 *Purchases* | |
| Paid | 98 317 |
| – Opening creditors | 10 316 |
| | 88 001 |
| + Closing creditors | 11 495 |
| | 99 496 |
| + Cash | 102 341 |
| | 201 837 |

*Balance Sheet as at 31.3.X9*

| Fixed assets | Cost | Dep. | NBV |
|---|---|---|---|
| | £ | £ | £ |
| Leasehold premises | 10 700 | 7 680 | 3 020 |
| Shop fittings | 20 125 | 3 900 | 16 225 |
| | 30 825 | 11 580 | 19 245 |
| *Current assets* | | | |
| Stock | 96 217 | | |
| Debtors | 18 190 | | |
| Prepayments | 4 298 | 118 705 | |
| *Current liabilities* | | | |
| Creditors | 11 495 | | |
| Accruals | 5 206 | | |
| Bank overdraft | 37 143 | 53 844 | |
| Working capital | | | 64 861 |
| | | | 84 106 |
| *Financed by*: | | | |
| Capital | 62 940 | | |
| Net profit | 84 268 | | |
| | 147 208 | | |
| Drawings | 63 102 | | |
| | | | 84 106 |

**4(a)**

*Trading Profit and Loss Account for Malcolm Biskett for the year ending 30.9.88*

| | £ | £ | £ |
|---|---|---|---|
| Sales (*Note 1*) | | | 206 740 |
| *less Cost of goods sold* | | | |
| Opening stock | | 5 106 | |
| + Purchases (*Note 2*) | | 182 269 | |
| | | 187 375 | |
| – Closing stock | | 7 564 | 179 811 |
| Gross profit | | | 26 929 |
| *add Income* | | | |
| Interest on deposit account | | | 34 |
| | | | 26 963 |
| *less Expenses* | | | |
| Bank charges | | 214 | |
| General expenses | | 779 | |
| Heat and light | 578 | | |
| + Owing | 120 | 698 | |
| Postage and telephone | | 316 | |
| Printing and stationery | | 76 | |
| Repairs | | 143 | |
| Travelling and van expenses | | 1 257 | |
| Wages and National Insurance | | 10 314 | |
| Accountancy fee | | 300 | |
| Depreciation of motor vehicle | | 2 832 | |
| Depreciation of equipment | | 883 | 17 812 |
| Net profit | | | 9 151 |

**(b)**

*Balance Sheet of Malcolm Biskett as at 30.9.88*

| | £ | £ | £ |
|---|---|---|---|
| *Fixed assets* | | | |
| Motor vehicles | | 15 105 | |
| – Depreciation | | 6 608 | 8 497 |
| Shop equipment | | 12 319 | |
| – Depreciation | | 7 313 | 5 006 |
| | | | 13 503 |
| *Current assets* | | | |
| Stock | | 7 564 | |
| Debtors | | 758 | |
| | | 8 322 | |
| *less Current liabilities* | | | |
| Creditors | 3 145 | | |
| *Accruals* | | | |
| Electricity | 120 | | |
| Accountancy | 300 | | |
| Bank overdraft | 3 042 | 6 607 | 1 715 |
| | | | 15 218 |
| Capital | | | 25 369 |
| + Net profit | | | 9 151 |
| | | | 34 520 |
| – Drawings | | | 19 302 |
| | | | 15 218 |

**(c)**

*Gross profit margin*

$$\frac{\text{Gross profit}}{\text{Sales}} \times 100$$

$$\frac{26\,929}{206\,740} \times 100 = 13.02\%$$

**(d)**

Purchase costs may have increased without such increases being passed on to their customers.

Sales prices might have been reduced

Stock may have been lost or stolen.

## ■ CHAPTER 9: PARTNERSHIP ACCOUNTS

*Trading Profit and Loss Account of Rowntree and Makintosh for the year ending 31.12.Y0*

| | £ | £ |
|---|---|---|
| Net profit | | 100 000 |
| appropriated as follows: | | |
| *add Interest on drawings:* | | |
| Rowntree | 5 000 | |
| Makintosh | 1 000 | 6 000 |
| | | 106 000 |
| *less Interest capital:* | | |
| Rowntree | 10 000 | |
| Makintosh | 10 000 | 20 000 |
| | | 86 000 |
| *less Salaries:* | | |
| Makintosh | 11 000 | |
| Rowntree | 20 000 | 31 000 |
| *Balance of profits shared:* | | 55 000 |
| Rowntree | 33 000 | |
| Makintosh | 22 000 | 55 000 |

*Balance Sheet extract of Rowntree and Makintosh as at 31.12.Y0*

| | £ | £ | £ |
|---|---|---|---|
| *Capital* | | | |
| Rowntree | | | 100 000 |
| Makintosh | | | 100 000 |
| | | | 200 000 |
| *Current account* | *Rowntree* | *Makintosh* | |
| Opening balance | 10 000 | (5 000) | |
| Share of profit | 33 000 | 22 000 | |
| Interest on capital | 10 000 | 10 000 | |
| Salary | 11 000 | 20 000 | |
| | 64 000 | 47 000 | |
| *less* Drawings | 25 000 | 5 000 | |
| | 39 000 | 42 000 | |
| *less* Interest on drawings | 5 000 | 1 000 | |
| | 34 000 | 41 000 | 75 000 |
| | | | 275 000 |

## ■ CHAPTER 10: THE ADMISSION OR RETIREMENT OF A PARTNER

**1(a)**

| | *Old ratio* | *Amount* | *New ratio* | *Amount* | *Loss/gain* |
|---|---|---|---|---|---|
| Matthew | 3 | £30 000 | 3 | £22 500 | (£7 500) |
| Mark | 2 | £20 000 | 2 | £15 000 | (£5 000) |
| Luke | 1 | £10 000 | 2 | £15 000 | +£5 000 |
| John | — | — | 1 | £7 500 | +£7 500 |
| | | £60 000 | | £60 000 | |

*Goodwill*

| | | | |
|---|---|---|---|
| (a) Capital account | £60 000 | Matthew (b) | £22 500 |
| | | Mark (b) | £15 000 |
| | | Luke (b) | £15 000 |
| | | John (b) | £7 500 |
| | £60 000 | | £60 000 |

*Matthew*

| | | | |
|---|---|---|---|
| Goodwill W/O (b) | £22 500 | Goodwill (a) | £30 000 |

*Mark*

| | | | |
|---|---|---|---|
| Goodwill W/O (b) | £15 000 | Goodwill (a) | £20 000 |

*Luke*

| | | | |
|---|---|---|---|
| Goodwill W/O (b) | £15 000 | Goodwill (a) | £10 000 |

*John*

| | | | |
|---|---|---|---|
| Goodwill W/O (b) | £7 500 | | |

**(b)**

While Luke's capital account has been reduced by £5 000, he has a larger claim on goodwill of £5 000 and hence his position has not altered.

**2**

| | *Old ratio* | *Amount* | *New ratio* | *Amount* | *Loss/gain* |
|---|---|---|---|---|---|
| Matthew | 3 | £37 500 | — | | (£37 500) |
| Mark | 2 | £25 000 | 2 | £40 000 | +£15 000 |
| Luke | 2 | £25 000 | 2 | £40 000 | +£15 000 |
| John | 1 | £12 500 | 1 | £20 000 | + £7 500 |
| | | £100 000 | | £100 000 | |

*Goodwill*

| | | | |
|---|---|---|---|
| (a) Capital A/c's | £100 000 | Mark (b) | £40 000 |
| | | Luke (b) | £40 000 |
| | | John (b) | £20 000 |

*Matthew*

| | | | |
|---|---|---|---|
| | | Goodwill (a) | £37 500 |

*Mark*

| | | | |
|---|---|---|---|
| Goodwill W/O (b) | £40 000 | Goodwill (a) | £25 000 |

*Luke*

| | | | |
|---|---|---|---|
| Goodwill W/O (b) | £40 000 | Goodwill (a) | £25 000 |

*John*

| | | | |
|---|---|---|---|
| Goodwill W/O (b) | £20 000 | Goodwill (a) | £12 500 |

1

*Trading Profit and Loss Account of Davidsons Ltd for the year ending 31.12.X8*

| | £ | £ | £ |
|---|---|---|---|
| Sales | | | 279 108 |
| *less Cost of goods sold* | | | |
| Opening stock | | 36 106 | |
| + Purchases | | 87 107 | |
| | | 123 213 | |
| – Closing stock | | 21 999 | 101 214 |
| Gross profit | | | 177 894 |
| *less Expenses* | | | |
| Wages | 16 091 | | |
| + Wages owing | 300 | 16 391 | |
| Rent | | 5 000 | |
| Rates | | 3 000 | |
| Motor expenses | 1 154 | | |
| – Prepaid | 159 | 995 | |
| Admin. expenses | | 2 189 | |
| Directors' remuneration | | 30 000 | |
| Debenture interest | | 1 000 | 58 575 |
| Net profit for the year before taxation | | | 119 319 |
| *less* Taxation | | | 10 000 |
| Net profit after taxation | | | 109 319 |
| *less Appropriation* | | | |
| Transfer to general revenue | | 5 000 | |
| Ordinary dividends | | | |
| Paid | 3 000 | | |
| Proposed | 30 000 | 33 000 | 38 000 |
| Retained profit | | | 71 319 |

2

*Trading Profit and Loss Account of Bernham Cars for the year ending 31.3.X9*

| | £ | £ | £ |
|---|---|---|---|
| Sales | | | 207 284 |
| *less* Returns in | | | 5 000 |
| | | | 202 284 |
| *less Cost of goods sold* | | | |
| Opening stock | | 42 107 | |
| + Purchases | 61 000 | | |
| *less* Returns out | 2 900 | 58 100 | |
| | | 100 207 | |
| *less* Closing stock | | 36 987 | 63 220 |
| Gross profit | | | 139 064 |
| *add* | | | |
| Discount received | | 3 109 | |
| Interest received | | 4 000 | 7 109 |
| | | | 146 173 |
| *less Expenses:* | | | |
| Wages | | 13 521 | |
| Rent and rates | 5 000 | | |
| + Rent owing | 1 500 | 6 500 | |
| Insurance | 2 500 | | |
| – Insurance prepaid | – 300 | 2 200 | |
| Motor expenses | | 2 000 | |
| Directors' remuneration | | 27 500 | |
| Auditors' remuneration | | 2 000 | |
| Provision for bad debts | | 400 | |
| Debenture interest | 4 000 | | |
| Debenture interest owing | 1 000 | 5 000 | |
| *Provision for depreciation* | | | |
| Motor vehicle | | 1 000 | |
| Equipment | | 4 500 | 64 621 |
| Net profit for the year before taxation | | | 81 552 |
| *less* Corporation tax | | | 24 000 |
| Net profit for the year after taxation | | | 57 552 |
| *less* Appropriation: | | | |
| Transfer to general reserves | | 1 000 | |
| Transfer to tax reserve | | 2 000 | |
| | | 3 000 | |
| Goodwill written off | | 500 | |
| Preference dividend proposed | 3 500 | | |
| Ordinary dividend paid | 500 | | |
| proposed | 1 500 | 5 500 | 9 000 |
| | | | 48 552 |

*Balance Sheet of Bernham Cars as at 31.3.X9*

| | £ | £ | £ | £ |
|---|---|---|---|---|
| *Fixed assets* | | | | |
| *Intangible assets* | | | | |
| Goodwill | | | | 1 000 |
| Goodwill Written off | | | | 500 |
| | | | | 500 |
| *Tangible assets* | | | | |
| Premises | | | 170 000 | |
| Equipment cost | | 70 000 | | |
| – Depreciation | | 29 500 | 40 500 | |
| Fixtures and fittings | | | 5 000 | |
| Motor vehicles | | 20 000 | | |
| – Depreciation | | 15 000 | 5 000 | 220 500 |
| | | | | 221 000 |
| *Current assets* | | | | |
| Stock | | | 36 987 | |
| Debtors | | 52 795 | | |
| *less* Provision for bad debts | | 2 000 | 50 795 | |
| Prepayment | | | 300 | |
| Bank | | | 7 508 | |
| Cash | | | 2 166 | |
| | | | 97 756 | |
| *less Creditors – amounts falling due within one year* | | | | |
| Creditors | | 31 704 | | |
| *Accruals* | | | | |
| Rent | 1 500 | | | |
| Debenture interest | 1 000 | 2 500 | | |
| *Proposed dividend*: | | | | |
| Preference | 3 500 | | | |
| Ordinary | 1 500 | 5 000 | | |
| Taxation | | 24 000 | 63 204 | |
| Net current assets | | | | 34 552 |
| | | | | 255 552 |
| *less Creditors – amounts falling due after more than one year* | | | | |
| 10% Debenture 1999 | | | | 50 000 |
| | | | | 205 552 |
| *Capital and reserves* | | | Authorised | Issued |
| Ordinary shares of £1 each | | | 100 000 | 92 000 |
| 7% pref. shares of £1 each | | | 50 000 | 50 000 |
| | | | 150 000 | 142 000 |
| *Reserves* | | | | |
| General reserve | | | 10 000 | |
| Tax reserve | | | 5 000 | |
| Retained profits | | | 48 552 | 63 552 |
| | | | | 205 552 |

## ■ CHAPTER 12: MANUFACTURING ACCOUNTS

**1(a)**

Insurance of the factory
Depreciation of machinery
Factory rates
Factory supervisor's wages

**(b)**

(i) Heat and light £800
(ii) Rent £6 000
(iii) Depreciation of premises £1 600
(iv) Insurance £2 000

**2**

*Manufacturing Account of Clothing Manufacturers Ltd for the year ending 31.12.Y0*

| | £ | £ |
|---|---|---|
| Opening stock of raw material | | 30 000 |
| + Purchases of raw material | 80 000 | |
| + Carriage in of raw material | 2 000 | 82 000 |
| | | 112 000 |
| – Closing stock of raw material | | 26 000 |
| Direct material | | 86 000 |
| Direct labour | | 50 000 |
| Direct expenses | | — |
| Prime cost of manufacture | | 136 000 |
| *add Works/factory overheads* | | |
| Factory supervisors | 10 000 | |
| Depreciation of factory machinery | 12 000 | |
| Rent | 6 250 | |
| Insurance | 5 000 | |
| Light and heat | 500 | 33 750 |
| | | 169 7550 |
| + *Add* Opening stock of WIP | | 41 000 |
| | | 210 750 |
| – Closing stock of WIP | | 31 500 |
| Cost of manufacture | | 179 250 |

3

*Manufacturing Account of Doric Beds Ltd for the year ending 31.12.Y0*

| | £ | £ |
|---|---|---|
| Opening stock of raw materials | | 7 105 |
| + Purchases of raw materials | 21 908 | |
| + Carriage in of raw materials | 700 | 22 608 |
| | | 29 713 |
| – Closing stock of raw materials | | 17 177 |
| Direct material | | 12 536 |
| Direct labour | | 27 000 |
| Direct expenses | | 1 000 |
| Prime cost of manufacture | | 40 536 |
| *add Factory overheads* | | |
| Heat and light | 2 000 | |
| Rent | 5 000 | |
| Foreman's wages | 10 000 | |
| Factory expenses | 2 176 | |
| | | 19 176 |
| | | 59 712 |
| + Opening stock of WIP | | 7 721 |
| | | 67 433 |
| – Closing stock of WIP | | 6 433 |
| Cost of manufacture | | 61 000 |

*Trading Profit and Loss Account of Doric Beds Ltd for the year ending 31.12.Y0*

| | £ | £ | £ |
|---|---|---|---|
| Sales | | | 376 173 |
| *less Cost of goods sold* | | | |
| Opening stock of finished goods | | 12 774 | |
| + Cost of manufacture | | 61 000 | |
| | | 73 774 | |
| – Closing stock of finished goods | | 10 616 | 63 158 |
| Gross profit | | | 313 015 |
| *add Income* | | | |
| Discounts received | | | 1 000 |
| | | | 314 015 |
| *less Expenses* | | | |
| *Administration*: | | | |
| Office expenses | 2 000 | | |
| + owing | 500 | 2 500 | |
| Heat and light | | 1 000 | |
| Rent | | 2 500 | |
| Office salaries | | 37 000 | |
| | | 43 000 | |
| *Selling and distribution*: | | | |
| Salesmen's salaries | 42 000 | | |
| Salesmen's commission | 8 000 | | |
| Warehouse expenses | 4 424 | | |
| Depreciation of salesman's car | 1 000 | 55 424 | |
| *Financial* | | | |
| Depreciation of equipment | 5 000 | | |
| Provision for bad debts | 1 000 | | |
| Bank charges | 485 | | |
| Discounts allowed | 1 106 | 7 591 | 106 015 |
| Net profit for the year before taxation | | | 208 000 |
| *less* Taxation | | | 60 000 |
| Net profit for the year after taxation | | | 148 000 |
| *less* Appropriations | | | |
| Transfer to reserves | | | 7 000 |
| | | | 141 000 |
| *Proposed dividend* | | | |
| Ordinary | | 10 000 | |
| Preference | | 2 000 | 12 000 |
| Retained profit | | | 129 000 |

*Balance Sheet of Doric Beds Ltd as at 31.12.Y0*

| | £ | £ | £ |
|---|---|---|---|
| *Fixed assets* | | | |
| Land and buildings (cost) | | | 500 000 |
| Equipment (cost) | | 125 000 | |
| *less* Depreciation | | 40 000 | 85 000 |
| Motor vehicles (cost) | | 20 000 | |
| *less* Depreciation | | 12 000 | 8 000 |
| Fixtures and fittings | | | 12 000 |
| | | | 605 000 |
| *Current assets* | | | |
| *Stock* | | | |
| Raw materials | 17 177 | | |
| WIP | 6 433 | | |
| Finished goods | 10 616 | 34 226 | |
| Debtors | 80 000 | | |
| *less* Provision for bad debts | 8 000 | 72 000 | |
| Bank | | 3 717 | |
| Cash | | 162 | |
| | | 110 105 | |
| *less Creditors – amounts falling due for payment within 12 months* | | | |
| Taxation | 60 000 | | |
| Proposed dividends | | | |
| Ordinary | 10 000 | | |
| Preference | 2 000 | | |
| Creditors | 47 105 | | |
| Accruals office expenses | 500 | 119 605 | (9 500) |
| | | | 595 500 |
| *less Creditors – amounts falling due for payment after 12 months* | | | |
| 10% Debentures | | | 96 500 |
| | | | 499 000 |
| *Capital and reserves* | | | |
| *Shareholders' capital employed* | | *Authorised* | *Issued* |
| £1 Ordinary shares | | 300 000 | 300 000 |
| 9% Preference shares | | 60 000 | 60 000 |
| | | 360 000 | 360 000 |
| *Reserves* | | | |
| General reserve | | 10 000 | |
| Profit and loss | | 129 000 | 139 000 |
| | | | 499 000 |

## ■ CHAPTER 13: SSAPs AND FRSs

**1**

See text

**2 *Great Clearance Stores***

(a) *Timber sleepers and finished gate posts*

Closing stocks = 4 100 unexamined sleepers
6 120 finished gate posts

(i) *Unexamined sleepers*

| | £ |
|---|---|
| Cost = £2 × 100 = | 8 200 |
| less 10% rotten | 820 |
| | 7 380 |

(ii) *Finished gate posts*

*Cost*

$\frac{6120}{4}$ = 1530 sleepers to manufacture the gate posts

+ 170 10% written off prior to sawing
1700

i.e. $\frac{1530}{90} \times 100 = 1700$

| | | |
|---|---|---|
| Sleepers cost | 1700 × £2 | = £3 400.00 |
| Sawing cost | 1530 × £1.78 | = £2 723.40 |
| | | £6 123.40 |

*Net realisable value*

| | | |
|---|---|---|
| Selling price | 1.85 | |
| – Delivery costs | 50 | |
| | 1.35 × 6120 | = £8 262.00 |

Value at lower of cost or net realisable value
= £6 123.40

(b) *Army Berets*

| | | £ | £ |
|---|---|---|---|
| *Cost* | Cost: Purchase | 2 000 | |
| | Dyeing cost | 680 | |
| | | 2 680 | |
| *Net realisable value* | | £ | £ |
| Sales 3185 × £2.75 | | | 8 758.75 |
| *less* | | | |
| Tassels | 3185 × £1.20 | 3 822.00 | |
| Postage | 3185 × £0.65 | 2 070.25 | |
| Advertising | | 550.00 | 6 442.25 |
| | | | 2 316.50 |

Value at lower of cost or net realisable value = 2 316.50

(c) *Plastic knives*
*Cost* Purchase 100

| *Net realisable value* | |
|---|---|
| Selling price 5p × 8000 (10 000 – 20%) | 400 |
| *less* | |
| Cost of grinding 10 000 × 2p | 200 |
| | 200 |

Value at lower of cost or net realisable value = £100

**3**

*Trading Account of DIY Stores Ltd for the month of January*

| | FIFO | | LIFO | | AVCO | |
|---|---|---|---|---|---|---|
| | £ | £ | £ | £ | £ | £ |
| Sales | | 700 | | 700 | | 700 |
| *less Cost of goods sold* | | | | | | |
| Opening stock | nil | | nil | | nil | |
| + Purchases | 710 | | 710 | | 710 | |
| | 710 | | 710 | | 710 | |
| – Closing stock | 236 | 474 | 186 | 524 | 213 | 497 |
| Gross profit | | 226 | | 176 | | 203 |

The higher the closing stock the higher the profit.

**4(a)**

*Ladders*

| | | |
|---|---|---|
| Purchase | 600 at £15 each | £9 000 |
| Sold | 325 at £29 each | £9 425 |
| Purchase | 400 at £19 each | £7 600 |
| Sold | 150 at £35 each | £5 250 |

(i) *FIFO*

| | | £ | £ |
|---|---|---|---|
| *Stock:* | Purchases | | 600 |
| | | | 400 |
| | | | 1 000 |
| | *less* sales | 325 | |
| | | 150 | 475 |
| | | | 525 |

Value The first in were first out
∴ 525 are valued at the latest
i.e. 400 at £19 = £7 600
125 at £15 = £1 875
525 9 475

(ii) *Average cost*

| | | |
|---|---|---|
| Stock | 525 units | |
| Purchase | 600 at £15 | |
| | 325 | |
| Stock | 275 at £15 = | £4 125 |
| Purchase | 400 at £19 = | £7 600 |
| | 675 | £11 725 |

$$\text{Average cost} = \frac{11\,725}{675} = £17.37$$

Stock: £17.37 × 525 = £9 199.44

**(b) (i) *Stockport Stores Ltd***

*A Periodic*

| | |
|---|---|
| Purchases | 190 units |
| – Sales | 95 units |
| Closing stock | 95 units |

*FIFO*

| | |
|---|---|
| 10 at £29 = | £290 |
| 30 at £28 = | £840 |
| 50 at £27 = | £1 350 |
| 90 | £2 480 |
| 5 at £25 = | £125 |
| 95 | £2 605 |

*LIFO*
95 at £25 £2 375

*AVCO*

100 at £25 = £2 500
50 at £27 = £1 350
30 at £28 = £840
10 at £29 = £290
190 £4 980

$\frac{£4\,980}{190}$ = £26.21 average price each

Closing stock = 95 × £26.21 = £2 490

*B Perpetual*

*FIFO*

| Date | Receipts Quantity | Receipts Price (£) | Receipts Value (£) | Issued Quantity | Issued Price (£) | Issued Value (£) | Stock Quantity | Stock Price (£) | Stock Value (£) |
|---|---|---|---|---|---|---|---|---|---|
| Sept 1 | 100 | 25.00 | 2500 | | | | 100 | 25.00 | 2500 |
| Sept 11 | 50 | 27.00 | 1350 | | | | 100 | 25.00 | 2500 |
| | | | | | | | 50 | 27.00 | 1350 |
| | | | | | | | 150 | | 3850 |
| Sept 12 | | | | 65 | 25.00 | 1625 | 35 | 25.00 | 875 |
| | | | | | | | 50 | 27.00 | 1350 |
| | | | | | | | 85 | | 2225 |
| Sept 16 | 30 | 28.00 | 840 | | | | 35 | 25.00 | 875 |
| | | | | | | | 50 | 27.00 | 1350 |
| | | | | | | | 30 | 28.00 | 840 |
| | | | | | | | 115 | | 3065 |
| Sept 17 | | | | 30 | 25.00 | 750 | 5 | 25.00 | 125 |
| | | | | | | | 50 | 27.00 | 1350 |
| | | | | | | | 30 | 28.00 | 840 |
| | | | | | | | 85 | | 2315 |
| Sept 27 | 10 | 29.00 | 290 | | | | 5 | 25.00 | 125 |
| | | | | | | | 50 | 27.00 | 1350 |
| | | | | | | | 30 | 28.00 | 840 |
| | | | | | | | 10 | 29.00 | 290 |
| | | | | | | | 95 | | 2605 |

*LIFO*

| Date | Receipts Quantity | Receipts Price (£) | Receipts Value (£) | Issued Quantity | Issued Price (£) | Issued Value (£) | Stock Quantity | Stock Price (£) | Stock Value (£) |
|---|---|---|---|---|---|---|---|---|---|
| Sept 1 | 100 | 25.00 | 2500 | | | | 100 | 25.00 | 2500 |
| Sept 11 | 50 | 27.00 | 1350 | | | | 100 | 25.00 | 2500 |
| | | | | | | | 50 | 27.00 | 1350 |
| | | | | | | | 150 | | 3850 |
| Sept 12 | | | | 50 | 27.00 | 1350 | 85 | 25.00 | 2125 |
| | | | | 15 | 25.00 | 375 | | | |
| | | | | 65 | | 1725 | | | |
| Sept 16 | 30 | 28.00 | 840 | | | | 85 | 25.00 | 2125 |
| | | | | | | | 30 | 28.00 | 840 |
| | | | | | | | 115 | | 2965 |
| Sept 17 | | | | 30 | 28.00 | 840 | 85 | 25.00 | 290 |
| Sept 27 | 10 | 29.00 | 290 | | | | 85 | 25.00 | 2125 |
| | | | | | | | 10 | 29.00 | 290 |
| | | | | | | | 95 | | 2 415 |

*AVCO*

| Date | Receipts Quantity | Receipts Price (£) | Receipts Value (£) | Issued Quantity | Issued Price (£) | Issued Value (£) | Stock Quantity | Stock Price (£) | Stock Value (£) |
|---|---|---|---|---|---|---|---|---|---|
| Sept 1 | 100 | 25.00 | 2500 | | | | 100 | 25.00 | 2500 |
| Sept 11 | 50 | 27.00 | 1350 | | | | 100 | 25.00 | 2500 |
| | | | | | | | 50 | 27.00 | 1350 |
| | | | | | | | 150 | | 3850 |
| | | | | | | | | 3850 | |
| | | | | | | | | 150 | |
| | | | | | | | 150 | 25.66 | 3850 |
| Sept 12 | | | | 65 | 25.66 | | 85 | 25.66 | 2181 |
| Sept 16 | 30 | 28.00 | 840 | | | | 85 | 25.66 | 2181 |
| | | | | | | | 30 | 28.00 | 840 |
| | | | | | | | 115 | | 3021 |
| | | | | | | | | 3021 | |
| | | | | | | | | 115 | |
| | | | | | | | 115 | 26.27 | 3021 |
| Sept 17 | | | | 30 | 26.27 | 788 | 85 | 26.27 | 2233 |
| Sept 27 | 10 | 29 | 290 | | | | 85 | 26.27 | 2233 |
| | | | | | | | 10 | 29.00 | 290 |
| | | | | | | | 95 | | 2523 |
| | | | | | | | | 2523 | |
| | | | | | | | | 95 | |
| | | | | | | | 95 | 26.55 | 2523 |

**(b) (ii)**

*Trading Account of Stockport Stores for the month of September*

| | FIFO | | LIFO | | AVCO | |
|---|---|---|---|---|---|---|
| *Periodic* | £ | £ | £ | £ | £ | £ |
| Sales | | 4 810 | | 4 810 | | 4 810 |
| *less Cost of goods sold* | | | | | | |
| Opening stock | nil | | nil | | nil | |
| + Purchases | 4 980 | | 4 980 | | 4 980 | |
| | 4 980 | | 4 980 | | 4 980 | |
| – Closing stock | 2 605 | 2 375 | 2 375 | 2 605 | 2 490 | 2 490 |
| Gross profit | | 2 445 | | 2 205 | | 2 320 |
| *Perpetual* | | | | | | |
| Sales | | 4 810 | | 4 810 | | 4 810 |
| *less Cost of goods sold* | | | | | | |
| Opening stock | nil | | nil | | nil | |
| + Purchases | 4 980 | | 4 980 | | 4 980 | |
| | 4 980 | | 4 980 | | 4 980 | |
| – Closing stock | 2 605 | 2 375 | 2 415 | 2 565 | 2 523 | 2 457 |
| Gross profit | | 2 435 | | 2 245 | | 2 353 |

**5**

*1 World Wide PLC*

ACT payable = £20 000 × $\frac{25}{100 - 25}$ = £6 666.66

| i.e. Based on dividend paid | |
|---|---|
| Corporation tax liability = | £100 000 |
| *less* ACT payable | £6 666 |
| Corporation tax payable | £93 334 |

2

| | *Year end* | *Next 6 April* | *Date payable* | *Delay period* |
|---|---|---|---|---|
| Dunstable PLC | 31.5.93 | 6.4.94 | 1.1.92 | 19 months |
| Winchester PLC | 31.11.93 | 6.4.94 | 1.1.92 | 13 months |
| Gem PLC | 28.2.93 | 6.4.93 | 1.1.91 | 10 months |

## ■ CHAPTER 14: CASH FLOW FORECASTS

**1(a)**

*See* page 285

**(b)**

Maximum overdraft = £ 8 700

Sales show an increase over the year. Can Louise support her estimates in any way?

Has she included all expenses, if not this would make the situation worse?

Based on the figures the cash swings into credit by the end of the year and the second year will not see expenses, such as the lease and equipment.

Louise is also willing to put in £15 000 of her own money and therefore, provided the figures can be justified, this proposition would appear worthwhile.

## ■ CHAPTER 15: CASH AND WORKING CAPITAL

**1(a)**

| | |
|---|---|
| Hi-fi Equipment Ltd | 2.68 : 1 |
| Stores UK plc | 0.65 : 1 |
| Engineering Co Ltd | 2.06 : 1 |
| Office Suppliers Inc. | 1.78 : 1 |
| Doncasters Ltd | 1 : 1 |

**(b)**

Working capital = £103 098 (Current assets £160 843 – Current liabilities £57 745)
Ratio = 2.78 = 1

**2(a)**

Creditors' payment period $= \frac{160}{1800} \times 360$ days

= 32 days

Debtors' collection period $= \frac{300}{2700} \times 360$ days

= 40 days

Stock turnover period $= \frac{305}{1830} \times 360$ days

= 60 days

**1(a)**

| | 1 | 2 | 3 | 4 | 5 | 6 | 7 | 8 | 9 | 10 | 11 | 12 | Dr/Cr | Total |
|---|---|---|---|---|---|---|---|---|---|---|---|---|---|---|
| | £ | £ | £ | £ | £ | £ | £ | £ | £ | £ | £ | £ | £ | £ |
| *Income* | | | | | | | | | | | | | | |
| Sales | 3 600 | 6 000 | 6 000 | 7 500 | 7 500 | 7 500 | 7 500 | 8 400 | 8 400 | 8 400 | 8 400 | 8 400 | | |
| Total Income | 3 600 | 6 000 | 6 000 | 7 500 | 7 500 | 7 500 | 7 500 | 8 400 | 8 400 | 8 400 | 8 400 | 8 400 | | |
| *Expenditure* | | | | | | | | | | | | | | |
| Lease | 10 000 | | | | | | | | | | | | | |
| Rent | 1 500 | | | 1 500 | | | 1 500 | | | 1 500 | | | | |
| Catering equipment | 8 000 | | | | | | | | | | | | | |
| Stock of china | 2 000 | | | | | | | | | | | | | |
| Wages | 2 000 | 2 000 | 2 000 | 2 800 | 2 800 | 2 800 | 2 800 | 2 800 | 2 800 | 2 800 | 2 800 | 2 800 | | |
| Drawings | 500 | 500 | 500 | 500 | 500 | 500 | 500 | 500 | 500 | 500 | 500 | 500 | | |
| Food etc | 1 200 | 2 000 | 2 000 | — | 2 500 | 2 500 | 2 500 | 2 500 | 2 800 | 2 800 | 2 800 | 2 800 | 2 800 | |
| Stock of food | 1 000 | | | | | | | | | | | | | |
| Rates | 800 | | | 2 000 | | | | | | 2 200 | | | | |
| Other expenses | 300 | 300 | 300 | 300 | 300 | 300 | 300 | 300 | 300 | 300 | 300 | 300 | | |
| Accountant's fee | | | | | | | | | | | | | 250 | |
| Total expenditure | 27 300 | 4 800 | 4 800 | 7 100 | 6 100 | 6 100 | 7 600 | 6 100 | 6 400 | 10 100 | 6 400 | 6 400 | 3 050 | |
| Income – expenditure | (23 700) | 1 200 | 1 200 | 400 | 1 400 | 1 400 | (100) | 2 300 | 2 000 | (1 700) | 2 000 | 2 000 | | |
| Opening balance | 15 000 | (8 700) | (7 500) | (3 300) | (2 900) | (1 500) | (100) | (200) | 2 100 | 4 100 | 2 400 | 4 400 | | |
| *Other injections* | | | | | | | | | | | | | | |
| Loan | | | 3 000 | | | | | | | | | | | |
| Cumulative balance | (8 700) | (7 500) | (3 300) | (2 900) | (1 500) | (100) | (200) | 2 100 | 4 100 | 2 400 | 4 400 | 6 400 | | |

**(b)**

The cash operating cycle can be shown as follows:

Day 1 – purchase goods
Day 32 – pay supplier (creditors' payment period = 32 days)
Day 60 – sell goods (stock turnover period = 60 days)
Day 100 – collect cash (debtors' collection period = 40 days)

Thus cash is collected from the customer on day 100, 68 days after the goods were paid for
Therefore cash operating cycle = 68 days

**3**

Either reduce stock or debtors; or increase creditors, e.g. reduce debtors to £280
How?

$\frac{\text{Debtors}}{\text{Sales}}$ = Number of days to settle debit

$\frac{280}{2700} \times 360 = 37.3$ days

Previously 40 days therefore reduce credit given by 2.7 days.

## ■ CHAPTER 16: CASH FLOW STATEMENTS

*Cash Flow Statement of Sandersons PLC for the year ended 31.12.Y2*

| | | |
|---|---|---|
| *Operating activities* | | |
| Profit for year before taxation (*Note 1*) | | 55 073 |
| Depreciation | | 10 000 |
| | | 65 073 |
| Increase in stock | (3 895) | |
| Decrease in debtors | 12 761 | |
| Decrease in prepayments | 161 | |
| Increase in creditors | 10 000 | |
| Increase in accruals | 1 800 | 20 827 |
| Net cash inflow from operating activities | | 85 900 |
| *Return on investments and services of finance* | | |
| Dividend paid | | (8 000) |
| *Taxation* | | |
| Tax paid | | (12 000) |
| *Investing activities* | | |
| Purchase of fixed assets | | (153 000) |
| *Net cash flow before financing* | | (87 100) |
| *Financing* | | |
| Issue of shares | 250 000 | |
| Issue of debenture | 20 000 | 45 000 |
| Decrease in cash/bank | | (42 100) |

*Analysis of changes in cash/bank during year*

| | | |
|---|---|---|
| *Balances at the beginning of the year* | | |
| Cash | | 100 |
| Bank | | (2 000) |
| | | (1 900) |
| *Balances at the end of the year* | | |
| Cash | 1 000 | |
| Bank | (45 000) | (44 000) |
| Decrease in cash/bank | | (42 100) |

i.e. The balance has gone from (1 900) to (44 000), a further reduction of £42 100.

*Note 1 Profit for year before taxation*

| | | |
|---|---|---|
| Profit before taxation | 55 073 | ↑ |
| *less* Taxation | 21 000 | |
| Profit before tax | 34 073 | |
| *less* Proposed dividend | 15 000 | |
| | 19 073 | |
| *less* Transfer to general reserve | 5 000 | |
| Profit for the year | 14 073 | |
| Retained profit c/d | 36 127 | Work |
| Balance of profit and loss a/c | 50 200 | backwards |

## ■ CHAPTER 17: RECONCILIATION STATEMENTS

**1(a)**

*Bank Reconciliation Statement 31 March*

| | £ | £ |
|---|---|---|
| Balance per bank statement | | 72.68 o/d |
| *add* Bankings not yet credited | 93.27 | |
| | 125.42 | 218.69 |
| | | 146.01 Cr |
| *less* Cheques not yet presented | 21.37 | |
| | 32.15 | |
| | 159.27 | |
| | 34.27 | |
| | 85.16 | 332.22 |
| | | 186.21 o/d |
| *add Outgoings not entered in cash book* | | |
| Standing order | 13.10 | |
| Bank charges | 25.70 | |
| Interest | 18.35 | 57.15 |
| | | 129.06 o/d |
| *less* Receipt not entered in cash book: | | |
| VAT refund | | 137.81 |
| Balance per cash book | | 266.87 o/d |

**(b)**

Bankings not yet credited: these will be entered in the account once Brown visits the bank. Should he have already paid these into his account he will need to enquire why they do not appear on his statement.

Cheques not yet presented: these will go through his account once the payees credit the cheques to their account.

Outgoings and receipts not entered in the cashbook: provided they are genuine transactions Mr Brown will need to record these in his cashbook.

**2**

*Bank Reconciliation Statement of West Bank Ltd for the month ending 28.2.Y0*

| | £ | £ |
|---|---|---|
| Balance as per statement | | 3 498.66 |
| *less Unpresented items* | | |
| Electricity | 50.00 | |
| Fixtures | 1 500.00 | 1 550.00 |
| *add Outgoings not entered in the cashbook* | | 1 948.66 |
| D D Water | 40.00 | 40.00 |
| *less Bankings not entered in the cashbook* | | 1 988.66 |
| Credit | 120.00 | 120.00 |
| | | 1 868.66 |

## ■ CHAPTER 18: RATIO ANALYSIS

**1 Poynton PLC**

| | *19Y1* £ | | |
|---|---|---|---|
| 1 Return of capital employers | $\frac{35\,000}{287\,000}$ | × 100 | 12.19% |
| 2 Gross profit margin | $\frac{250\,000}{400\,000}$ | × 100 | 62.5% |
| 3 Net profit margin | $\frac{35\,000}{400\,000}$ | × 100 | 8.75% |
| 4 Rate of stock turnover | $\frac{30\,000}{150\,000}$ | × 365 | 73 Days |
| 5 Debtors' settlement period | $\frac{65\,000}{400\,000}$ | × 365 | 59.3 Days |
| 6 Creditors' settlement period | $\frac{50\,000}{165\,000}$ | × 365 | 110.6 Days |
| 7 Working capital ratio | 99 000 : 62 000 | | 1.59 : 1 |
| 8 Liquidity ratio | 69 000 : 62 000 | | 1.1 : 1 |
| 9 Gearing | $\frac{20\,000}{287\,000}$ | × 100 | 6.9% |

| 10 Debt : Equity | 20 000 : 267 000 | 0.07 : 1 |
|---|---|---|

**2**

See text

**3**

See text

## ■ CHAPTER 19: BREAK EVEN ANALYSIS

**1**

(a) 17 500 units
(b) 4 000 units
(c) £20 000
(d) £85 000
(e) £8.83
(f) £0.30
(g) £2.55
(h) £0.90

**2(a)**

| | | £ | £ | per unit | |
|---|---|---|---|---|---|
| Contribution = | Sales | | 1 400 000 | | 14 |
| | *less* Variable costs | | | | |
| | Direct material | 400 000 | | 4.00 | |
| | Direct labour | 60 000 | | 0.60 | |
| | Variable overheads | 140 000 | 600 000 | 1.40 | 6 |
| | Contribution | | 800 000 | | 8 |

Break even point = *Fixed costs* ÷ Contribution per unit

$$\frac{300\,000 + 140\,000}{8} = 55\,000 \text{ units}$$

**(b)**

*Contribution to sales ratio*

| | £ | |
|---|---|---|
| Sales | 14 | 100% |
| *less* Variable costs | 6 | 43% |
| Contribution | 8 | 57% |

$$\text{Contribution : Sales Ratio} \quad \frac{\text{Contribution}}{\text{Sales}} \times 100$$

$$\frac{£800\,000}{£1\,400\,000} \times 100 = 57\%$$

**(c)**

*Margin of Safety*

| | | | |
|---|---|---|---|
| Forecasts sales | £1 400 000 | or | 100 000 units |
| Break even point | £770 000 | | 55 000 units |
| Margin of safety | £630 000 | | 45 000 units |

**(d)**

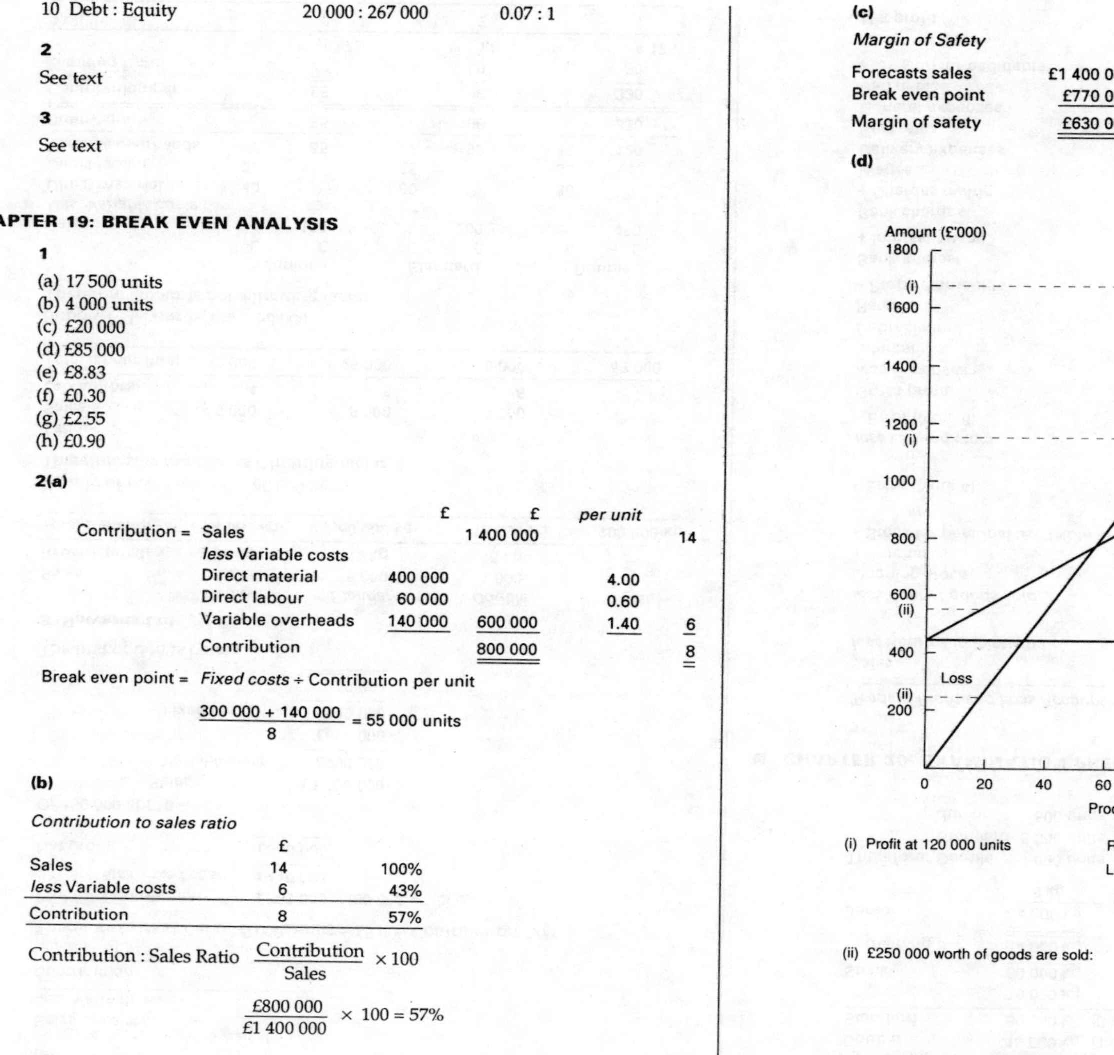


| | | |
|---|---|---|
| (i) Profit at 120 000 units | Revenue = 120 000 x £14 = | 1 680 000 |
| | Less costs | 1 160 000 |
| | | £ 520 000 |
| (ii) £250 000 worth of goods are sold: | Revenue | 250 000 |
| | Costs | 547 143 |
| | | (£ 297 143) |

**Figure 6 Break even analysis chart**

**(e)**

| | |
|---|---|
| Sales price at | £7 |
| *less* Variable costs | £6 |
| Contribution | £1 |

Therefore extra order of 5 000 units = £5 000 Contribution

| | | |
|---|---|---|
| Profit = Contribution | £805 000 | (800 000 + 5 000) |
| *less* Fixed cost | £440 000 | |
| Net profit | £365 000 | |

Or 150 000 at £10 =

| | |
|---|---|
| Sales | £1 500 000 |
| – Variable cost | £900 000 |
| | £600 000 |
| – Fixed cost | £440 000 |
| | £160 000 |

The first option is better.

**3 Howards Ltd**

| | *Junior* | *Standard* | *Double* | *Total* |
|---|---|---|---|---|
| Sales | 3 000 | 5 000 | 1 000 | |
| Raw materials | 8 kg | 12 kg | 16 kg | |
| Total material | 24 000 kg | 60 000 kg | 16 000 kg | 100 000 kg |

Supply of raw material = 80 000 kg
Therefore raw material is a limiting factor.

| *Labour* | | | | |
|---|---|---|---|---|
| Sales | 3 000 | 5 000 | 1 000 | |
| Labour (hrs) | 4 | 5 | 6 | |
| Total labour (hrs) | 12 000 | 25 000 | 6 000 | 43 000 |

Supply of labour hours = 50 000
Therefore labour is not a limiting factor.

| | Junior | | Standard | | Double | |
|---|---|---|---|---|---|---|
| | £ | £ | £ | £ | £ | £ |
| Sales | | 120 | | 200 | | 450 |
| *less Variable costs* | | | | | | |
| Direct material | 40 | | 60 | | 80 | |
| Direct labour | 20 | | 25 | | 30 | |
| Variable overheads | 5 | 65 | 7 | 92 | 10 | 120 |
| Contribution | | 55 | | 108 | | 330 |
| Contribution per | | 55 | | 108 | | 330 |
| limiting factor | | 40 | | 60 | | 80 |
| | | 1.375 | | 1.8 | | 4.125 |
| Rank | | 3 | | 2 | | 1 |

*Optimum production level*

| | | |
|---|---|---|
| Double | 16 000 kg | (1 000 × 16 kg) |
| Standard | 60 000 kg | (5 000 × 12 kg) |
| | 76 000 kg | |
| Stock | 80 000 kg | |
| Remaining | 4 000 kg | |

Junior $\frac{4\,000 \text{ kg}}{8 \text{ kg}}$ = 500 units

Therefore: Double 1 000 units
Standard 5 000 units
Junior 500 units

## ■ CHAPTER 20: EXAMINATION PREPARATION/REVISION

**1**

*Trading Profit and Loss Account of Tower for the year ending 31.12.91*

| | | | |
|---|---|---|---|
| Sales | | | 800 |
| *less* Returns in (Note 6) | | | 16 |
| | | | 784 |
| *less Cost of goods sold* | | | |
| Opening stock | | 125 | |
| + Purchases | 620 | | |
| – Stock for personal use (Note 1) | 3 | | |
| | 617 | | |
| – Error (Note 4) | 5 | 612 | |
| | | 737 | |
| *less* Closing stock | 136 | | |
| – Error (Note 6) | 6 | 130 | 607 |
| Gross profit | | | 177 |
| *less Expenses* | | | |
| Interest | | 6 | |
| Depreciation | | 8 | |
| Rates | 16 | | |
| – Prepaid amounts | 2 | 14 | |
| Bank interest | 1 | | |
| + Interest owing | 1 | 2 | |
| Bank charges | 2 | | |
| + Charges owing | 2 | 4 | |
| Wages | | 31 | |
| Delivery expenses | | 7 | |
| Heat, etc. | | 9 | |
| General expenses | | 21 | |
| Bad debts | | 4 | |
| Provision for bad debts | | 9 | 115 |
| Net profit | | | 62 |

*Balance Sheet of Tower as at 31.12.91*

| | | | |
|---|---|---|---|
| Premises | | | 108 |
| Fixtures and fittings at cost (25+ 5) | | 30 | |
| *less* Accumulated depreciation | | 18 | |
| | | | 12 |
| Fixed assets | | | 120 |
| Stock | | 130 | |
| Debtors | 64 | | |
| – Returned goods (Note 6) | 16 | | |
| | 48 | | |
| – Bad debts written off (Note 7) | 4 | | |
| | 44 | | |
| – Provision for bad debts (Note 7) | 9 | 35 | |
| Prepayment | | 2 | |
| Current assets | | 167 | |
| Creditors | | 38 | |
| Bank | | 7 | |
| Interest due | | 6 | |
| Bank interest accrued | | 2 | |
| Bank charges accrued | | 1 | |
| Current liabilities | | 54 | |
| Working capital | | | 113 |
| | | | 233 |
| Loan | | | 50 |
| | | | 183 |
| Opening capital | | | 148 |
| Profit | | | 62 |
| Drawings | | | – 27 |
| Closing capital | | | 183 |

*Depreciation for the year equals:*

| | |
|---|---|
| Fixtures and fittings at cost | 25 |
| + Additional fixtures and fittings | 5 |
| | 30 |
| – Accumulated depreciation to date | 10 |
| | 20 |
| 20 × 40% = | 8 |

**2**

(a) *See* text

(b) *See* text

(c) Assets which represent capital expenditure:

- Land
- Motor vehicles
- Goodwill

Goodwill can be dealt with according to SSAP 22 as follows:

1 Capitalise and amortise. The value of goodwill is entered in the balance sheet as a fixed asset and this is written off through the profit and loss account over its estimated life. It must not be carried as a permanent balance. Over the years the value in the balance sheet declines to zero.

2 Write off immediately. The purchase of goodwill is capital expenditure, but a permissible, and preferred, accounting treatment is to write it off immediately on acquisition. Therefore, under this approach, no value appears in the balance sheet, and reserves are reduced by the value of goodwill acquired.

**3**

(a) Owner capital, Loans and Debentures, Retained profits — *see* text

(b) *See* text, Chapter 14. Overtrading is a condition which arises when a company attempts to do too much too quickly, e.g. where short-term funds are used to finance long-term assets.

Symptoms include:

- Heavy expenditure on fixed assets
- Fall in cash
- Sharp rise in creditors
- Poor working capital and liquidity ratios

(c) Where short-term funds are used to finance long-term applications, the firm may not, as a result, be able to meet their debts as they fall due, and may show the above symptoms.

**4**

| **(a)**(i) | *Method 1* | *Method 2* |
|---|---|---|
| Selling price per unit | 33 | 33 |
| Materials | 13 | 15 |
| Labour | 8 | 14 |
| | 21 | 29 |
| Contribution | 12 | 4 |
| (ii) | | |
| Fixed cost 100 000 × | 7 | 2 |
| = | 700 000 | 200 000 |
| Depreciation* | 200 000 | 40 000 |
| | 900 000 | 240 000 |
| Break even point in units | 900 000/12 | 240 000/4 |
| = | 75 000 | 60 000 |
| Value | £2 475 000 | £1 980 000 |

(iii)

| | | |
|---|---|---|
| Contribution at maximum output | | |
| 150 000 × 12 | 1 800 000 | |
| 120 000 × 4 | | 480 000 |
| Fixed costs | 900 000 | 240 000 |
| Profit | 900 000 | 240 000 |
| (iv) Maximum loss | £900 000 | £240 000 |
| (v) Contribution at 100 000 units | 1 200 000 | 400 000 |
| Fixed costs | 900 000 | 240 000 |
| Profit | 300 000 | 160 000 |
| *Depreciation** | | |
| Purchase of fixed assets | 1 200 00 | 200 000 |
| – Residual value | 200 000 | — |
| Total depreciation over life | 1 000 000 | 2 000 000 |
| ÷ life | 5 yr | 5 yr |
| Annual depreciation | 200 000 | 40 000 |

**(b)**

| | *Merits* | *Drawbacks* |
|---|---|---|
| Method 1 | Great potential/profit at expected level of sales and if sales exceed forecasts | More risk<br>Higher break even point<br>More loss may be incurred |
| Method 2 | Less risk (lower break even point) | Does not offer same profit potential |

Additional information:

- reliability of forecasts
- likelihood of changes in costs

**5(a)**

*Trading Profit and Loss and Appropriation Account of Maurice Ltd for the year ending 31.12.91*

| | |
|---|---|
| Trading profit for the year | 530 |
| – Corporation tax | 185 |
| | 345 |
| – Dividend | 150 |
| | 195 |
| Profit brought forward | 740 |
| Profit carried forward | 935 |

*Note 1*

Dividend – 25p per ordinary share

| | |
|---|---|
| Ordinary shares as at 1.1.91 | 400 |
| Ordinary shares new issue | 200 |
| | 600 × 25p = 150 |

**(b)**

*Balance Sheet of Maurice Ltd as at 31.12.91*

| | | |
|---|---|---|
| *Fixed assets* | | |
| Premises (as per revaluation) | | 2 000 |
| Plant at cost (as at 1.1.91) | 1 500 | |
| + Additional plant | 1 000 | |
| | 2 500 | |
| – Depreciation | 1 000 | 1 500 |
| | | 3 500 |
| Stock | 210 | |
| Debtors | 250 | |
| Cash (Note 2) | 430 | |
| | 890 | |
| Trade creditors | 120 | |
| Dividend for 1991 | 150 | |
| Tax for 1991 | 185 | |
| | 455 | |
| | | 435 |
| | | 3 935 |
| Debenture | | 500 |
| | | 3 435 |
| Ordinary shares (400 + 200) | | 600 |
| Share premium (200 + 200) | | 400 |
| Profit and loss account | | 935 |
| Revaluation reserve | | 1 500 |
| | | 3 435 |

*Note 2*

*Cash account*

| | | | | |
|---|---|---|---|---|
| Opening balance | | 25 | Plant | 1 000 |
| Share issue | | 400 | Salaries and wages | 760 |
| Debenture issue | | 500 | Delivery costs | 125 |
| Sales | 4 800 | | Expenses | 105 |
| + Opening debtors | 225 | | Debenture interest | 50 |
| | 5 025 | | Dividend | 100 |
| – Closing debtors | 250 | 4 775 | Tax | 135 |
| | | | Purchases | 2 995 |
| | | | Closing balance | 430 |
| | | 5 700 | | 5 700 |

*Sales for year ended 31.12.91*

| Opening debtors | Sales | Closing debtors |
|---|---|---|
| £225 | £4 800 | £250 |

| | |
|---|---|
| Sales | 4 800 |
| + Opening debtors | 225 |
| | 5 025 |
| – Closing debtors | 250 |
| | 4 775 |

*Purchases for year ended 31.12.91*

| Opening creditors | Purchases | Closing creditors |
|---|---|---|
| £115 | | £120 |

| | |
|---|---|
| Purchases | 3 000 |
| + Opening creditors | 115 |
| | 3 115 |
| – Closing creditors | 120 |
| | 2 995 |

**6 Ratios**

| | *Relay* | | *Baton* | |
|---|---|---|---|---|
| GP% | 100/200 | = 50% | 50/150 | = 33.33% |
| NP% | 20/200 | = 10% | 20/150 | = 13.33% |
| ROCE | 20/197 | = 10.15% | 20/283 | = 7.07% |
| Working capital | 66/69 | = 0.96:1 | 74/11 | = 6.73:1 |
| Liquidity | 16/69 | = 0.23:1 | 14/11 | = 1.27:1 |
| Gearing | 100/197 | = 50.76% | 0.283 | = — |
| (or, with overdraft) | 110/197 | = 55.84% | | |

*See* text for comments and limitations.

**7**

(a) *See* text

(b)

| | | |
|---|---|---|
| Fixed assets | | 6 000 |
| Stock | 3 300 | |
| Debtors | 2 500 | |
| Prepayment | 260 | |
| | 6 060 | |
| Creditors | 1 125 | |
| Overdraft | 2 700 | |
| Electricity | 70 | |
| Bank interest | 110 | |
| Loan interest | 120 | |
| | 4 125 | |
| | | 1 935 |
| | | 7 935 |
| Loan | | 4 000 |
| | | 3 935 |
| Opening capital | | 10 000 |
| Capital introduced | | 1 000 |
| | | 11 000 |
| Profit (balancing figure) | | 7 935 |
| | | 18 935 |
| Drawings | | 15 000 |
| | | 3 935 |

# Appendix B: Answers to self-assessment questions

## ■ CHAPTER 1 AN INTRODUCTION TO ACCOUNTING

*See* text

## ■ CHAPTER 2 THE BALANCE SHEET

**1**

*See* text

**2**

(a) 40 000
(b) 22 000
(c) 50 000
(d) 15 500
(e) 35 000
(f) 5 000

**3**

*See* text

**4**

*See* text

**5**

| | *Assets* | *Capital* | *Liabilities* |
|---|---|---|---|
| (a) | Stock + 2 000 | | Creditors + £2 000 |
| (b) | Van + £5 000 | | |
| | Cash – £5 000 | | |
| (c) | Cash + £2 500 | Capital + £2 500 | |
| (d) | Stock – £1 000 | Profit + £2 000 | |
| | Cash + £3 000 | | |
| (e) | Cash + £7 000 | | Loan £7 000 |
| (f) | Debtors – £1 000 | | |
| | Cash + £1 000 | | |

**6**

| | |
|---|---|
| Creditors | – Current liability |
| Debtors | – Current asset |
| Drawings | – Deduct from capital + net profit |
| Bank loan | – Long-term liability |
| Bank overdraft | – Current liability |
| Cash | – Current asset |
| Stock | – Current asset |
| Profit | – Add to capital |

**7**

| | | |
|---|---|---|
| Stock | £2 000 | Some |
| Debtors | £5 000 | Dogs |
| Bank | £1 000 | Bite |
| Cash | £500 | Cats |

**8**

*Balance Sheet of The Spud Shop as at 30.9.Y0*

| | £ | £ | | £ |
|---|---|---|---|---|
| *Fixed assets* | | | Capital | 31 000 |
| Premises | | 30 000 | add Net profit | — |
| Equipment | | 2 000 | | |
| | | 32 000 | – Drawings | 1 000 |
| | | | | 30 000 |
| *Current assets* | | | | |
| Stock | 5 000 | | *Current liabilities* | |
| Debtors | 5 000 | | Creditors | 2 000 |
| Bank | — | | | |
| Cash | — | 10 000 | *Long-term liabilities* | |
| | | | Loan | 10 000 |
| | | 42 000 | | 42 000 |

## ■ CHAPTER 3 DOUBLE ENTRY BOOKKEEPING

**1**

| | *Debit* | *Credit* |
|---|---|---|
| (a) | Purchases | Cash |
| (b) | A Barlow | Returns out |
| (c) | Wages | Cash |
| (d) | Cash | Capital |
| (e) | Loan | Bank |

**2**

*Cash*

| Date | Details | £ | Date | Details | £ |
|---|---|---|---|---|---|
| 1.9 | Capital | 40 000 | 2.9 | Bank | 29 000 |
| 9.9 | Sales | 200 | 12.9 | Drawings | 2 000 |
| 22.9 | Sales | 500 | 16.9 | Rent | 50 |
| | | | 16.9 | Gas | 30 |
| | | | 16.9 | Wages | 400 |
| | | | 20.9 | Drawings | 2 000 |
| | | | 28.9 | Wages | 300 |
| | | | 30.9 | Balance | 6 920 |
| | | 40 700 | | | 40 700 |
| 1.10 | Balance | 6 920 | | | |

*Bank*

| Date | Details | £ | Date | Details | £ |
|---|---|---|---|---|---|
| 2.9 | Cash | 29 000 | 4.9 | Van | 8 000 |
| 3.9 | Loan | 10 000 | 4.9 | Equipment | 3 000 |
| | | | 4.9 | Fixtures | 3 000 |
| | | | 5.9 | Purchases | 2 000 |
| | | | 26.9 | Delta | 480 |
| | | | 30.9 | Balance | 22 520 |
| | | 39 000 | | | 39 000 |
| 1.10 | Balance | 22 520 | | | |

*Capital*

| Date | Details | £ | Date | Details | £ |
|---|---|---|---|---|---|
| 30.9 | Balance | 40 000 | 1.9 | Cash | 40 000 |
| | | | 1.10 | Balance | 40 000 |

*Loan*

| Date | Details | £ | Date | Details | £ |
|---|---|---|---|---|---|
| 30.9 | Balance | 10 000 | 3.9 | Balance | 10 000 |
| | | | 1.10 | Balance | 10 000 |

*Van*

| Date | Details | £ | Date | Details | £ |
|---|---|---|---|---|---|
| 4.9 | Bank | 8 000 | 30.9 | Balance | 8 000 |
| 1.10 | Balance | 8 000 | | | |

*Equipment*

| Date | Details | £ | Date | Details | £ |
|---|---|---|---|---|---|
| 4.9 | Bank | 3 000 | | | |
| 10.9 | Delta | 500 | 30.9 | Balance | 3 500 |
| | | 3 500 | | | 3 500 |
| 1.10 | Balance | 3 500 | | | |

*Fixtures and fittings*

| Date | Details | £ | Date | Details | £ |
|---|---|---|---|---|---|
| 4.9 | Bank | 3 000 | 30.9 | Balance | 3 000 |

*Purchases*

| Date | Details | £ | Date | Details | £ |
|---|---|---|---|---|---|
| 5.9 | Bank | 2 000 | | | |
| 15.9 | Wainwright | 1 000 | 30.9 | Balance | 3 000 |
| | | 3 000 | | | 3 000 |
| 1.10 | Balance | 3 000 | | | |

*Sales*

| Date | Details | £ | Date | Details | £ |
|---|---|---|---|---|---|
| | | | 9.9 | Cash | 200 |
| | | | 11.9 | A Iqbal | 100 |
| | | | 22.9 | Cash | 500 |
| 30.9 | Balance | 1 100 | 23.9 | B White | 300 |
| | | 1 100 | | | 1 100 |

*Delta Equipment*

| Date | Details | £ | Date | Details | £ |
|---|---|---|---|---|---|
| 26.9 | Dis Rec'd | 20 | 10.9 | Equipment | 500 |
| 26.9 | Bank | 480 | | | |
| | | 500 | | | 500 |

*A Iqbal*

| Date | Details | £ | Date | Details | £ |
|---|---|---|---|---|---|
| 11.9 | Sales | 100 | 30.9 | Balance | 100 |
| 1.10 | Balance | 100 | | | |

*C Wainwright*

| Date | Details | £ | Date | Details | £ |
|---|---|---|---|---|---|
| 30.9 | Balance | 1 000 | 15.9 | Purchase | 1 000 |
| | | | 1.10 | Balance | 1 000 |

*Rent*

| Date | Details | £ | Date | Details | £ |
|---|---|---|---|---|---|
| 16.9 | Cash | 50 | 30.9 | Balance | 50 |
| 1.10 | Balance | 50 | | | |

*Gas*

| Date | Details | £ | Date | Details | £ |
|---|---|---|---|---|---|
| 16.9 | Cash | 30 | 30.9 | Balance | 30 |
| 1.10 | Balance | 30 | | | |

*Wages*

| Date | Details | £ | Date | Details | £ |
|---|---|---|---|---|---|
| 16.9 | Cash | 400 | | | |
| 28.9 | Wages | 300 | 30.9 | Balance | 700 |
| | | 700 | | | 700 |
| 1.10 | Balance | 700 | | | |

*Drawings*

| Date | Details | £ | Date | Details | £ |
|---|---|---|---|---|---|
| 12.9 | Cash | 2 000 | 30.9 | Balance | 4 000 |
| 20.9 | Cash | 2 000 | | | |
| 1.10 | Balance | 4 000 | | | |

*B White*

| | £ | | £ |
|---|---|---|---|
| 23.9 | | 30.9 | |
| Sales | 300 | Balance | 300 |
| 1.10 | | | |
| Balance | 300 | | |

*Discount Received*

| | £ | | £ |
|---|---|---|---|
| 30.9 | | 26.9 | |
| Balance | 20 | Delta | 20 |
| | | 1.10 | |
| | | Balance | 20 |

*Trial Balance of Dave's Pantry as at 30.9.X9*

| | Debit £ | Credit £ |
|---|---|---|
| Cash | 6 920 | |
| Bank | 22 520 | |
| Capital | | 40 000 |
| Loan | | 10 000 |
| Van | 8 000 | |
| Equipment | 3 500 | |
| Fixtures | 3 000 | |
| Purchases | 3 000 | |
| Sales | | 1 100 |
| Delta Equipment | — | |
| A Iqbal | 100 | |
| Rent | 50 | |
| Wages | 700 | |
| Gas | 30 | |
| C Wainwright | | 1 000 |
| Drawings | 4 000 | |
| B White | 300 | |
| Discount received | | 20 |
| | 52 120 | 52 120 |

**3**

*See* text

## ■ CHAPTER 4 ERRORS AND CONTROL ACCOUNTS

**1**

*See* text

**2**

(a) Post the difference to a suspense account
Make investigations to fund using control accounts

*Suspense*

| | £ | | £ |
|---|---|---|---|
| Sales | 5 000 | Difference as per trial balance | 1 000 |
| Bank | 14 000 | Cash | 2 000 |
| | | D Black | 16 000 |
| | 19 000 | | 19 000 |

(b)

*Sales*

| | |
|---|---|
| | Suspense £5 000 |

*D Black*

| | |
|---|---|
| Suspense £16 000 | |

*Bank*

| | |
|---|---|
| | Suspense £14 000 |

*Cash*

| | |
|---|---|
| Suspense £2 000 | |

**3**

*See* text

**4**

*Sales ledger control account*

| | | | |
|---|---|---|---|
| Balance b/d | 95 617 | Balance b/d | 613 |
| Sales | 759 348 | Returns inwards | 3 549 |
| Balance c/d | 161 | Cash received | 703 195 |
| | | Discounts | 25 355 |
| | | Bad debts | 5 123 |
| | | Balance c/d | 117 291 |
| | 855 126 | | 855 126 |

*Purchase ledger control account*

| | | | |
|---|---|---|---|
| Balance b/d | 782 | Balance b/d | 78 298 |
| Returns outwards | 4 581 | Purchases | 621 591 |
| Cash paid | 612 116 | Balance c/d | 329 |
| Discounts received | 8 570 | | |
| Balance c/d | 74 169 | | |
| | 700 218 | | 700 218 |

## ■ CHAPTER 5 TRADING PROFIT AND LOSS ACCOUNT

**1**

*See* text

**2**

*See* text

**3**

*Trading Profit and Loss Account of R Ford for the year ending 31.10.X9*

| | £ | £ |
|---|---|---|
| Sales | | 279 105 |
| *less Cost of goods sold* | | |
| Opening stock | 57 955 | |
| + Purchases | 104 829 | |
| | 162 784 | |
| – Closing stock | 41 295 | 121 489 |
| Gross profit | | 157 616 |
| *less Expenses* | | |
| Wages | 31 106 | |
| Electricity | 991 | |
| Rent | 1 000 | |
| Rates | 1 500 | |
| Gas | 350 | |
| Insurance | 200 | |
| Carriage out | 107 | |
| Discount allowed | 500 | 34 754 |
| Net profit | | 121 862 |

*Balance Sheet of R Ford as at 31.10.X9*

| | £ | £ | | £ |
|---|---|---|---|---|
| *Fixed assets* | | | Capital | 100 000 |
| Premises | 100 000 | | + Net profit | 121 862 |
| Fittings | 24 000 | | | 221 862 |
| Van | 26 000 | 150 000 | – Drawings | 60 000 |
| | | | | 161 862 |
| *Current assets* | | | *Deferred liabilities* | |
| Stock | 41 295 | | | |
| Debtors | 5 105 | | Loan | 30 000 |
| Bank | 3 500 | | | |
| Cash | 100 | 50 000 | *Current liabilities* | |
| | | | Creditors | 8 138 |
| | | 200 000 | | 200 000 |

**4**

*Trading Profit and Loss Account of D Eyles for the year ending 31.11.X9*

| | £ | £ | £ |
|---|---|---|---|
| Sales | | | 510 927 |
| *less* Returns in | | | 814 |
| | | | 510 113 |
| *less Cost of goods sold* | | | |
| Opening stock | | 39 509 | |
| + Purchases | 72 108 | | |
| *less* Returns out | 519 | | |
| | 71 589 | | |
| + Carriage in | 616 | 72 205 | |
| | | 111 714 | |
| – Closing stock | | 21 509 | 90 205 |
| Gross profit | | | 419 908 |
| *add Income* | | | |
| Rent received | | 1 898 | |
| Discounts received | | 215 | |
| Interest received | | 100 | 2 213 |
| | | | 422 121 |
| *less Expenses* | | | |
| Rates | | 5 100 | |
| Wages | | 25 900 | |
| Electricity | | 3 908 | |
| Carriage out | | 500 | |
| Discount allowed | | 750 | |
| Motor expenses | | 1 287 | 37 445 |
| | | | 384 676 |

*Balance Sheet of D Eyles as at 31.11.X9*

| | £ | £ | | | £ |
|---|---|---|---|---|---|
| *Fixed assets* | | | Capital | | 500 000 |
| Land and buildings | 450 000 | | + Net profit | | 384 670 |
| Machinery | 200 000 | | | | 884 670 |
| Fixtures | 39 871 | | – Drawings | | 200 670 |
| Van | 10 129 | 700 000 | | | 684 000 |
| *Current assets* | | | *Deferred liabilities* | | |
| Stock | 21 509 | | Loan | | 30 000 |
| Debtors | 51 000 | | | | |
| Cash | 7 591 | 80 100 | *Current liabilities* | | |
| | | | Creditors | 56 100 | |
| | | | Bank overdraft | 10 000 | 66 100 |
| | | 780 100 | | | 780 100 |

**5**

*Trading Profit and Loss Account for A Jackson for the year ending 31.12.X9*

| | £ | £ | £ |
|---|---|---|---|
| Sales | | | 101 995 |
| *less* Returns in | | | 3 000 |
| | | | 98 995 |
| *less Cost of goods sold* | | | |
| Opening stock | | 36 109 | |
| + Purchases | 52 379 | | |
| + Carriage in | 300 | 52 679 | |
| | | 88 788 | |
| – Closing stock | | 11 810 | 76 978 |
| | | | 22 017 |
| *less Expenses* | | | |
| Motor expenses | | 2 005 | |
| Insurance | | 1 000 | |
| Rent | | 5 105 | |
| Rates | | 2 000 | |
| Wages | | 17 000 | |
| Electricity | | 1 510 | |
| Discount allowed | | 3 000 | |
| Carriage out | | 397 | 32 017 |
| Net loss | | | (10 000) |

*Balance Sheet of A Jackson as at 31.12.X9*

| | £ | £ | | | £ |
|---|---|---|---|---|---|
| *Fixed assets* | | | Capital | | 50 000 |
| Premises | 50 000 | | – Net loss | | 10 000 |
| Fixtures | 6 698 | | | | 40 000 |
| Equipment | 8 213 | | | | |
| | | 64 911 | *Long-term liabilities* | | |
| | | | Loan | | 15 000 |
| *Current assets* | | | | | |
| Stock | 11 810 | | *Current liabilities* | | |
| Debtors | 15 000 | | Creditors | 26 105 | |
| Bank | — | | Bank overdraft | 10 616 | 36 721 |
| Cash | — | 26 810 | | | |
| | | 91 721 | | | 91 721 |

## ■ CHAPTER 6 TRADING PROFIT AND LOSS ACCOUNT AND BALANCE SHEET – EXTRA MATTERS

**1**

*See* text

**2**

*See* text

**3**

*See* text

**4**

*See* text

**5(a)**

*Debtors*

| | | | | | |
|---|---|---|---|---|---|
| 30.6.89 | Balance | £35 208 | | | |

*Provision for bad debt*

| | | | | | |
|---|---|---|---|---|---|
| | | | 30.6.89 | Debtors | £450 |

| | £ | Provision | Provision £ |
|---|---|---|---|
| Invoiced within the last month | 24 906 | 1% | 249.06 |
| Invoiced 1–2 months ago | 8 476 | 3% | 254.28 |
| Invoiced over 2 months ago | 1 826 | 5% | 91.30 |
| | | | 594.64 |

i.e. increase provision by £144.64, say £145 (£595 – £450)

(i) *Balance Sheet Extract as at 30.6.89*

| | £ |
|---|---|
| Debtors | 35 208 |
| *less* Provision for bad debts | 595 |
| | 34 613 |

(ii) *Profit and Loss Extract Expenses*

| | |
|---|---|
| Provision for bad debt | 145 |

**(b)**

Loan £5 000
Monthly repayments £200 + interest of 1.5% per month

| *Date* | | *Payments* £ | *Receipts* £ | *Balance* £ |
|---|---|---|---|---|
| 1.4.8 | Loan | | | 5 000 |
| 30.4.89 | Interest | 75 | | 5 075 |
| 1.5.89 | Repayment | | 275 | 4 800 |
| 31.5.89 | Interest | 72 | | 4 872 |
| 1.6.89 | Repayment | | 272 | 4 600 |
| 30.6.89 | Interest | 69 | | 4 669 |
| 1.7.89 | Repayment | | 269 | 4 400 |
| 31.2.89 | Interest | 66 | | 4 466 |
| Loan interest charged | | 282 | | |

*Balance Sheet Extract*

| | |
|---|---|
| *Current liability* | |
| Loan | 2 400 |
| Accrual Loan Interest | 66 |
| *Long-term liability* | |
| Loan | 2 000 |

**(c)**

*Telephone expenses*

| | £ | | £ |
|---|---|---|---|
| Oct 88 | | 31.8.88 | |
| Bank | 138 | Opening balance owing | 92 |
| Jan 89 | | | |
| Bank | 94 | | |
| Apr 89 | | | |
| Bank | 93 | | |
| Jun 89 | | | |
| Bank | 144 | | |
| Aug 89 | | | |
| Balance owing* | 112 | Balance profit and loss | 489 |
| | 581 | | 581 |
| | | 1.9.88 | |
| | | Balance owing | 112 |

*Aug 89 = 2/3 of £168

*(i) Profit and Loss Account Extract*

| | |
|---|---|
| *Expenses* | |
| Telephone charges | £489 |

*(ii) Balance Sheet Extract as at 31.8.89*

| | |
|---|---|
| *Current liabilities* | |
| Accruals – telephone | £112 |

**6(a)**

*Trading Profit and Loss Account of F Norman for the year ending 31.12.89*

| | £ | £ | £ |
|---|---|---|---|
| Sales | | | 169 421 |
| *less Cost of goods sold* | | | |
| Opening stock | | 36 108 | |
| + Purchases | 79 210 | | |
| *less* Returns Out | 410 | 78 800 | |
| | | 114 908 | |
| – Closing stock | | 20 000 | 94 908 |
| Gross profit | | | 74 513 |
| *add Income* | | | |
| Discount received | | | 1 100 |
| | | | 75 613 |
| *less Expenses* | | | |
| Rent | | 269 | |
| Rates | | 1 500 | |
| Office expenses | 269 | | |
| + owing | 80 | 349 | |
| Insurance | 670 | | |
| – prepaid | 100 | 570 | |
| Wages | | 7 500 | |
| Provision for bad debts | | 1 000 | 11 188 |
| Net profit | | | 64 425 |

*Balance Sheet as at 31.12.89 of F Norman*

| | £ | £ | £ |
|---|---|---|---|
| *Fixed assets* | | | |
| Premises | | | 70 000 |
| Machinery | | | 40 000 |
| Fixtures and fitting | | | 20 686 |
| | | | 130 686 |
| *Current assets* | | | |
| Stock | | 20 000 | |
| Debtors | 12 000 | | |
| *less* Provision for bad debts | 2 000 | 10 000 | |
| Prepayments | | 100 | |
| Bank | | 7 510 | |
| Cash | | 100 | |
| | | 37 710 | |
| *less* | | | |
| *Current liabilities* | | | |
| Creditors | 20 000 | | |
| Accruals | 80 | 20 080 | 17 630 |
| | | | 148 316 |
| Capital | | | 100 000 |
| Net profit | | | 64 425 |
| | | | 164 425 |
| – Drawings | | | 36 109 |
| | | | 128 316 |
| *Long-term liabilities* | | | |
| Loan | | | 20 000 |
| | | | 148 316 |

## ■ CHAPTER 7 DEPRECIATION

**1**

*See* text

**2(a)**

*See* text

**(b)**

*See* text

**(c)**

Cost £6 500
Estimated life 5 years
Estimated residual value £500

(i) *Straight line*

Total depreciation = £6 500 – 500 = £6 000

$\frac{£6\,000}{5} = £1\,200$ p.a.

(ii) *Reducing balance*

$r = 1 - n\sqrt{s/c}$

$r = 1 - 5\sqrt{\frac{500}{6500}}$ = Approx 40%

| | *Straight line* £ | *Reducing balance* £ |
|---|---|---|
| Cost | 6 500 | 6 500 |
| Depreciation charge Year 1 | 1 200 | 2 600 |
| | 5 300 | 3 900 |
| Depreciation charge Year 2 | 1 200 | 1 560 |
| | 4 100 | 2 340 |
| Depreciation charge Year 3 | 1 200 | 936 |
| | 2 900 | 1 404 |
| Depreciation charge Year 4 | 1 200 | 561.60 |
| | 1 700 | 842.40 |
| Depreciation charge Year 5 | 1 200 | 336.96 |
| Book value end of Year 5 | 500 | 505.44 |

**3**

*See* text

**4**

Depreciation incorrectly charged.

| | *Motor lorries 20%* £ | *Shop fittings 30%* £ |
|---|---|---|
| Cost | 192 000 | 126 000 |
| Year 1 | 38 400 | 37 800 |
| | 153 600 | 88 200 |
| Year 2 | 30 720 | 26 460 |
| | 122 880 | 61 740 |
| Year 3 | 24 576 | 18 522 |
| | 98 304 | 43 218 |

Working backwards we are able to derive the costs then work forward with the correct rates.

| | *Motor lorries 30%* £ | *Shop fittings 20%* £ |
|---|---|---|
| Cost | 192 000 | 126 000 |
| Year 1 | 57 600 | 25 200 |
| | 134 400 | 100 800 |
| Year 2 | 40 320 | 20 160 |
| | 94 080 | 80 640 |
| Year 3 | 28 224 | 16 128 |
| | 65 856 | 64 512 |
| Year 4 | 19 756 | 12 902 |
| | 46 100 | 51 610 |

(a) *Profit and Loss Account Extract Year 4*

| | | £ |
|---|---|---|
| Depreciation: Motor lorries | | 19 756 |
| Shop fitting | | 12 902 |
| Prior year adjustment | | 11 154 |
| i.e. | £ | |
| Motor lorries £98 304 – 65 856 = | 32 448 shortfall | |
| Shop fittings £43 218 – 64 512 = | 21 294 surplus | |
| | 11 154 | |

(b) *Balance Sheet Extract*

| *Fixed assets* | £ | £ |
|---|---|---|
| Motor lorries (cost) | 192 000 | |
| – depreciation | 145 900 | 46 100 |
| Shop fittings (cost) | 126 000 | |
| – depreciation | 74 390 | 51 610 |

**5**

*North Down Bus Co.*

(a)

*Bus account*

| | | £ | | | |
|---|---|---|---|---|---|
| Jul 76 | No. 22 | 15 200 | | | |
| Apr 84 | No. 23 | 25 600 | | | |
| Jan 87 | No. 24 | 52 000 | | | |
| | | 92 800 | | | |

*Provision for depreciation*

| | | | | | £ |
|---|---|---|---|---|---|
| | | | 1.7.88 | Balance c/d No. 22 | 15 200 |
| | | | 1.7.88 | Balance c/d No. 23 | 12 800 |
| | | | 1.7.88 | Balance c/d No. 24 | 10 400 |

*Provision for depreciation as at 1.7.88*

July 76 — July 89

| 77 | 78 | 79 | 80 | 81 | 82 | 83 | 84 | 85 | 86 | 87 | 88 |
|---|---|---|---|---|---|---|---|---|---|---|---|

*No.* 22 12 years @ £1 520 per annum (15 200 × 10%)
= £18 240
*But* cost = £15 200
∴ Book value is written down to 0 by charging depreciation of £15 200
*No.* 23 5 years @ £2 560 = £12 800
*No.* 24 2 years @ £5 200 = £10 400
(b) (i) Open a disposal account and transfer the cost and balance of depreciation of No. 22
(ii) Enter the purchase of No. 25

| | |
|---|---|
| Bank/cash | £54 500 |
| Trade in | £3 500 |
| | £58 000 |

The trade in being part of the disposal of No. 22 and purchase of No. 25.
(iii) Transfer the cost and provision for depreciation of No. 23 to the disposal account.
(iv) Insurance money received is part of the disposal of No. 23.
(v) Enter details of the price of No. 26.
(vi) The profit on disposals £1 200 is transferred to the profit and loss account.

*Bus account*

| | | | £ | £ | | | £ |
|---|---|---|---|---|---|---|---|
| | July 76 | No. 22 | | 15 200 | Disposal of | No. 22 | 15 200 (i) |
| | Apr 84 | No. 23 | | 25 600 | | No. 23 | 25 600 (iii) |
| | Jan 87 | No. 25 | | 52 000 | | | |
| (ii) | Aug 88 | No. 25 | | | | | |
| | Trade in | | 3 500 | | | | |
| (ii) | Bank | | 54 500 | 58 000 | | | |
| (v) | Dec 88 | No. 26 | | 14 000 | Balance c/d | | 124 000 |
| | | | | 164 800 | | | 164 800 |

*Provision for depreciation*

| | | £ | | | | £ |
|---|---|---|---|---|---|---|
| (i) | Disposal No. 22 | 15 200 | July 88 | Balance | No. 22 | 15 200 |
| (iii) | Disposal No. 23 | 12 800 | | | No. 23 | 12 800 |
| | | | | | No. 24 | 10 400 |
| | | | | | | 38 400 |
| | | | June 89 | P & L | No. 24 | 5 200 (vii) |
| | | | | | No. 25 | 5 800 (viii) |
| | Balance c/d | 22 800 | | | No. 26 | 1 400 (ix) |
| | | 50 800 | | | | 50 800 |
| | | | Balance c/o | | | 22 800 |

*Disposal account*

| | | £ | | £ |
|---|---|---|---|---|
| (i) | No. 22 Cost | 15 200 | Provision for depreciation No. 22 | 15 200 (i) |
| (iii) | No. 23 Cost | 25 600 | Trade in No. 25 | 3 500 (ii) |
| | | | Provision for depreciation No. 23 | 12 800 (iii) |
| | Balance P & L | 1 200 | Bank (Ins. Co.) No. 23 | 10 500 (iv) |
| | | 42 000 | | 42 000 |

(c) *Depreciation for year ending 30 June 1989*
(vii) No. 24 10% × £52 000 = £5 200
(viii) No. 25 10% × £58 000 = £5 800
(ix) No. 26 10% × £14 000 = £1 400
N.B. Do not forget the profit on disposals which will also be transferred to the Profit and Loss Account, i.e. £1 200.

(d) *See* text.

**6**

*Trading Profit and Loss Account of Hugh for the year ending 31.12.86*

| | £ | £ | £ |
|---|---|---|---|
| Sales | | | 48 100 |
| *less Cost of goods sold* | *Livestock* | *Other* | |
| Purchases | 16 560 | 19 209 | |
| – Closing stock | 3 400 | 1 750 | |
| | 13 160 | 17 459 | 30 619 |
| Gross profit | | | 17 481 |
| *less Expenses* | | | |
| Advertising | | 1 863 | |
| Rent | | 5 000 | |
| Rates | 2 500 | | |
| Prepaid | – 550 | 1 950 | |
| Wages | | 6 220 | |
| Vet's fees | | 316 | |
| Bank interest | | 2 478 | |
| Heat and light | 417 | | |
| owing | + 58 | 475 | |
| Other expenses | | 3 143 | |
| Accountancy fees | | 200 | |
| Depreciation: Fittings and cages | | 860 | |
| Amortise lease | | 960 | 23 465 |
| Net loss | | | (5 984) |

*Balance Sheet of Hugh as at 31.12.86*

| | £ | £ | £ |
|---|---|---|---|
| *Fixed assets* | *Cost* | *Dep* | *WDV* |
| Cages | 8 600 | 860 | 7 740 |
| Lease | 4 800 | 960 | 3 840 |
| | 13 400 | 1 820 | 11 580 |
| *Current assets* | | | |
| Stock: Livestock | 3 400 | | |
| Other | 1 750 | | |
| | 5 150 | | |
| Prepayments | 550 | 5 700 | |
| *Current liabilities* | | | |
| Creditors | 9 086 | | |
| Bank overdraft | 6 120 | | |
| Loan | 2 000 | | |
| Accruals | 258 | 17 474 | |
| Working capital | | | (11 764) |
| | | | (184) |
| Capital | 5 000 | | |
| – Net loss | 5 984 | | |
| | (984) | | |
| Drawings | 5 200 | | (6 184) |
| Loan | | | 6 000 |
| | | | (184) |

## ■ CHAPTER 9 PARTNERSHIP ACCOUNTS

**1**

*See* text

**2**

*See* text

**3(a)**

Profits are shared equally hence each receives 93 000/3 = 31 000

| | *Horley* | *Horsham* | *Hayward* |
|---|---|---|---|
| Share of profit | 31 000 | 31 000 | 31 000 |
| less: Drawings | 19 000 | 21 000 | 23 000 |
| Current account balance | 12 000 | 10 000 | 8 000 |

**(b)**

| | *Horley* | *Horsham* | *Hayward* | *Total* |
|---|---|---|---|---|
| Interest on capital | 7 500 | 6 500 | 5 000 | 19 000 |
| Salary | 20 000 | 17 000 | 16 000 | 53 000 |
| Residue | 7 000 | 7 000 | 7 000 | 21 000 |
| Total | 34 500 | 30 500 | 28 000 | 93 000 |
| less: Drawings | 19 000 | 21 000 | 23 000 | 63 000 |
| Current account balance | 15 500 | 9 500 | 5 000 | 30 000 |

**(c)**

*See* text

**4**

*Trading Profit and Loss and Appropriation Account of Wave and Trough for the year ending 30.6.90*

| | £ | £ | £ |
|---|---|---|---|
| Sales | | | 611 300 |
| *less Cost of goods sold* | | | |
| Opening stock | | 35 500 | |
| + Purchases | 426 100 | | |
| Personal use (note 4) | 1 500 | 424 600 | |
| | | 460 100 | |
| – Closing stock | | 42 700 | 417 400 |
| Gross profit | | | 193 900 |
| *less Expenses* | | | |
| Wages | | 36 900 | |
| Rates prepaid | 15 000 | | |
| | 4 000 | 11 000 | |
| Motor expenses | | 6 300 | |
| Depreciation: | | | |
| Motor vehicle | | 3 000 | |
| Fixtures and fittings | | 5 000 | |
| Bank charges | | 3 600 | |
| Advertising (note 3) | 21 200 | | |
| | 4 300 | 25 500 | |
| Discounts allowed | | 9 800 | |
| Loan interest | | 5 000 | |
| | | | 106 100 |
| Net profit | | | 87 800 |
| Discounts received | | | 2 700 |
| | | | 90 500 |
| *Appropriated as follows* | | | |
| Interest: Wave | 10 800 | | |
| Trough | 9 000 | | |
| Salary: Wave | 20 000 | | |
| Trough | 30 000 | | |
| Residue: Wave | 10 350 | | |
| Trough | 10 350 | | |
| | | 90 500 | |

*Balance Sheet of Wave and Trough as at 30.6.90*

| | £ | £ | £ |
|---|---|---|---|
| *Fixed assets* | | | |
| Freehold land at cost | | | 134 000 |
| Motor vehicle at cost | | 20 000 | |
| *less* Accumulated depreciation | | 6 000 | |
| | | | 14 000 |
| Fixtures and fittings at cost | | 55 200 | |
| *less* Accumulated depreciation | | 15 000 | |
| | | | 40 200 |
| | | | 188 200 |
| *Current assets* | | | |
| Stock | | 42 700 | |
| Debtors | | 101 800 | |
| Prepayment | | 4 000 | |
| | | 148 500 | |
| *Current liabilities* | | | |
| Creditors | | 35 500 | |
| Overdraft | | 15 100 | |
| Accrual | | 4 300 | |
| | | 54 900 | |
| *Working capital* | | | 93 600 |
| | | | 281 800 |
| *less* Loan | | | 50 000 |
| | | | 231 800 |
| Financed by | | | |
| | *Wave* | *Trough* | *Total* |
| *Capital accounts* | 90 000 | 75 000 | 165 000 |
| Current accounts | | | |
| Balance | (1 000) | 10 600 | |
| Stock drawings | (1 500) | | |
| Interest | 10 800 | 9 000 | |
| Salary | 20 000 | 30 000 | |
| Residue | 10 350 | 10 350 | |
| Drawings | (16 000) | (15 800) | |
| | 22 650 | 44 150 | 66 800 |
| | | | 231 800 |

## ■ CHAPTER 10 THE ADMISSION OR RETIREMENT OF A PARTNER

**1**
*See* text

**2**
*See* text

**3**
*See* text

**4**
*See* text

**5**

| | *Old ratio* | *Amount* £ | *New ratio* | *Amount* £ | *Loss/gain* £ |
|---|---|---|---|---|---|
| Rye | 3 | 37 500 | 3 | 30 000 | (7 500) |
| Wheat | 1 | 12 500 | 1 | 10 000 | (2 500) |
| Barley | | | 1 | 10 000 | 10 000 |
| | — | 50 000 | | 50 000 | |

(a) *Cash paid privately* to the existing partners will not affect their capital accounts unless they subsequently choose to pay the money received into the company.
(b) *Cash paid into the business.*

*Cash*

| | | | |
|---|---|---|---|
| Capital | £10 000 | | |

*Capital: Rye*

| | | | |
|---|---|---|---|
| | | Cash | £7 500 |

*Capital: Wheat*

| | | | |
|---|---|---|---|
| | | Cash | £2 500 |

(c) *Goodwill account*

*Goodwill*

| | | | | |
|---|---|---|---|---|
| (a) | | | | |
| Capital | £50 000 | Rye | £30 000 | (b) |
| | | Wheat | £10 000 | (b) |
| | | Barley | £10 000 | (b) |

*Capital: Rye*

| | | | | |
|---|---|---|---|---|
| (b) | | | | (a) |
| Goodwill w/o | £30 000 | Goodwill | £37 500 | |

*Capital: Wheat*

| | | | | |
|---|---|---|---|---|
| (b) | | | | (a) |
| Goodwill w/o | £10 000 | Goodwill | £12 500 | |

*Capital: Barley*

| | | | |
|---|---|---|---|
| (b) | | | |
| Goodwill w/o | £10 000 | | |

(a) Credit the goodwill to the partners' capital account in their existing profit sharing ratio;
(b) write off the goodwill account in the new profit sharing ratio
in the case of (b) and (c) ...

Rye's capital has increased by £7 500 and Wheat's by £2 500... in order to compensate them for their loss of goodwill. Therefore their position is unaltered.

**6**

| | *Old ratio* | *Amount* £ | *New ratio* | *Amount* £ | *Loss/gain* £ |
|---|---|---|---|---|---|
| Rye | 3 | 45 000 | 2 | 50 000 | + 5 000) |
| Wheat | 1 | 15 000 | — | — | (15 000) |
| Barley | 1 | 15 000 | 1 | 25 000 | + 10 000) |
| | | 70 000 | | 75 000 | |

– a goodwill account is used to compensate Wheat for his loss of goodwill.

*Goodwill*

| | | | |
|---|---|---|---|
| (a) | | | |
| Capital | £75 000 | Rye | £50 000(b) |
| | | Barley | £25 000(b) |

*Rye Capital*

| | | | | |
|---|---|---|---|---|
| (b) | | | | |
| Goodwill w/o | £50 000 | Goodwill | £45 000 | (a) |

*Wheat Capital*

| | | | | |
|---|---|---|---|---|
| (b) | | | | |
| Goodwill w/o | £25 000 | Goodwill | £15 000 | (a) |

*Barley Capital*

| | | | | |
|---|---|---|---|---|
| | | Goodwill | £15 000 | (b) |

(a) Credit the goodwill to the partners' capital account in their existing profit sharing ratio;
(b) write off the goodwill in the new profit sharing ratio.

**7**

(a) *Open a revaluation account*
N.B. The double entry would be made in the ledger of the various assets.

*Revaluation Account*

| *Decreases in assets* | £ | *Increases in assets* | £ |
|---|---|---|---|
| (a) Equipment | 5 000 | Goodwill | 20 000 (a) |
| (a) Fixtures and fittings | 4 500 | Premises | 40 000 (a) |
| (a) Debtors | 5 000 | | 60 000 |
| | 14 500 | | |
| (b) Simmons | 17 062 | | |
| (b) Bond | 11 375 | | |
| (b) Blackshaw | 11 375 | | |
| (b) Allen | 5 688 | | |
| | 60 000 | | 60 000 |

(b) The balance remaining, i.e. an increase of £45 500 (60 000 – 14 500) is distributed to the existing partners in their profit sharing ratios, i.e:

| | *Ratio* | *Amount* £ |
|---|---|---|
| Simmons | 3 | 17 062 |
| Bond | 2 | 11 375 |
| Blackshaw | 2 | 11 375 |
| Allen | 1 | 5 688 |
| | | 45 500 |

| Simmons Capital | Bond Capital |
|---|---|
| Reval. Inc. £17 062 | Reval. Inc. £11 375 |

| Blackshaw Capital | Allen Capital |
|---|---|
| Reval. Inc. £11 375 | Reval. Inc. £5 688 |

## ■ CHAPTER 11 LIMITED COMPANY ACCOUNTS

**1**

*See* text

**2**

*See* text

**3**

*See* text

**4**

(i) Share capital is normally in round figures, e.g. £10 000 or £15 000. It is acceptable to transfer some to a loan account. But Wendy will need to be able to repay this loan at a future date.
(ii) The article does not mean a company does not need an ordinary business insurance policy, all companies will need one.
(iii) Reserves – *see* Chapter 11.
(iv) ACT – *see* Chapter 13 SSAPs and FRSs.
(v) Advantages: Limited liability
Increase capital more easily by issuing shares
Disadvantages: Need to publish accounts
More formal

**5**

*Sportsman*

| | £ | £ |
|---|---|---|
| Net profit before taxation | | 521 886 |
| *less* Corporation tax | | 150 000 |
| Net profit after tax | | 371 886 |
| *Appropriated as follows* | | |
| Transfer to general reserve | | 20 000 |
| | | 351 886 |
| Proposed dividend: | | |
| Ordinary | 10 000 | |
| Preference | 20 000 | 30 000 |
| Retained profit for the year | | 321 886 |

*Balance Sheet of Sportsman Ltd as at 31.4.X9*

| | £ | £ | £ |
|---|---|---|---|
| *Fixed assets* | | | |
| *Intangible assets* | | | |
| Goodwill | | | 50 000 |
| *Tangible assets* | | | |
| Land and buildings | | | 460 000 |
| Equipment | | | 50 000 |
| Motor vehicles | | 30 000 | |
| *less* Depreciation | | 5 000 | 25 000 |
| Fixtures | | 10 000 | |
| *less* Depreciation | | 2 000 | 8 000 |
| | | | 593 000 |
| *Current assets* | | | |
| Stock | | 146 000 | |
| Debtors | 120 000 | | |
| *less* Provision for bad debts | 4 000 | 116 000 | |
| Bank | | 30 000 | |
| Cash | | 4 081 | |
| | | 296 081 | |
| *less Current liabilities* | | | |
| Creditors | 37 195 | | |
| Taxation | 150 000 | | |
| Proposed dividend: | | | |
| Ordinary | 10 000 | | |
| Preference | 20 000 | 217 195 | 78 886 |
| | | | 671 886 |
| *Capital and reserves* | | *Authorised* | *Issued* |
| £1 Ordinary shares | | 100 000 | 100 000 |
| 10% Preference shares | | 200 000 | 200 000 |
| | | 300 000 | 300 000 |
| *Reserves* | | | |
| General reserves | | 30 000 | |
| Retained profits | | 321 886 | 351 886 |
| | | | 651 886 |
| *Long-term liabilities* | | | |
| 12% Debenture | | | 20 000 |
| | | | 671 886 |

**6**

*Trading Profit and Loss Account of Milestone PLC for the year ending 31.8.X9*

| | £ | £ | £ |
|---|---|---|---|
| Sales | | | 196 666 |
| *less* Returns in | | | 170 |
| | | | 196 496 |
| *less Cost of goods sold* | | | |
| Opening stock | | 27 776 | |
| + Purchases | 79 104 | | |
| + Carriage in | 205 | | |
| | 79 309 | | |
| – Returns out | 260 | 79 049 | |
| | | 106 825 | |
| – Closing stock | | 30 000 | 76 825 |
| Gross profit | | | 119 671 |
| *add Income* | | | |
| Discount received | | | 5 100 |
| | | | 124 771 |
| *less Expenses* | | | |
| Discounts allowed | | 3 000 | |
| Wages | 11 790 | | |
| + owing | 4 000 | 15 790 | |
| Electricity | 2 407 | | |
| – prepaid | 500 | 1 907 | |
| Rent and rates | | 5 000 | |
| Gas | | 3 105 | |
| Office expenses | 2 198 | | |
| – prepayments | 376 | 1 822 | |
| Bad debts | | 700 | |
| Provision for bad debts | | | |
| Auditors' remuneration | | 2 000 | |
| Debenture interest | 3 000 | | |
| + owing | 200 | 3 200 | |
| Depreciation: | | | |
| Motor vehicles | | 1 275 | |
| Equipment | | 2 500 | |
| Provision for bad debt | | (500) | 39 799 |
| Net profit before taxation | | | 84 972 |
| *less* Taxation | | | 42 486 |
| Net profit after taxation | | | 42 486 |
| Retained profits | | | 20 000 |
| | | | 62 486 |
| *less Appropriations* | | | |
| Transfer to general reserve | | | 5 000 |
| | | | 57 486 |
| Goodwill written off | | | 2 000 |
| | | | 55 486 |
| Dividends paid: Ordinary | | 2 000 | |
| Proposed dividend: Preference shares | | 10 500 | |
| Ordinary shares | | 7 500 | 20 000 |
| Retained profit | | | 35 486 |

*Balance Sheet of Milestone PLC as at 31.8.X9*

| | £ | £ | £ | £ |
|---|---|---|---|---|
| *Fixed assets* | | | | |
| *Intangible assets* | | | | |
| Goodwill | | | | 12 000 |
| – Goodwill written off | | | | 2 000 |
| | | | | 10 000 |
| *Tangible assets* | | | | |
| Premises (cost) | | | | 499 000 |
| Equipment (cost) | | | 25 000 | |
| – Depreciation | | | 7 500 | 17 500 |
| Motor vehicles (cost) | | | 10 000 | |
| – Depreciation | | | 2 775 | 7 225 |
| | | | | 533 725 |
| *Current assets* | | | | |
| Stock | | | 30 000 | |
| Debtors | | 36 166 | | |
| – Provision for bad debts | | 2 500 | 33 666 | |
| Prepayments: | | | | |
| Office expenses | | 376 | | |
| Electricity | | 500 | 876 | |
| | | | 64 542 | |
| *less Current liabilities* | | | | |
| Creditors | | 41 095 | | |
| Accruals: | | | | |
| Wages | 4 000 | | | |
| Debenture interest | 200 | 4 200 | | |
| Bank | | 2 000 | | |
| Proposed Dividend | | | | |
| Preference | 10 500 | | | |
| Ordinary | 7 500 | 18 000 | | |
| Taxation | | 42 486 | 107 781 | (43 239) |
| | | | | 490 486 |
| *Capital and reserves* | | | *Authorised* | *Issued* |
| £1 Ordinary shares | | | 250 000 | 230 000 |
| 7% Preference shares | | | 150 000 | 150 000 |
| | | | 400 000 | 380 000 |
| *Reserves* | | | | |
| General reserve | | | 35 000 | |
| Retained profits | | | 35 486 | 70 486 |
| | | | | 450 486 |
| *Long-term liabilities* | | | | |
| 8% Debenture | | | | 40 000 |
| | | | | 490 486 |

**7**

*Trading Profit and Loss and Appropriation Account of Nospe Ltd for the year ending 31.12.90*

| | £000 | £000 |
|---|---|---|
| Sales | | 640 |
| *less Cost of goods sold* | | |
| Purchases | 410 | |
| *less* Closing stock | 42 | |
| Cost of goods sold | | 368 |
| Gross profit | | 272 |
| Interest (100 × 12% × ¾) | 9 | |
| Depreciation of lease | 11 | |
| Depreciation of fixtures and fittings | 15 | |
| Rates (14 – 6/2) | 11 | |
| Light and heat (8 + 4) | 12 | |
| Guarantee provision | 7 | |
| Wages | 86 | |
| Insurance | 5 | |
| Delivery | 21 | |
| General expenses | 27 | |
| Advertising | 32 | |
| | | 236 |
| Net trading profit | | 36 |
| Corporation tax (36 × 25%) | | 9 |
| | | 27 |
| Dividend (150 × 10p) | | 15 |
| Retained profit | | 12 |

*Balance Sheet of Nospe Ltd as at 31.12.90*

| | £000 | £000 |
|---|---|---|
| *Fixed asset* | | |
| Lease | | 209 |
| – Written off | | 11 |
| | | 198 |
| Fixtures and fittings | 50 | |
| – Depreciation | 15 | 35 |
| | | 244 |
| *Current assets* | | |
| Stock | 42 | |
| Debtors | 34 | |
| Cash | 15 | |
| Prepayment | 3 | |
| | 94 | |
| *Current liabilities* | | |
| Creditors | 32 | |
| Accrued light and heat | 4 | |
| Interest due | 9 | |
| Guarantee provision | 7 | |
| Corporation tax | 9 | |
| Dividend | 15 | |
| | 76 | |
| Working capital | | 18 |
| | | 262 |
| Long-term loan | | 100 |
| | | 162 |
| Financed by: | | |
| Ordinary shares of £1 each | | 150 |
| Retained profit | | 12 |
| | | 162 |

**8**

*Trading Profit for Driver Ltd for the year to 31.7.90*

| | £000 | £000 |
|---|---|---|
| Profit as per balance sheet | | 125 |
| *Adjustments* | | |
| Depreciation charge (note 1) | | |
| Straight line [(100 000 – 10 000) ÷ 6] | 15 | |
| Reducing balance (100 000 × 30%) | 30 | |
| Additional charge | (15) | |
| Stock adjustment (note 2) | | |
| X should be NRV not cost value (95 – 75) | | (20) |
| Goods on sale or return (note 3) | | (15) |
| Audit fee (note 7) | | (7) |
| Revised profit | | 68 |

*Revised Balance Sheet of Driver as at 31.7.90*

| | £000 | £000 | £000 |
|---|---|---|---|
| *Fixed assets* | | | |
| Freehold premises at cost | | | 250 |
| Plant and machinery | | | |
| at cost | | 300 | |
| less: Accumulated depreciation | | 115 | |
| | | | 185 |
| | | | 435 |
| *Current assets* | | | |
| Stocks | | 190 | |
| Goods out on sale or return (note 3) | | 30 | |
| Debtors | | 250 | |
| Cash | | 40 | |
| | | 510 | |
| *Current liabilities* | | | |
| Creditors | 142 | | |
| Accrual – audit fee | 7 | | |
| Proposed dividend | 15 | | |
| | | 164 | |
| | | | 346 |
| | | | 781 |
| less: Debentures | | | 200 |
| | | | 581 |
| Financed by: | | | |
| Ordinary shares of £1 each | | | 300 |
| Profit and loss account (see below) | | | 281 |
| Revaluation reserve | | | 0 |
| Capital reserve | | | 0 |
| | | | 581 |

*Profit and Loss Account*

| | |
|---|---|
| Balance at 1.8.89 | 228 |
| + Revised profit for year to 31.7.90 | 68 |
| | 296 |
| – Dividend 5p × 300 000 shares | 15 |
| (100 + 200 bonus issue) | 281 |

## ■ CHAPTER 12 MANUFACTURING ACCOUNTS

**1**

*Wrenbury Gifts Ltd*

| | £ |
|---|---|
| Opening stock of raw material | 56 000 |
| + Purchases of raw material | 117 119 |
| | 173 119 |
| – Closing stock of raw material | 41 000 |
| Direct material | 132 119 |
| Direct labour | 37 212 |
| Direct expenses | 5 000 |
| Prime cost of manufacture | 174 331 |

**2**

*Manufacturing Account of Alvanley Cabinet Makers Ltd for the year ending 31.12.Y0*

| | £ | £ |
|---|---|---|
| Opening stock of raw material | | 41 888 |
| + Purchases of raw material | 46 166 | |
| – Returns out of raw material | 5 000 | 41 166 |
| | | 83 054 |
| – Closing stock of raw material | | 30 106 |
| Direct material | | 52 948 |
| Direct labour | | 32 166 |
| Direct expenses | | — |
| Prime cost of manufacture | | 85 114 |
| *add Factory overheads* | | |
| Rent | 9 375 | |
| Insurance | 6 333 | |
| Light and heat | 5 250 | |
| Foreman's wages | 15 000 | 35 958 |
| | | 121 072 |
| + Opening stock of work in progress | | 9 620 |
| | | 130 692 |
| – Closing stock of work in progress | | 11 177 |
| | | 119 515 |

**3**

*Manufacturing Trading Profit and Loss Account of Siddington Ltd for the year ending 31.12.Y0*

| | £ | £ | £ |
|---|---|---|---|
| Opening stock of raw material | | | 26 109 |
| + Purchases of raw material | | | 86 111 |
| | | | 112 220 |
| – Closing stock of raw material | | | 17 777 |
| Direct material | | | 94 443 |
| Direct labour | | | 52 000 |
| Direct expenses | | | — |
| | | | 146 443 |
| *add Works overheads* | | | |
| Rent | | 5 500 | |
| Electricity | | 7 500 | |
| Gas | | 1 500 | |
| Depreciation of machinery | | 6 966 | 21 466 |
| | | | 167 909 |
| + Opening stock of work in progress | | | 11 717 |
| | | | 179 626 |
| – Closing stock of work in progress | | | 12 616 |
| Cost of manufacture | | | 167 010 |
| Sales | | | 312 105 |
| *less Cost of goods sold* | | | |
| Opening stock of finished goods | | 26 106 | |
| + Cost of manufacture | | 167 010 | |
| | | 193 116 | |
| Closing stock of finished goods | | 31 777 | 161 339 |
| Gross profit | | | 150 766 |
| *add Income* | | | |
| Discount received | | | 3 100 |
| | | | 153 866 |
| *less Expenses* | | | |
| *Administration* | | | |
| Rent | | 5 500 | |
| Electricity | | 7 500 | |
| Gas | | 1 500 | |
| Telephone | 1 560 | | |
| – Prepaid | 150 | 1 410 | |
| Expenses (office) | | 4 176 | |
| Salaries (office) | | 76 000 | |
| Depreciation of fixtures and fittings | | 2 000 | |
| | | 98 086 | |

| *Selling and distribution* | £ | £ | £ |
|---|---|---|---|
| Motor expenses | 2 000 | | |
| + Owing | 300 | | |
| | 2 300 | | |
| Depreciation of motor vehicle | 3 100 | 5 400 | |
| *Financial* | | | |
| Bad debts | 2 000 | | |
| Discounts allowed | 2 000 | | |
| Provision for bad debts | 5 710 | 9 710 | 113 196 |
| Net profit (loss) before tax | | | 40.670 |
| *less* Taxation | | | 10 000 |
| Net profit after tax | | | 30 670 |
| *less* Dividends: | | | |
| Proposed | | 10 000 | |
| Paid | | 1 000 | 11 000 |
| Profit for the year | | | 19 670 |
| + Balance of profits | | | 100 000 |
| Retained profits | | | 119 670 |

*Balance Sheet of Siddington Ltd as at 31.12.Y0*

| | £ | £ | £ |
|---|---|---|---|
| Fixed assets | | | |
| Land and buildings (cost) | | | 200 000 |
| Machinery (cost) | | 86 000 | |
| – Provision for depreciation | | 23 306 | 62 694 |
| Motor vehicles (cost) | | 31 000 | |
| – Provision for depreciation | | 9 100 | 21 900 |
| Fixtures and fittings (cost) | | 26 000 | |
| – Provision for depreciation | | 13 000 | 13 000 |
| | | | 297 594 |
| *Current assets* | | | |
| Stock of raw material | | 17 777 | |
| work in progress | | 12 616 | |
| finished goods | | 31 777 | |
| | | 62 170 | |
| Debtors | 57 100 | | |
| – Provision for bad debts | 5 710 | 51 390 | |
| Prepayments: Telephone | | 150 | |
| Cash | | 407 | |
| | | 114 117 | |
| *less Current liabilities* | | | |
| Creditors | 36 161 | | |
| Accruals: Motor expenses | 300 | | |
| Bank overdraft | 65 580 | | |
| Proposed dividend: Ordinary | 10 000 | | |
| Taxation | 10 000 | 122 041 | (7 924) |
| | | | 289 670 |
| *Authorised and Issued Share Capital* | | *Authorised* | *Issued* |
| £1 ordinary shares f.p. | | 150 000 | 150 000 |
| *Reserves* | | | |
| Balance of profits | | 119 670 | |
| General reserve | | 20 000 | 139 670 |
| | | | 289 670 |

**4**

*Manufacturing Account of Reigate for the year ending 31.12.90*

| | £000 |
|---|---|
| Opening stock of raw materials | 13 |
| Purchases | 126 |
| Closing stock of raw materials | 15 |
| Materials consumed | 124 |
| Wages | 73 |
| Depreciation (164 – 14)/10 | 15 |
| Rent (24 + 8) × 75% | 24 |
| Expenses | 34 |
| Rates (15 – 3) × 75% | 9 |
| Light, heat and power (28 × 75%) | 21 |
| Cost of goods manufactured | 300 |

*Trading Profit and Loss Account of Reigate for the year ending 31.12.90*

| | £000 | £000 |
|---|---|---|
| Sales | | 500 |
| Opening stock of finished goods | 28 | |
| Cost of manufacture | 300 | |
| Closing stock of finished goods | 33 | |
| Cost of goods sold | | 295 |
| Gross profit | | 205 |
| Interest | 12 | |
| Depreciation (100 – 25)/3 | 25 | |
| Rent (24 + 8) × 25% | 8 | |
| Salaries | 28 | |
| Expenses | 11 | |
| Rates (15 – 3) × 25% | 3 | |
| Delivery wages | 30 | |
| Light, heat and power (28 × 25%) | 7 | |
| Vehicle expenses | 13 | |
| Advertising | 23 | |
| Bad debts | 4 | |
| | | 164 |
| Net profit | | 41 |

*Balance Sheet of Reigate as at 31.12.90*

| | £000 | £000 |
|---|---|---|
| *Fixed assets* | | |
| Plant: Cost | 164 | |
| less: Accumulated depreciation (75 + 15) | 90 | |
| | | 74 |
| Vehicles: Cost | 100 | |
| less: Accumulated depreciation (25 + 25) | 50 | |
| | | 50 |
| | | 124 |
| *Current assets* | | |
| Stock (15 + 33) | 48 | |
| Debtors | 56 | |
| Cash | 24 | |
| Rates prepaid | 3 | |
| | 131 | |
| *Current liabilities* | | |
| Creditors | 32 | |
| Rent accrued | 8 | |
| | 40 | |
| Working capital | | 91 |
| *Long-term liabilities* | | 215 |
| Long-term loan | | 100 |
| | | 115 |
| Financed by: | | |
| Opening capital | | 110 |
| Profit | | 41 |
| | | 151 |
| less: Drawings | | 36 |
| | | 115 |

## ■ CHAPTER 13 STATEMENTS OF STANDARD ACCOUNTING PRACTICE

**1**

*See* text

**2(a)**

See 'Why do we need SSAPs and FRSs?' in this chapter.

**(b) *Examples***

'Why do we need SSAPs and FRSs?' illustrates the effect of two companies adopting different depreciation policies.

The effect of using different methods of valuing stock, e.g. FIFO and LIFO, would have provided another example, *see* Chapter 13.

**3**

*See* text

**4**
*See* text

**5**
*See* text

**6**
*See* text

## ■ CHAPTER 14 CASH FLOW FORECASTS

**1**
*See* text

**2**
*See* text

**3**
*See* opposite for Cash Budget of Telephone Pizza.

*Note 1 Ingredients*:
As stock is maintained at a constant level Mr and Mrs Deepan will need to replace what they sell. However, as shown below, this will only cost them 20% of their selling price.

*Replacement purchases*

| Month | 1 | 2 | 3 | 4 | 5 | 6 |
|---|---|---|---|---|---|---|
| Sales (£) | 300 | 500 | 600 | 700 | 800 | 1 000 |
| *Cost* of purchases 20% (£) | 60 | 100 | 120 | 140 | 160 | 200 |

In addition to replacing stock sold, the stock is to be increased in Month 3 to £300 and in Month 5 to £500, i.e.

*Month 3 purchases*

| | |
|---|---|
| Replacement purchases (as above) | £120 |
| Increase in stock (£200 – £300) | £100 |
| | £220 |

*Month 5 purchases*

| | |
|---|---|
| Replacement purchases (as above) | £160 |
| Increase in stock (£300 – £400) | £100 |
| | £260 |

**3**

*Cash Budget of Telephone Pizza for the six months ending ...*

| | 1<br>£ | 2<br>£ | 3<br>£ | 4<br>£ | 5<br>£ | 6<br>£ | Dr/Cr<br>£ | Total<br>£ |
|---|---|---|---|---|---|---|---|---|
| *Income* | | | | | | | | |
| Sales | 300 | 500 | 600 | 700 | 800 | 1 000 | | |
| Total income | 300 | 500 | 600 | 700 | 800 | 1 000 | | 3 900 |
| *Expenditure* | | | | | | | | |
| Advertising | 200 | 200 | 150 | 150 | 50 | 50 | | 800 |
| *Ingredients (Note 1)* | | | | | | | | |
| Initial stock | 200 | | | | | | | 200 |
| Purchases | 60 | 100 | 220 | 140 | 260 | 200 | | 980 |
| Lease premium | 1 000 | | | | | | | 1 000 |
| Rental | 500 | | | 500 | | | | 1 000 |
| Legal fees | 200 | | | | | | | 200 |
| Assistant cook | | | | | | 100 | | 100 |
| Shop expenses | 150 | 150 | 150 | 150 | 150 | 150 | | 900 |
| Insurance | 350 | | | | | | | 350 |
| HP Catering equipment | 180 | 35 | 35 | 35 | 35 | 35 | | 355 |
| Motor cycle expenses | 30 | 30 | 30 | 30 | 30 | 30 | | 180 |
| Drawings | 300 | 300 | 300 | 300 | 300 | 300 | | 1 800 |
| Total expenditure | (3 170) | (815) | (885) | (1 305) | (825) | (865) | | (7 865) |
| Total income – total expenditure | (2 870) | (315) | (285) | (605) | (25) | 135 | | |
| Opening balance | 900 | (1 970) | (2 285) | (2 570) | (3 175) | (3 200) | | |
| Other injections | | | | | | | | |
| Running balance | (1 970) | (2 285) | (2 570) | (3 175) | (3 200) | (3 065) | | |

**4**

*Forecast Trading Profit and Loss Account of Telephone Pizza for the six months ending ...*

| | £ | £ | £ |
|---|---|---|---|
| Sales | | | 3 900 |
| *less Cost of goods sold* | | | |
| Opening stock | | 200 | |
| + Purchases | | 980 | |
| | | 1 180 | |
| – Closing stock | | 400 | 780 |
| Gross profit | | | 3 120 |
| *less Expenses* | | | |
| Advertising | | 800 | |
| Rent | | 1 000 | |
| Legal fees | | 200 | |
| Wages (Assistant cook) | | 100 | |
| Shop expenses | | 900 | |
| Insurance (*Note 1*) | 350 | | |
| *less* Insurance prepaid | 175 | 175 | |
| Motor cycle expenses | | 180 | |
| Interest on HP (*Note 2*) | | 86 | |
| Depreciation of lease (*Note 3*) | | 167 | |
| Depreciation of equipment (*Note 4*) | | 82 | |
| Depreciation of motor cycle (*Note 5*) | | 120 | 3 810 |
| Net profit/(loss) | | | (690) |

*Note 1 Insurance*
1 year's premium has been paid
∴ at the end of 6 months half, i.e. £175, has been prepaid.
*Note 2 Interest on HP* given as per Note 1.
*Note 3 Depreciation of lease*
Lease cost £1 000

$$\text{Depreciation} = 1/6 = \frac{1000}{6} = \underline{\underline{£167}}$$

*Note 4 Depreciation of equipment*
Cost £820
Depreciation = 20% per annum = £164 per annum
∴ 6 months = £82

*Note 5 Depreciation of motor cycle*
Value £1 200
Depreciation = 20% per annum = £240
∴ 6 months = £120

*Balance Sheet of Telephone Pizza as at ...*

| | £ | £ |
|---|---|---|
| *Fixed assets* | | |
| Lease | 1 000 | |
| – Depreciation | 167 | 833 |
| Equipment | 820 | |
| – Depreciation | 82 | 738 |
| Motor Cycle | 1 200 | |
| – Depreciation | 120 | 1 080 |
| | | 2 651 |
| *Current assets* | | |
| Stock | 400 | |
| Prepayments insurance | 175 | 575 |
| | | 3 226 |
| *Financed by:* | | |
| Capital: | | |
| Cash | | 900 |
| Motor cycle (*Note 6*) | | 1 200 |
| | | 2 100 |
| + Net profit (loss) | | (690) |
| | | 1 410 |
| – Drawings | | (1800) |
| | | (390) |
| *Current liabilities* | | |
| Creditors: HP (*Note 7*) | 348 | |
| Bank overdraft | 3 065 | 3 413 |
| | | 3 023 |
| *Long-term liabilities* | | |
| Creditors: HP (*Note 7*) | | 203 |
| | | 3 226 |

*Note 6 Capital*
Capital is not only the amount of cash invested in the company by the owners, but also the value of any assets the owners contribute. When Mr Deepan started the business the bookkeeping entries for the motor cycle would therefore have been:

*Motor cycle*

| | |
|---|---|
| Capital £1 200 | |

*Capital*

| | |
|---|---|
| | Motor cycle £1 200 |

*Note 7 HP*
Catering equipment is brought into the accounts at the cash price, i.e. £820.

To find the amount outstanding, i.e. creditors, we must deduct the amount which has been repaid, namely:

| | £ |
|---|---|
| Deposit | 180 |
| 5 × £35 per month | 175 |
| | 355 |
| – Interest | 86 |
| Capital repaid | 269 |

∴ Outstanding (creditors) = £820
– £269
£551

As the HP agreement calls for 24 monthly repayments Mr and Mrs Deepan have another 19 payments to make.

∴ £551 = 19 monthly payments

∴ $\frac{551}{19}$ = £29 per month

∴ *Current liability* (amount due within 12 months)

12 × £29 = £348

∴ *Long-term liability* (amount due over 12 months)

= 7 × £29 = £203

or £551 – £348 = £203

The monthly repayments are quoted as being £35, which represents both capital £29 plus interest £6.

**5**

*Cash Flow Forecast at Merstham's for the six months ending 31.11.91*

| Income | June | July | August | Sept | Oct | Nov |
|---|---|---|---|---|---|---|
| Capital | 7 000 | | | | | |
| Sales – cash | 4 000 | 4 000 | 4 000 | 6 400 | 6 400 | 6 400 |
| – credit | | 6 000 | 6 000 | 6 000 | 9 600 | 9 600 |
| | 11 000 | 10 000 | 10 000 | 12 400 | 16 000 | 16 000 |
| *Expenditure* | | | | | | |
| Stock | 4 000 | | | | 4 000 | |
| Purchases – cash | 5 000 | 5 000 | 5 000 | | | |
| – credit | | | | | 8 000 | 8 000 |
| Fixtures and fittings | | 4 500 | | | | |
| Rent | 4 300 | | | | | |
| Insurance | 1 650 | | | | | |
| Wages | 1 000 | 1 000 | 1 000 | 1 000 | 1 000 | 1 000 |
| General expenses | 750 | 750 | 750 | 750 | 750 | 750 |
| Drawings | 1 250 | 1 250 | 1 250 | 1 250 | 1 250 | 1 250 |
| | 17 950 | 12 500 | 8 000 | 3 000 | 15 000 | 11 000 |
| Income – expenditure | (6 950) | (2 500) | 2 000 | 9 400 | 1 000 | 5 000 |
| Opening balance | – | (6 950) | (9 450) | (7 450) | 1 950 | 2 950 |
| Cumulative balance | (6 950) | (9 450) | (7 450) | 1 950 | 2 950 | 7 950 |

**6**

*See* the cash flow forecast on the next page.

## ■ CHAPTER 15 CASH AND WORKING CAPITAL

**1**

(a) 3 : 1
(b) 2.73 : 1
(c) 0.55 : 1
(d) 1.08 : 1

**2**

*Current assets*

| | £ | £ |
|---|---|---|
| Stock | | 215 000 |
| Debtors | | 100 000 |
| Prepayments | | 7 500 |
| Bank Investment Account | | 20 000 |
| Cash | | 10 000 |
| | | 352 500 |
| *less Current liabilities* | | |
| Creditors | 60 000 | |
| Accruals | 10 000 | |
| Bank overdraft | 16 000 | 86 000 |
| Working capital | | 266 500 |

Ratio = 1.32 : 1

**3**

$$\text{Stock turnover} = \frac{\text{Stock}}{\text{Cost of goods sold}} \times 365$$

$$\frac{150}{1\,750} \times 365 = 31.28 \text{ days}$$

$$\text{Debtors' settlement period} = \frac{\text{Debtors}}{\text{Sales}} \times 365$$

$$\frac{850}{10\,000} \times 365 = 31.025 \text{ days}$$

$$\text{Creditors' settlement period} = \frac{\text{Creditors}}{\text{Purchases}} \times 365$$

$$\frac{1\,960}{7\,700} \times 365 = 92.9 \text{ days}$$

| | |
|---|---|
| Stock turnover | 31 days |
| Debtors' settlement | 31 days |
| Creditors' settlement | 62 days |

**6**

***Ivor Shop***

(a)

| Income | J | A | S | O | N | D | J | F | M | A | M | J |
|---|---|---|---|---|---|---|---|---|---|---|---|---|
| | £ | £ | £ | £ | £ | £ | £ | £ | £ | £ | £ | £ |
| Receipts | 3 000 | 3 600 | 4 500 | 4 500 | 6 000 | 6 000 | 7 500 | 7 500 | 9 000 | 9 000 | 12 000 | 12 000 |
| Total receipts | 3 000 | 3 600 | 4 500 | 4 500 | 6 000 | 6 000 | 7 500 | 7 500 | 9 000 | 9 000 | 12 000 | 12 000 |
| *Expenditures* | | | | | | | | | | | | |
| Rent | 2 000 | | | 2 000 | | | 2 000 | | | 2 000 | | |
| Legal costs | 400 | | | | | | | | | | | |
| Shop fittings | 2 500 | 215 | 215 | 215 | 215 | 215 | 215 | 215 | 215 | 215 | 215 | 215 |
| Rates | | 360 | | 960 | | | | | | 980 | | |
| Wages | | | 500 | 500 | 500 | 500 | 500 | 500 | 500 | 500 | 500 | 500 |
| Purchases | 2 000 | 2 400 | 3 000 | 3 000 | 4 000 | 4 000 | | 5 000 | 5 000 | 6 000 | 6 000 | 8 000 |
| Stock | 15 000 | | | | | | | | | | | |
| Other expenses | 250 | 250 | 250 | 250 | 250 | 250 | 250 | 250 | 250 | 250 | 250 | 250 |
| Loan repayment | | | | | | | 5 000 | | | | | |
| Drawings | 400 | 400 | 400 | 400 | 400 | 400 | 400 | 400 | 400 | 400 | 400 | 400 |
| Total expenditure | 22 550 | 3 625 | 4 365 | 7 325 | 5 365 | 5 365 | 8 365 | 6 365 | 6 365 | 10 345 | 7 365 | 9 365 |
| Income – expenditure | (19 550) | (25) | 135 | (2 825) | 635 | 635 | (865) | 1 135 | 2 635 | (1 345) | 4 635 | 2 635 |
| Opening balance (Capital) | 10 000 | (4 550) | (4 575) | (4 440) | (7 265) | (6 630) | (5 995) | (6 860) | (5 725) | (3 090) | (4 435) | 200 |
| Other injections | 5 000 | | | | | | | | | | | |
| Balance | (4 550) | (4 575) | (4 440) | (7 265) | (6 630) | (5 995) | (6 860) | (5 725) | (3 090) | (4 435) | 200 | 2 835 |

(b) The biggest overdraft he will need is £7 265 in October.

(c) The above budget shows credit given by suppliers after 6 months. If credit was given after 3 months there would be no purchase in October and the purchases for November, December and January would be 3 000, 4 000 and 4 000 respectively. February onwards would be as shown.

Under such circumstances the largest overdraft would be £ 6 860 in January.

**4**

$$\text{Debtors' settlement period} = \frac{\text{Debtors}}{\text{Sales}} \times 365$$

$$72 \text{ days} = \frac{\text{Debtors}}{200\,000} \times 365$$

$$\text{Debtors} = \frac{72}{365} \times 200\,000$$

$$39\,452$$

$$\text{Creditors' settlement period} = \frac{\text{Creditors}}{\text{Purchases}} \times 365$$

$$30 \text{ days} = \frac{\text{Creditors}}{150\,000} \times 365$$

$$\text{Creditors} = \frac{30}{365} \times 150\,000$$

$$12\,328.75$$

**5**

*See* text

**6**

*See* text

**7(a)**

| Suggestion | Overdraft £ | Working capital £ | Working capital ratio |
|---|---|---|---|
| (i) | + 44 000 | 0 | 1:0.90 |
| (ii) | + 50 000 | + 50 000 | 1:1.33 |
| (iii) | 0 | 0 | 1:0.93 |
| (iv) | + 20 000 | 0 | 1:0.93 |
| (v) | + 30 000 | + 30 000 | 1:1.13 |

*Workings*:

| Suggestion... | | (i) | (ii) | (iii) | (iv) | (v) |
|---|---|---|---|---|---|---|
| Stock | 65 | 65 | 65 | 65 | 65 | 65 |
| Debtors | 88 | 44 | 88 | 88 | 88 | 88 |
| | 153 | 109 | 153 | 153 | 153 | 153 |
| Creditors | 55 | 55 | 55 | 55 | 75 | 55 |
| Overdraft | 110 | 66 | 60 | 110 | 90 | 80 |
| | 165 | 121 | 115 | 165 | 165 | 135 |
| Working capital | (12) | (12) | 38 | (12) | (12) | 18 |
| Ratio | | 109/121 | 153/115 | 153/165 | 153/165 | 153/135 |

**(b)**

(i) Will it force customers to go elsewhere?
Are some debtors more than two months overdue?
How will it be enforced?
Will we need to offer discounts – and at what cost?

(ii) Loans, cost interest
It does improve working capital – amount and ratio

(iii) No effect

(iv) Will suppliers allow you longer credit?
Our creditors will increase but our overdraft reduce hence working capital and ratio are unchanged

(v) The £30 000 would reduce the overdraft and therefore improve the working capital and ratio
Can the asset be sold?
Will we need to replace it?

## ■ CHAPTER 16 CASH FLOW STATEMENTS

**1**

*Cash Flow Statement of... for the year ending 30.4.89*

| | | |
|---|---|---|
| *Operating activities* | | |
| Net profit for the year | | 21 871 |
| Add depreciation, shop fittings | 5 942 | |
| Add depreciation, TV sets for rental | 10 537 | |
| Add depreciation, motor vehicles | 5 070 | 21 549 |
| | | 43 420 |
| Increase in stock | (4 901) | |
| Decrease in debtors | 1 967 | |
| Increase in prepaids | (834) | |
| Decrease in creditors | (3 784) | |
| Increase in accruals | 68 | (7 484) |
| Net cash inflow from operating activities | | 35 936 |
| Return on investments and servicing of finance | | |
| Dividends paid | | (1 000) |
| *Taxation* | | |
| Tax paid | | (4 300) |
| *Investing activities* | | |
| Purchase of shop fittings | (5 000) | |
| Purchase of motor vehicles | (21 500) | |
| Sale of motor vehicles | 4 250 | |
| Net cashflow from investing activities | | (22 250) |
| Net cashflow before financing | | 8 386 |
| *Financing* | | |
| Issue of shares | | 10 000 |
| Increase in cash/bank | | 18 386 |
| *Analysis of changes in cash/bank during year* | | |
| Balance at start of year | | (7 186) |
| Balance at end of year | | 11 120 |
| Increase in cash/bank | | 18 386 |

*Workings re motor vehicles* (not essential to be shown)

| | *Cost* | *Aggregate depreciation* |
|---|---|---|
| B/fwd | £27 200 | £8 135 |
| Sales | (10 500) | (6 535) |
| | 16 700 | 1 600 |
| Purchases (balancing figure) | 21 500 | |
| Depreciation for year | | 5 070 |
| Balance sheet 1989 | 38 200 | 6 670 |

**2(a)**

*Cash Flow Statement of Trapper for the year ending 30.6.91*

| | | |
|---|---|---|
| *Operating activities* | | |
| Profit for year | | 50 |
| Depreciation | | 30 |
| | | 80 |
| Increase in stock | (30) | |
| Increase in debtors | (40) | |
| Increase in creditors | 25 | (45) |
| Net cash inflow from operating activities | | 35 |
| *Investing activities* | | |
| Purchase of fixed assets | | (100) |
| Net cash flow before financing | | (65) |
| *Financing* | | |
| Loan raised | 40 | |
| Drawings | (45) | |
| Net cash flow from financing | | (5) |
| Decrease in cash/bank | | (70) |
| *Analysis of changes in cash/bank during year* | | |
| Balance at start of year | | 50 |
| Balance at end of year | | (20) |
| | | (70) |

**(b)**

| | *1990* | *1991* |
|---|---|---|
| Working capital ratio | 3.6:1 | 2.4:1 |
| Liquidity ratio | 2.2:1 | 1.3:1 |

**(c)**

- Progress appears good – extra profit as a result of the expansion.
- The above ratios have come down to a better level though still possibly too high.
- The overdraft is manageable and could be repaid from internal sources.
- We are told that these results will be repeated in the future.

**3(a)**

| | |
|---|---|
| Capital at end of year | 37 100 |
| Capital at start of year | 25 530 |
| Increase in capital | 11 570 |
| *add* Drawings | 13 000 |
| *less* Capital introduced | −1 000 |
| Profit for year | 23 570 |

**(b)**

*Cash Flow Statement of Schooner for the year ended 31.3.90*

| | | |
|---|---|---|
| *Operating activities* | | |
| Profit | | 23 570 |
| Depreciation for the year | | 5 000 |
| | | 28 570 |
| Increase in stock | (6 500) | |
| Increase in debtors | (2 130) | |
| Increase in creditors | 3 550 | (5 080) |
| Net cash inflow from operating activities | | 23 490 |
| *Investing activities* | | |
| Purchase of fixed assets | | (25 000) |
| Net cash flow before financing | | (1 510) |
| Financing | | |
| Capital introduced | 1 000 | |
| Drawings | (13 000) | |
| Loan repaid | (5 000) | |
| Net cash flow from financing | | (17 000) |
| Decrease in cash/bank | | (18 510) |
| | | |
| Analysis of changes in cash/bank during year | | |
| Balance at start of year | | 2 310 |
| Balance at end of year | | (16 200) |
| | | 18 510 |

**(c)**

The major uses of funds have been:

- the purchase of a van (25 000);
- drawings of £13 000; and
- repayment of loan (5 000)

The purchase of a van has therefore been financed by the increase in overdraft rather than long-term funds.

## ■ CHAPTER 17 RECONCILIATION STATEMENTS

**1(a)**

*Bank Reconciliation Statement at 30.9.87*

| | £ | £ |
|---|---|---|
| Balance as per bank statement | | 64 o/d |
| *add debits not in cash book* | | |
| Sept 17 085 | 117 | |
| 18 Returned cheque | 782 | |
| 23 D D Moon Ins Co. | 375 | |
| 30 Bank charges | 97 | 1 371 |
| | | 1 307 |
| *less cheques not yet presented* | | |
| Sept 11 Johnson & Co. | 257 | |
| 26 Thames Water | 110 | 367 |
| | | 940 |
| *add bankings not credited* | | |
| Sept 29 Victor | 178 | |
| 30 Watson | 3 | 213 |
| | | 1 153 |
| *less credits not in cash book* | | |
| Sept 9 B G C Jones | 825 | |
| 23 Dividend Excelsior | 335 | 860 |
| | | 293 |

**(b)**

*See* text

**2**

(a) The reasons why Ken's cash position is worse are identified in the reconciliation statement below, i.e.

- purchase of shop fittings;
- purchase of a new car;
- increase in stock;
- high drawings, which although less than the net profit for the year did not leave sufficient finance for the above purchases;
- while Ken increased creditors and reduced debtors this was not enough to cover the purchases.

**(b)**

| | £ | £ |
|---|---|---|
| *Bank balance as at 30.6.86* | | 3 417 |
| *add* | | |
| Net profit on trading (*Note 1*) | 20 691 | |
| Sale proceeds of car (*Note 2*) | 950 | |
| Decrease in debtors | 373 | |
| Increase in creditors | 1 864 | 23 878 |
| | | 27 295 |
| *less* | | |
| Purchase of new shop fittings | 1 575 | |
| Purchase of new car | 6 250 | |
| Increase in stock | 9 144 | |
| Drawings | 14 768 | 30 737 |
| Bank balance as at 30.6.87 | | 3 442 o/d |

| *Note 1* | £ |
|---|---|
| Net profit | 19 871 |
| *less* Book profit on sale of car | 400 |
| | 19 471 |
| *add* Depreciation | 1 220 |
| | 20 691 |

i.e. the profit on sale of car and depreciation are *bookkeeping entries only* and must therefore be added or deducted from the profit for the year.

| *Note 2* | £ |
|---|---|
| Motor car (at cost) 30.6.86 | 2 510 |
| less depreciation | 1 960 |
| Net book value | 550 |
| Profit on sale | 400 |
| Sale proceeds | 950 |

**3(a)**

*Cash Account*

| | | | |
|---|---|---|---|
| Buyit | 3 200 | Balance b/d | 27 392 |
| Balance c/d | 27 745 | Charges | 1 853 |
| | | Rates | 1 700 |
| | 30 945 | | 30 945 |

**(b)**

| | |
|---|---|
| Balance per statement | (23 570) |
| + cheque wrongly charged | 532 |
| – outstanding cheques | (15 326) |
| + outstanding lodgements | 10 619 |
| Balance per cash account | (27 745) |

(c) Follow up outstanding items in subsequent reconciliations to ensure they are all correctly cleared.
Report the cheque charged in error to the bank.
Review the age of outstanding cheques.
(d) Checks the accuracy of the bank statement and cash account.
Provides management with a regular check on cash records.

**4(a)**

*Cash Account of Mr Matrix for year to 30 June 1991*

| | | | |
|---|---|---|---|
| Capital | 7 000 | Van | 6 000 |
| Sales | 15 000 | Ladders | 550 |
| | | Sign writing | 450 |
| | | Sundry costs | 1 025 |
| | | Motor expenses | 1 500 |
| | | Casual labour | 2 500 |
| | | Drawings | 9 000 |
| | | Balance c/d | 975 |
| | 22 000 | | 22 000 |
| Balance b/d | 975 | | |

**(b)**

| | |
|---|---|
| Cash account balance | 975 |
| plus: Uncleared cheque | 890 |
| less: Outstanding lodgements | (50) |
| Balance on bank statement | 1 815 |

**(c)**

| | |
|---|---|
| Cost of van | 6 000 |
| add: Sign writing | 450 |
| | 6 450 |
| less: Residual value | 750 |
| Total depreciation | 5 700 |
| Cost of van | 6 000 |
| + Sign writing | 450 |
| | 6 450 |
| – Value as at 30.6.91 | 5 310 |
| Depreciation to date | 1 140 |

$$\frac{\text{Total depreciation}}{\text{Life of asset}} \quad \frac{5\,700}{5} = 1\,140 \text{ pa}$$

∴ Straight line method is being adopted.

**(d)**

*Profit and Loss Account for the year ending 30.6.91 for Mr Matrix*

| | | | |
|---|---|---|---|
| Sales | | | 15 000 |
| + Outstanding | | | 750 |
| | | | 15 750 |
| *less* | | | |
| Materials | 1 025 | | |
| + Owing | 75 | 1 100 | |
| Motor expenses | 1 500 | | |
| + Owing | 85 | 1 585 | |
| Labour | | 2 500 | |
| Depreciation Ladders | | 145 | |
| Van | | 1 140 | 6 470 |
| Net profit | | | 9 280 |

*Balance Sheet of Mr Matrix as at 30.6.91*

| | | |
|---|---|---|
| *Fixed assets* | | |
| Van | 6 450 | |
| – Depreciation | 1 140 | 5 310 |
| Ladders | 550 | |
| – Depreciation | 145 | 405 |
| | | 5 715 |
| *Current assets* | | |
| Debtors | 750 | |
| Cash | 975 | |
| | 1 725 | |
| *Current liabilities* | | |
| Accrued sundry materials | 75 | |
| Accrued motor expenses | 85 | |
| | 160 | |
| Working capital | | 1 565 |
| | | 7 280 |
| Financed by: | | |
| Opening capital | | 7 000 |
| add: Profit for year | | 9 280 |
| less: Drawings | | (9 000) |
| | | 7 230 |

## ■ CHAPTER 18 RATIO ANALYSIS

**1**

Gee-Whiz: May 1988

| *Ratio* | *Calculation* | *1986* | *1987* |
|---|---|---|---|
| Gross margin | $\frac{\text{Gross profit}}{\text{Sales}} \times 100$ | $\frac{732\ 420}{2\ 154\ 203} \times 100$ | $\frac{894\ 915}{3\ 196\ 124} \times 100$ |
| | | 34% | 28% |
| Net margin | $\frac{\text{Net profit}}{\text{Sales}} \times 100$ | $\frac{150\ 794}{2\ 154\ 203} \times 100$ | $\frac{267\ 096}{3\ 196\ 124} \times 100$ |
| | | 7% | 8.35% |
| Working capital | Current assets: Current liabilities | 551 749:77 571<br>7.1:1 | 599 503:145 308<br>4.12:1 |
| Acid test | Liquid assets: Current liabilities (i.e. not stock) | 425 532:77 571<br>5.5:1 | 451 286:145 308<br>3.1:1 |
| Rate of stock turnover | $\frac{\text{Cost of goods sold}}{\text{Average stock}}$ | $\frac{1\ 421\ 774}{125\ 217}$ | $\frac{2\ 301\ 209}{148\ 217}$ |
| | | 11.35 times | 15.5 times |
| Debtors' collection period | $\frac{\text{Debtors}}{\text{Sales}} \times 365$ | $\frac{317\ 412}{2\ 154\ 203} \times 365$ | $\frac{352\ 140}{3\ 196\ 124} \times 365$ |
| | | 53.7 days | 40.2 days |
| Creditors' collection period | $\frac{\text{Creditors}}{\text{Purchases}} \times 365$ | $\frac{77\ 571}{1\ 421\ 774} \times 365$ | $\frac{145\ 308}{2\ 301\ 209} \times 365$ |
| | | 19.9 days | 23 days |

N.B. As we do not have a figure for purchases cost of sales has been used. This is therefore a rough estimate only.

| *Ratio* | *Calculation* | *1986* | *1987* |
|---|---|---|---|
| Return on capital employed | $\frac{\text{Net profit}}{\text{Capital employed}} \times 100$ | $\frac{150\ 794}{649\ 095} \times 100$ | $\frac{267\ 096}{822\ 707} \times 100$ |
| | | 23.23% | 32.46% |

Comments: *see* text.

**2**

A Gross profit margin has increased due to either:
(a) increase in selling price, and/or
(b) reduction in cost of goods sold.
Increase in debtors indicates long credit given to customers.

It therefore appears that customers have been given longer credit but asked to pay increased prices.

B Gross profit margin has increased due to either:
(a) increase in selling price, and/or
(b) reduction in cost of goods sold (e.g. purchases).
The company now take considerably less credit, paying immediately by cheque (4-day clearance).

It therefore appears that Company B are paying for purchases immediately and therefore obtaining a discount and as a result a lower cost of goods sold.

C If the gross profit percentage is constant, yet the amount doubled, something has resulted in a doubling of sales, e.g. advertising campaign.

The net margin has doubled as the increased gross profit figure would result in a higher net profit figure, without a proportional increase in expenses.

D The increase in sales is likely to be due to reduced prices. The company have, however, been unable to reduce their cost of goods sold by an equal amount, hence the reduction in gross profit margin 50%–25%.

The net margin has increased as the amount of gross profit will have increased as a result of the increased sales. Expenses, however, have been controlled as most of these will be fixed costs.

**3**

(i) Disagree – the sales increase may be at a reduced selling price.
(ii) Disagree – the increase in gross profit may be offset by increases in expenses.
(iii) Disagree – depreciation is a bookkeeping entry only and does not represent cash.
(iv) Disagree – debtors may increase if larger credit is offered and hence working capital may increase, if all other factors remain constant.
(v) Disagree – net profit and drawings are only two items which affect the cash/bank; there are many more factors affecting working capital.
(vi) Agree
(vii) Disagree – a corresponding reduction in debtors will enable creditors to be paid quicker.
(viii) Disagree – depreciation is a bookkeeping entry only.

**4(a)**

*Profit and Loss Statements of Departments A, B and C of Flag Ltd for year ended 30.6.91*

| Department | A | B | C | Total |
|---|---|---|---|---|
| Sales | 200 | 350 | 450 | 1 000 |
| Cost of goods sold | 100 | 140 | 189 | 429 |
| | 100 | 210 | 261 | 571 |
| Departmental costs | 60 | 70 | 90 | 220 |
| Rent | 70 | 70 | 70 | 210 |
| | 130 | 140 | 160 | 430 |
| Departmental net profit (loss) | (30) | 70 | 101 | 141 |
| Central administration costs | | | | 45 |
| Overall net profit | | | | 96 |

**(b)**

| | A | B | C | Total |
|---|---|---|---|---|
| Gross profit % | 50 | 60 | 58 | 57.1 |
| Net profit % | (15) | 20 | 22.4 | 14.1 |
| Departmental cost as % of sales | 30 | 20 | 20 | 22 |
| Rent | Apportioned equally | | | |

*See* text

**(c)**

The managing director suggests closing all departments reporting a loss, i.e. A, which could be rented out to gain £25 000 p.a.

- Whilst closing A would save departmental costs of £60 it would lose gross profit of £100, i.e. a gain of £40.
- The only thing which makes A a loss-making department is the rent which could not be saved by closing the department (it is a fixed cost).
- Therefore whilst we would gain £25 rent, we would lose £40 contribution.

Are there any alternatives?

- Sell other goods in Department A to increase profits.
- Reduce costs.
- Rent part of the space out.
- It cost £70 rent for Flag Ltd. Why will they only receive £25?

**5(a)**

| | Moa | Dodo |
|---|---|---|
| Current assets | 180 | 210 |
| Current liabilities | 80 | 150 |
| Working capital | 100 | 60 |
| Working capital ratio | 2.25:1 | 1.4:1 |
| Quick ratio | 1.1:1 | 0.53:1 |
| Gearing ratio | 0 | 16.67 |
| Gross profit on sales | 24% | 12% |
| Net profit on sales | 4% | 4% |

**(b)**

*See* text

## ■ CHAPTER 19 BREAK EVEN ANALYSIS

**1**

(a) 17.25 − 8.50 = 8.75

$\frac{20\,000}{8.75} = \underline{\underline{2\,285.7 \text{ units}}}$

(b) 11.79 − 10.20 = 1.59

$\frac{5\,000}{1.59} = \underline{\underline{3\,144.6 \text{ units}}}$

(c) 36.12 − 20.00 = 16.12

$\frac{x}{16.12} = \underline{\underline{2\,000 \text{ units}}}$

$x = 2\,000 \times 16.12 = \underline{\underline{£32\,240}}$

(d) 11.00 − 5.00 = 6.00

$\frac{x}{6.00} = 60\,000 \text{ units}$

$x = 60\,000 \times 6.0 = \underline{\underline{£360\,000}}$

(e) 0.50 − x = y

$\frac{10\,000}{y} = 40\,000$

$\therefore y = \frac{10\,000}{40\,000} = 0.25$

$\therefore x = 0.50 - x$ → 0.25, $\underline{\underline{x = 0.25}}$

(f) 110.00 − x = y

$\frac{160\,000}{y} = 3\,200$

$\therefore y = \frac{160\,000}{3\,200} = 50$

$\therefore x = 110.00 - x$ → 50.00, $\underline{\underline{x = £60}}$

(g) x − 2.30 = y

$\frac{20\,000}{y} = 9\,000$

$y = \frac{20\,000}{9\,000} = 2.22$

x = x − 2.30 → 2.22

$\underline{\underline{x = £5.52}}$

(h) x − 1.80 = y

$\frac{100\,000}{y} = 5\,000$

$y = \frac{100\,000}{5\,000} = 20$

x = x − 1.80 → 20.00

$\underline{\underline{x = 21.80}}$

**2(a)**

| | £ | £ |
|---|---|---|
| Budgeted sales (4 000 × 47 wk) | | 188 000 |
| *less Variable costs* | | |
| Factory cost (£2 000 × 47 wk) | 94 000 | |
| Salesman's commission (£4 000 × 7.5% × 47 wk) | 14 100 | 108 100 |
| Contribution | | 79 900 |
| *less Fixed costs* | | |
| Advertising (£2 000 × 12 mth) | 24 000 | |
| Salesman (£100 × 52 wk) | 5 200 | |
| Van rental (£200 × 52 wk) | 10 400 | |
| Craftsman (£200 × 52 wk) | 10 400 | |
| Labourer (£150 × 52 wk) | 7 800 | |
| Van running cost (£50 × 47 wk) | 2 350 | |
| Bank charges and interest | 1 000 | |
| Office expenses | 1 500 | |
| Dennis | 10 000 | 72 650 |
| Budgeted net profit | | 7 250 |

*Break even point*

| | % | £ |
|---|---|---|
| Sales | 100 | 188 000 |
| – Variable costs | 57.5 | 108 100 |
| Contribution | 42.5 | 79 900 |
| – Fixed costs | 38.64 | 72 650 |
| Budgeted net profit | 3.86 | 7 250 |

BEP = Where Contribution = £72 650, i.e. fixed costs
∴ Where £72 650 = 42.5%

$\therefore \text{Sales} = \frac{£72\,650}{42.5} \times 100 = \underline{\underline{£170\,941}}$

**(b)**

Dennis will not need to employ a second team as his first team can achieve the sales of £188 000 above.

**3(a)**

| | Scheme A | Scheme B |
|---|---|---|
| | £ | £ |
| Selling price (unit | 200 | 200 |
| *less* Variable cost | 150 | 120 |
| Contribution | 50 | 80 |
| Break even point | *Fixed costs* / 50 | *Fixed costs* / 80 |
| *Fixed costs* | £ | £ |
| Depreciation | 280 000 / 4 yrs | 400 000 / 4 yrs |
| | 70 000 | 100 000 |
| Other fixed expenses | 130 000 | 300 000 |
| | 200 000 | 400 000 |
| (i) Break even point | 200 000 / 50 | 400 000 / 80 |
| | 4 000 units or £800 000 | 5 000 units or £1 000 000 |
| (ii) *Forecast profit* | £ | £ |
| Total contribution (7 000 units) | 350 000 | 560 000 |
| *less* fixed costs | 200 000 | 400 000 |
| | 150 000 | 160 000 |
| (iii) *Margin of safety* | £ | £ |
| Budgeted sales | 1 400 000 (100%) | 1 400 000 (100%) |
| BEP (£) | 800 000 | 1 000 000 |
| Margin of safety | 600 000 (42.85%) | 400 000 (28.5%) |

**(b)**

Profit = (Units × Contribution) – Fixed costs

∴ the number of units to generate the same profit is

$$\left[\begin{array}{c}\text{Units} \times \text{Contribution} \\ - \text{Fixed costs}\end{array}\right] A = \left[\begin{array}{c}\text{Units} \times \text{Contribution} \\ - \text{Fixed costs}\end{array}\right] B$$

Units × £50 – £200 000 = Units × £80 – £400 000

∴ (£400 000 – £200 000) = (£80 – 50) units

$$\therefore \text{Units} = \frac{£200\,000}{£30} = 6\,667 \text{ units}$$

**(c)**

*Scheme A*

- requires less capital
- has less fixed costs
- has a greater margin of safety
- a lower break even point

*Scheme B*

- based on the estimates is ultimately more profitable (but for more capital employed).

*Recommendation:* Adopt Scheme A.

**4(a)**

*Forecast Profit for the Years 1992–1996 for Brigton Ltd*

| | 1992 | 1993 | 1994 | 1995 | 1996 | Total |
|---|---|---|---|---|---|---|
| Sales | 500 | 600 | 700 | 800 | 900 | |
| Option 1 | | | | | | |
| Variable costs | 250 | 300 | 350 | 400 | 450 | |
| Fixed costs | 75 | 75 | 75 | 75 | 75 | |
| Depreciation | 200 | 200 | 200 | 200 | 200 | |
| | 525 | 575 | 625 | 675 | 725 | |
| Net profit (loss) | (25) | 25 | 75 | 125 | 175 | 375 |
| Option 2 | | | | | | |
| Variable costs | 150 | 180 | 210 | 240 | 270 | |
| Fixed costs | 60 | 60 | 60 | 60 | 60 | |
| Depreciation | 350 | 350 | 350 | 350 | 350 | |
| | 560 | 590 | 620 | 650 | 680 | |
| Net profit | (60) | 10 | 80 | 150 | 220 | 400 |
| Option 3 | | | | | | |
| Variable costs | 450 | 540 | 630 | 720 | 810 | |
| Fixed costs | 10 | 10 | 10 | 10 | 10 | |
| | 460 | 550 | 640 | 730 | 820 | |
| Net profit | 40 | 50 | 60 | 70 | 80 | 300 |

**(b)**

| | | |
|---|---|---|
| Investment | Option 1 | 1 000 000 |
| | Option 2 | 2 000 000 |
| | Option 3 | Nil |
| Findings | Option 2 | Shows the highest cumulative profit<br>*But* involves an investment of £2M<br>Does not show a profit until year 2<br>Here is very risky |
| | Option 1 | Also requires a substantial investment and does not show a return until year 2<br>*But* is less likely than Option 2 |
| | Option 3 | Does not require any investment and shows a return immediately<br>It is not as profitable overall and management must trade off risk v. return. |

**5**

| | (a) With advertising Method 1 | (a) With advertising Method 2 | (b) No advertising Method 2 | (b) No advertising Method 2 |
|---|---|---|---|---|
| Break even point | | | | |
| Selling price per unit | 5.00 | 5.00 | 5.00 | 5.00 |
| Variable cost per unit | 0.50 | 1.00 | 0.50 | 1.00 |
| Contribution per unit | 4.50 | 4.00 | 4.50 | 4.00 |
| Fixed production costs | 420 000 | 370 000 | 420 000 | 370 000 |
| Depreciation | 300 000 | 100 000 | 300 000 | 100 000 |
| Advertising | 135 000 | 135 000 | — | — |
| Total | 855 000 | 605 000 | 720 000 | 470 000 |
| Fixed cost/contribution | 855/4.5 | 605/4 | 720/4.5 | 470/4 |
| Break even point (units) | 190 000 | 151 250 | 160 000 | 117 500 |
| Min sales | 200 000 | 200 000 | 200 000 | 100 000 |
| Maximum profit | | | | |
| Contribution at 250 000 units | 1 125 000 | 1 000 000 | 1 125 000 | 1 000 000 |
| Fixed costs | 855 000 | 605 000 | 720 000 | 470 000 |
| Profit | 270 000 | 395 000 | 405 000 | 530 000 |

**(c)**

*Method* 2 is far superior – Lower break even (less risk)
– high profit (more return)

Whether with or without advertising

Therefore we know we are going for method 2, the question now is, is it with or without advertising?

*Method 2*

Method 2 without advertising has a lower break even point and a higher profit *but* the break even point is *above* the minimum expected sales and *hence* a risky proposition. Therefore go for Method 2, with advertising.

**6(a)**

| | Thin £000 | Thin £000 | Stout £000 | Stout £000 |
|---|---|---|---|---|
| Sales | | 1 400 | | 1 400 |
| Materials | 420 | | 420 | |
| Labour | 280 | | 70 | |
| Depreciation | 100 | | 250 | |
| | | 800 | | 740 |
| | | 600 | | 660 |
| Other expenses: | | | | |
| Fixed | 150 | | 200 | |
| Variable | 210 | | 140 | |
| | | 360 | | 340 |
| Net profit | | 240 | | 320 |

**(b)**

Assumptions (any four from):

1 Variable costs linear: each additional unit sold incurs the same additional variable cost
2 No extra capacity required
3 Sell each unit for the same price
4 Straight line depreciation used
5 The fixed costs are truly fixed

**(c)**

Stout's profits are substantial compared to Thin's, which as we can see is as a result of lower costs.

# Index


Accountancy 1
  an introduction to accounts 1–5
  equation 8
  procedure 39
Accounting concepts and conventions 54–67
  accruals concepts 56–62
  business entity concept 54
  consistency concept 55
  going concern concept 55
  historical cost concept 54
  matching concept 55–6
  materiality concept 55
  money measurement concept 55
  prudence concept 62
  realisation concept 55
Accruals concept 56–62
  accruals 56
  accruals and prepayments at the beginning and end of the accounting period 60–2
  dealing with accruals and prepayments 56–60
  prepayments 56
Advance corporation tax (ACT) 161
Appropriation account (limited company) 124
Appropriation account (partnership) 100
Assets 7
  current 7, 8
  fixed 7, 8
  intangible 113, 126–7
Auditor's remuneration 124
Authorised share capital 127
Average cost (AVCO) 157
  periodic 157
  perpetual 159

Bad debts 66–7
Balance sheet
  horizontal format 6–15
  principles of 6–15
  specimen layouts
    limited company 126–7
    partnership 103
    sole trader 93
Bank reconciliation statements 204–16
  what are they? 204–8
  different opening balances 209–10
  producing a bank reconciliation statement 205–8
  updating the cashbook 208–9
Break even analysis 227–43
  assumptions/limitations 237
  break-even charts 229–30
  calculating the break even point 228–9
  contribution/sales ratio 229
  definition 227
  effects of changes in sales volume and costs 231–2
  fixed costs 227
  margin of safety 231
  use of, as a decision making tool and planning aid 232–7
  variable costs 227
Business entity concept 54

Calculating depreciation 73–6
Capital reserves 127–8
Carriage
  inwards 19, 43
  outwards 19, 43
Cash and working capital 181–90
Cash cycle/flow of funds 184–5
Cashflow forecasts 169–86
  construction 170–4
  definition 169
  producing a forecast trading profit and loss account and balance sheet 175–6
  purpose 169
Cashflow statements 190–203
  cashflows in and out 190–1
  example presentation 191–2

preparing a cashflow statement 192–5
purchase/sale of fixed assets 196–7
analysis of cashflow statements 198
Causes of depreciation 73
Closing stock 40–1
Concepts and conventions (*see* Accounting concepts and conventions)
Consistency concept 55
Contribution 228
Contribution/sales ratio 229
Control accounts 33–4
purchase ledger 34
sales ledger 34
Corporation tax 126, 127–8
Cost (*see* Stock: valuation of stock) 154
Creditor 9–10
Creditors' settlement period 184, 218, 220
Cumulative preference shares 127
Current assets 8
Current liability 9

Day books 20–1
Debenture 124, 127
Debenture interest 124
Debt/equity ratio 219, 221
Debtor 10–1
Debtors settlement period 184, 218, 220
Deferred liability 10
Deferred taxation 162–4
Depreciation 72–89
causes of 73
dealing with, in the trading profit and loss account and balance sheet 75–82
definition 72
disposal or scrapping of a fixed asset 82–5
effects of, on the trading profit and loss account and balance sheet 76–8
methods of calculating 73–6
reducing balance method 74–5
straight line method 74–5
Direct expenses 139
Direct labour 139, 227
Direct material 139, 227
Directors' remuneration 124
Discount allowed 44–5
Discount received 44–5
Discounts 22
cash 22–4
trade 22
Disposal or scrapping of a fixed asset 82–5
Dividends (proposed) 124
Double entry bookkeeping 16–30
balancing off the ledgers 24
procedure 17–30
Drawings 11–2

Errors and control account 31–7
compensating error 31
error of commission 31
error of omission 31
error of original entry 31
error of principle 31
errors and the reported profit figure 46–7
passing correcting entries 33

Factory overheads (*see* Manufacturing overheads)
FRS 1: Cashflow Statements 190, 250–7
FIFO (first in first out) 156
periodic 157
perpetual 158
Financial information
purpose of recording 2–3
recorded 1–2
Financial policy 198
Financial Reporting Standards (FRSs) 149–68
Financing long-term investments 198
Fixed assets 8
Fixed costs 227
Fluctuating capital account (partnerships) 101
Foreseeable losses 62
Franked investment income 162

Gearing 219, 221
Going concern concept 55
Goodwill 108–10
as an intangible asset 113
methods of valuing 109–10
reasons for 109
Gross profit 39–40
Gross profit margin 218, 219